AGE AT MARRIAGE IN INDIA: VISION AND REALITY

AGE AT MARRIAGE IN INDIA: VISION AND REALITY

D. RADHA DEVI

SERIALS PUBLICATIONS
NEW DELHI

In Association with Malabar Institute for Development Research
Thrissur (Kerala)

First Published - 2006

ISBN : 81-8387-051-1

Published by

SERIALS PUBLICATIONS
4830/24, Ansari Road, Darya Ganj
New Delhi-110002 (India)
Phone : 91-11-23245225
Fax : 91-11-23272135
E-mail: serials@satyam.net.in,
serialspublications@vsnl.net
Website : www.serielaspub.com

CONTENTS

PREFACE

To call this, a study that satisfies all that one would like to know about age at marriage in India would be impertinent. The main objective of this research is to identify the areas in India where age at marriage is low and to show how far or close the country is in attaining its vision of eliminating child/early marriage of both girls and boys.

Timing of marriage has been a concern of all the Governments that ruled this country from the beginning of 20th century when child/early marriage was the norm and practice. Even as early as 1929 the then Government of India passed the Child Marriage Restraint Act limiting the minimum age at marriage for girls as 14 years and for boys as 18 years. After attaining independence, the minimum age at marriage for girls was revised to 15 years in 1948. Subsequently, with increased commitment in reducing fertility, improving the health of women and children, strengthening the status of women in general and their education in particular, to have mature and responsible parents, the Government raised the age at marriage for both boys and girls to 21 and 18 years respectively in 1978 through an Amendment to the Child Marriage Restraint Act of 1929. The latest in this series of attempts by the Government manifested in the form of a policy statement that appeared in the New Population Policy 2000, where it was stated that the girls should preferably be married only after they complete 20 years of age, at least not before 18 years, a vision to be achieved by 2010.

However, though the Government has been repeatedly raising the age at marriage for both girls and boys through legislation, there were pressing social, religious and economic factors that helped in reducing the pace with which the age at marriage has been increasing. Since all the marriages in this country are not registered, the true state of affairs at the grass root level is not clearly known. Hence the district level Rapid Household Survey of the Reproductive and Child Health Project of the Government of India during 1998-99, sought the age at marriage information from all the selected households for all the marriages that were conducted five years prior to the survey. This is the first time in India that age at marriage information was collected from all the districts in the country based on marriages conducted during a specified time period. The present study made use of this data which was collected almost two decades after the legal minimum age at marriage was raised to 18 years for girls and 21 years for boys.

The originality of this study lies in its attempt to show the current situation of age at marriage of both boys and girls in each and every district in this country using information on marriages conducted during a specified time period. It made clear that legislations alone are not sufficient to bring about changes in age at marriage by showing that there are many districts in this country where the children, particularly girls, get married before they complete 18 years of age. However, it is fully understood that this study would have been enriched had there been information of the achieved characteristics of the people who got married, the circumstances in which they grew up, the basic characteristics of the household to which they belong/belonged. But such information is not available in the data set used in this study. Further it should be stressed that age at marriage of boys was not given the importance it deserves in any of the prior studies.

Nevertheless, the age at which people enter into matrimony in itself is very important as it has many social, economic, demographic, health and emotional consequences. *Ceteris paribus,* early marriage will deprive a person of the chances of education and better employment, leads to high fertility and poor health of mother/child, results in greater risk of domestic violence and subjugation of women, lessen inter-spouse communication and understanding, and increases maternal mortality. Early marriage is also seen as a violation of human rights. Article 16(2) of the Convention of All Forms of Discrimination Against Women specifically addresses age at marriage. It is stated that a person marrying before 18 years of age shall have no legal effect and all member states should pass minimum age at marriage legislation and all marriages should be registered.

In this research, I was helped by many persons directly and indirectly and I would like to put on record my gratitude to one and all. However, a few names need special mention. Dr. Manoj Alagarajan was primarily responsible for creating a data file specifically for this study without which it would have been very difficult for me to complete this report. Further, he along with Mr.Bipul Hazarika has helped in bringing out some of the tables and we had several sessions of discussion on the subject. Some technical assistance was provided by Ms. Purabi Pathak. Prof. T.K. Roy patiently went through the initial draft and gave me suggestions which helped in improving the report enormously. While thanking them all, I would like to assert here that any drawback or errors that may remain in this report should be attributed solely to me.

D. Radha Devi

LIST OF ABBREVIATIONS

A M	Acceptable Marriage
A P	Andhra Pradesh
A&N	Andaman & Nicobar
ARP	Arunachal Pradesh
ASM	Assam
BIH	Bihar
C M	Child Marriage
CHA	Chandigarh
D&D	Daman & Diu
D & NH	Dadra & Nagar Haveli
DEL	Delhi
E M	Early Marriage
E S	Economic Status
FLR	Female Literacy Rate
GUJ	Gujarat
H P	Himachal Pradesh
HAR	Haryana
J&K	Jammu & Kashmir
KAR	Karnataka
KER	Kerala
LAK	Lakshadweep
M P	Madhya Pradesh
MAH	Maharashtra
MAN	Manipur
MEG	Meghalaya
MIZ	Mizoram

NAG	Nagaland
O C	Other Castes
OBC	Other Backward class
ORI	Orissa
P M	Preferred Marriage
PON	Pondicherry
PUN	Punjab
RAJ	Rajasthan
RCH	Reproductive and Child Health
S C	Scheduled Caste
S T	Scheduled Tribe
SIK	Sikkim
T N	Tamil Nadu
TRI	Tripura
U P	Uttar Pradesh
U T	Union Territory
W B	West Bengal

Chapter - 1

INTRODUCTION

IMPORTANCE OF THE STUDY

Age at marriage is a subject of great practical importance as it is related to both socio-economic antecedents and attainments (Call and Otto, 1977) though its importance is recognized mostly by demographers than scholars of other disciplines. Davis and Blake (1956) treated age at marriage as a prominent variable in the context of reproductive control. McDonald (1981) writes that "in demography age at marriage occupies a predominant place as one of the proximate determinants of fertility and any respectable discussion of fertility trends or determinants refers to the level of age at marriage, at least for women".

Age at marriage is also a key intervening variable in the status attainment process (Bartz and Nye, 1970). This is based on the assumption that, other things remaining constant, late marriage will help to give opportunities for increase in educational attainment and obtain better occupation and better income-all of which are regarded as status indicators. "All these opportunities, which are virtually closed to a girl who marries at 15 or 16, will not only help women understand the value of spacing children and limiting family size later, but also will enable them to play more active roles in family, community, and national development (Population Reports, 1979). However, whether the availability of opportunities for education with a high social demand foı education leads to late marriage or *vice versa* is a matter of contention. Nonetheless, studies have shown the existence of a strong association between girl's age at marriage and level of education.

It is also argued that postponement of marriage will make both girls and boys mature mentally and emotionally. A mature couple will have high quality verbal interaction which can affect emotional closeness and sharing of private thoughts, values and concerns-all necessary ingredients for marital adjustments-than a couple that start marriage at an early age (Westoff and Ryder, 1977).

The effect of late marriage on reproduction through shortening the reproductive life span has been recognized even from the time of Thomas Robert Malthus who advocated postponement of marriage as a preventive check to high fertility (Malthus, 1798). Since then many scholars have made known its fertility depressing effect in varying social set up (Davis and Blake, 1956; Freedman, 1979; Goyal, 1964; Coale, 1965; Agarwala, 1966; Van de Valle, 1972; Coale, 1973; Westoff and Ryder, 1977; Malhotra, 1997). However, reproduction is not the only function of marriage. Marriage heralds the beginning of a new family unit with all the complicated roles and statuses which the members of this unit are expected to play. As such, it is wrong to perceive it only as a reproductive unit, though it is difficult to separate the specific functions of marriage from the broader functions of the family as marriage is an integral part of the institution of the family (McDonald, 1981). In all the societies of the world there are four main functions for a family - reproduction, maintenance, placement and socialization (Davis, 1973), though the stress on each of these functions vary widely from culture to culture. Thus, the age at which a person enters into the formation of a family unit is of immense importance as it involves multifarious activities.

In India, marriage is universal and all marriages are not registered. Most of the marriages are solemnized through religious functions. Moreover, there are still areas in this country where early marriage is the norm. Many reasons are given for an early age at marriage in ancient India, mostly based on religion and social customs. Beliefs like having an unmarried girl of 10 years at home will take the parents to hell; that it will reduce the social prestige of the parents; that it reflects the low status and lack of affluence of the family, etc. are some such reasons (For a detailed version see Reddy, 1998). Further, marriage restrictions based on the endogenous character of different caste groups reduced the field of selection for a partner and hence the parents took the first opportunity to get their girls married and at an early age. With the passing of time early marriage became a norm and deviation from it was seen as a matter of social disapproval and even social disgrace. As in any other social aspect, the low caste people in their eagerness to imitate the higher caste people married the girls even in infancy (Reddy, 1998).

Age at marriage in India, is given particular importance in the context of fertility. In many parts of the country, high fertility is still the norm-mostly in places where the son preference is very strong. In the absence of large scale use of contraception, early marriage generally leads to early and repeated pregnancies in quick succession, which is injurious to the health of both mother and child. Recognizing the adverse effect of early marriage and early parenthood on the mental and physical health of the girl, the then Government passed the Child Marriage Restraint Act, 1929 which is an important mile stone in the path to raise the age at marriage for girls and boys. This Act fixed the minimum age of marriage for girls to 14 years and for boys to 18 years. Later, the Government of India in its avowed policy of improving the health of women, reducing the fertility level and increasing the status of women, found the legal minimum prescribed in the 1929 Act to be too low. Hence the 1929 Act was amended in 1949 raising the minimum age at marriage for girls from 14 to 15 years (IIPS, 1995). But the age at marriage remained low and fertility was reluctant to come down. The Government then passed the Child Marriage Restraint (Amendment) Act, 1978 that increased the minimum age at marriage for girls to 18 years and for boys to 21 years and offences under this Act are made cognisable.

Though the Government has been repeatedly raising the age at marriage for both girls and boys through legislation, there were pressing social, religious and economic factors that helped in reducing the pace with which the age at marriage has been increasing. Of the social variables that affect age at marriage, education stands out as a major one. Since education for girls after marriage is a very rare phenomenon in India, it stands to reason that those who spend more years in school naturally tend to get married late. The relationship between economic aspects and age at marriage has also been studied by many (Driver, 1963; Radha Devi, 1984; Singh and Richard, 1989) which indicates that low age at marriage is more common among the lower income groups or lower occupational groups.

POPULATION RELATED GENERAL INFORMATION

Before examining the age at marriage *per se* it is worth having a look at some selected characteristics of the population (Table 1.1). In 1991 the fifteen major states in India (states with a population of at least 10 million) together accounted for almost 96 per cent of the total Indian population. (The share of these states remained more or less the same in 2001 also). Hence the Tables in this section will show only data relating to these 15 states. Another important point to note here is that in this whole report where ever state-wise information is given the three new states (Jharkhand, Uttaranchal, Chhatisgad) will not be shown separately as they were not formed at the time of data collection.

In 2001, of the 32 states and union territories, 6 major states together accounted for 60 per cent of the total population. These states are Uttar Pradesh (17.0%), Bihar (10.7%), Maharashtra (9.4%), Madhya Pradesh (7.9%), West Bengal (7.8%) and Andhra Pradesh (7.4%). This indicates that with respect to any aspect, the situation prevailing in these states will get reflected at the all-India level. These six states can also be grouped into two, with Andhra Pradesh, Maharashtra and West Bengal in one and Bihar, Madhya Pradesh and Uttar Pradesh in the other according to the total fertility rate (TFR). The TFR of the former group varied between 2.5 and 2.8 in 1996 while that of the second group varied between 4.1 and 4.9.

However, among the major 15 states, the lowest TFR is found in Kerala, but its share in the total Indian population is just 3.1 per cent.

The growth rate of the population during 1991-2001 is found to be more than 25 per cent in Bihar, Haryana, Rajasthan and Uttar Pradesh. This is the lowest in Kerala (9.3), Tamil Nadu (11.1) and Andhra Pradesh (13.8). The proportion of literates in 1998-99, according to National Family Health Survey-2 (IIPS and ORC Macro, 2000), is the lowest in Bihar (34.5%) followed by Rajasthan (37.1%). At the other extreme is Kerala with 85.1 per cent literate women followed by Punjab (64.9%) and Maharashtra (61.4%). Male literacy is higher than that of females in all the states. Again the lowest level is in Bihar (63.2%) and the highest in Kerala (92.8%). It is also observed that except in Andhra Pradesh and Bihar, all other states have at least 70 per cent of literate males. The median number of years of schooling is also given in Table 1 which shows that the median age for females to be zero years in Andhra Pradesh, Bihar, Madhya Pradesh, Rajasthan and Uttar Pradesh. Kerala has the highest median number of years for both males and females, 8.1 and 7.6 years respectively.

At the risk of repetition, it should be mentioned here that the TFR of Bihar, Madhya Pradesh, Rajasthan and Uttar Pradesh varied between 4.1 and 4.9. The Crude Birth Rate for these states in 1999 varied between 31 and 33.

In 1999, the infant mortality rate (IMR) for these states are also high at 63 for Bihar, 90 for Madhya Pradesh, 81 for Rajasthan and 84 for Uttar Pradesh. However, the highest IMR of 97 was found in Orissa. Madhya Pradesh and Uttar Pradesh are among the states with a crude death rate of above 10. In Assam, Madhya Pradesh and Orissa the expectation of life at birth in 1996-2001 was below 60 years for both males and females.

Thus, on the whole it can be said that educationally and demographically Bihar, Madhya Pradesh, Rajasthan and Uttar Pradesh are comparatively backward and the all-India situation is only a reflection of the conditions prevailing in these four states as they together account for two-fifths of the total Indian population.

KNOWLEDGE OF LEGAL MINIMUM AGE AT MARRIAGE AMONG EVER MARRIED WOMEN

India is a vast country marked more by heterogeneity than by homogeneity. The customs and norms vary from state to state; from religion to religion. Cultural variations by caste, place of residence, education and level of wealth are general knowledge. But marriage is an institution, which is common to all and is universal.

Marriage in India, generally, is not just a concern between two individuals but is the establishment of a relationship between two families, the bride and the groom serving as the connecting link. Hence marriages are often arranged by the parents of the girls and boys taking into

Table 1
Population Related General Information in Major States of India

Sr. No.	Major states	Population (million)		Growth rate	% share total in pop.	Education (1998-99)				TFR	CBR	IMR	CDR	e^{o}_{o}	
						Literate (%)		Median no. of years of schooling							
		1991	2001	1991-2001	2001	Female	Male	Female	Male	1996	1999	1999	1999	1996-2001 Female	Male
1.	Andhra Pradesh	66.5	75.7	13.8	7.4	46.0	66.9	0.0	4.9	2.5	21.7	66.0	8.2	63.7	61.6
2.	Assam	22.4	26.6	18.8	2.6	59.1	74.6	2.5	4.7	3.2	27.0	76.0	9.7	58.8	57.3
3.	Bihar	86.4	109.8	27.1	10.7	34.8	63.2	0.0	3.6	4.5	31.5	63.0	8.9	62.1	63.6
4.	Gujarat	41.3	50.6	22.5	4.9	53.6	76.7	3.2	6.3	3.0	25.4	63.0	7.9	62.8	61.5
5.	Haryana	16.5	21.1	27.9	2.1	57.3	78.8	2.4	6.2	3.5	26.8	68.0	7.7	67.4	63.9
6.	Karnataka	45.0	52.7	17.1	5.1	55.5	74.3	3.2	6.0	2.6	22.3	58.0	7.7	65.4	61.7
7.	Kerala	29.1	31.8	9.3	3.1	85.1	92.8	7.6	8.1	1.8	18.0	14.0	6.4	75.0	70.7
8.	Madhya Pradesh	66.2	81.2	22.7	7.9	44.5	72.1	0.0	4.8	4.1	31.1	90.0	10.4	57.2	56.8
9.	Maharashtra	78.9	96.8	22.7	9.4	61.4	82.7	4.1	7.1	2.8	21.1	48.0	7.5	68.2	65.3
10.	Orissa	31.7	36.7	15.8	3.6	51.3	76.0	1.2	5.1	3.1	24.1	97.0	10.7	58.1	58.5
11.	Punjab	20.3	24.3	19.7	2.4	64.9	77.9	5.0	6.4	2.8	21.5	53.0	7.4	71.4	68.4
12.	Rajasthan	44.0	56.5	28.4	5.5	37.1	71.8	0.0	5.0	4.2	31.1	81.0	8.4	61.4	60.3
13.	Tamil Nadu	55.9	62.1	11.1	6.0	58.2	79.7	4.5	6.4	2.1	19.3	52.0	8.0	67.6	65.2
14.	Uttar Pradesh	139.1	174.5	25.4	17.0	42.7	71.8	0.0	5.0	4.9	32.8	84.0	10.5	61.1	61.2
15.	West Bengal	68.1	80.2	17.8	7.8	57.4	76.0	2.1	4.7	2.6	20.7	52.0	7.1	67.2	64.5
	INDIA	846.4	1027.0	21.3	100.0	51.4	74.5	1.6	5.5	3.4	26.1	70.0	8.7	63.4	62.4

Note: TFR = Total Fertility Rate; CBR = Crude Birth Rate; IMR = Infant Mortality Rate; CDR = Crude Death Rate; e^{o}_{o} = Expectation of Life at Birth.

Source: Census of India 1991 & 2001; Family Welfare Programme in India Year Book 1997-98; SRS Bulletin, April 2001, Vol. 35 (1); IIPS & ORC Macro, 2000.

consideration the family status, economic position, caste, religion, region and the like. Another important factor that plays a major role in the timing of marriage now-a-days in India is dowry-an octopus that is spreading its tentacles across the society and squeezes it mercilessly irrespective of caste, creed or class[1].

Knowledge of the provisions of Child Marriage Restraint Act alone will not be able to decide when a girl/boy should get married. But this knowledge will help to know when a girl/boy should not get married. Further, when there is a minimum age at marriage legally decided, then the first step in the direction of implementation is to let every family in this country know about it. In this context it is worth knowing the extent of knowledge of the adult men and women about the legal minimum age at marriage. However, such data are hardly available. This knowledge among the ever married women in the 13-49 age group has been collected by the National Family Health Survey (IIPS, 1995) and the same is presented in Table 2.

This Table shows that two-thirds of the respondents could not identify age 18 as the correct legal minimum age at marriage for girls and 80 per cent could not identify age 21 as the correct legal minimum age of marriage for boys. It is a very disturbing finding as this is a situation evaluated 14-15 years after the 1978 legislation came into vogue.

Table 2

Per cent of ever Married Women Age 13-49 who knew the Correct Legal Minimum Age at Marriage for Girls and Boys, 1992-93

Sr. No.	*Major States*	*Per cent of women reporting correct knowledge of legal minimum age at marriage for*	
		Female	*Male*
1.	Andhra Pradesh	38.0	27.0
2.	Assam	18.8	3.8
3.	Bihar	18.9	12.8
4.	Gujarat	33.7	23.6
5.	Haryana	40.9	27.5
6.	Karnataka	40.9	23.7
7.	Kerala	65.3	27.6
8.	Madhya Pradesh	24.6	15.9
9.	Maharashtra	49.1	31.4
10.	Orissa	19.1	6.5
11.	Punjab	41.1	33.0
12.	Rajasthan	26.9	18.0
13.	Tamil Nadu	38.9	19.6
14.	Uttar Pradesh	26.9	17.7
15.	West Bengal	31.6	10.7
	INDIA	33.2	19.8

Source: IIPS, 1995.

The proportion of women having the correct knowledge of legal minimum age at marriage for boys and girls is the lowest in Assam. While one in every three respondent could report correct legal minimum age at marriage for boys in Punjab, the corresponding number in Assam was one in every 25. Correct knowledge of legal minimum age at marriage for girls was the highest in Kerala where two-thirds of the respondents reported it correctly. The Government having not made any specific effort to make the provisions of the Child Marriage Restraint Amendment Act to reach the public after this finding, it can safely be assumed that the level of knowledge will not be much different even to-day.

However, India is still a male dominant society, and knowledge of women on any aspect is not sufficient yet, to bring about any change in any situation. As stated by the Government of India (2000) "gender inequalities in patriarchal societies ensure that men play a critical role in determining the education and employment of family members, *age at marriage*, besides access to and utilization of health, nutrition, and family welfare services for women and children" (Italics added). Thus, men are still the major decision-makers of family matters and if they are knowledgeable that will go a long way in bringing about changes in this matter. However, no data are available to gauge the knowledge of men in this aspect.

TREND OF AGE AT MARRIAGE IN INDIA

The age at marriage estimations for girls and boys made using census data is given in Table 3. It shows that the mean age at marriage for girls till 1951 was below 15 years-quite an unacceptable situation. The increase since then also was not very fast as can be seen from the last but one column of Table 3.

Table 4 gives the singulate mean age at marriage (SMAM) for girls in the major states from 1971 to 1998-99. The socio-cultural and economic diversity in the country is also reflected in the mean age at marriage. In 1971 in all the 15 major states the SMAM was at least 15 years (the then prevailing legal minimum age at marriage). But it was just about 15 years in Bihar, Madhya Pradesh, Rajasthan and Uttar Pradesh. In these four states, the increase in female age at marriage during 1971-99 periods was relatively high. The least increase was observed in Kerala where the age at marriage for girls was the highest even in 1971-21.3 years (a situation of 1.3 years above the envisioned age at marriage of 20 years in the New National Population Policy, 2000).

Furthermore, the proportion married in the age group 15-29 is also of interest as it reflects the age at marriage. Since the details of age and marital status for 2001 census of India is not yet available the proportion married in the three age groups, viz. 15-19, 20-24 and 25-29 in 1991 is given in Table 5. The age group 15-19 in Table 5 includes ages below legal minimum and, therefore, should have only a comparatively smaller proportion married and in a country where early and universal marriage is the norm, by the time one reaches the age group 25-29 almost all are expected to be married.

Table 3
Singulate mean Age at Marriage in India by Sex

Year	*Singulate Mean age at marriage*		*Addition made to age at marriage over the previous decade (years)*	
	Girls	*Boys*	*Girls*	*Boys*
1901	13.1	20.0	**	**
1911	13.2	20.3	0.1	0.3
1921	13.7	20.7	0.5	0.4
1931	12.7	18.6	-1.0	-2.1
1941	14.7	19.9	2.0	1.3
1951	15.6	19.9	0.9	0
1961	16.1	21.4	0.5	1.5
1971	17.2	22.6	1.1	1.2
1981	18.4	23.5	1.2	0.9
1991	19.3	24.0	0.9	0.5
1998-99	19.7	24.9	0.4	0.9

Source: Agarwala, 1966 and IIPS and ORC Macro, 2000.

Table 4
Singulate mean Age at Marriage for Girls in India and Major States

Sr. No.	*Major States*	*Singulate Mean Age at Marriage (Census) t*				
		1971	*1981*	*1991*	*1998-99*	*Diff. in SMAM 1971-99*
1.	Andhra Pradesh	16.3	17.3	18.3	18.3	2.0
2.	Assam	18.7	Na	Na	21.7	3.0
3.	Bihar	15.3	16.6	17.5	18.8	3.5
4.	Gujarat	18.5	19.6	19.9	20.2	1.7
5.	Haryana	17.7	17.9	18.8	19.8	2.1
6.	Karnataka	17.9	19.3	20.1	20.1	2.2
7.	Kerala	21.3	22.1	22.2	21.5	0.2
8.	Madhya Pradesh	15.0	16.6	17.8	18.9	3.9
9.	Maharashtra	17.6	18.8	19.7	19.8	2.2
10.	Orissa	17.3	19.1	20.2	21.2	3.9
11.	Punjab	20.1	21.1	21.0	22.1	2.0
12.	Rajasthan	15.1	16.1	17.5	18.3	3.2
13.	Tamil Nadu	19.6	20.3	20.9	20.9	1.3
14.	Uttar Pradesh	15.5	16.7	18.0	19.0	3.5
15.	West Bengal	18.0	19.3	19.7	19.6	1.6
	INDIA	17.2	18.4	19.3	19.7	2.5

Source: IIPS and ORC Macro, 2000.

Table 5
Proportion of Women Married in Age Group 15-29, 1991 in Major States

Sr. No.	*Major States*	*Proportion married in specific age group in 1991 (%)*		
		15-19	*20-24*	*25-29*
1.	Andhra Pradesh	25.5	87.4	94.9
2.	Assam	23.2	66.5	87.1
3.	Bihar	55.3	92.0	97.2
4.	Gujarat	22.4	80.9	85.2
5.	Haryana	34.7	88.2	97.7
6.	Karnataka	27.1	75.1	92.0
7.	Kerala	11.3	55.5	83.5
8.	Madhya Pradesh	51.4	89.9	96.0
9.	Maharashtra	19.0	81.0	93.9
10.	Orissa	22.0	76.7	93.7
11.	Punjab	12.3	70.7	95.6
12.	Rajasthan	55.9	93.5	98.2
13.	Tamil Nadu	17.8	70.2	90.6
14.	Uttar Pradesh	46.7	91.2	97.6
15.	West Bengal	33.0	78.8	91.0
	INDIA	35.3	81.8	94.0

Source: Registrar General, India, 1991 Census, Table C-1.

Fifty to fifty six per cent of women aged 15-19 years in Bihar, Madhya Pradesh and Rajasthan were married at the time of 1991 Census. Conversely, in Kerala and Punjab, the proportion was only 11 and 12 per cent respectively. More than 70 per cent of the girls aged 20-24 years were married at the time of 1991 census except in Assam (66.5%) and in Kerala (55.5%). In Bihar, Madhya Pradesh, Rajasthan and Uttar Pradesh, at least 90 per cent of the women in this age group were married. And as expected almost all women in the 25-29 age group were married at the time of enumeration with the lowest per cent of 83.5 in Kerala and 85.2 in Gujarat.

PURPOSE OF THE STUDY

The vision India cherishes is to have the girls married off only after they attain 20 years of age, at least not before 18 years. This is clearly stated as one of the goals set by the National Population Policy, 2000 to be achieved by 2010 (Government of India, 2000). The policy stress is on decentralized planning which calls for information on age at marriage at the micro level not only to prepare the action plan but also to evaluate whether changes are really taking place as desired by the policy at the grass root level. In this context a study on currently prevailing age at marriage at district[2] level is, indeed, a necessity.

Available district level studies on age at marriage are based on small samples and restricted to a few districts (Audinarayana, 1990) or based on estimations obtained from census data (Bhagat, 2002). State level studies based on large scale surveys are also estimations (IIPS and ORC-MACRO, 2000) and conceal a large amount of internal variations. Studies based on actual data on age at marriage of those who got married during a specified time period at the district level for all the districts in the country has not yet been undertaken. It is felt that such a study will portray the real age at marriage situation than any estimations.

The primary focus of this study is to understand the ages at which the girls and boys in India get married. Such a study is overdue considering the fact that an evaluation of the effect of the Minimum Age at Marriage Act on the behaviour patterns of the people has not yet taken place, even though the Government has been increasing the legal minimum age at marriage from time to time.

Most often, if not always, the age at marriage of boys are ignored in research. Perhaps the studies that addresses the age at marriage are those that deal with reproduction, where the age at marriage of girls is more important than that of boys. But it is also of great importance to know when men begin their married lives which will define their sexual activity, fertility behaviour, their family obligations, conjugal roles, bases of financial and social support and future opinions which will be in a manner different from that of women (Malhotra, 1997). Hence this study will examine the age at marriage pattern of both girls and boys.

DATA SOURCE

The data for the study came from the recently concluded Rapid Household Survey on Reproductive and Child Health (RCH). Since the Government is committed to promote RCH programme in India with a stress on decentralized planning, information on programme variables at micro level are needed. In the absence of such recent information at the district level, the Department of Family Welfare, Ministry of Health and Family Welfare, Government of India launched a district level Rapid Household Survey in the country in 1998-99. From each district, samples of 1100 households were selected[3].

The household schedule of this survey has inserted two questions specifically relating to the current age at marriage of girls and boys. The survey was carried out in two phases and the reference period used for marriage data was three years prior to the survey. The questions were:

> *Was there any marriage among the usual residents of this household since 1st January 1995?*
>
> *If Yes, Who got married (boy or girl) and what was the age of that person at the time of marriage?*

The reference period for the second phase was 1st January 1996. The specific instruction given to the investigators was to enumerate all the marriages that took place during the reference period among the usual residents of the household and enter the sex and age of only that person who was/is a usual resident of the household and *not* the age of his/her spouse[4]. This is the data set that is used for this study.

METHODOLOGY

In 1995, India was divided into 506 districts and data were collected from 504[5]. On the whole, a total of 54030 marriages of girls and 66144 marriages of boys were reported from the 529,777 households enumerated in India. However, there were a total of 620 marriages among girls (1.1 per cent of total reported marriages) where the age at marriage was below 10 years. These cases are excluded from this report[6]. Since the grooms are, more often than not, older than the brides, the cut off age for boys was taken as 14 years and there were a total of 653 marriages of boys aged less than 14 years who were also not included in this analysis[7]. That means the age at marriage data for girls analysed here relates only to those who got married at age 10 and above and for boys, those who got married at the age of 14 and above. Table 6 gives the total number of surveyed districts, the total number of households surveyed and the total number of marriages that are reported from these households.

In this study, for easy reference, marriages will be classified into four categories based on age at marriage. For girls, the categories will be 10-14 years (child marriage), 15-17 years (early marriage), 18-19 years (acceptable marriage) and 20 years and above (preferred marriage). These demarcations of ages are not totally arbitrary. Taking a cue from the generally accepted classification of population below 15 years of age as children, those marriages are classified as child marriage. The legal minimum age at marriage for girls being 18 years, all marriages after completion of 15 years and before completing 18 years are taken as early marriage. However, as stated elsewhere in this report, the Government of India would prefer to have "all marriages of girls to be postponed till they attained 20 years of age, at least not before 18 years". Thus, marriages at ages 18 and 19 are taken as "acceptable marriage" and marriages after the completion of age 20 is considered as "preferred marriage". Marriages before 18 years "had profound physical, intellectual and psychological consequences for girls. It also meant premature pregnancy and often lead to a life time of domestic and sexual subservience" (French, 2001).

The age at marriage category for boys is slightly different from that of the girls though the age interval in all the age at marriage categories (except the child marriage category) is kept the same as that for girls. All marriages from 14 years to 17 years are taken as "child marriage". Age 21 being the legal minimum age at marriage for boys; marriages at ages 18 to 20 years

Table 6
Number of Districts, Households Surveyed and Number of Marriages Reported from each State and Union Territory

Sr. No.	State/UT Names	Short forms	No. of districts	No. of households surveyed	No. of reported marriages Girls (age 10+)	Boys (age 14+)
MAJOR STATES						
1.	Andhra Pradesh	AP	23	24,034	1,610	2,241
2.	Assam	ASM	22	23,817	1,734	2,964
3.	Bihar	BIH	43	46,138	6,168	7,201
4.	Gujarat	GUJ	19	20,748	2,349	3,292
5.	Haryana	HAR	17	17,537	2,104	2,888
6.	Karnataka	KAR	20	21,253	2,450	2,906
7.	Kerala	KER	14	14,396	2,151	2,102
8.	Madhya Pradesh	MP	45	46,355	4,186	5,321
9.	Maharashtra	MAH	30	32,176	3,542	4,230
10.	Orissa	ORI	30	32,214	2,890	3,930
11.	Punjab	PUN	17	18,014	2,282	2,954
12.	Rajasthan	RAJ	30	29,519	3,214	4,137
13.	Tamil Nadu	TN	23	23,850	2,355	2,556
14.	Uttar Pradesh	UP	68	72,262	7,245	9,014
15.	West Bengal	WB	18	19,923	2,238	2,784
SMALLER STATES/UNION TERRITORIES						
16.	Andaman & Nicobar	A&N	2	2,175	121	144
17.	Arunachal Pradesh	ARP	13	13,576	532	517
18.	Chandigarh	CHA	1	998	43	54
19.	Dadra & Nagar Haveli	D & NH	1	974	81	116
20.	Daman & Diu	D&D	2	2,177	234	307
21.	Delhi	DEL	1	1,000	119	102
22.	Goa	GOA	2	2,137	161	248
23.	Himachal Pradesh	HP	12	12,355	937	1,703
24.	Jammu & Kashmir	J&K	14	13,409	1,641	871
25.	Lakshadweep	LAK	1	1,095	159	98
26.	Manipur	MAN	8	8,405	628	768
27.	Meghalaya	MEG	7	7,240	425	147
28.	Mizoram	MIZ	3	3,315	203	249
29.	Nagaland	NAG	7	7,239	660	446
30.	Pondicherry	PON	4	4,181	527	479
31.	Sikkim	SIK	4	4,181	170	312
32.	Tripura	TRI	3	3,084	251	410
	TOTAL		504	529,777	53,410	65,491

Source: IIPS, 2001.

are treated as "early marriage". Since the Government of India is silent on the preferred age at marriage for boys, it is assumed that the same age difference will be expected even in this case as is the case with legal minimum age at marriage for girls. Thus "acceptable marriage" for boys will be from age 21 to 22 and "preferred marriage" will be from age 23 onwards. The classification is given in Table 7.

The *rapid* household survey of RCH did not include many background characteristics to save time. Hence, the analysis in this study will be carried out only on the basis of limited characteristics, viz. place of residence, caste and economic status. Note that all these variables reflect the socio-economic status of the household in one way or the other. In the absence of data on education of the concerned married person, the district level female literacy rate is considered in this study which is an acceptable development variable. The median age will also be calculated and classified on the basis of the above age at marriage categories for the analysis.

Table 7
Marriage Categories

Sr. No.	*Marriage category*	*Age category (age in completed years)*	
		Girls	*Boys*
1.	Child (CM)	10-14	14-17
2.	Early (EM)	15-17	18-20
3.	Acceptable (AM)	18-19	21-22
4.	Preferred (PM)	20+	23+
	Total	10+	14+

Place of residence is either rural or urban. The socio-economic and cultural differences between the rural and urban areas is an almost certain phenomenon in almost all countries of the world even though the rural to urban migration helps to dilute the situation a bit. However, in the major part of India this divide is still persisting and hence the need to differentiate and examine the prevailing age at marriage situation by place of residence. Generally, observation of traditional values and attitudes are more likely to be found in rural areas than in urban. Besides, in most cases the rural persons are comparatively less literate and less economically well off compared to those in urban areas. Hence place of residence will reflect the socio-economic status differences to a certain extent.

There are too many castes in India to have an individual classification. However, generally castes are grouped into a few categories. There are many castes that are socially and economically backward. With an intention to uplift their situation, the President of India is constitutionally empowered to declare a few castes as scheduled (SC) referring to their listing in Government rosters or schedules. Similarly there are tribes which are more like ethnic groups than castes who also need to be brought to the mainstream of the society. They are all categorised into one group called scheduled tribes (ST). Apart from these two, there are still some group of people who belong to low socio-economic class and are, therefore, categorised into what is called "Other Backward Class" (OBC). According to the Government policy these three categories are entitled to positive discrimination. All the rest of the castes which include mostly forward castes are usually referred to as "Other Castes" (OC). In this study the castes will be grouped into two categories, viz. SC, ST and OBC in one group and OC in the other.

Type of house is used as a proxy for economic status. Houses where the selected households were residing are classified into *Pucca*, Semi-*pucca* and *Kachcha* on the basis of the materials used for construction of houses. Good construction is classified as *pucca* and very bad construction mainly by mud, leaves, tin etc. are classified as *kachcha*. Semi-*pucca* falls in between *Pucca* and *Kachcha*. *Pucca*, semi-*pucca* and *Kachcha* houses represents high, medium and low economic status respectively.

Female literacy rate (FLR) is also classified as high, medium and low. If the FLR is less than 33.4 per cent, it is taken as low literacy level, between 33.4 and 66.6 is taken as medium literacy level and at least 66.7 per cent is taken as high literacy level. Though female literacy rate has its own direct relationship with girls' marriage age, it is also a very important development variable. Hence this variable will be used in the analysis of male age at marriage also.

Generally, for age at marriage analysis, only the average is used. However, here the actual data will also be analysed as such, to show the details that will be concealed once the average is calculated. It will show the districts where child marriages and early marriages still persist and therefore requires special attention from the administrators/policy makers–the main aim of this study.

Table 8 gives the background characteristics of the surveyed households in major state. It shows that, of the total selected households 78.9 per cent are from rural areas, 82 per cent belonged to Hindu religion, 61 per cent belonged to SC/ST/OBC and those living in Kachcha houses formed 39 per cent and those living in Pucca houses formed 29 per cent. The regional variation can be viewed from the said Table which shows that most of the major states follow almost the same pattern though with differences in magnitude.

LIMITATIONS OF THE DATA

There are basically three limitations in this data set: (i) no information is available on the achieved characteristics of the persons married, (ii) no information is available on many of the household characteristics and (iii) the order of marriage has also not been ascertained.

Table 8
Selected Back Ground Characteristics of Surveyed Households

Sr. No.	States	Residence Rural	Religion Hindu	Muslim	Caste SC/ST/ OBC	Type of house Kachcha	Pucca
1.	Andhra Pradesh	73.2	086.4	8.0	71.4	31.6	33.9
2.	Assam	88.8	69.6	27.4	44.2	66.1	13.7
3.	Bihar	87.9	84.7	13.8	79.3	62.3	16.8
4.	Gujarat	66.0	90.1	7.9	57.6	21.6	48.1
5.	Haryana	76.0	90.2	4.3	44.9	6.6	42.4
6.	Karnataka	69.3	85.4	11.0	54.4	18.8	20.8
7.	Kerala	74.6	59.2	21.4	66.2	9.7	56.1
8.	Madhya Pradesh	76.5	93.4	4.6	76.5	66.7	17.4
9.	Maharashtra	61.8	78.5	11.0	51.4	28.7	29.7
10.	Orissa	86.2	95.6	2.0	73.3	70.9	14.6
11.	Punjab	72.5	36.1	1.1	45.0	5.6	42.0
12.	Rajasthan	77.6	90.0	6.8	53.7	31.8	50.2
13.	Tamil Nadu	66.0	89.4	5.1	95.7	25.4	27.8
14.	Uttar Pradesh	81.1	82.3	16.9	64.8	38.9	27 .3
15.	West Bengal	73.0	74.6	24.2	37.0	60.9	20.5
	TOTAL	78.9	82.1	11.8	60.6	39.0	29.2

Source: IIPS, 2001.

ARRANGEMENT OF THE REPORT

This report will have four chapters. The first is introduction incorporating the importance of the study, data source, methodology and limitations of the data. Chapter II will deal with the age at marriage of girls and Chapter III will deal with the age at marriage of boys. Fourth and the last chapter will discuss the major findings and draw conclusions.

NOTES

1. Dowry or *Dahej* is the payment in cash or/and kind by the bride's family to the bridegroom's family along with the giving away of the bride, called *Kanyadaan* in India. *Kanyadanam* is an important part of Hindu marital rites. *Kanya* means daughter, and *daan* means gift. Dowry, which initially started as some kind of pocket money to the groom among the affluent has spread like wild fire among all and sundry. Now besides money, material goods like car, apartments, refrigerator, music system, utensils of all variety etc etc. are also finding its place in the dowry basket and not only for the groom but also for the groom's family members! The practice of dowry is prohibited by law through the Dowry Prohibition Act of 1961. However, the practice is still continuing with increased vigour in all the regions of the country irrespective of caste or class to such an extent that the parents of a girl will start worrying about dowry from the time of her birth. Arguably, earlier the marriage, lesser the dowry.
2. The smallest administrative unit.

3. From each district 50 primary sampling units (PSUs), i.e. villages/urban wards, were selected using the sampling technique Probability Proportional to Size (PPS). The 1991 population census data was used to decide the population size. From each PSU, 20 households were selected with 10 percent over sampling to take care of non-response. Thus from each district, samples of 1100 households were selected using circular systematic random sampling technique.
4. This was to avoid duplication in case one of the partners came from another selected household.
5. The data could not be collected from districts Kokrajhar (Assam) and Dhalai (Tripura) due to different problems that prevailed at the time of data collection.
6. Since marriages in India are still parentally decided, age has never been a problem, particularly in some parts of the country. However, marriage age below 10 years need be treated only as engagements as the girls will continue to stay with their parents even after the "marriage". On attainment of puberty, after another ceremony though small in magnitude, the girl will be sent to her in-law's house. Even so, most of these "marriages" are concentrated in three states, viz. Madhya Pradesh (16.8%), Rajasthan (45.2%) and Uttar Pradesh (14.0%).
7. Eighty five percent of these marriages were in Bihar (10.7), Madhya Pradesh (18.8), Rajasthan (28.9) and Uttar Pradesh (26.3).

Chapter - 2

AGE AT MARRIAGE OF GIRLS

GENERAL SITUATION

All the reported marriages of girls are classified into the four categories of marriage mentioned in the methodology, viz. child, early, acceptable and preferred. Among the total 53,410 marriages reported, 9.1, 26.2, 29.1 and 35.6 per cent respectively are child, early, acceptable and preferred marriages.

Most of the total 4850 child marriages are concentrated in four major states, viz. Bihar (22.4%), Madhya Pradesh (13.3%), Rajasthan (13.1%), and Uttar Pradesh (21.3%), together accounting for 70.1 per cent. West Bengal also has a fairly high per cent share (6.8) of the total child marriages.

The important point to note here, however, is that almost two-thirds of the total marriages were conducted only after the girl attained legally acceptable age of 18 years. This comprised of 29.1 per cent of acceptable and 35.6 per cent preferred marriages.

Marriages among the SC/ST/OBC accounted for 62 per cent and that among the castes other than SC/ST/OBC formed 35 per cent with 3 per cent having no caste data. The distribution among the different economic class shows that 28 per cent are from among the high economic status category, 39 per cent from low economic status category and the remaining 33 per cent from the medium economic status category. Ten per cent of the total marriages are reported from districts with low FLR, 70 per cent from districts with medium FLR and the remaining 20 per cent are from districts with high FLR.

DISTRIBUTION OF MARRIAGES/DISTRICTS IN STATES BY AGE AT MARRIAGE

The state-wise distribution of age at marriage by marriage category is given in Table 1. Of the total reported marriages more than 10 per cent of child marriage is observed only in Bihar (17.6%), Madhya Pradesh (15.4%),

Rajasthan (19.8%), Uttar Pradesh (14.3%), West Bengal (14.8%) and Dadra and Nagar Haveli (14.8%). Conversely from Kerala, Andaman and Nicobar, Chandigarh, Delhi, Lakshadweep and Mizoram no child marriage is reported.

Table 1
Percentage Distribution of Marriages by Marriage Category (Girls)

Sr. No.	State/Union Territories	Marriage category				Total reported marriages	
		Child	Early	Acceptable	Preferred	Percent	Number
	MAJOR STATES						
1.	Andhra Pradesh	7.9	29.1	35.8	27.1	100.0	1610
2.	Assam	4.3	21.9	25.6	48.3	100.0	1734
3.	Bihar	17.6	39.8	25.1	17.5	100.0	6168
4.	Gujarat	4.9	20.0	31.2	43.9	100.0	2349
5.	Haryana	4.4	25.1	34.9	35.6	100.0	2104
6.	Karnataka	9.8	24.1	26.9	39.2	100.0	2450
7.	Kerala	0.0	8.5	23.2	68.3	100.0	2151
8.	Madhya Pradesh	15.4	36.2	28.0	20.4	100.0	4186
9.	Maharashtra	6.2	26.0	38.3	29.4	100.0	3542
10.	Orissa	4.4	28.3	24.4	43.0	100.0	2890
11.	Punjab	1.3	9.6	27.6	61.6	100.0	2282
12.	Rajasthan	19.8	35.2	25.9	19.1	100.0	3214
13.	Tamil Nadu	1.3	16.4	28.5	53.8	100.0	2355
14.	Uttar Pradesh	14.3	32.9	30.1	22.7	100.0	7245
15.	West Bengal	14.8	35.9	23.3	26.0	100.0	2238
	SMALLER STATES/UNION TERRITORIES						
16.	Andaman &Nicobar	0.0	9.9	26.4	63.6	100.0	121
17.	Arunachal Pradesh	3.2	28.4	36.5	32.0	100.0	532
18.	Chandigarh	0.0	0.0	16.3	83.7	100.0	43
19.	Dadra & Nagar Haveli	14.8	35.8	27.2	22.2	100.0	81
20.	Daman & Diu	0.4	16.2	36.3	47.0	100.0	234
21.	Delhi	0.0	6.7	25.2	68.1	100.0	119
22.	Goa	0.6	2.5	6.8	90.1	100.0	161
23.	Himachal Pradesh	0.1	3.3	27.7	68.8	100.0	937
24.	Jammu & Kashmir	0.2	2.4	44.1	53.3	100.0	1641
25.	Lakshadweep	0.0	18.2	33.3	48.4	100.0	159
26.	Manipur	1.3	13.1	18.0	67.7	100.0	628
27.	Meghalaya	0.5	1.6	44.9	52.9	100.0	425
28.	Mizoram	0.0	13.8	32.5	53.7	100.0	203
29.	Nagaland	0.2	23.0	35.9	40.9	100.0	660
30.	Pondicherry	0.4	6.6	28.1	64.9	100.0	527
31.	Sikkim	0.6	14.1	28.2	57.1	100.0	170
32.	Tripura	4.4	28.3	25.9	41.4	100.0	251
	Total	9.1	26.2	29.1	35.6	100.0	53410

In Chandigarh no girl got married before attaining the legal minimum age at marriage of 18 years during the reference period. In Goa, Himachal Pradesh, Jammu & Kashmir and Meghalaya only less than five per cent of the total marriages are found to be below 18 years of age.

The mean and median age at marriage calculated for the states/Union Territories is given in Table 2. The median age at marriage is less than 18 years in Bihar, Madhya Pradesh, Rajasthan and West Bengal (in the case of mean age at marriage replace West Bengal by Uttar Pradesh). The highest median of 24 years is in Goa. Among the major states the highest median age of 21 years is in Kerala which is closely followed by Punjab and Tamil Nadu with a median age of 20 years.

Table 2
Average Age at Marriage and Marriage Category based on Median Age in States and Union Territories (Girls)

Sr. No.	State and union territories	Mean	Median	Coefficient of variation	Marriage category based on median age: Districts Percent EM	AM	PM	Total %	Total Number
MAJOR STATES									
1.	Andhra Pradesh	18.2	18.0	0.040	4.3	87.0	8.7	100	23
2.	Assam	19.7	19.0	0.056	4.5	54.5	40.9	100	22
3.	Bihar	16.9	17.0	0.047	72.1	27.9	0.0	100	43
4.	Gujarat	19.4	19.0	0.047	5.3	52.6	42.1	100	19
5.	Haryana	18.6	18.0	0.059	0.0	76.5	23.5	100	17
6.	Karnataka	18.9	18.0	0.086	20.0	50.0	30.0	100	20
7.	Kerala	21.7	21.0	0.071	0.0	7.1	92.9	100	14
8.	Madhya Pradesh	17.4	17.1	0.052	51.1	48.9	0.0	100	45
9.	Maharashtra	18.7	18.0	0.064	16.7	73.3	10.0	100	30
10.	Orissa	19.3	19.0	0.071	26.7	46.7	26.7	100	30
11.	Punjab	20.4	20.0	0.031	0.0	5.9	94.1	100	17
12.	Rajasthan	17.0	17.0	0.046	63.3	36.7	0.0	100	30
13.	Tamil Nadu	20.2	20.0	0.050	0.0	34.8	65.2	100	23
14.	Uttar Pradesh	17.5	18.0	0.076	48.5	42.6	7.4	98.5	68
15.	West Bengal	18.0	17.1	0.070	50.0	44.4	5.6	100	18
SMALLER STATES/UNION TERRITORIES									
16.	Andaman & Nicobar	20.6	19.0	0.052	0.0	50.0	50.0	100	2
17.	Arunachal Pradesh	18.9	18.0	0.039	0.0	92.3	7.7	100	13
18.	Chandigarh	22.7	22.0	0.000	0.0	0.0	100.0	100	1
19.	Dadra & Nagar Haveli	17.5	17.0	0.000	100.0	0.0	0.0	100	1
20.	Daman & Diu	19.7	19.0	0.002	0.0	100.0	0.0	100	2
21.	Delhi	20.7	21.0	0.000	0.0	0.0	100.0	100	1
22.	Goa	23.8	24.0	0.008	0.0	0.0	100.0	100	2
23.	Himachal Pradesh	20.9	21.0	0.023	0.0	0.0	100.0	100	12
24.	Jammu & Kashmir	20.4	20.0	0.057	0.0	21.4	78.6	100	14
25.	Lakshadweep	19.9	19.0	0.000	0.0	100.0	0.0	100	1
26.	Manipur	23.8	23.0	0.075	0.0	0.0	100.0	100	8
27.	Meghalaya	20.2	20.0	0.018	0.0	57.1	42.9	100	7
28.	Mizoram	21.4	20.0	0.049	0.0	33.3	66.7	100	3
29.	Nagaland	19.2	19.0	0.040	14.3	57.1	28.6	100	7
30.	Pondicherry	21.5	21.0	0.054	0.0	25.0	75.0	100	4
31.	Sikkim	21.2	21.0	0.029	0.0	25.0	75.0	100	4
32.	Tripura	20.3	19.0	0.059	0.0	66.7	33.3	100	3

Note: 1. Weighted mean and median.
2. District Maharajganj of Uttar Pradesh is the only district with a median age at marriage falling in the child marriage category (14.5 years)

Of the major states, Haryana, Kerala, Punjab and Tamil Nadu have no district with a median below 18 years of age and among smaller states and Union Territories all except Dadra & Nagar Haveli and one district in Nagaland (Kohima) fall in this category. However, a median of at least 20 years is found only in Chandigarh, Delhi, Goa, Himachal Pradesh, Jammu and Kashmir, Kerala, Manipur, Meghalaya, Mizoram, Pondicherry, Punjab, Sikkim and Tamil Nadu which together accounts for a mere 15 per cent of the total Indian population. Table 3 gives the per cent of districts by per cent share of marriages below legal minimum age.

Table 3
Percentage Distribution of Districts by per cent Share of Marriages below 18 years of age (Girls)

Sr. No.	*State/Union territory*	*Percentage distribution of districts by per cent share of marriages below legal minimum age at marriage*							
		0	*<10*	*10-19.9*	*20-29.9*	*30-49.9*	*50+*	*Total %*	*#*
MAJOR STATES									
1.	Andhra Pradesh	**	4.3	**	17.4	73.9	4.3	100.0	23
2.	Assam	**	27.3	13.6	22.7	31.8	4.5	100.0	22
3.	Bihar	**	**	**	4.7	23.3	72.1	100.0	43
4.	Gujarat	**	5.3	36.8	21.1	31.6	5.3	100.0	19
5.	Haryana	**	11.8	17.6	11.8	58.8	**	100.0	17
6.	Karnataka	**	5.0	25.0	15.0	35.0	20.0	100.0	20
7.	Kerala	42.9	21.4	28.6	**	7.1	**	100.0	14
8.	Madhya Pradesh	**	2.2	**	4.4	42.2	51.1	100.0	45
9.	Maharashtra	**	13.3	20.0	16.7	33.3	16.7	100.0	30
10.	Orissa	**	3.3	23.3	10.0	36.7	26.7	100.0	30
11.	Punjab	**	47.1	35.3	17.6	**	**	100.0	17
12.	Rajasthan	**	**	**	**	36.7	63.3	100.0	30
13.	Tamil Nadu	4.3	21.7	34.8	30.4	8.7	**	100.0	23
14.	Uttar Pradesh	**	5.9	13.2	8.8	23.5	48.5	100.0	68
15.	West Bengal	**	**	5.6	5.6	38.9	50.0	100.0	18
SMALLER STATES/UNION TERRITORIES									
16.	Andaman &Nicobar	**	**	50.0	**	**	50.0	100.0	2
17.	Arunachal Pradesh	7.7	7.7	7.7	7.7	69.2	**	100.0	13
18.	Chandigarh	100.0	**	**	**	**	**	100.0	1
19.	Dadra & Nagar Haveli	**	**	**	**	**	100.0	100.0	1
20.	Daman & Diu	**	**	100.0	**	**	**	100.0	2
21.	Delhi	**	100.0	**	**	**	**	100.0	1
22.	Goa	**	100.0	**	**	**	**	100.0	2
23.	Himachal Pradesh	8.3	83.3	8.3	**	**	**	100.0	12
24.	Jammu & Kashmir	28.6	64.3	**	7.1	**	**	100.0	14
25.	Lakshadweep	**	**	100.0	**	**	**	100.0	1
26.	Manipur	**	12.5	62.5	25.0	**	**	100.0	8
27.	Meghalaya	28.6	42.9	28.6	**	**	**	100.0	7
28.	Mizoram	**	66.7	**	33.3	**	**	100.0	3
29.	Nagaland	**	14.3	28.6	28.6	14.3	14.3	100.0	7
30.	Pondicherry	**	75.0	**	25.0	**	**	100.0	4
31.	Sikkim	**	**	100.0	**	**	**	100.0	4
32.	Tripura	**	**	33.3	**	66.7	**	100.0	3
	Total	3.4	13.9	15.5	10.9	29.0	27.4	100.0	504

** No district.

Of the total marriages, the per cent share of marriages conducted before the girl attained the legal minimum age at marriage of 18 years and the per cent of districts with a median age at marriage below 18 years is charted for each state and union territory in Fig. F-1. All the states and Union territories in India (except Chandigarh) have reported marriages below legal minimum age of 18 years though the median age at marriage below 18 years is noted only in 13 (of which 11 are major states) of the 32 states and Union territories. The highest share is noted in Bihar with 72 per cent of the districts reporting marriages below legal minimum age. The other major states with a high per cent of districts in this category are Rajasthan (63%), Madhya Pradesh (51%), West Bengal (50%) and Uttar Pradesh (49%). Dadra and Nagar Haveli is one district with a median age at marriage of 17 years and hence the 100 per cent shown in Figure F-1.

Fig. F-1: Percent share of Marriages Conducted before the girl attained 18 years of age and the percent of Districts with a Median Age Marriage below 18 years by state/UT

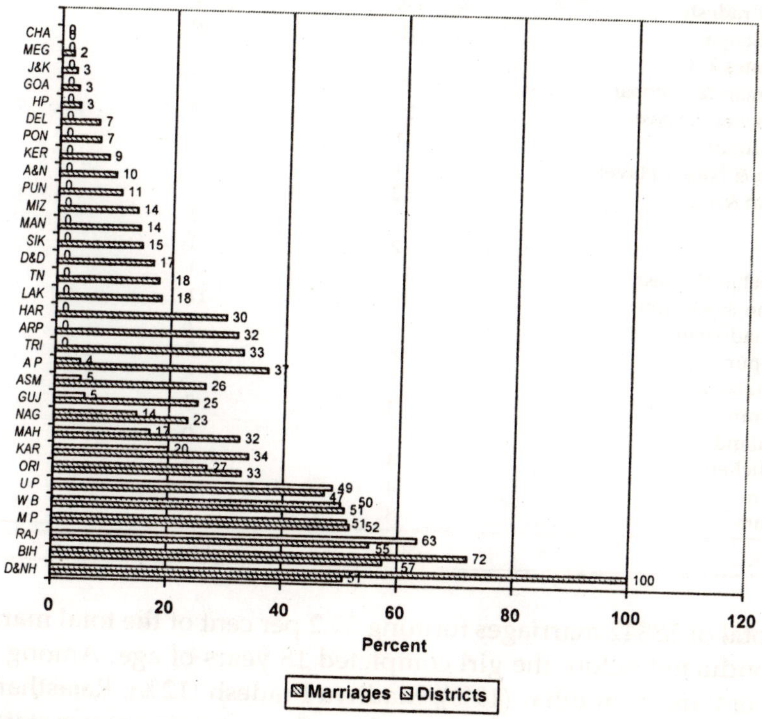

DISTRICT-WISE ANALYSIS

General Situation

The distribution of marriages in each district by marriage category, average age at marriage and per cent of marriages below legal minimum age of 18 years is given in Appendix I.

Table 4
Number of Districts with no child/early Marriage in each State/UT (Girls)

Sr. No.	State/UT	Number of Total districts	Number of districts with no CM	Number of districts with no EM
	Major states			
1.	Andhra Pradesh	23	1	0
2.	Assam	22	7	0
3.	Bihar	43	0	0
4.	Gujarat	19	3	0
5.	Haryana	17	2	0
6.	Karnataka	20	2	0
7.	Kerala	14	14	6
8.	Madhya Pradesh	45	0	0
9.	Maharashtra	30	6	0
10.	Orissa	30	3	0
11.	Punjab	17	6	0
12.	Rajasthan	30	0	0
13.	Tamil Nadu	23	10	1
14.	Uttar Pradesh	68	7	0
15.	West Bengal	18	0	0
	Smaller States/UT			
16.	Andaman & Nicobar	2	2	0
17.	Arunachal Pradesh	13	8	1
18.	Chandigarh	1	1	1
19.	Dadra & Nagar Haveli	1	0	0
20.	Daman & Diu	2	1	0
21.	Delhi	1	1	0
22.	Goa	2	1	0
23.	Himachal Pradesh	12	11	1
24.	Jammu & Kashmir	14	11	4
25.	Lakshadweep	1	1	0
26.	Manipur	8	3	0
27.	Meghalaya	7	5	2
28.	Mizoram	3	3	0
29.	Nagaland	7	6	0
30.	Pondicherry	4	2	0
31.	Sikkim	4	3	0
32.	Tripura	3	0	0
	TOTAL	504	120	16

A total of 18842 marriages forming 35.2 per cent of the total marriages were conducted before the girl completed 18 years of age. Among them, 58 per cent are from Bihar (19%), Madhya Pradesh (12%), Rajasthan (9%) and Uttar Pradesh (18%), 38 per cent from the remaining major states and 4 per cent from all the smaller states and Union territories. Further, majority of the below legal minimum age marriages in all these states are from Hindu families except Assam (Muslims: 60%), Kerala (Muslims: 80%) and Punjab (Sikhs: 70%).

The number of districts with no child/early marriage in each state and Union territory given in Table 4 shows that there are 120 districts with no child marriage and 16 districts with no marriage below legal minimum age of 18 years. These districts are one each from Chandigarh, Delhi, Daman & Due, Goa, Lakshdweep and Andhra Pradesh; two each from Andaman & Nicobar, Haryana, Karnataka and Pondicherry; three each from Gujarat, Manipur, Mizoram, Orissa and Sikkim; five from Meghalaya; six each from Maharashtra, Nagaland and Punjab; seven each from Assam and Uttar Pradesh; eight from Arunachal Pradesh; ten from Tamil Nadu; eleven each from Himachal Pradesh and Jammu and Kashmir; and fourteen from Kerala.

The per cent of districts with at least one child marriage, with at least 25 per cent child marriages and at least 25 per cent marriages below legal minimum age at marriage based on actual reported ages at marriage is given in Table 5. This Table also gives the per cent of districts with child marriage and the per cent of districts with below legal minimum age at marriage, both based on median age. While in all the major states (except Kerala) child marriages are reported from one district or the other, the same is reported from all the districts in Bihar, Madhya Pradesh, Rajasthan and West Bengal. The per cent of districts with at least one child marriage is also fairly high in Andhra Pradesh, Gujarat, Haryana, Karnataka, Maharashtra, Orissa and Uttar Pradesh.

Marriages below legal minimum age forming at least 25 per cent of the total marriages given in column 6 of Table 5 shows that of the major states all except Kerala, Punjab and to a certain extent Tamil Nadu have a sizable per cent of districts falling in this category.

Table 5

Per cent of Districts with Child and Early Marriages based on Actual and Median Age at Marriage in each State/UT (Girls)

Sr. No.	*State/UT*	*Total # of districts*	*Per cent of districts with (Based on actual age at marriage)*			*Per cent of districts with*	
			C M (<15 years)	*At least 25% CM*	*At least 25% marriages below legal minimum*	*Median age < 15 years*	*Median age below 18 years*
MAJOR STATES							
1.	Andhra Pradesh	23	95.7	0.0	91.3	0.0	4.3
2.	Assam	22	68.2	0.0	40.9	0.0	4.5
3.	Bihar	43	100.0	16.3	100.0	0.0	72.1
4.	Gujarat	19	84.2	0.0	52.6	0.0	5.3
5.	Haryana	17	88.2	0.0	70.6	0.0	0.0
6.	Karnataka	20	90.0	10.0	60.0	0.0	20.0
7.	Kerala	14	0.0	0.0	7.1	0.0	0.0
8.	Madhya Pradesh	45	100.0	15.6	95.6	0.0	51.1
9.	Maharashtra	30	80.0	0.0	63.3	0.0	16.7

Contd...

Sr. No.	State/UT	Total # of districts	Per cent of districts with (Based on actual age at marriage)			Per cent of districts with	
			C M (<15 years)	At least 25% CM	At least 25% marriages below legal minimum	Median age < 15 years	Median age below 18 years
10.	Orissa	30	90.0	3.3	70.0	0.0	26.7
11.	Punjab	17	64.7	0.0	5.9	0.0	0.0
12.	Rajasthan	30	100.0	26.7	100.0	0.0	63.3
13.	Tamil Nadu	23	56.5	0.0	30.4	0.0	0.0
14.	Uttar Pradesh	68	89.7	20.6	77.9	1.5	48.5
15.	West Bengal	18	100.0	11.1	94.4	0.0	50.0
SMALLER STATES/UNION TERRITORIES							
16.	Andaman & Nicobar	2	0.0	0.0	0.0	0.0	0.0
17.	Arunachal Pradesh	13	38.5	0.0	76.9	0.0	0.0
18.	Chandigarh	1	0.0	0.0	0.0	0.0	0.0
19.	Dadra & Nagar Haveli	1	100.0	100.0	100.0	0.0	100.0
20.	Daman & Diu	2	50.0	0.0	0.0	0.0	0.0
21.	Delhi	1	0.0	0.0	0.0	0.0	0.0
22.	Goa	2	50.0	0.0	0.0	0.0	0.0
23.	Himachal Pradesh	12	8.3	0.0	0.0	0.0	0.0
24.	Jammu & Kashmir	14	21.4	0.0	7.1	0.0	0.0
25.	Lakshadweep	1	0.0	0.0	0.0	0.0	0.0
26.	Manipur	8	62.5	0.0	0.0	0.0	0.0
27.	Meghalaya	7	28.6	0.0	0.0	0.0	0.0
28.	Mizoram	3	0.0	0.0	33.3	0.0	0.0
29.	Nagaland	7	14.3	0.0	42.9	0.0	14.3
30.	Pondicherry	4	50.0	0.0	0.0	0.0	0.0
31.	Sikkim	4	25.0	0.0	0.0	0.0	0.0
32.	Tripura	3	100.0	0.0	66.7	0.0	0.0
	TOTAL	504	76.2	8.3	62.9	0.2	27.2

The names of the districts with no child marriage are given in Table 6.

Even though there are 384 districts with at least one child marriage reported, there are only 42 districts where at least one in every four marriages is found to be below 15 years of age'. These districts are from Dadra and Nagar Haveli (1), Bihar (7), Dadra and Nagar Haveli (1), Karnataka (2), Madhya Pradesh (7), Orissa (1), Rajasthan (8), Uttar Pradesh (14) and West Bengal (2). Half the marriages reported from Maharajganj district of Uttar Pradesh during the reference period are below 15 years of age. The names of these 42 districts are given in Table 7.

Early marriages are found in almost all the districts with degrees of differences. But 53.5 per cent of the total early marriages are from the districts of Rajasthan (8.1), Madhya Pradesh (10.8) Uttar Pradesh (17.0) and Bihar (17.5). The per centage distribution of districts by marriages

Table 6
Districts with no child marriage (Girls)

Sr. No.	*District (State)*	*Sr. No.*	*District (State)*	*Sr. No.*	*District (State)*
1.	Aizwal(MIZ)	41.	Kangra(HP)	81.	Poonch(J&K)
2.	Alappuzha(KER)	42.	Kanniyakumari(TN)	82.	Pulawama(J&K)
3.	Almora(UP)	43.	Kannur(KER)	83.	Raigarh(MAH)
4.	Amravali(MAH)	44.	Kanpur Nagar(UP)	84.	Rajori(J&K)
5.	Amreli(GUJ)	45.	Kapurthala(PUJ)	85.	Ramanathapuram(TN)
6.	Anantnag(J&K)	46.	Karbi Anglong(ASM)	86.	Ri Bhoi (MEG)
7.	Andaman(A&N)	47.	Kasaragod(KER)	87.	Rupnagar(PUJ)
8.	Bangalore (KAR)	48.	Kathua(J&K)	88.	Sambalpur(ORI)
9.	Baramulla(J&K)	49.	Kohima(NAG)	89.	Senapati(MAN)
10.	Barpeta(ASM)	50.	Kollam(KER)	90.	Shimla(HP)
11.	Bhandara(MAH)	51.	Kottayam(KER)	91.	Shivganganagar(TN)
12.	Bijnor(UP)	52.	Kozhikode(KER)	92.	Sindhudurg(MAH)
13.	Bilaspur(HP)	53.	Kullu(HP)	93.	Sirmaur(HP)
14.	Bishnupur(MAN)	54.	Kupuwada(J&K)	94.	Solan(HP)
15.	Budgam(J&K)	55.	Kurukshetra(HAR)	95.	South Garo Hills(MEG)
16.	Chamba(HP)	56.	Lahul & Spiti(HP)	96.	South Goa(GOA)
17.	Chandigarh(CHN)	57.	Lakshadweep	97.	South Sikkim(SIK)
18.	Chennai(TN)	58.	Lohit(ARP)	98.	S.urendranagar(GUJ)
19.	Chhimtuipui(MIZ)	59.	Ludhiana(PUJ)	99.	Tawang(ARP)
20.	Coimbatore(TN)	60.	Lungeli(MIZ)	100.	Tehri Garwal(UP)
21.	Cuttak(ORI)	61.	Mahe(PON)	101.	Thanjavur(TN)
22.	Dakshina Kannada (KAR)	62.	Malappuram(KER)	102.	Thirunelveli(TN)
23.	Delhi	63.	Mandi(HP)	103.	Thiruvanathapuram(KER)
24.	Dhemaji(ASM)	64.	Meerut(UP)	104.	Thrissur(KER)
25.	Dibrugarh(ASM)	65.	Mokokchung(NAG)	105.	Tinsukia(ASM)
26.	Diu (D&D)	66.	Mon(NAG)	106.	Tirap (ARP)
27.	Doda(J&K)	67.	Namakkal(TN)	107.	Tuensang(NAG)
28.	East Garo Hills(MEG)	68.	Nawanshahar(PUJ)	108.	Udhampur(J&K)
29.	East Siang(ARP)	69.	Nicobar(A&N)	109.	Ukhrul(MAN)
30.	Ernakulam(KER)	70.	Nilgiris(TN)	110.	Una(HP)
31.	Greater Bombay (MAH)	71.	North Cachar Hill (ASM)	111.	Upper Siang(ARP)
32.	Gurdaspur(PUJ)	72.	North Sikkim(SIK)	112.	Uttarkashi(UP)
33.	Hamirpur(HP)	73.	Palghat(KER)	113.	Wardha(MAH)
34.	Hoshiarpur(PUJ)	74.	Panipat(HAR)	114.	Wayanad(KER)
35.	Hyderabad(AP)	75.	Papumpare(ARP)	115.	West Garo Hills(MEG)
36.	Idukki(KER)	76.	Pathanamthitta(KER)	116.	West Kameng(ARP)
37.	Jammu(J&K)	77.	Pauri Garhwal(UP)	117.	West Khasi Hills(MEG)
38.	Jamnagar(GUJ)	78.	Periyar(TN)	118.	West Siang(ARP)
39.	Jharsuguda(ORI)	79.	Phek(NAG)	119.	West Sikkim(SIK)
40.	Jorhat(ASM)	80.	Pondicherry	120.	Wokha(NAG)

Table 7

Districts with at least 25 per cent of total Reported Marriages Falling in the Child Marriage Category (Girls)

Sr. No.	*District (State)*	*Sr. No.*	*District (State)*	*Sr. No.*	*District (State)*
1.	Ajmer(RAJ)	15.	Faizabad(UP)	29.	Ratlam(MP)
2.	Ambedkarnagar(UP)	16.	Gaya(BIH)	30.	Rohtas(BIH)
3.	Azamgarh(UP)	17.	Gonda(UP)	31.	Samastipur(BIH)
4.	Bahraich(UP)	18.	Jhalawar(RAJ)	32.	Shahdol(MP)
5.	Banda(UP)	19.	Lalitpur(UP)	33.	Shajahanabad(UP)
6.	Basti(UP)	20.	Maharajganj(UP)	34.	Shajapur(MP)
7.	Bhilwara(RAJ)	21.	Murshidabad(WB)	35.	Sidhart Nagar(UP)
8.	Bidar(KAR)	22.	Nagaur(RAJ)	36.	Sidhi(MP)
9.	Bijapur(KAR)	23.	Nawada(BIH)	37.	Sonbhadra(UP)
10.	Bundi(RAJ)	24.	Nawrangapura(ORI)	38.	Sultanpur(UP)
11.	Chattarpur(MP)	25.	Palamu(BIH)	39.	Tikamgarh(MP)
12.	Dadra & nagar Haveli	26.	Patna(BIH)	40.	Tonk(RAJ)
13.	Dausa(RAJ)	27.	Puruliya(WB)	41.	Udaipur(RAJ)
14.	Deoghar(BIH)	28.	Rajgarh(MP)	42.	Varanasi(UP)

below legal minimum age of 18 years based on reported age at marriage is given in Figure F-2.

Fig. F-2: Percentage Distribution of Districts by Marriages below 18 years of Age based on Reported Marriages (Girls)

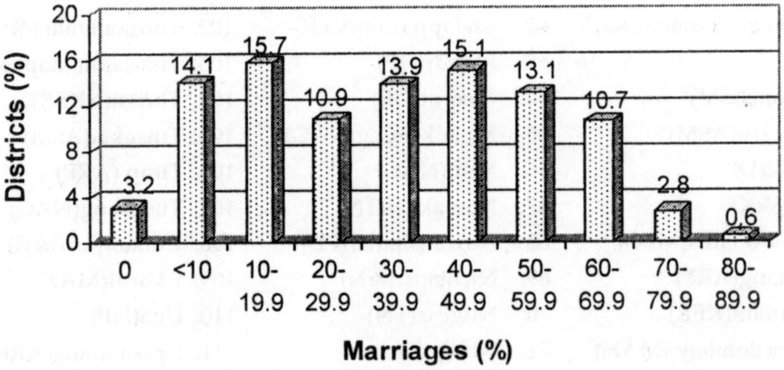

There is no marriage below 18 years in 3.2 per cent of the districts (16 in number) and these districts are from Kerala (6), Tamil Nadu (1), Andaman and Nicobar (1), Chandigarh (1), Himachal Pradesh (1), Jammu & Kashmir (4) and Meghalaya (2). The names of these districts are given in Table 8.

Fourteen per cent of the districts have only less than 10 per cent of their total marriages below 18 years and another 16 per cent have only 10-20 per cent of the marriages in this category. At the other extreme, 3.4 per cent of the total districts (17 in number) reported more than 70 per cent of marriages falling below legal minimum age at marriage. These districts are from five states - Bihar (2), Madhya Pradesh (3), Rajasthan (4), Uttar Pradesh (6) and West Bengal (2) and their names are given in Table 9.

Table 8
Districts with no Marriage below legal Minimum Age at Marriage of 18 years (Girls)

Sr. No.	*District (State)*	*Sr. No.*	*District (State)*	*Sr. No.*	*District (State)*
1.	Alappuzha (Kerala)	7.	Kanniyakumari (Tamil Nadu)	13.	Kupwara (Jammu & Kashmir)
2.	Ernakulam (Kerala)	8.	Tawang (Arunachal Pradesh)	14.	Pulwama (Jammu & Kashmir)
3.	Kollam (Kerala)	9.	Chandigarh (Chandigarh)	15.	East Garo Hills (Meghalaya)
4.	Kottayam (Kerala)	10.	Lahul & Spiti (Himachal Pradesh)	16.	South Garo Hills (Meghalaya)
5.	Pathanamthitta (Kerala)	11.	Doda (Jammu & Kashmir)		
6.	Thiruvananthapuram (Kerala)	12.	Kathua (Jammu & Kashmir)		

Table 9
Districts with at least Seventy per cent Marriages below 18 years of Age (Girls)

Sr. No.	*District (State)*	*Sr. No.*	*District (State)*	*Sr. No.*	*District (State)*
1.	Bahraich(UP)	7.	Dausa(RAJ)	13.	Patna(BIH)
2.	Banda(UP)	8.	Lalitpur(UP)	14.	Puruliya(WB)
3.	Basti(UP)	9.	Maharajganj(UP)	15.	Shajapur(MP)
4.	Bhilwara(RAJ)	10.	Morena(MP)	16.	Tonk(RAJ)
5.	Bundi(RAJ)	11.	Murshidabad(WB)	17.	Varanasi(UP)
6.	Chattarpur(MP)	12.	Nawada(BIH)		

Turning to marriages conducted after attainment of legal minimum age at marriage, there are 374 districts with at least 50 per cent of marriages conducted after the girl attained 18 years of age. Among them, 18 districts have 50-60 per cent of the marriages that could be classified as acceptable (age at the time of marriage being 18-20 years). These districts are one each from Arunachal Pradesh (Lohit), Assam (Karbi Aglong), Karnataka (Bangalore Rural) and Nagaland (Mon), two each from Jammu and Kashmir (Rajauri & Udhampur) and Maharashtra (Kolhapur & Satara), three each from Meghalaya (Rai Bhoi, South Garo Hills & West Garo Hills) and Uttar Pradesh (Pauri Garhwal, Rampur & Tehri Garhwal) and four from Madhya Pradesh (Balaghat, Betul, Mandla & Raigarh). Raigarh in Madhya Pradesh and Rajouri in Jammu & Kashmir have 62 per cent and 81 per cent respectively of acceptable marriages.

In 143 districts, at least 50 per cent of marriages were conducted only after the girl attained the preferred age at marriage of 20 years. Whereas all the districts in Chandigarh, Delhi, Goa, Himachal Pradesh and Manipur have at least 50 per cent of marriages in the preferred category, there is no district in Bihar, Madhya Pradesh, Rajasthan, Dadra & Nagar Haveli, Daman & Diu and Lakshadweep that fall into this category of marriage. Ninety three to ninety four per cent of the districts in Kerala and Punjab, about fourth-fifths of the districts in Jammu and Kashmir, three-fourths of the districts in Pondicherry and Sikkim, two-thirds of the districts in Tamil Nadu and Mizoram also reported preferred marriages of at least 50 per cent of the total marriages.

In 191 districts at least 75 per cent of marriages were conducted only after the girl attained 18 years of age. Further, in 139 of *these* districts at least 50 per cent of marriages were effected only after the girl completed 20 years of age. The names of these 139 districts are given in Table 10.

On the whole, going by the total reported ages at marriage in each state and Union Territory, at least 75 per cent were conducted after completion of 18 years in 18 of the 32 states/Union Territories. They are Andaman & Nicobar, Chandigarh, Daman & Diu, Delhi, Goa, Gujarat, Himachal Pradesh, Jammu & Kashmir, Kerala, Lakshadweep, Manipur, Meghalaya, Mizoram, Nagaland, Pondicherry, Punjab, Sikkim and Tamil Nadu. However, the total population of these 18 states/Union Territories together accounts for only 20.5 per cent of the total Indian population.

Table 10
Districts with at least 75 per cent of Marriages after Completion of 18 years and at least 50 per cent of Marriages after Completion of age 20 years (Girls)

Sr. No.	*District (State)*	*Sr. No.*	*District (State)*	*Sr. No.*	*District (State)*
1.	Aizwal(MIZ)	47.	Jagatsinghpur(ORI)	93.	North Sikkim(SIK)
2.	Alappuzha(KER)	48.	Jaintia Hill(MEG)	94.	Palghat(KER)
3.	Ambala(HAR)	49.	Jajpur(ORI)	95.	Pathanamthitta(KER)
4.	Amritsar(PUJ)	50.	Jalandhar(PUJ)	96.	Patiala(PUJ)
5.	Anantnag(J&K)	51.	Jammu(J&K)	97.	Periyar(TN)
6.	Badgam(J&K)	52.	Jamnagar(GUJ)	98.	Pondichery(PON)
7.	Bangalore (KAR)	53.	Jorhat(ASM)	99.	Pudukottai(TN)
8.	Baramulla(J&K)	54.	Junagadh(GUJ)	100.	Pulawama(J&K)
9.	Bathinda(PUJ)	55.	Kamrup(ASM)	101.	Punch(J&K)
10.	Bhadrak(ORI)	56.	Kangra(HP)	102.	Puri(ORI)
11.	Bhandara(MAH)	57.	Kanniyakumari(TN)	103.	Rajkot(GUJ)
12.	Bharuch(GUJ)	58.	Kannur(KER)	104.	Ramanathapuram(TN)
13.	Bilaspur(HP)	59.	Kanpur Nagar(UP)	105.	Rupnagar(PUJ)
14.	Bishnupur(MAN)	60.	Kapurthala(PUJ)	106.	Sangrur(PUJ)
15.	Cachar(ASM)	61.	Karaikal(PON)	107.	Senapati(MAN)
16.	Chamba(HP)	62.	Karimganj(ASM)	108.	Shimla(HP)
17.	Chamoli(UP)	63.	Kasaragod(KER)	109.	Shimoga(KAR)
18.	Chandel(MAN)	64.	Kathua(J&K)	110.	Shivganganagar(TN)
19.	Chandigarh(CHN)	65.	Kendrapara(ORI)	111.	Sibsagar(ASM)

Contd....

Sr. No.	*District (State)*	*Sr. No.*	*District (State)*	*Sr. No.*	*District (State)*
20.	Chengalpattu(TN)	66.	Khordha(ORI)	112.	Sindhudurg(MAH)
21.	Chennai(TN)	67.	Kinnaur(HP)	113.	Sirmaur(HP)
22.	Chikmaglur(KAR)	68.	Kodagu(KAR)	114.	Solan(HP)
23.	Chittor(AP)	69.	Kolkata(WB)	115.	Sonipat(HAR)
24.	Churachandpur(MAN)	70.	Kollam(KER)	116.	South Goa(GOA)
25.	Coimbatore(TN)	71.	Kottayam(KER)	117.	South Sikkim(SIK)
26.	Cuttak(ORI)	72.	Kozhikode(KER)	118.	Srinagar(J&K)
27.	Dakshina Kannada(KAR	73.	Kullu(HP)	119.	Surat(GUJ)
28.	Darjeeling(WB)	74.	Kupuwada(J&K)	120.	Surendranagar(GUJ)
29.	Dehradun(UP)	75.	Kurukshetra(HAR)	121.	Tamenglong(MAN)
30.	Delhi	76.	Lahul & Spiti(HP)	122.	Tawang(ARP)
31.	Dhemaji(ASM)	77.	Leh(J&K)	123.	Thanjavur(TN)
32.	Doda(J&K)	78.	Ludhiana(PUJ)	124.	The Nilgiris(TN)
33.	East Garo Hill(MEG)	79.	Lungeli(MIZ)	125.	Thirunelveli(TN)
34.	East Sikkim(SIK)	80.	Mahe(PON)	126.	Thiruvanathapuram(KE)
35.	Ernakulam(KER)	81.	Mandi(HP)	127.	Thoubal(MAN)
36.	Faridkot(PUJ)	82.	Mansa(PUJ)	128.	Thrissur(KER)
37.	Fatehgarh Sahib(PUJ)	83.	Meerut(UP)	129.	Tuensang(NAG)
38.	Greater Bombay(MAH)	84.	Moga(PUJ)	130.	Tutikorin(TN)
39.	Gurdaspur(PUJ)	85.	Mokokchung(NAG)	131.	Ukhrul(MAN)
40.	Hailakandi(ASM)	86.	Muktsar(PUJ)	132.	Una(HP)
41.	Hamirpur(HP)	87.	Nalbari(ASM)	133.	Uttar Kannada(KAR)
42.	Hardwar(UP)	88.	Namakkal(TN)	134.	Valsad(GUJ)
43.	Hoshiarpur(PUJ)	89.	Nawanshahar(PUJ)	135.	Virudunagar(TN)
44.	Hyderabad(AP)	90.	Nicobar(A&N)	136.	Wayanad(KER)
45.	Idukki(KER)	91.	North Cachar Hill(AS	137.	West Khasi Hills (MEG)
46.	Imphal(MAN)	92.	North Goa(GOA)	138.	West Tripura(TRI)
				139.	Yamunanagar(HAR)

Median age at Marriage

Median age also shows that among the major states there is no district with a median age below 18 years in Haryana, Kerala, Punjab and Tamil Nadu. The names of the 137 districts with a median age at marriage below legal minimum age of 18 years are given in Table 11.

Table 11

Districts with Median Age at Marriage below 18 years of Age (Girls)

Sr. No.	*District(state)*	*Sr. No.*	*District(state)*	*Sr. No.*	*District(state)*
1.	Allahabad(UP)	47.	Dholpur(RAJ)	93.	Nagaur(RAJ)
2.	Alwar(RAJ)	48.	Dhubri(ASM)	94.	Nalanda(BIH)
3.	Ambedkarnagar(UP)	49.	Etah(UP)	95.	Nanded(MAH)
4.	Araria(BIH)	50.	Faizabad(UP)	96.	Nawada(BIH)
5.	Aurangabad(BIH)	51.	Firozabad(UP)	97.	Nawrangapura(ORI)
6.	Aurangabad(MAH)	52.	Ganjam(ORI)	98.	Nayagarh(ORI)
7.	Azamgarh(UP)	53.	Gaya(BIH)	99.	Palamu(BIH)
8.	Bahraich(UP)	54.	Ghazipur(UP)	100.	Pali(RAJ)
9.	Ballia(UP)	55.	Giridih(BIH)	101.	Panna(MP)

Contd....

Sr. No.	District(state)	Sr. No.	District(state)	Sr. No.	District(state)
10.	Banas Kantha(GUJ)	56.	Godda(BIH)	102.	Patna(BIH)
11.	Banda(UP)	57.	Gonda(UP)	103.	Pilibhit(UP)
12.	Bankura(WB)	58.	Gopalganj(BIH)	104.	Pratapgarh(UP)
13.	Banswara(RAJ)	59.	Gorakhpur(UP)	105.	Purba Champaran(BIH)
14.	Barabanki(UP)	60.	Guna(MP)	106.	Puruliya(WB)
15.	Barddhaman(WB)	61.	Hanumangarh(RAJ)	107.	Raichur(KAR)
16.	Barmer(RAJ)	62.	Hazaribag(BIH)	108.	Raipur(MP)
17.	Basti(UP)	63.	Jaisalmer(RAJ)	109.	Rajgarh(MP)
18.	Beed(MAH)	64.	Jalaun(UP)	110.	Rajnandgaon(MP)
19.	Begusarai(BIH)	65.	Jalna(MAH)	111.	Rewa(MP)
20.	Belgaum(KAR)	66.	Jaunpur(UP)	112.	Rohtas(BIH)
21.	Bhadohi(UP)	67.	Jehanabad(BIH)	113.	Sagar(MP)
22.	Bhagalpur(BIH)	68.	Jhabua(MP)	114.	Saharsa(BIH)
23.	Bharatpur(RAJ)	69.	Jhalawar(RAJ)	115.	Sahibganj(BIH)
24.	Bhilwara(RAJ)	70.	Jodhpur(RAJ)	116.	Samastipur(BIH)
25.	Bhind(MP)	71.	Kalahandi(ORI)	117.	Saran(BIH)
26.	Bhojpur(BIH)	72.	Khagaria(BIH)	118.	Satna(MP)
27.	Bidar(KAR)	73.	Kheri(UP)	119.	Shahdol(MP)
28.	Bijapur(KAR)	74.	Kohima(NAG)	120.	Shajahanabad(UP)
29.	Bikaner(RAJ)	75.	Kooch Bihar(WB)	121.	Shajapur(MP)
30.	Birbhum(WB)	76.	Koraput(ORI)	122.	Shivpuri(MP)
31.	Bolangir(ORI)	77.	Kota(RAJ)	123.	Sidhart Nagar(UP)
32.	Boudh(ORI)	78.	Lalitpur(UP)	124.	Sidhi(MP)
33.	Budaun(UP)	79.	Latur(MAH)	125.	Sitamarhi(BIH)
34.	Bundi(RAJ)	80.	Madhepura(BIH)	126.	Sitapur(UP)
35.	Buxar(BIH)	81.	Madhubani(BIH)	127.	Sonbhadra(UP)
36.	Chattarpur(MP)	82.	Maharajganj(UP)	128.	Sultanpur(UP)
37.	Churu(RAJ)	83.	Mahoba(UP)	129.	Surguja(MP)
38.	Dadra	84.	Mainpuri(UP)	130.	Tikamgarh(MP)
39.	Dakshin Dinajpur(WB)	85.	Maldah (WB)	131.	Tonk(RAJ)
40.	Damoh(MP)	86.	Malkangiri(ORI)	132.	Udaipur(RAJ)
41.	Darbhanga(BIH)	87.	Mandsaur(MP)	133.	Uttar Dinajpur(WB)
42.	Dausa(RAJ)	88.	Mirzapur(UP)	134.	Vaishali(BIH)
43.	Deoghar(BIH)	89.	Morena(MP)	135.	Varanasi(UP)
44.	Deoria(UP)	90.	Munger(BIH)	136.	Vidisha(MP)
45.	Dewas(MP)	91.	Murshidabad(WB)	137.	Vishakhapatanam(AP)
46.	Dhar(MP)	92.	Muzaffarpur(BIH)		

The per centage distribution of these 137 districts by median age at marriage is given in Figure F-3 below.

It is of some relief to know that half the districts with median age at marriage below 18 years are concentrated in the 17.0 to 17.9 years category, indicating, perhaps, that the day will not be too far when all marriages of girls will be conducted after the girl completed 18 years of age. Considering the fact that the singulate mean age at marriage for the country as a whole was only 15.6 years in 1951, this is a great achievement for a vast country like India with all her diverse characteristics/culture.

Fig. F-3: Percentage Distribution of the Districts with Median Age at Marriage below 18 years of Age (Girls)

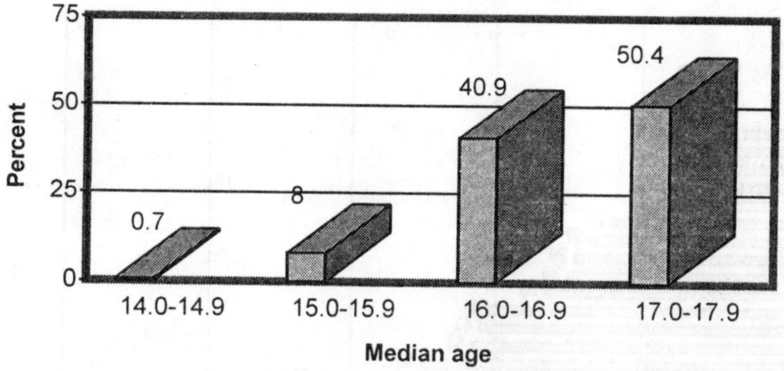

Ninety per cent of the total 137 districts with a median of less than 18 years are located in six states: viz. Bihar, Madhya Pradesh, Rajasthan, Orissa, Uttar Pradesh and West Bengal (Figure F-4).

Fig. F-4: Percentage Distribution of Districts with Age at Marriage below 18 years in selected States (Girls)

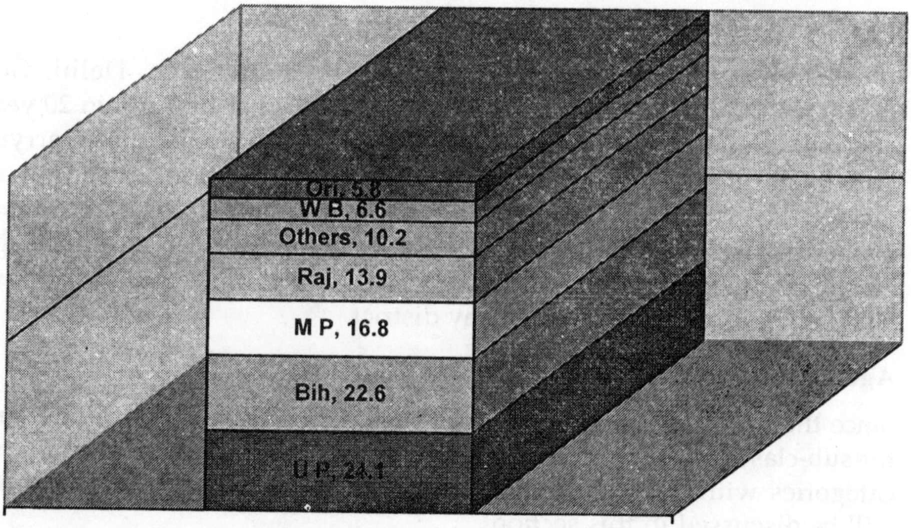

Of the 85 districts belonging to the smaller states and Union territories, 83 districts have median age at marriage of at least 18 years (the two exceptions are Dadra & Nagar Haveli and Kohima in Nagaland with a median of 17 years). Also it is found that 50 of these districts have a median age at marriage of at least 20.

The per cent of districts in each state/ union territory having a median age at marriage of at least 20 years is given in Figure F-5.

Fig. F-5: Percentage of Districts in each State/UT with a Median Age at Marriage of at least 20 years (Girls)

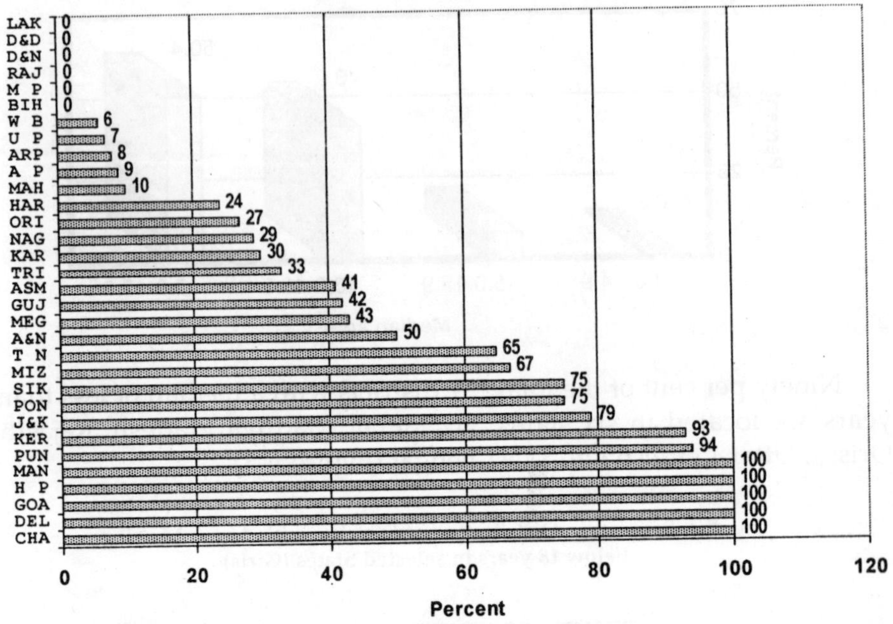

Going by median age at marriage, in Chandigarh, Delhi, Goa, Himachal Pradesh and Manipur, girls marrying after they attain 20 years of age have already became the norm. In Kerala and Punjab also marrying after attainment of at least 20 years have become the norm except in one district each (Malappuram in Kerala and Firozpur in Punjab). However, in the districts of Bihar, Madhya Pradesh, Rajasthan, Dadra and Nagar Haveli, Daman and Diu and Lakshadweep the median age at marriage has not yet reached 20 years in any district.

Age at Marriage by Characteristics

Since the number of marriages from each district is not sufficiently large for sub-classification into the four categories of age at marriage, only two categories with the legal minimum age at marriage as the cut off point will be discussed in this section.

(a) Place of Residence

No marriage of girls was reported from the rural areas of six districts and the urban areas of 26 districts. Appendix II gives the district-wise information on per cent share of marriages below the legal minimum age at marriage, mean and median age at marriage along with the number of marriages reported from each district by place of residence. The per cent of marriages below legal minimum age at marriage varies in rural areas from zero in 22 districts to 86.6 per cent in Lalitpur (Uttar Pradesh) and in urban areas, from zero in 95 districts to 86.7 per cent in Patna (Bihar)[1]. The summary picture is provided in the Figure F-6.

Fig. F-6: Percentage Distribution of Districts by per cent share of Marriages below 18 years of Age in Rural and Urban areas (Girls)

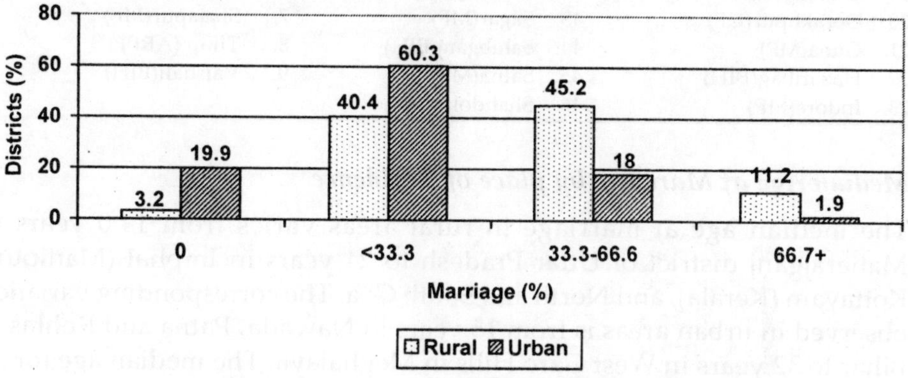

Whereas 11 per cent of the districts in rural areas have at least two-thirds of the marriages below legal minimum age at marriage, the corresponding per centage in urban areas is only 2 per cent. At the other end, there are just 3 per cent of the districts with no marriage below legally permissible age in rural areas compared to 20 per cent in urban areas. In 56 districts (11.2 %) at least two-thirds of the marriages in rural areas are below 18 years and the corresponding share for urban is only nine (1.9 %). The names of these districts are given in Table 12.

Table 12

Districts with Marriages below 18 years Forming at least two-thirds of the Total Marriages in Rural and Urban areas (Girls)

Sr. No.	*District (State)*	*Sr. No.*	*District (State)*	*Sr. No.*	*District (State)*
	RURAL		**RURAL**		**RURAL**
1.	Ahmadabad(GUJ)	24.	Jhalawar(RAJ)	47.	Shajapur(MP)
2.	Ajmer(RAJ)	25.	Jodhpur(RAJ)	48.	Shivpuri(MP)
3.	Ambedkarnagar(UP)	26.	Koraput(ORI)	49.	Sidhi(MP)
4.	Bahraich(UP)	27.	Kota(RAJ)	50.	Sitapur(UP)
5.	Banda(UP)	28.	Lalitpur(UP)	51.	Sonbhadra(UP)
6.	Basti(UP)	29.	Madhepura(BIH)	52.	Tikamgarh(MP)
7.	Bhadohi(UP)	30.	Maharajganj(UP)	53.	Tonk(RAJ)
8.	Bhilwara(RAJ)	31.	Mahoba(UP)	54.	Udaipur(RAJ)
9.	Bhopal(MP)	32.	Morena(MP)	55.	Varanasi(UP)
10.	Bidar(KAR)	33.	Murshidabad(WB)	56.	Vidisha(MP)
11.	Bijapur(KAR)	34.	Nagaur(RAJ)		
12.	Bikaner(RAJ)	35.	Nanded(MAH)		**URBAN**
13.	Bundi(RAJ)	36.	Nawada(BIH)		
14.	Chattarpur(MP)	37.	Nawrangapura(ORI)	1	Azamgarh(UP)

Contd....

Sr. No.	District (State)	Sr. No.	District (State)	Sr. No.	District (State)
15.	Churu(RAJ)	38.	Palamu(BIH)	2.	Godda(BIH)
16.	Dakshin Dinajpur(WB)	39.	Patna(BIH)	3.	Madhubani(BIH)
17.	Dausa(RAJ)	40.	Puruliya(WB)	4.	Murshidabad(WB)
18.	Deoghar(BIH)	41.	Rajgarh(MP)	5.	Patna(BIH)
19.	Gonda(UP)	42.	Rohtas(BIH)	6.	Rohtas(BIH)
20.	Gorakhpur(UP)	43.	Sagar(MP)	7.	Shajapur(MP)
21.	Guna(MP)	44.	Sahibganj(BIH)	8.	Tirap (ARP)
22.	Hazaribag(BIH)	45.	Satna(MP)	9.	Vaishali(BIH)
23.	Indore(MP)	46.	Shahdol(MP)		

Median Age at Marriage by place of Residence

The median age at marriage in rural areas varies from 14.0 years in Maharajganj district of Uttar Pradesh to 24 years in Imphal (Manipur), Kottayam (Kerala), and North and South Goa. The corresponding variation observed in urban areas is from 15 years in Nawada, Patna and Rohtas in Bihar to 32 years in West Garo Hills in Meghalaya. The median age for all the marriages reported in rural areas works out to be 18 years and that for urban areas is 20 years–a clear difference of two years.

In 30 districts the median age at marriage in the rural areas is found to be higher than that of the urban areas and in another 74 districts there is no difference in the median. However, in all the remaining districts reporting marriages, the urban median age at marriage is found to be higher than that of the rural, and in 120 districts the difference is even higher by 2.5 years.

The percentage distribution of districts by marriage category, based on median age, in rural and urban areas is given in Figure F-7. It is clear from the figure that districts with early marriages are high in rural areas and preferred marriages are high in urban areas, as one would expect.

Fig. F-7: Percentage Distribution of Districts by Marriages category based on Median Age in Rural and Urban areas (Girls)

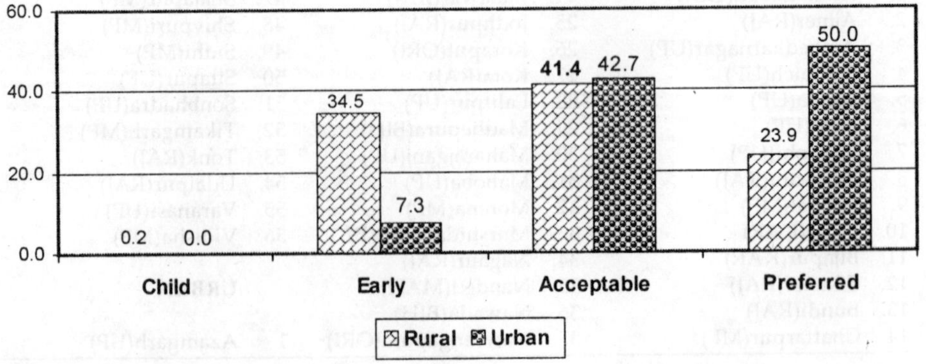

There are 173 districts with rural median age at marriage below 18 years and 35 such districts in urban areas. The per cent share of selected states of these districts is shown in Figure F-8.

Fig. F-8: Percentage share of Selected States of Districts with Median Age at Marriage below 18 years by place of Residence (Girls)

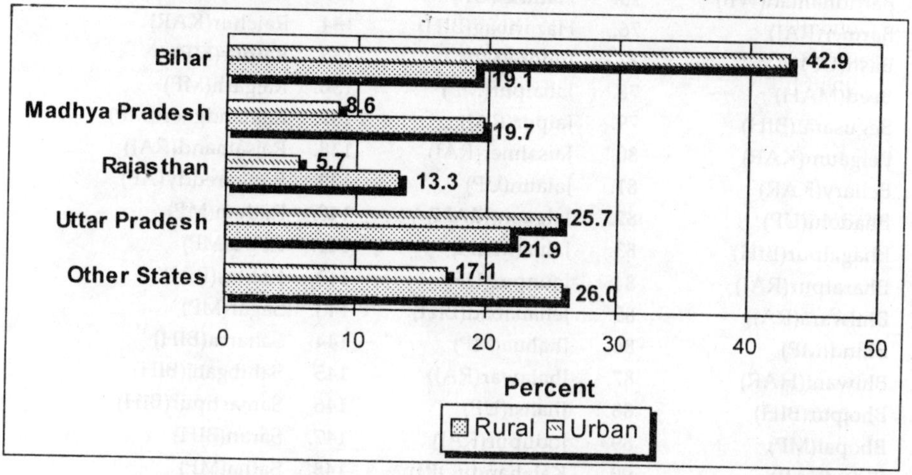

The four states (Bihar, Madhya Pradesh, Rajasthan and Uttar Pradesh) together accounts for 74 per cent of the total number of districts with rural girls marrying below 18 years of age and the corresponding per cent of districts for urban areas is 83. The names of districts with below legal minimum median age at marriage for rural and urban areas are given below in Table 13(a) and 13 (b) respectively.

Table 13(a)
Districts with Median age below 18 years in Rural areas (Girls)

Sr. No.	District (State)	Sr. No.	District (State)	Sr. No.	District (State)
1.	Ahmadabad(GUJ)	59.	Faizabad(UP)	117.	Nalanda(BIH)
2.	Ajmer(RAJ)	60.	Fathepur(UP)	118.	Nanded(MAH)
3.	Allahabad(UP)	61.	Firozabad(UP)	119.	Narsimhapur(MP)
4.	Alwar(RAJ)	62.	Ganjam(ORI)	120.	Nawada(BIH)
5.	Ambedkarnagar(UP)	63.	Gaya(BIH)	121.	Nawrangapura(ORI)
6.	Araria(BIH)	64.	Ghazipur(UP)	122.	Nayagarh(ORI)
7.	Aurangabad(BIH)	65.	Giridih(BIH)	123.	North 24 Parganas(WB)
8.	Aurangabad(MAH)	66.	Godda(BIH)	124.	Palamu(BIH)
9.	Azamgarh(UP)	67.	Gonda(UP)	125.	Pali(RAJ)
10.	Bahraich(UP)	68.	Gopalganj(BIH)	126.	Panna(MP)
11.	Ballia(UP)	69.	Gorakhpur(UP)	127.	Parbhani(MAH)
12.	Banas Kantha(GUJ)	70.	Gulbarga(KAR)	128.	Pashchim Champaran(BIH)
13.	Banda(UP)	71.	Guna(MP)	129.	Patna(BIH)

Contd....

Sr. No.	District (State)	Sr. No.	District (State)	Sr. No.	District (State)
14.	Bankura(WB)	72.	Gwalior(MP)	130.	Pilibhit(UP)
15.	Banswara(RAJ)	73.	Hamirpur(UP)	131.	Pratapgarh(UP)
16.	Barabanki(UP)	74.	Hanumangarh(RAJ)	132.	Purba Champaran(BIH)
17.	Barddhaman(WB)	75.	Hathras(UP)	133.	Puruliya(WB)
18.	Barmer(RAJ)	76.	Hazaribag(BIH)	134.	Raichur(KAR)
19.	Basti(UP)	77.	Indore(MP)	135.	Raipur(MP)
20.	Beed(MAH)	78.	Jabalpur(MP)	136.	Rajgarh(MP)
21.	Begusarai(BIH)	79.	Jaipur(RAJ)	137.	Rajnandgaon(MP)
22.	Belgaum(KAR)	80.	Jaisalmer(RAJ)	138.	Rajsamand(RAJ)
23.	Bellary(KAR)	81.	Jalaun(UP)	139.	Rangareddy(AP)
24.	Bhadohi(UP)	82.	Jalgaon(MAH)	140.	Ratlam(MP)
25.	Bhagalpur(BIH)	83.	Jalna(MAH)	141.	Rewa(MP)
26.	Bharatpur(RAJ)	84.	Jaunpur(UP)	142.	Rohtas(BIH)
27.	Bhilwara(RAJ)	85.	Jehanabad(BIH)	143.	Sagar(MP)
28.	Bhind(MP)	86.	Jhabua(MP)	144.	Saharsa(BIH)
29.	Bhiwani(HAR)	87.	Jhalawar(RAJ)	145.	Sahibganj(BIH)
30.	Bhojpur(BIH)	88.	Jhansi(UP)	146.	Samastipur(BIH)
31.	Bhopal(MP)	89.	Jodhpur(RAJ)	147.	Saran(BIH)
32.	Bidar(KAR)	90.	Kalahandi(ORI)	148.	Satna(MP)
33.	Bijapur(KAR)	91.	Katihar(BIH)	149.	Sawaimadhopur(RAJ)
34.	Bikaner(RAJ)	92.	Khagaria(BIH)	150.	Sehore(MP)
35.	Birbhum(WB)	93.	Kheri(UP)	151.	Shahdol(MP)
36.	Bolangir(ORI)	94.	Kishanganj(BIH)	152.	Shajahanabad(UP)
37.	Boudh(ORI)	95.	Kohima(NAG)	153.	Shajapur(MP)
38.	Budaun(UP)	96.	Kooch Bihar(WB)	154.	Shivpuri(MP)
39.	Bundi(RAJ)	97.	Koraput(ORI)	155.	Sidhart Nagar(UP)
40.	Buxar(BIH)	98.	Kota(RAJ)	156.	Sidhi(MP)
41.	Chattarpur(MP)	99.	Lalitpur(UP)	157.	Sitamarhi(BIH)
42.	Chittorgarh(RAJ)	100.	Latur(MAH)	158.	Sitapur(UP)
43.	Churu(RAJ)	101.	Madhepura(BIH)	159.	Sonbhadra(UP)
44.	Dadra	102.	Madhubani(BIH)	160.	South 24 Parganas(WB)
45.	Dakshin Dinajpur(WB)	103.	Maharajganj(UP)	161.	Srikakulam(AP)
46.	Damoh(MP)	104.	Mahendragarh(HAR)	162.	Sultanpur(UP)
47.	Darbhanga(BIH)	105.	Mahoba(UP)	163.	Surguja(MP)
48.	Datia(MP)	106.	Mainpuri(UP)	164.	Tikamgarh(MP)
49.	Dausa(RAJ)	107.	Maldah (WB)	165.	Tonk(RAJ)
50.	Deoghar(BIH)	108.	Malkangiri(ORI)	166.	Udaipur(RAJ)
51.	Deoria(UP)	109.	Mandsaur(MP)	167.	Ujjain(MP)
52.	Dewas(MP)	110.	Mirzapur(UP)	168.	Uttar Dinajpur(WB)
53.	Dhar(MP)	111.	Morena(MP)	169.	Vaishali(BIH)
54.	Dholpur(RAJ)	112.	Munger(BIH)	170.	Varanasi(UP)
55.	Dhubri(ASM)	113.	Murshidabad(WB)	171.	Vidisha(MP)
56.	East Godavari(AP)	114.	Muzaffarpur(BIH)	172.	Vishkhapatanam(AP)
57.	East Nimar(MP)	115.	Mysore(KAR)	173.	Warangal(AP)
58.	Etah(UP)	116.	Nagaur(RAJ)		

Table 13(b)
Districts with Median Age below 18 years in Urban areas (Girls)

Sr. No.	District (State)	Sr. No.	District (State)	Sr. No.	District (State)
1.	Aurangabad(BIH)	13.	Gonda(UP)	25.	Nawada(BIH)
2.	Azamgarh(UP)	14.	Hazaribag(BIH)	26.	Patna(BIH)
3.	Begusarai(BIH)	15.	Khammam(AP)	27.	Phek(NAG)
4.	Bhadohi(UP)	16.	Kheri(UP)	28.	Rohtas(BIH)
5.	Bidar(KAR)	17.	Kohima(NAG)	29.	Shajahanabad(UP)
6.	Buxar(BIH)	18.	Lalitpur(UP)	30.	Shajapur(MP)
7.	Churu(RAJ)	19.	Madhepura(BIH)	31.	Shivpuri(MP)
8.	Dholpur(RAJ)	20.	Madhubani(BIH)	32.	Sidhart Nagar(UP)
9.	Dumka(BIH)	21.	Mahoba(UP)	33.	Sitamarhi(BIH)
10.	Ghazipur(UP)	22.	Morena(MP)	34.	Tirap (ARP)
11.	Giridih(BIH)	23.	Murshidabad(WB)	35.	Vaishali(BIH)
12.	Godda(BIH)	24.	Nalanda(BIH)		

(b) Caste

An examination of the age at marriage in each caste group in each district shows that the percentage share of marriages at below legal minimum age at marriage is high among the SC/ST/OBC group than the "other group" in many districts. Appendix III gives the district-wise picture of per cent share of marriages below the legal minimum age at marriage and the average age at marriage with the number of marriages in each category in each district. In 21 districts no marriage was reported among the castes other than SC/ST/OBC. The variation in the per cent share of marriages below legal minimum age at marriage is from zero in 26 districts to 96 per cent in Lalitpur district in the case of SC/ST/OBC and from zero in 66 districts to 79 per cent in Shajapur (MP)[2]. The summary situation is shown in Figure F-9.

Fig. F-9: Percentage Distribution of Districts by per cent share of Marriages below 18 years of Age in each Caste Group (Girls)

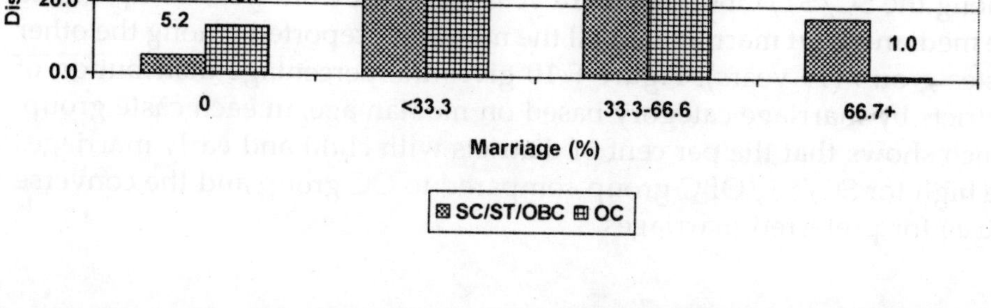

In seventeen per cent of the districts, the per cent share of marriages below 18 years is at least two-thirds among the SC/ST/OBC group compared to a mere 1 per cent among the other caste group. The names of these districts are given below in Table 14.

Table 14
Districts with Marriages below 18 years of Age Forming at least two-thirds of the Total Marriages in each Caste Group (Girls)

Sr. No.	District (State)	Sr. No.	District (State)	Sr. No.	District (State)
	SC/ST/OBC		**SC/ST/OBC**		**SC/ST/OBC**
1.	Alwar(RAJ)	31.	Godda(BIH)	61.	Raichur(KAR)
2.	Ambedkarnagar(UP)	32.	Gonda(UP)	62.	Rajgarh(MP)
3.	Aurangabad(BIH)	33.	Gorakhpur(UP)	63.	Rewa(MP)
4.	Azamgarh(UP)	34.	Gulbarga(KAR)	64.	Rohtas(BIH)
5.	Bahraich(UP)	35.	Guna(MP)	65.	Sagar(MP)
6.	Ballia(UP)	36.	Hazaribag(BIH)	66.	Samastipur(BIH)
7.	Banda(UP)	37.	Jhalawar(RAJ)	67.	Satna(MP)
8.	Barddhaman(WB)	38.	Jodhpur(RAJ)	68.	Shahdol(MP)
9.	Basti(UP)	39.	Kalahandi(ORI)	69.	Shajahanabad(UP)
10.	Begusarai(BIH)	40.	Khagaria(BIH)	70.	Shajapur(MP)
11.	Belgaum(KAR)	41.	Koraput(ORI)	71.	Shivpuri(MP)
12.	Bhadohi(UP)	42.	Kota(RAJ)	72.	Sidhart Nagar(UP)
13.	Bhilwara(RAJ)	43.	Lalitpur(UP)	73.	Sidhi(MP)
14.	Bhind(MP)	44.	Latur(MAH)	74.	Sitamarhi(BIH)
15.	Bhojpur(BIH)	45.	Madhepura(BIH)	75.	Sitapur(UP)
16.	Bidar(KAR)	46.	Madhubani(BIH)	76.	Sonbhadra(UP)
17.	Bijapur(KAR)	47.	Maharajganj(UP)	77.	Sultanpur(UP)
18.	Bikaner(RAJ)	48.	Mahoba(UP)	78.	Tikamgarh(MP)
19.	Birbhum(WB)	49.	Mandsaur(MP)	79.	Tonk(RAJ)
20.	Bundi(RAJ)	50.	Morena(MP)	80.	Udaipur(RAJ)
21.	Buxar(BIH)	51.	Murshidabad(WB)	81.	Vaishali(BIH)
22.	Chattarpur(MP)	52.	Nagaur(RAJ)	82.	Varanasi(UP)
23.	Churu(RAJ)	53.	Nanded(MAH)	83.	Vidisha(MP)
24.	Darbhanga(BIH)	54.	Nawada(BIH)	84.	Vishakhapatanam(AP)
25.	Dausa(RAJ)	55.	Nawrangapura(ORI)		**OTHER CASTES**
26.	Deoghar(BIH)	56.	Palamu(BIH)	1.	Dibang Valley(ARP)
27.	Dholpur(RAJ)	57.	Patna(BIH)	2.	Dindigul(TN)
28.	Etah(UP)	58.	Pilibhit(UP)	3.	Murshidabad(WB)
29.	Gaya(BIH)	59.	Purba Champaran(BIH)	4.	Shajapur(MP)
30.	Ghazipur(UP)	60.	Puruliya(WB)	5.	Virudunagar(TN)

Median age at Marriage by Caste

On the whole, the median age at marriage for all the marriages reported among the SC/ST/OBC group (18 years) is less by one year compared to the median age at marriage for all the marriages reported among the other castes group (19 years). Figure F-10 gives the percentage distribution of districts by marriage category based on median age, in each caste group, which shows that the per cent of districts with child and early marriages are high for SC/ST/OBC group compared to OC group and the converse is true for preferred marriages.

Fig. F-10: Percentage Distribution of Districts by Marriage Category based on Median Age in each Caste Group (Girls)

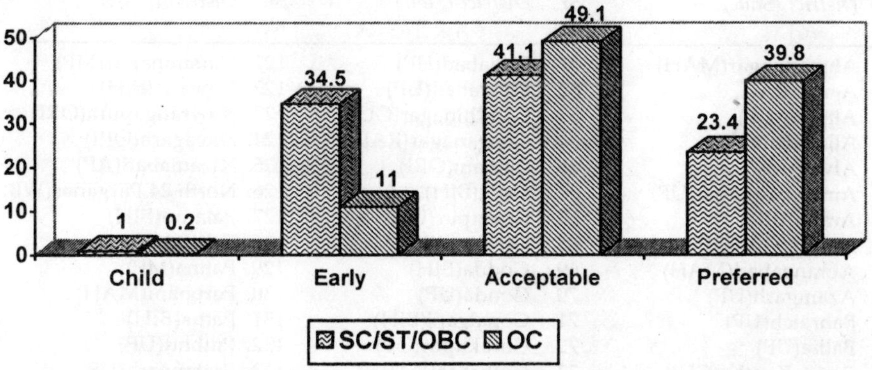

The median age at marriage among the SC/ST/OBC ranged from 14 years in Bahraich, Gonda, Lalitpur, Maharajganj and Sidhartnagar (all from Uttar Pradesh) to 24 years in Imphal (Manipur) and Pulawama (Jammu & Kashmir). Similar variation observed in the other castes group is from 15 years in Shajapur (Madhya Pradesh) and Sonbhadra (Uttar Pradesh)[3] to 25.5 years in Imphal[4]. Median age at marriage of less than 18 years among the SC/ST/OBC group is found in 179 districts and among the other castes group in 54 districts. Among the SC/ST/OBC group three out of every four districts with median age below legal minimum age are from Bihar, Madhya Pradesh, Rajasthan or Uttar Pradesh (Figure F-11). Similarly among the "other castes" group also a large proportion of marriages below legal minimum age (57.4%) are from these states.

Fig. F-11: Percentage share of Selected States of Districts with Median Age at Marriage below 18 years by Caste (Girls)

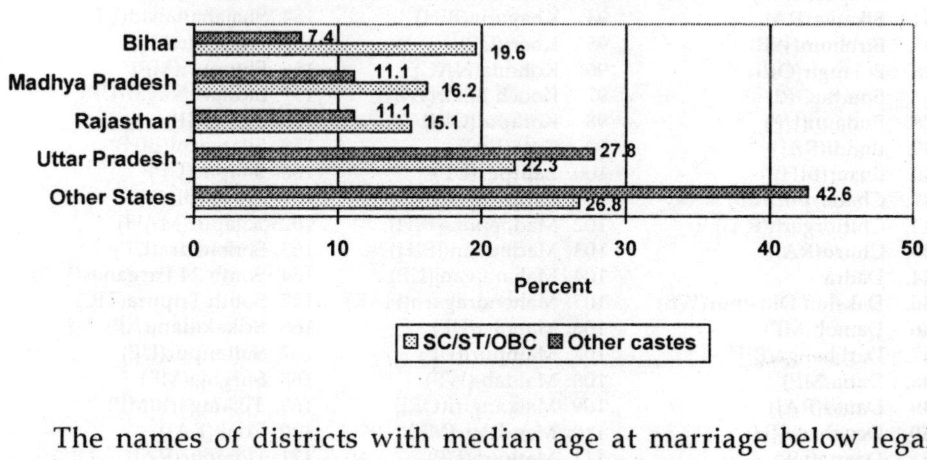

The names of districts with median age at marriage below legal minimum age at marriage for SC/ST/OBC and "other caste" group are given below in Table 15(a) and 15(b) respectively.

Table 15(a)
Districts with Median Age at Marriage below 18 years for SC/ST/OBC (Girls)

Sr. No.	District (State)	Sr. No.	District (State)	Sr. No.	District (State)
1.	Ahmadnagar(MAH)	61.	Faizabad(UP)	121.	Narsimhapur(MP)
2.	Ajmer(RAJ)	62.	Firozabad(UP)	122.	Nawada(BIH)
3.	Aligarh(UP)	63.	Gandhinagar(GUJ)	123.	Nawrangapura(ORI)
4.	Allahabad(UP)	64.	Ganganagar(RAJ)	124.	Nayagarh(ORI)
5.	Alwar(RAJ)	65.	Ganjam(ORI)	125.	Nizamabad(AP)
6.	Ambedkarnagar(UP)	66.	Gaya(BIH)	126.	North 24 Parganas(WB)
7.	Araria(BIH)	67.	Ghazipur(UP)	127.	Palamu(BIH)
8.	Aurangabad(BIH)	68.	Giridih(BIH)	128.	Pali(RAJ)
9.	Aurangabad(MAH)	69.	Godda(BIH)	129.	Panna(MP)
10.	Azamgarh(UP)	70.	Gonda(UP)	130.	Parbhani(MAH)
11.	Bahraich(UP)	71.	Gopalganj(BIH)	131.	Patna(BIH)
12.	Ballia(UP)	72.	Gorakhpur(UP)	132.	Pilibhit(UP)
13	Banas Kantha(GUJ)	73.	Gulbarga(KAR)	133.	Pratapgarh(UP)
14.	Banda(UP)	74.	Guna(MP)	134.	Purba Champaran(BIH)
15.	Bankura(WB)	75.	Gwalior(MP)	135.	Purnia(BIH)
16.	Banswara(RAJ)	76.	Hamirpur(UP)	136.	Puruliya(WB)
17.	Barabanki(UP)	77.	Hanumangarh(RAJ)	137.	Raichur(KAR)
18.	Barddhaman(WB)	78.	Hathras(UP)	138.	Raipur(MP)
19.	Barmer(RAJ)	79.	Hazaribag(BIH)	139.	Raisen(MP)
20.	Basti(UP)	80.	Jaipur(RAJ)	140.	Rajgarh(MP)
21.	Beed(MAH)	81.	Jaisalmer(RAJ)	141.	Rajsamand(RAJ)
22.	Begusarai(BIH)	82.	Jalaun(UP)	142.	Ratlam(MP)
23.	Belgaum(KAR)	83.	Jalna(MAH)	143.	Rewa(MP)
24.	Bellary(KAR)	84.	Jalore(RAJ)	144.	Rohtas(BIH)
25.	Bhadohi(UP)	85.	Jaunpur(UP)	145.	Sagar(MP)
26.	Bhagalpur(BIH)	86.	Jehanabad(BIH)	146.	Saharsa(BIH)
27.	Bharatpur(RAJ)	87.	Jhabua(MP)	147.	Sahibganj(BIH)
28.	Bhilwara(RAJ)	88.	Jhalawar(RAJ)	148.	Samastipur(BIH)
29.	Bhind(MP)	89.	Jhansi(UP)	149.	Saran(BIH)
30.	Bhiwani(HAR)	90.	Jhunjhunu(RAJ)	150.	Satna(MP)
31.	Bhojpur(BIH)	91.	Jodhpur(RAJ)	151.	Sawaimadhopur(RAJ)
32.	Bidar(KAR)	92.	Kalahandi(ORI)	152.	Sehore(MP)
33.	Bijapur(KAR)	93.	Katihar(BIH)	153.	Shahdol(MP)
34.	Bikaner(RAJ)	94.	Khagaria(BIH)	154.	Shajahanabad(UP)
35.	Birbhum(WB)	95.	Kheri(UP)	155.	Shajapur(MP)
36.	Bolangir(ORI)	96.	Kohima(NAG)	156.	Shivpuri(MP)
37.	Boudh(ORI)	97.	Kooch Bihar(WB)	157.	Sidhart Nagar(UP)
38.	Budaun(UP)	98.	Koraput(ORI)	158.	Sidhi(MP)
39.	Bundi(RAJ)	99.	Kota(RAJ)	159.	Sitamarhi(BIH)
40.	Buxar(BIH)	100.	Lalitpur(UP)	160.	Sitapur(UP)
41.	Chattarpur(MP)	101.	Latur(MAH)	161.	Siwan(BIH)
42.	Chittorgarh(RAJ)	102.	Madhepura(BIH)	162.	Solapur(MAH)
43.	Churu(RAJ)	103.	Madhubani(BIH)	163.	Sonbhadra(UP)
44.	Dadra	104.	Maharajganj(UP)	164.	South 24 Parganas(WB)
45.	Dakshin Dinajpur(WB)	105.	Mahendragarh(HAR)	165.	South Tripura(TRI)
46.	Damoh(MP)	106.	Mahoba(UP)	166.	Srikakulam(AP)
47.	Darbhanga(BIH)	107.	Mainpuri(UP)	167.	Sultanpur(UP)
48.	Datia(MP)	108.	Maldah (WB)	168.	Surguja(MP)
49.	Dausa(RAJ)	109.	Malkangiri(ORI)	169.	Tikamgarh(MP)
50.	Deoghar(BIH)	110.	Mandsaur(MP)	170.	Tonk(RAJ)
51.	Deoria(UP)	111.	Mathura(UP)	171.	Udaipur(RAJ)
52.	Dewas(MP)	112.	Mirzapur(UP)	172.	Ujjain(MP)

Contd....

Sr. No.	*District (State)*	*Sr. No.*	*District (State)*	*Sr. No.*	*District (State)*
53.	Dhanbad(BIH)	113.	Morena(MP)	173.	Unnao(UP)
54.	Dhar(MP)	114.	Munger(BIH)	174.	Uttar Dinajpur(WB)
55.	Dharwad(KAR)	115.	Murshidabad(WB)	175.	Vaishali(BIH)
56.	Dhenkanal(ORI)	116.	Muzaffarpur(BIH)	176.	Varanasi(UP)
57.	Dholpur(RAJ)	117.	Mysore(KAR)	177.	Vidisha(MP)
58.	Dhubri(ASM)	118.	Nagaur(RAJ)	178.	Vishkhapatanam(AP)
59.	Etah(UP)	119.	Nalanda(BIH)	179.	Warangal(AP)
60.	Etawah(UP)	120.	Nanded(MAH)		

Table 15 (b)
Districts with Median Age at Marriage below 18 years for other Caste Group (Girls)

Sr. No.	*District (State)*	*Sr. No.*	*District (State)*	*Sr. No.*	*District (State)*
1.	Ambedkarnagar(UP)	19.	Dindigul(TN)	37.	Patna(BIH)
2.	Bahraich(UP)	20.	Dumka(BIH)	38.	Phulbani(ORI)
3.	Banda(UP)	21.	East Khasi Hills(MEG)	39.	Pratapgarh(UP)
4.	Basti(UP)	22.	Faizabad(UP)	40.	Puruliya(WB)
5.	Beed(MAH)	23.	Goalpara(ASM)	41.	Ramanathapuram(TN)
6.	Bhadohi(UP)	24.	Godda(BIH)	42.	Rewa(MP)
7.	Bhilwara(RAJ)	25.	Gonda(UP)	43.	Sahibganj(BIH)
8.	Bidar(KAR)	26.	Jalaun(UP)	44.	Satna(MP)
9.	Bijapur(KAR)	27.	Jalna(MAH)	45.	Shajahanabad(UP)
10.	Bikaner(RAJ)	28.	Kishanganj(BIH)	46.	Shajapur(MP)
11.	Birbhum(WB)	29.	Latur(MAH)	47.	Sonbhadra(UP)
12.	Budaun(UP)	30.	Maharajganj(UP)	48.	Sultanpur(UP)
13.	Chattarpur(MP)	31.	Maldah (WB)	49.	Tonk(RAJ)
14.	Churu(RAJ)	32.	Malkangiri(ORI)	50.	Udaipur(RAJ)
15.	Dakshin Dinajpur(WB)	33.	Morena(MP)	51.	Uttar Dinajpur(WB)
16.	Dhar(MP)	34.	Murshidabad(WB)	52.	Varanasi(UP)
17.	Dhubri(ASM)	35.	Nagaur(RAJ)	53.	Virudunagar(TN)
18.	Dibang Valley(ARP)	36.	Nanded(MAH)	54.	West Garo Hills(MEG)

(c) Economic status

Economic status as assessed by the type of house they live in shows that there was no marriage conducted during the reference period among the high economic status (HES) group in 14 districts. The corresponding number of districts among the medium economic status (MES) group is 2 and among the low economic status (LES) group is 9. Appendix IV provides the district-wise situation of per cent share of marriages below the legal minimum age at marriage, average age at marriage, and the number of marriages in each category in each district by economic status.

The proportion of marriages below legal minimum age at marriage is much less among those who are well off than the poor group. The share of such marriages vary from zero in the case of 104 districts to 77.3 per cent in Maharajganj district of Uttar Pradesh[5] among the economically well off persons. The corresponding situation among those who are in the MES category is 40 districts with no such marriages to 96 per cent in Lalitpur (Uttar Pradesh)[6]. Similarly among the LES group, the variation is from zero in the case of 49 districts to 100 per cent in Gandhinagar (Gujarat) and Jhunjhunu (Rajasthan)[7]. The summary situation is given in Figure F-12.

Fig. F-12: Percentage Distribution of Districts by per cent share of Marriage below 18 years of Age by Economic Status (Girls)

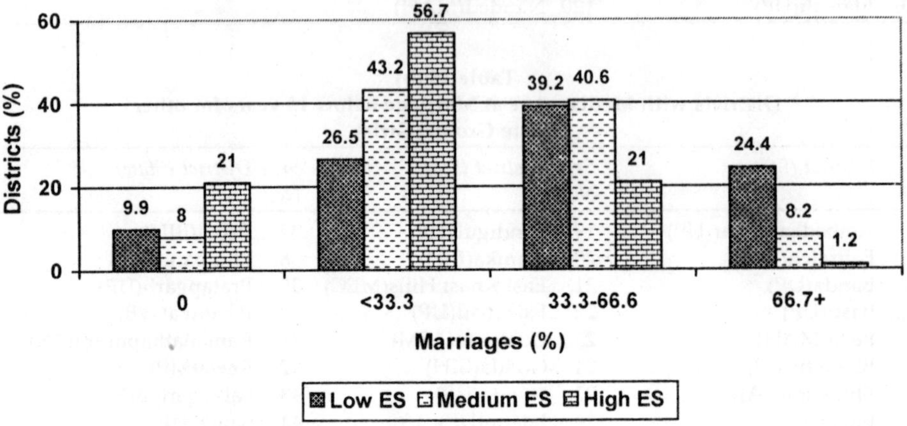

While there is only one per cent of districts with at least two-thirds of the marriages falling below 18 years among those who are economically well off, there is 8 per cent among the medium group and 24 per cent among the poor. The names of these districts are provided in Tables 16(a) and 16 (b) respectively for low and high/medium economic status groups.

Table 16(a)
Districts with Marriages below 18 years of Age Forming at least two-thirds of the Total Marriages Among low Economic Status Group (Girls)

Sr. No.	District (Sate)	Sr. No.	District (Sate)	Sr. No.	District (Sate)
1.	Agra(UP)	42.	Ghazipur(UP)	83.	Nawada(BIH)
2.	Ajmer(RAJ)	43.	Godda(BIH)	84.	Nawrangapura(ORI)
3.	Aligarh(UP)	44.	Gonda(UP)	85.	Palamu(BIH)
4.	Allahabad(UP)	45.	Gopalganj(BIH)	86.	Pali(RAJ)
5.	Alwar(RAJ)	46.	Gorakhpur(UP)	87.	Pashchim Champaran(BIH)
6.	Ambedkarnagar(UP)	47.	Guna(MP)	88.	Patna(BIH)
7.	Aurangabad(BIH)	48.	Gwalior(MP)	89.	Pilibhit(UP)
8.	Azamgarh(UP)	49.	Hazaribag(BIH)	90.	Purba Champaran(BIH)
9.	Bahraich(UP)	50.	Indore(MP)	91.	Puruliya(WB)
10.	Ballia(UP)	51.	Jaipur(RAJ)	92.	Raichur(KAR)
11.	Banas Kantha(GUJ)	52.	Jalaun(UP)	93.	Raipur(MP)
12.	Banda(UP)	53.	Jalgaon(MAH)	94.	Rajgarh(MP)
13.	Barddhaman(WB)	54.	Jalna(MAH)	95.	Rajsamand(RAJ)
14.	Basti(UP)	55.	Jehanabad(BIH)	96.	Rangareddy(AP)
15.	Begusarai(BIH)	56.	Jhalawar(RAJ)	97.	Ratlam(MP)

Contd....

Sr. No.	*District (Sate)*	*Sr. No.*	*District (Sate)*	*Sr. No.*	*District (Sate)*
16.	Belgaum(KAR)	57.	Jhansi(UP)	98.	Rohtas(BIH)
17.	Bhadohi(UP)	58.	Jhunjhunu(RAJ)	99.	Sagar(MP)
18.	Bhagalpur(BIH)	59.	Jodhpur(RAJ)	100.	Sahibganj(BIH)
19.	Bhilwara(RAJ)	60.	Kaithal(HAR)	101.	Samastipur(BIH)
20.	Bhiwani(HAR)	61.	Kalahandi(ORI)	102.	Satna(MP)
21.	Bhojpur(BIH)	62.	Khagaria(BIH)	103.	Shahdol(MP)
22.	Bidar(KAR)	63.	Kodagu(KAR)	104.	Shajahanabad(UP)
23.	Bijapur(KAR)	64.	Koraput(ORI)	105.	Shajapur(MP)
24.	Bikaner(RAJ)	65.	Kota(RAJ)	106.	Shivpuri(MP)
25.	Birbhum(WB)	66.	Lalitpur(UP)	107.	Sidhart Nagar(UP)
26.	Bundi(RAJ)	67.	Latur(MAH)	108.	Sidhi(MP)
27.	Buxar(BIH)	68.	Madhepura(BIH)	109.	Sitamarhi(BIH)
28.	Chattarpur(MP)	69.	Madhubani(BIH)	110.	Sonbhadra(UP)
29.	Churu(RAJ)	70.	Maharajganj(UP)	111.	Sultanpur(UP)
30.	Dakshin Dinajpur(WB)	71.	Mahbubnagar(AP)	112.	Theni(TN)
31.	Darbhanga(BIH)	72.	Mahesana(GUJ)	113.	Tikamgarh(MP)
32.	Dausa(RAJ)	73.	Mahoba(UP)	114.	Tonk(RAJ)
33.	Deoghar(BIH)	74.	Mandsaur(MP)	115.	Tumkur(KAR)
34.	Dharwad(KAR)	75.	Mathura(UP)	116.	Udaipur(RAJ)
35.	Etah(UP)	76.	Morena(MP)	117.	Vadodara(GUJ)
36.	Faizabad(UP)	77.	Munger(BIH)	118.	Vaishali(BIH)
37.	Faridabad(HAR)	78.	Murshidabad(WB)	119.	Varanasi(UP)
38.	Faridkot(PUJ)	79.	Mysore(KAR)	120.	Vidisha(MP)
39.	Firozabad(UP)	80.	Nagaur(RAJ)	121.	Vishakhapatanam(AP)
40.	Gandhinagar(GUJ)	81.	Nalanda(BIH)		
41.	Gaya(BIH)	82.	Nanded(MAH)		

Table 16(b)

Districts with Marriages below 18 years of Age Forming at least two-thirds of the Total Marriages Among high and Medium Economic Status Groups (Girls)

Sr. No.	*District (State)*	*Sr. No.*	*District (State)*	*Sr. No.*	*District (State)*
	HIGHES		MEDIUM ES		MEDIUM ES
1.	East Kameng(ARP)	10.	Bhilwara(RAJ)	27.	Maldah (WB)
2.	Maharajganj(UP)	11.	Bikaner(RAJ)	28.	Malkangiri(ORI)
3.	Murshidabad(WB)	12.	Bundi(RAJ)	29.	Morena(MP)
4.	Patna(BIH)	13.	Chittorgarh(RAJ)	30.	Murshidabad(WB)
5.	Shahdol(MP)	14.	Churu(RAJ)	31.	Nagaur(RAJ)
6.	Sultanpur(UP)	15.	Dausa(RAJ)	32.	Nawada(BIH)
		16.	Dhanbad(BIH)	33.	Palamu(BIH)
	MEDIUM	17.	Dholpur(RAJ)	34.	Rajgarh(MP)
1.	Ajmer(RAJ)	18.	East Siang(ARP)	35.	Rohtas(BIH)
2.	Alwar(RAJ)	19.	Giridih(BIH)	36.	Shajapur(MP)
3.	Ambedkarnagar(UP)	20.	Gonda(UP)	37.	Sonbhadra(UP)
4.	Bahraich(UP)	21.	Jhalawar(RAJ)	38.	Tirap (ARP)
5.	Banas Kantha(GUJ)	22.	Jhunjhunu(RAJ)	39.	Tonk(RAJ)
6.	Banda(UP)	23.	Kota(RAJ)	40.	Udaipur(RAJ)
7.	Barddhaman(WB)	24.	Lalitpur(UP)	41.	Varanasi(UP)
8.	Basti(UP)	25.	Latur(MAH)		
9.	Bhadohi(UP)	26.	Maharajganj(UP)		

Median age at Marriage by Economic Status

The median age at marriage among those who are in high economic condition is found to be 19 years as against 18 years for the other two categories. The variation in the median age at marriage in the former group is from 15 years in Patna (Bihar), Maharajganj and Sultanpur (both in Uttar Pradesh) to 27 years in Chandel, Churachandpur and Imphal (all in Manipur)[8]. Among the poor class the lowest median age of 13 years is found in Sidhartnagar (Uttar Pradesh) and a maximum of 26 years is found in Pattanamthitta (Kerala)[9]. Among the medium economic status group the lowest median age of 14 years is found in Bhilwara, Bundi, Kota (all in Rajasthan), Lalitpur and Maharajganj (both in Uttar Pradesh) and the highest median age of 27 years is foiund in Imphal (Manipur), Sibsagar (Assam) and West Garo Hills (Meghalaya).

The percentage distribution of districts in each economic status category by category of marriage is given in Figure F-13.

Fig. F-13: Percentage Distribution of Districts in each Economic Status Group by Marriage Category based on Median Age (Girls)

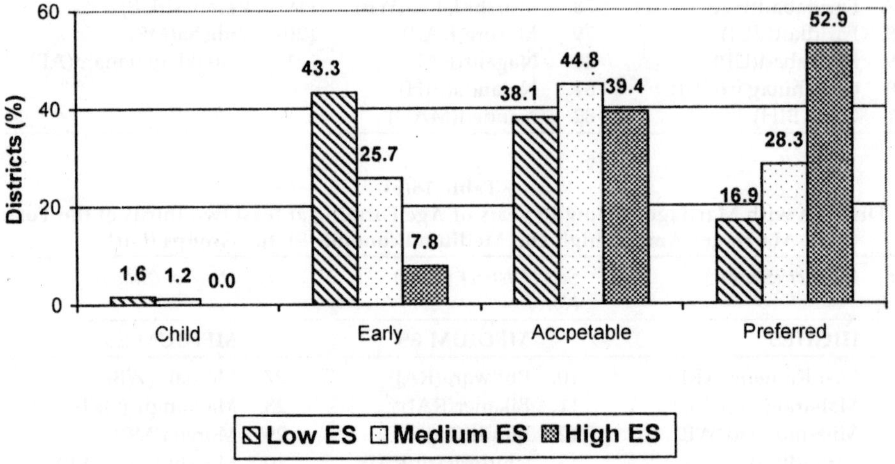

There is no child marriage among those who are in high economic condition and the proportion of early marriage forms only about 8 per cent. This includes two districts each from Arunachal Pradesh, Maharashtra, Nagaland and West Bengal, three each from Andhra Pradesh and Bihar, five from Madhya Pradesh, seven from Rajasthan and 12 from Uttar Pradesh.

The highest per cent of districts with preferred marriages is among the economically better off category (52.9%), and the highest per cent of districts with early marriages is found among the economically poor households (43.3%).

A very negligible proportion of districts reported child marriage with a median age at marriage below 15 years. There are 14 such districts six from the medium economic status group (Bhilwara, Bundi, Kota and Jhalawar from Rajasthan and Lalitpur and Maharajganj from Uttar Pradesh) and eight from the economically poor group (Bahraich, Basti, Gonda, Lalitpur, and Sidhartnagar from Uttar Pradesh, Bhilwara and Jhunjhunu from Rajasthan, and Mysore from Karnataka).

Figure F-14 gives the per cent share of selected states of the districts with median age below 18 years of age for each economic status category. While the poor households from 223 districts reported below legal minimum median age at marriage the corresponding number of districts for economically better off households is only 38 and that of medium households it is only 135. Bihar, Madhya Pradesh, Rajasthan and Uttar Pradesh together accounts for at least two-thirds of these districts in all the economic status category. The names of these districts are given below in Table 17(a), 17(b) and 17(c) respectively for high, medium and low economic status group.

Fig. F-14: Percent Share of Selected States of Districts with Median Age at Marriage below 18 years of Age of Economic Status (ES)

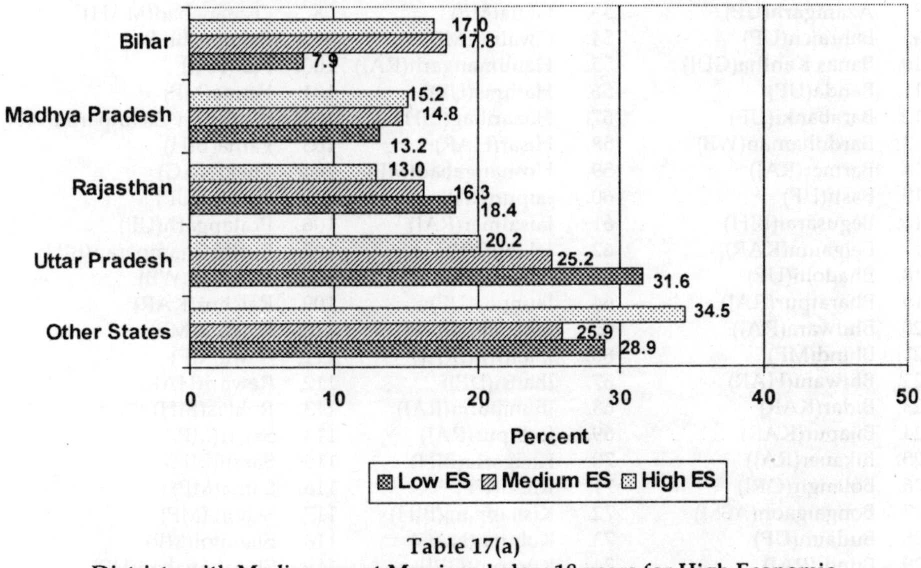

Table 17(a)

Districts with Median age at Marriage below 18 years for High Economic Status Group (Girls)

Sr. No.	*District (State)*	*Sr. No.*	*District (State)*	*Sr. No.*	*District (State)*
1.	Adilabad(AP)	14.	Gonda(UP)	27.	Puruliya(WB)
2.	Bahraich(UP)	15.	Gorakhpur(UP)	28.	Shahdol(MP)
3.	Ballia(UP)	16.	Jalaun(UP)	29.	Shivpuri(MP)
4.	Beed(MAH)	17.	Karimnagar(AP)	30.	Sidhart Nagar(UP)

Contd....

Sr. No.	District (State)	Sr. No.	District (State)	Sr. No.	District (State)
5.	Bharatpur(RAJ)	18.	Kohima(NAG)	31.	Sitapur(UP)
6.	Bhilwara(RAJ)	19.	Lalitpur(UP)	32.	Srikakulam(AP)
7.	Bhind(MP)	20.	Maharajganj(UP)	33.	Sultanpur(UP)
8.	Bikaner(RAJ)	21.	Morena(MP)	34.	Tikamgarh(MP)
9.	Churu(RAJ)	22.	Murshidabad(WB)	35.	Tonk(RAJ)
10.	Dausa(RAJ)	23.	Nagaur(RAJ)	36.	Upper Siang(ARP)
11.	East Kameng(ARP)	24.	Patna(BIH)	37.	Varanasi(UP)
12.	Gadchiroli(MAH)	25.	Pratapgarh(UP)	38.	Zunheboto(NAG)
13.	Giridih(BIH)	26.	Purba Champaran(BIH)		

Table 17(b)

Districts with Median Age at Marriage below 18 years for Medium Economic Status Group (Girls)

Sr. No.	District (State)	Sr. No.	District (State)	Sr. No.	District (State)
1.	Ahmadabad(GUJ)	46.	Etah(UP)	91.	Morena(MP)
2.	Ajmer(RAJ)	47.	Faizabad(UP)	92.	Murshidabad(WB)
3.	Aligarh(UP)	48.	Firozabad(UP)	93.	Muzaffarpur(BIH)
4.	Alwar(RAJ)	49.	Gaya(BIH)	94.	Nagaur(RAJ)
5.	Ambedkarnagar(UP)	50.	Ghazipur(UP)	95.	Nanded(MAH)
6.	Aurangabad(BIH)	51.	Giridih(BIH)	96.	Nawada(BIH)
7.	Aurangabad(MAH)	52.	Gonda(UP)	97.	Nayagarh(ORI)
8.	Azamgarh(UP)	53.	Guna(MP)	98.	Osmanabad(MAH)
9.	Bahraich(UP)	54.	Gwalior(MP)	99.	Palamu(BIH)
10.	Banas Kantha(GUJ)	55.	Hanumangarh(RAJ)	100.	Pali(RAJ)
11.	Banda(UP)	56.	Hathras(UP)	101.	Panna(MP)
12.	Barabanki(UP)	57.	Hazaribag(BIH)	102.	Pashchim Champaran(BIH)
13.	Barddhaman(WB)	58.	Hisar(HAR)	103.	Patna(BIH)
14.	Barmer(RAJ)	59.	Hoshangabad(MP)	104.	Phek(NAG)
15.	Basti(UP)	60.	Jaipur(RAJ)	105.	Pilibhit(UP)
16.	Begusarai(BIH)	61.	Jaisalmer(RAJ)	106.	Pratapgarh(UP)
17.	Belgaum(KAR)	62.	Jalaun(UP)	107.	Purba Champaran(BIH)
18.	Bhadohi(UP)	63.	Jalna(MAH)	108.	Puruliya(WB)
19.	Bharatpur(RAJ)	64.	Jaunpur(UP)	109.	Raichur(KAR)
20.	Bhilwara(RAJ)	65.	Jehanabad(BIH)	110.	Rajgarh(MP)
21.	Bhind(MP)	66.	Jhalawar(RAJ)	111.	Rewa(MP)
22.	Bhiwani(HAR)	67.	Jhansi(UP)	112.	Rewari(HAR)
23.	Bidar(KAR)	68.	Jhunjhunu(RAJ)	113.	Rohtas(BIH)
24.	Bijapur(KAR)	69.	Jodhpur(RAJ)	114.	Sagar(MP)
25.	Bikaner(RAJ)	70.	Khagaria(BIH)	115.	Saran(BIH)
26.	Bolangir(ORI)	71.	Kheri(UP)	116.	Satna(MP)
27.	Bongaigaon(ASM)	72.	Kishanganj(BIH)	117.	Sehore(MP)
28.	Budaun(UP)	73.	Kohima(NAG)	118.	Shahdol(MP)
29.	Bundi(RAJ)	74.	Koraput(ORI)	119.	Shajahanabad(UP)
30.	Buxar(BIH)	75.	Kota(RAJ)	120.	Shajapur(MP)
31.	Chittorgarh(RAJ)	76.	Kurnool(AP)	121.	Shivpuri(MP)
32.	Churu(RAJ)	77.	Lakhimpur(ASM)	122.	Sidhart Nagar(UP)
33.	Dadra	78.	Lalitpur(UP)	123.	Sitamarhi(BIH)
34.	Damoh(MP)	79.	Latur(MAH)	124.	Sitapur(UP)
35.	Datia(MP)	80.	Madhepura(BIH)	125.	Siwan(BIH)
36.	Dausa(RAJ)	81.	Maharajganj(UP)	126.	Sonbhadra(UP)
37.	Deoghar(BIH)	82.	Mahendragarh(HAR)	127.	Sultanpur(UP)

Contd...

Sr. No.	*District (State)*	*Sr. No.*	*District (State)*	*Sr. No.*	*District (State)*
38.	Deoria(UP)	83.	Mahesana(GUJ)	128.	Tikamgarh(MP)
39.	Dewas(MP)	84.	Mahoba(UP)	129.	Tirap (ARP)
40.	Dhanbad(BIH)	85.	Mainpuri(UP)	130.	Tonk(RAJ)
41.	Dhar(MP)	86.	Maldah (WB)	131.	Udaipur(RAJ)
42.	Dholpur(RAJ)	87.	Malkangiri(ORI)	132.	Vaishali(BIH)
43.	Dhubri(ASM)	88.	Mandsaur(MP)	133.	Varanasi(UP)
44.	Dumka(BIH)	89.	Mathura(UP)	134.	Vishkhapatanam(AP)
45.	East Siang(ARP)	90.	Mirzapur(UP)	135.	Warangal(AP)

Table 17(c)

Districts with Median Age at Marriage below 18 years of Age for Low Economic Status Group (Girls)

Sr. No.	*District (State)*	*Sr. No.*	*District (State)*	*Sr. No.*	*District (State)*
1.	Adilabad(AP)	76.	Gaya(BIH)	151.	North 24 Parganas(WB)
2.	Agra(UP)	77.	Ghazipur(UP)	152.	Osmanabad(MAH)
3.	Ajmer(RAJ)	78.	Giridih(BIH)	153.	Palamu(BIH)
4.	Aligarh(UP)	79.	Godda(BIH)	154.	Pali(RAJ)
5.	Allahabad(UP)	80.	Gonda(UP)	155.	Panna(MP)
6.	Alwar(RAJ)	81.	Gopalganj(BIH)	156.	Parbhani(MAH)
7.	Ambedkarnagar(UP)	82.	Gorakhpur(UP)	157.	Pashchim Champaran(BIH)
8.	Araria(BIH)	83.	Gulbarga(KAR)	158.	Patna(BIH)
9.	Aurangabad(BIH)	84.	Guna(MP)	159.	Pilibhit(UP)
10.	Aurangabad(MAH)	85.	Gwalior(MP)	160.	Prakasam(AP)
11.	Azamgarh(UP)	86.	Hamirpur(UP)	161.	Pratapgarh(UP)
12.	Bahraich(UP)	87.	Hanumangarh(RAJ)	162.	Pune(MAH)
13.	Ballia(UP)	88.	Hathras(UP)	163.	Purba Champaran(BIH)
14.	Banas Kantha(GUJ)	89.	Hazaribag(BIH)	164.	Purbi Singhbhum(BIH)
15.	Banda(UP)	90.	Indore(MP)	165.	Purnia(BIH)
16.	Bankura(WB)	91.	Jaipur(RAJ)	166.	Puruliya(WB)
17.	Banswara(RAJ)	92.	Jaisalmer(RAJ)	167.	Raibareilly(UP)
18.	Barabanki(UP)	93.	Jalaun(UP)	168.	Raichur(KAR)
19.	Barddhaman(WB)	94.	Jalgaon(MAH)	169.	Raipur(MP)
20.	Barmer(RAJ)	95.	Jalna(MAH)	170.	Raisen(MP)
21.	Basti(UP)	96.	Jalore(RAJ)	171.	Rajgarh(MP)
22.	Beed(MAH)	97.	Jaunpur(UP)	172.	Rajnandgaon(MP)
23.	Begusarai(BIH)	98.	Jehanabad(BIH)	173.	Rajsamand(RAJ)
24.	Belgaum(KAR)	99.	Jhabua(MP)	174.	Rangareddy(AP)
25.	Bellary(KAR)	100.	Jhalawar(RAJ)	175.	Ratlam(MP)
26.	Bhadohi(UP)	101.	Jhansi(UP)	176.	Rewa(MP)
27.	Bhagalpur(BIH)	102.	Jhunjhunu(RAJ)	177.	Rohtas(BIH)
28.	Bharatpur(RAJ)	103.	Jodhpur(RAJ)	178.	Sagar(MP)
29.	Bhilwara(RAJ)	104.	Kaithal(HAR)	179.	Saharsa(BIH)
30.	Bhind(MP)	105.	Kalahandi(ORI)	180.	Sahibganj(BIH)
31.	Bhiwani(HAR)	106.	Kanpur Dehat(UP)	181.	Salem(TN)
32.	Bhojpur(BIH)	107.	Kasaragod(KER)	182.	Samastipur(BIH)
33.	Bidar(KAR)	108.	Katihar(BIH)	183.	Saran(BIH)
34.	Bijapur(KAR)	109.	Khagaria(BIH)	184.	Satna(MP)
35.	Bikaner(RAJ)	110.	Kheda(GUJ)	185.	Sawaimadhopur(RAJ)
36.	Bilaspur(MP)	111.	Kheri(UP)	186.	Sehore(MP)
37.	Birbhum(WB)	112.	Kishanganj(BIH)	187.	Shahdol(MP)

Contd....

Sr. No.	*District (State)*	*Sr. No.*	*District (State)*	*Sr. No.*	*District (State)*
38.	Bolangir(ORI)	113.	Kodagu(KAR)	188.	Shajahanabad(UP)
39.	Boudh(ORI)	114.	Kohima(NAG)	189.	Shajapur(MP)
40.	Budaun(UP)	115.	Kolkata(WB)	190.	Shivpuri(MP)
41.	Bundi(RAJ)	116.	Kooch Bihar(WB)	191.	Sidhart Nagar(UP)
42.	Buxar(BIH)	117.	Koraput(ORI)	192.	Sidhi(MP)
43.	Chattarpur(MP)	118.	Kota(RAJ)	193.	Sikar(RAJ)
44.	Chittorgarh(RAJ)	119.	Lalitpur(UP)	194.	Sirohi(RAJ)
45.	Churu(RAJ)	120.	Latur(MAH)	195.	Sirsa(HAR)
46.	Dadra	121.	Madhepura(BIH)	196.	Sitamarhi(BIH)
47.	Dakshin Dinajpur(WB)	122.	Madhubani(BIH)	197.	Sitapur(UP)
48.	Damoh(MP)	123.	Maharajganj(UP)	198.	Siwan(BIH)
49.	Darbhanga(BIH)	124.	Mahbubnagar(AP)	199.	Solapur(MAH)
50.	Datia(MP)	125.	Mahendragarh(HAR)	200.	Sonbhadra(UP)
51.	Dausa(RAJ)	126.	Mahesana(GUJ)	201.	Sonipat(HAR)
52.	Deoghar(BIH)	127.	Mahoba(UP)	202.	South 24 Parganas(WB)
53.	Deoria(UP)	128.	Mainpuri(UP)	203.	Srikakulam(AP)
54.	Dewas(MP)	129.	Maldah (WB)	204.	Sultanpur(UP)
55.	Dhanbad(BIH)	130.	Malkangiri(ORI)	205.	Surat(GUJ)
56.	Dhar(MP)	131.	Mandsaur(MP)	206.	Surguja(MP)
57.	Dharmapuri(TN)	132.	Mandya(KAR)	207.	The Dangs(GUJ)
58.	Dharwad(KAR)	133.	Mathura(UP)	208.	Theni(TN)
59.	Dholpur(RAJ)	134.	Mirzapur(UP)	209.	Tikam[illegible]
60.	Dhubri(ASM)	135.	Morena(MP)	210.	Tonk(RAJ)
61.	Dhule(MAH)	136.	Muktsar(PUJ)	211.	Tumkur(KAR)
62.	East Godavari(AP)	137.	Munger(BIH)	212.	Udaipur(RAJ)
63.	East Nimar(MP)	138.	Murshidabad(WB)	213.	Ujjain(MP)
64.	Etah(UP)	139.	Muzaffarpur(BIH)	214.	Unnao(UP)
65.	Etawah(UP)	140.	Mysore(KAR)	215.	Uttar Dinajpur(WB)
66.	Faizabad(UP)	141.	Nadia((WB)	216.	Vadodara(GUJ)
67.	Faridabad(HAR)	142.	Nagaon(ASM)	217.	Vaishali(BIH)
68.	Faridkot(PUJ)	143.	Nagaur(RAJ)	218.	Varanasi(UP)
69.	Farrukhabad(UP)	144.	Nalanda(BIH)	219.	Vidisha(MP)
70.	Fathepur(UP)	145.	Nanded(MAH)	220.	Vishkhapatanam(AP)
71.	Firozabad(UP)	146.	Narsimhapur(MP)	221.	Vizianagaram(AP)
72.	Firozpur(PUJ)	147.	Nawada(BIH)	222.	Warangal(AP)
73.	Gandhinagar(GUJ)	148.	Nawrangapura(ORI)	223.	West Nimar(MP)
74.	Ganganagar(RAJ)	149.	Nayagarh(ORI)		
75.	Ganjam(ORI)	150.	Nizamabad(AP)		

(d) Female Literacy Rate

The per cent share of marriages below the legal minimum age at marriage, mean and median age at marriage and number of reported marriages in each district by female literacy rate is given in Appendix V. In districts with low literacy rate, the variation in the per cent share of marriages below legal minimum age at marriage is from zero in three districts to 83.9 in Lalitpur (Uttar Pradesh). Among districts with medium literacy rate the variation in the per cent of marriages below legal minimum age of 18 years is from zero in the case of five districts to 82.4 per cent in

Shajapur (Madhya Pradesh). The corresponding variation for the high literacy rate group is from zero in 8 districts to 50 per cent in Rajnandgaon district of Madhya Pradesh. The per centage distribution of districts by their per cent share of marriages below legal minimum age at marriage is given in a summary form in Figure F-15.

Fig. F-15: Percentage Distribution of Districts by per cent Share of Marriages below 18 years of Age in each Category of Literacy (Girls)

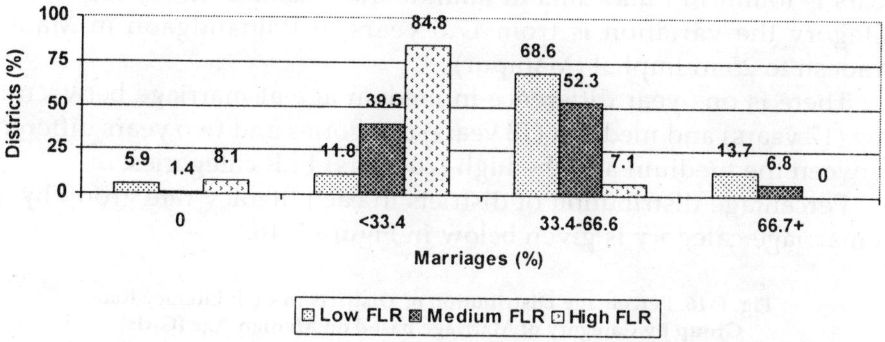

When the literacy level is high, the proportion of child and early marriages is found to be less and vice versa. Most of the districts in the high literacy category have only less than one-third of the marriages below legal minimum age and there is no district with two-thirds marriage in this category. The list of districts with at least two-thirds of the marriages falling in the below legal minimum age at marriage is given below in Table 18.

Table 18
Districts with Marriages below 18 years of Age Forming at Least two-thirds of the Total Marriages in each category of Female Literacy Rate

Sr. No.	*District (State)*	*Sr. No.*	*District (State)*	*Sr. No.*	*District (State)*
	Low FLR		**Medium FLR**		**Medium FLR**
1.	Bahraich(UP)	1.	Ambedkarnagar(UP)	13.	Jhalawar(RAJ)
2.	Gonda(UP)	2.	Banda(UP)	14.	Morena(MP)
3.	Lalitpur(UP)	3.	Basti(UP)	15.	Murshidabad(WB)
4.	Maharajganj(UP)	4.	Bhadohi(UP)	16.	Patna(BIH)
5.	Nawada(BIH)	5.	Bhilwara(RAJ)	17.	Puruliya(WB)
6.	Nawrangapura(ORI)	6.	Bidar(KAR)	18.	Rohtas(BIH)
7.	Tonk(RAJ)	7.	Bundi(RAJ)	19.	Shahdol(MP)
		8.	Chattarpur(MP)	20.	Shajapur(MP)
		9.	Churu(RAJ)	21.	Shivpuri(MP)
		10.	Dausa(RAJ)	22.	Sidhi(MP)
		11.	Guna(MP)	23.	Tikamgarh(MP)
		12.	Hazaribag(BIH)	24.	Varanasi(UP)

Median Age at Marriage by Female Literacy Rate

On the whole, the median age at marriage for districts with low FLR varies from a minimum of 14.5 in Maharajganj district of Uttar Pradesh to 22 in Anantnag of Jammu and Kashmir. Correspondingly, the lowest median age observed among the districts with medium FLR is 15 years (Basti in Uttar Pradesh, Bundi and Jhalawar in Rajasthan, Patna in Bihar and Shajapur in Madhya Pradesh). In this group, the highest median age of 23 years is found in Pulawama in Jammu and Kashmir. In the highest FLR category the variation is from 17.5 years in Rajnandgaon in Madhya Pradesh to 25 in Imphal (Manipur).

There is one year difference in median age at marriage between the low (17 years) and medium (18 years) categories and two years difference between the medium and the high (20 years) FLR categories.

Percentage distribution of districts in each literacy rate group by age at marriage category is given below in Figure F-16.

Fig. F-16: Percentage Distribution of Districts in each Literacy Rate Group by Category of Marriage based on Median Age (Girls)

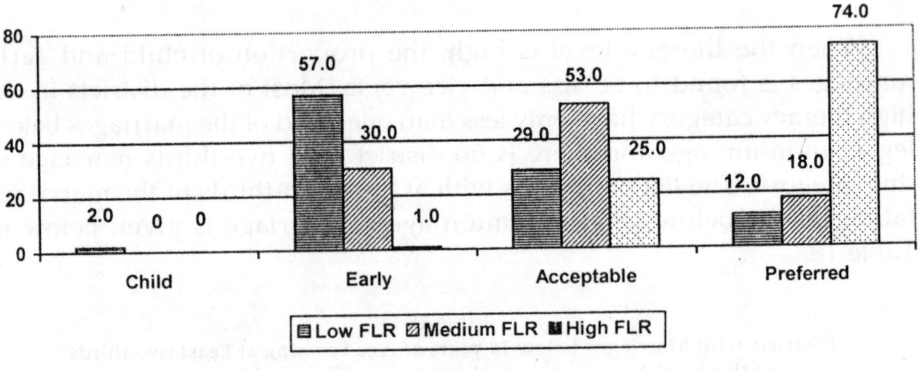

The only district with a median age at marriage below 15 years (Maharajganj) is in the low FLR group. Fifty seven per cent of the districts in this FLR group had a median age falling in the early marriage category. More than half the districts with medium FLR have acceptable median age at marriage. Preferred age of at least 20 years is found only in 18 per cent of districts in this category. When literacy rate is the highest, all but one per cent of the district has either acceptable or preferred median age at marriage with 74 per cent falling into the latter category.

Of the 137 districts with a median age at marriage below 18 years, the distribution by FLR group is 30, 106 and 1 respectively for low, medium and high. Seventy seven per cent of these districts are located in Bihar (22%), Madhya Pradesh (17%), Rajasthan (14%) and Uttar Pradesh (24%). The single district in the high FLR category with a median age at marriage less than 18 years is Rajnandgaon of Madhya Pradesh with a median age of 17.5 years. The per cent share of selected states of the districts with a median below 18 years in the low and median category of FLR group is given in Figure F-17.

Fig. F-17: Per cent Share of Selected States of Districts with Median Age at Marriage below 18 years of Age by Female Literacy Rate (Girls)

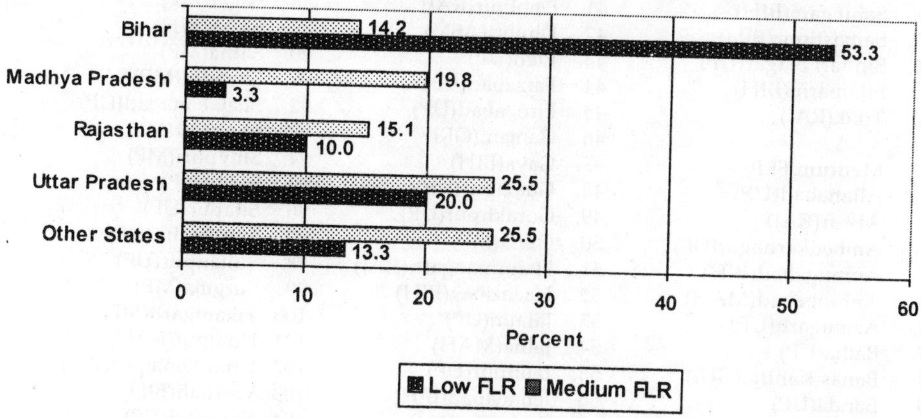

The names of all the districts with below legal minimum median age at marriage for the three FLR categories are given below in Table 19.

Table 19
Districts with Median Age at Marriage below 18 years of Age by Female Literacy Rate Group (Girls)

Sr. No.	District (State)	Sr. No.	District (State)	Sr. No.	District (State)
	Low FLR		**Medium FLR**		**Medium FLR**
1.	Araria(BIH)	16.	Begusarai(BIH)	63.	Latur(MAH)
2.	Bahraich(UP)	17.	Belgaum(KAR)	64.	Mahoba(UP)
3.	Banswara(RAJ)	18.	Bhadohi(UP)	65.	Mainpuri(UP)
4.	Budaun(UP)	19.	Bhagalpur(BIH)	66.	Maldah (WB)
5.	Darbhanga(BIH)	20.	Bharatpur(RAJ)	67.	Mandsaur(MP)
6.	Deoghar(BIH)	21.	Bhilwara(RAJ)	68.	Mirzapur(UP)
7.	Giridih(BIH)	22.	Bhind(MP)	69.	Morena(MP)
8.	Godda(BIH)	23.	Bhojpur(BIH)	70.	Munger(BIH)
9.	Gonda(UP)	24.	Bidar(KAR)	71.	Murshidabad(WB)
10.	Gopalganj(BIH)	25.	Bijapur(KAR)	72.	Muzaffarpur(BIH)
11.	Jaisalmer(RAJ)	26.	Bikaner(RAJ)	73.	Nagaur(RAJ)
12.	Jhabua(MP)	27.	Birbhum(WB)	74.	Nalanda(BIH)
13.	Kalahandi(ORI)	28.	Bolangir(ORI)	75.	Nanded(MAH)
14.	Khagaria(BIH)	29.	Boudh(ORI)	76.	Nayagarh(ORI)
15.	Koraput(ORI)	30.	Bundi(RAJ)	77.	Pali(RAJ)
16.	Lalitpur(UP)	31.	Buxar(BIH)	78.	Panna(MP)
17.	Madhepura(BIH)	32.	Chattarpur(MP)	79.	Patna(BIH)
18.	Madhubani(BIH)	33.	Churu(RAJ)	80.	Pilibhit(UP)
19.	Maharajganj(UP)	34.	Dadra	81.	Pratapgarh(UP)
20.	Malkangiri(ORI)	35.	Dakshin Dinajpur(WB)	82.	Puruliya(WB)

Contd....

Sr. No.	District (State)	Sr. No.	District (State)	Sr. No.	District (State)
21.	Nawada(BIH)	36.	Damoh(MP)	83.	Raichur(KAR)
22.	Nawrangapura(ORI)	37.	Dausa(RAJ)	84.	Raipur(MP)
23.	Palamu(BIH)	38.	Deoria(UP)	85.	Rajgarh(MP)
24.	Purba Champaran(BIH)	39.	Dewas(MP)	86.	Rewa(MP)
25.	Saharsa(BIH)	40.	Dhar(MP)	87.	Rohtas(BIH)
26.	Sahibganj(BIH)	41.	Dholpur(RAJ)	88.	Sagar(MP)
27.	Samastipur(BIH)	42.	Dhubri(ASM)	89.	Saran(BIH)
28.	Sidhart Nagar(UP)	43.	Etah(UP)	90.	Satna(MP)
29.	Sitamarhi(BIH)	44.	Faizabad(UP)	91.	Shahdol(MP)
30.	Tonk(RAJ)	45.	Firozabad(UP)	92.	Shajahanabad(UP)
		46.	Ganjam(ORI)	93.	Shajapur(MP)
	Medium FLR	47.	Gaya(BIH)	94.	Shivpuri(MP)
1.	Allahabad(UP)	48.	Ghazipur(UP)	95.	Sidhi(MP)
2.	Alwar(RAJ)	49.	Gorakhpur(UP)	96.	Sitapur(UP)
3.	Ambedkarnagar(UP)	50.	Guna(MP)	97.	Sonbhadra(UP)
4.	Aurangabad(BIH)	51.	Hanumangarh(RAJ)	98.	Sultanpur(UP)
5.	Aurangabad(MAH)	52.	Hazaribag(BIH)	99.	Surguja(MP)
6.	Azamgarh(UP)	53.	Jalaun(UP)	100.	Tikamgarh(MP)
7.	Ballia(UP)	54.	Jalna(MAH)	101.	Udaipur(RAJ)
8.	Banas Kantha(GUJ)	55.	Jaunpur(UP)	102.	Uttar Dinajpur(WB)
9.	Banda(UP)	56.	Jehanabad(BIH)	103.	Vaishali(BIH)
10.	Bankura(WB)	57.	Jhalawar(RAJ)	104.	Varanasi(UP)
11.	Barabanki(UP)	58.	Jodhpur(RAJ)	105.	Vidisha(MP)
12.	Barddhaman(WB)	59.	Kheri(UP)	106.	Vishakhapatanam(AP)
13.	Barmer(RAJ)	60.	Kohima(NAG)		
14.	Basti(UP)	61.	Kooch Bihar(WB)		**High FLR**
15.	Beed(MAH)	62.	Kota(RAJ)	1.	Rajnandgaon(MP)

NOTES

1. The single marriage at age 17 in Godda, two marriages at age 16 in Madhubani (Bihar) and one marriage at 16 in Tirap (Arunachal Pradesh) are not considered.
2. The single marriage at the age of 14 years in district Dibang Valley (Arunachal Pradesh) is not considered.
3. Same as foot note 9.
4. The single marriage at age 29 reported in the district The Nilgiris of Tamil Nadu is not considered.
5. The single marriage at age 16 reported from East Kameng district of Arunachal Pradesh is not considered.
6. The single marriage at age 16 reported from Tirap district of Arunachal Pradesh is not considered.
7. The single marriage at age 15 reported from Faridkot district of Punjab and the single marriage at age 16 reported from Kaithal district of Haryana are not considered.
8. The single marriage each at age 27 in Mokokchung (Nagaland) and Tamenglong (Manipur) are not considered.
9. The single marriage at the age of 29 years in North Goa is not considered.

Chapter - 3

AGE AT MARRIAGE OF BOYS

GENERAL SITUATION

No male marriage was reported from South Garo Hills of Meghalaya during the reference period and hence the analysis in this chapter will be based on marriages reported from the remaining 503 districts. A total of 65491 marriages of boys were reported during the reference period, of which only 30 per cent of marriages are found to be below the legal minimum age at marriage of 21 years (comprising of 6.3% child marriage and 23.7% early marriages. The important point to note here is that 70 per cent of the total marriages were conducted after the boy attained legally acceptable age and among them three-fourths were preferred marriages (after attaining 23 years of age).

Of the 4156 reported child marriages among the boys 78 per cent are from Bihar (18.3%), Madhya Pradesh (17.1%), Rajasthan (16.9%) and Uttar Pradesh (25.8%).

Of the total marriages, the share of SC/ST/OBC is 61 per cent and that of castes other than SC/ST/OBC was 36 per cent. Caste information is not available for the remaining 3 per cent of marriages. Thirty per cent of the total marriages are among those with high economic status, 33 per cent among those with medium economic status and 37 per cent among those in the low economic status group. Ten per cent of the total marriages are from districts with low FLR, 70 per cent from those with medium FLR and the remaining 20 per cent from districts with high FLR.

DISTRIBUTION OF MARRIAGES/DISTRICTS IN STATES BY AGE AT MARRIAGE

The state-wise distribution of age at marriage of the boys by marriage category (Table 1) shows that of the total reported marriages more than 10 per cent of child marriage is observed only in Bihar (10.5%), Madhya Pradesh (13.3%), Rajasthan (17.0%) and Uttar Pradesh (11.9%). Conversely, from Kerala, Andaman and Nicobar, Chandigarh, Goa, Lakshadweep and Pondicherry, no child marriage is reported. Boys getting married before they reach the legal minimum age at marriage of 21 years are very rare in Kerala (only 2.9%), Andaman and Nicobar (2.1), Goa (1.6) and Pondicherry (3.3).

Table 1

Per centage Distribution of Marriages by Marriage Category (Boys)

Sr. No.	State/Union Territories	*Marriage category* Child	Early	Accep-table	Preferred	*Total* Per cent	Number
	MAJOR STATES						
1.	Andhra Pradesh	3.3	24.9	20.0	51.7	100.0	2241
2.	Assam	0.8	7.1	9.2	82.9	100.0	2964
3.	Bihar*	10.5	34.4	20.1	34.9	100.0	7201
4.	Gujarat	6.3	27.9	25.0	40.9	100.0	3292
5.	Haryana	5.0	26.9	25.2	43.0	100.0	2888
6.	Karnataka	2.3	11.1	14.3	72.3	100.0	2906
7.	Kerala	0.0	2.9	7.0	90.1	100.0	2102
8.	Madhya Pradesh*	13.3	33.1	20.2	33.3	100.0	5321
9.	Maharashtra	1.5	13.5	21.9	63.1	100.0	4230
10.	Orissa	1.8	16.2	15.8	66.2	100.0	3930
11.	Punjab	1.8	19.8	23.2	55.2	100.0	2954
12.	Rajasthan	17.0	37.4	19.6	26.1	100.0	4137
13.	Tamil Nadu	0.4	7.0	13.2	79.3	100.0	2556
14.	Uttar Pradesh*	11.9	38.4	21.2	28.5	100.0	9014
15.	West Bengal	3.5	19.8	18.1	58.7	100.0	2784
	SMALLER STATES/UNION TERRITORIES						
16.	Andaman & Nicobar	0.0	2.1	17.4	80.6	100.0	144
17.	Arunachal Pradesh	2.9	29.8	18.0	49.3	100.0	517
18.	Chandigarh	0.0	9.3	11.1	79.6	100.0	54
19.	Dadra & Nagar Haveli	9.5	37.1	20.7	32.8	100.0	116
20.	Daman & Diu	0.7	13.7	20.5	65.1	100.0	307
21.	Delhi	1.0	11.8	16.7	70.6	100.0	102
22.	Goa	0.0	1.6	5.2	93.1	100.0	248
23.	Himachal Pradesh	0.4	6.8	15.4	77.4	100.0	1703
24.	Jammu & Kashmir	0.5	8.5	11.9	79.1	100.0	871
25.	Lakshadweep	0.0	9.2	13.3	77.6	100.0	98
26.	Manipur	2.2	15.5	12.2	70.1	100.0	768
27.	Meghalaya	2.0	44.9	17.0	36.1	100.0	147
28.	Mizoram	2.4	18.9	16.9	61.8	100.0	249
29.	Nagaland	3.6	21.3	19.5	55.6	100.0	446
30.	Pondicherry	0.0	3.3	9.2	87.5	100.0	479
31.	Sikkim	2.9	16.0	16.7	64.4	100.0	312
32.	Tripura	1.5	5.6	9.8	83.2	100.0	410
	Total	6.3	23.7	18.6	51.4	100.0	65491

* Refers to undivided states.

The mean and median age at marriage and the marriage category based on median age for the states is given in Table 2. Among the major states the median age at marriage is the lowest, 20 years, in Uttar Pradesh and Rajasthan which is one year below the legally prescribed minimum age at marriage for boys for boys. The highest median age at marriage among this group of states is 27 years in Assam and Kerala. In all the smaller states and union territories the median age at marriage is found to be at least 21 years. Further, based on median age, all the districts have preferred age at marriage in Kerala, Tamil Nadu, Andaman & Nicobar, Chandigarh, Daman & Diu, Delhi, Goa, Himachal Pradesh, Lakshadweep, Manipur, Mizoram, Pondicherry and Tripura.

Table 2
Average Age at Marriage and Marriage Category based on Median Age in states/union Territories (Boys)

Sr. No.	State and union territories	Mean	Median	Coefficient of variation	Marriage category based on median age: Districts Percent EM	AM	PM	Total %	Total Number
MAJOR STATES									
1.	Andhra Pradesh	23.1	23.0	0.047	0.0	47.8	52.2	100	23
2.	Assam	27.0	27.0	0.059	0.0	4.5	95.5	100	22
3.	Bihar	21.7	21.0	0.056	34.9	51.2	14.0	100	43
4.	Gujarat	22.2	22.0	0.048	10.5	57.9	31.6	100	19
5.	Haryana	22.3	22.0	0.033	0.0	70.6	29.4	100	17
6.	Karnataka	25.2	25.0	0.061	0.0	5.0	95.0	100	20
7.	Kerala	27.4	27.0	0.045	0.0	0.0	100.0	100	14
8.	Madhya Pradesh	21.4	21.0	0.063	46.7	33.3	20.0	100	45
9.	Maharashtra	24.1	24.0	0.051	0.0	13.3	86.7	100	30
10.	Orissa	24.5	24.0	0.055	3.3	16.7	80.0	100	30
11.	Punjab	23.5	23.0	0.040	0.0	47.1	52.9	100	17
12.	Rajasthan	20.7	20.0	0.035	70.0	30.0	0.0	100	30
13.	Tamil Nadu	26.0	26.0	0.035	0.0	0.0	100.0	100	23
14.	Uttar Pradesh	21.1	20.0	0.062	54.4	38.2	7.4	100	68
15.	West Bengal	24.4	24.0	0.046	0.0	16.7	83.3	100	18
SMALLER STATES/UNION TERRITORIES									
16.	Andaman & Nicobar	26.4	25.5	0.040	0.0	0.0	100.0	100	2
17.	Arunachal Pradesh	23.2	22.0	0.041	15.4	38.5	46.2	100	13
18.	Chandigarh	24.9	25.0	0.000	0.0	0.0	100.0	100	1
19.	Dadra & Nagar Haveli	21.4	21.0	0.000	0.0	100.0	0.0	100	1
20.	Daman & Diu	24.3	24.0	0.002	0.0	0.0	100.0	100	2
21.	Delhi	24.4	28.2	0.000	0.0	0.0	100.0	100	1
22.	Goa	28.8	29.0	0.009	0.0	0.0	100.0	100	2
23.	Himachal Pradesh	25.0	25.0	0.029	0.0	0.0	100.0	100	12
24.	Jammu & Kashmir	24.9	24.4	0.076	0.0	14.3	85.7	100	14
25.	Lakshadweep	25.7	26.0	0.000	0.0	0.0	100.0	100	1
26.	Manipur	25.8	29.5	0.039	0.0	0.0	100.0	100	8
27.	Meghalaya	21.8	21.0	0.071	50.0	0.0	50.0	100	6
28.	Mizoram	24.9	24.0	0.036	0.0	0.0	100.0	100	3
29.	Nagaland	23.2	23.0	0.071	14.3	42.9	42.9	100	7
30.	Pondicherry	27.7	27.0	0.064	0.0	0.0	100.0	100	4
31.	Sikkim	24.7	24.0	0.038	0.0	25.0	75.0	100	4
32.	Tripura	27.8	33.8	0.022	0.0	0.0	100.0	100	3

Note: (1) Weighted mean and median
(2) No district had a median age < 18 years which falls into the child marriage category
(3) EM = Early marriage; AM = Acceptable marriage; PM = Preferred marriage.

Among the states/Union Territories, the proportion of boys marrying before completing 21 years of age is given in Figure M-1 along with the per cent of districts with a median age at marriage below 21 years.

Fig. M-1: Per cent Share of Marriage Conducted before the Boy attained 21 years of Age and the per cent of Districts with a Median Age at Marriage below 21 years by State/UT

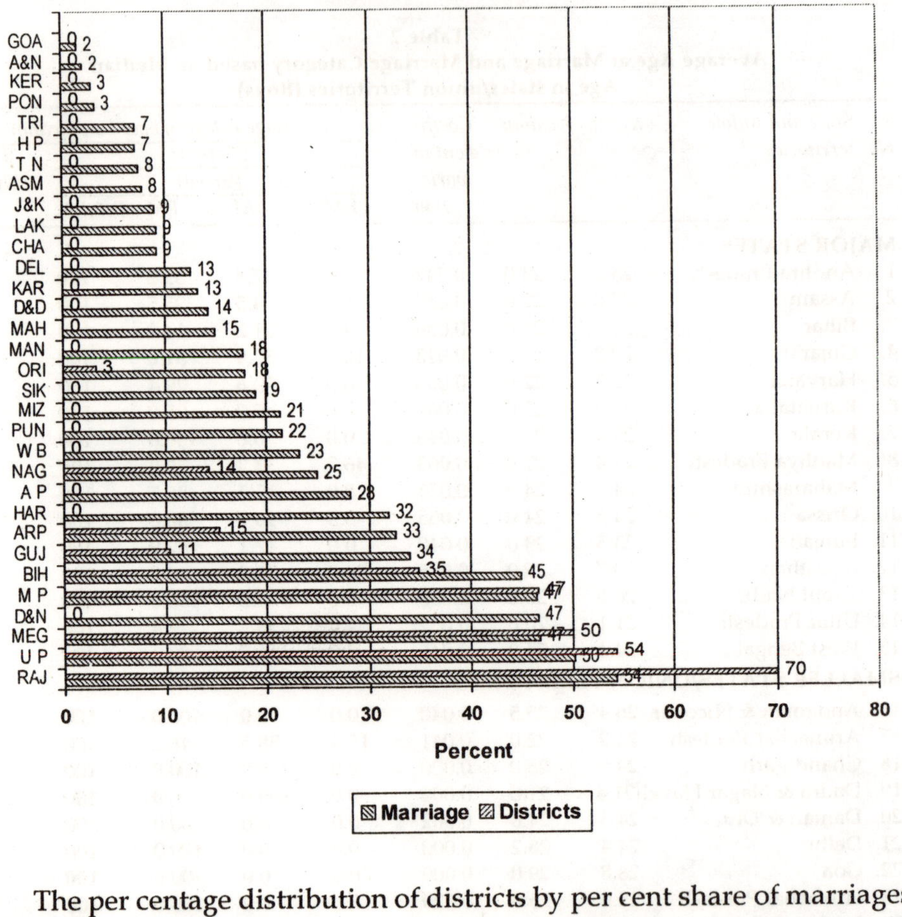

The per centage distribution of districts by per cent share of marriages below legal minimum age in each state and Union territory is given in Table 3.

The per cent share of marriages below legal minimum age forms at least 50 per cent of the total marriages in 70 per cent of the districts in Rajasthan. The other states that fall with a higher per cent of districts in this category are Bihar (35% of the districts), Madhya Pradesh (47% of districts), Meghalaya (50% of the districts), and Uttar Pradesh (54% of the districts). In just six districts out of a total of 503 districts (forming 1.2%), there were no marriages below 21 years. These districts are Kannur and Pathanamthitta in Kerala, Thirunelveli in Tamil Nadu, Nicobar of

Andaman & Nicobar, Jammu of Jammu & Kashmir and Jainta Hills of Meghalaya.

Table 3
Per centage Distribution of Districts by per cent Share of Marriages below 21 years of Age (Boys)

Sr. No.	*State/Union territory*	*Per cent of districts by per cent share of marriages below legal minimum age at marriage of 21 years*							
		0	*<10*	*10-19.9*	*20-29.9*	*30-49.9*	*50+*	*Total %*	*#*
MAJOR STATES									
1.	Andhra Pradesh	0.0	4.3	8.7	43.5	43.5	0.0	100.0	23
2.	Assam	0.0	54.5	36.4	4.5	4.5	0.0	100.0	22
3.	Bihar	0.0	2.3	2.3	16.3	44.2	34.9	100.0	43
4.	Gujarat	0.0	5.3	10.5	26.3	52.6	5.3	100.0	19
5.	Haryana	0.0	0.0	17.6	23.5	58.8	0.0	100.0	17
6.	Karnataka	0.0	55.0	20.0	15.0	10.0	0.0	100.0	20
7.	Kerala	14.3	85.7	0.0	0.0	0.0	0.0	100.0	14
8.	Madhya Pradesh	0.0	0.0	4.4	22.2	26.7	46.7	100.0	45
9.	Maharashtra	0.0	36.7	30.0	23.3	10.0	0.0	100.0	30
10.	Orissa	0.0	33.3	33.3	13.3	16.7	3.3	100.0	30
11.	Punjab	0.0	5.9	47.1	23.5	23.5	0.0	100.0	17
12.	Rajasthan	0.0	0.0	0.0	0.0	30.0	70.0	100.0	30
13.	Tamil Nadu	4.3	73.9	21.7	0.0	0.0	0.0	100.0	23
14.	Uttar Pradesh	0.0	4.4	2.9	8.8	29.4	54.4	100.0	68
15.	West Bengal	0.0	0.0	38.9	50.0	11.1	0.0	100.0	18
SMALLER STATES/UNION TERRITORIES									
16.	Andaman & Nicobar	50.0	50.0	0.0	0.0	0.0	0.0	100.0	2
17.	Arunachal Pradesh	0.0	7.7	15.4	23.1	38.5	15.4	100.0	13
18.	Chandigarh	0.0	100.0	0.0	0.0	0.0	0.0	100.0	1
19.	Dadra & Nagar Haveli	0.0	0.0	0.0	0.0	100.0	0.0	100.0	1
20.	Daman & Diu	0.0	0.0	100.0	0.0	0.0	0.0	100.0	2
21.	Delhi	0.0	0.0	100.0	0.0	0.0	0.0	100.0	1
22.	Goa	0.0	100.0	0.0	0.0	0.0	0.0	100.0	2
23.	Himachal Pradesh	0.0	66.7	33.3	0.0	0.0	0.0	100.0	12
24.	Jammu & Kashmir	7.1	42.9	28.6	7.1	14.3	0.0	100.0	14
25.	Lakshadweep	0.0	100.0	0.0	0.0	0.0	0.0	100.0	1
26.	Manipur	0.0	0.0	75.0	25.0	0.0	0.0	100.0	8
27.	Meghalaya	16.7	0.0	0.0	0.0	33.3	50.0	100.0	6
28.	Mizoram	0.0	0.0	33.3	66.7	0.0	0.0	100.0	3
29.	Nagaland	0.0	42.9	0.0	14.3	28.6	14.3	100.0	7
30.	Pondicherry	0.0	75.0	25.0	0.0	0.0	0.0	100.0	4
31.	Sikkim	0.0	25.0	0.0	75.0	0.0	0.0	100.0	4
32.	Tripura	0.0	100.0	0.0	0.0	0.0	0.0	100.0	3
	Total	1.2	21.9	16.7	16.3	23.7	20.3	100.0	503

Of the 20 per cent of districts with marriages below 21 years reaching a level of at least 50 per cent of the respective total marriages, ninety two per cent are from four states, viz. Bihar (14.7%), Madhya Pradesh (20.6%), Rajasthan (20.6%) and Uttar Pradesh (36.3%). Among the 84 districts from the smaller states and union territories only six districts fall in this category.

DISTRICT-WISE ANALYSIS

General situation

The distribution of marriages in each district by marriage category, average age at marriage and per cent of marriages below legal minimum age at marriage of 21 years is given in Appendix VI. Though most of the districts have marriages below 21 years of age, there are still some districts with no child or early marriage. Table 3.4 shows that there is no male child marriage in 124 districts and no marriage below legal minimum age of 21 years in 6 districts.

Table 4
Number of Districts with no child/early Marriage in each state/UT (Boys)

Sr. No.	*State/UT*	*Total # of districts*	*# of districts with no CM*	*# of districts with no EM*
MAJOR STATES				
1.	Andhra Pradesh	23	10	0
2.	Assam	22	9	0
3.	Bihar	43	1	0
4.	Gujarat	19	1	0
5.	Haryana	17	0	0
6.	Karnataka	20	6	0
7.	Kerala	14	14	2
8.	Madhya Pradesh	45	3	0
9.	Maharashtra	30	10	0
10.	Orissa	30	8	0
11.	Punjab	17	3	0
12.	Rajasthan	30	0	0
13.	Tamil Nadu	23	14	1
14.	Uttar Pradesh	68	3	0
15.	West Bengal	18	2	0
SMALLER STATES/UNION TERRITORIES				
16.	Andaman & Nicobar	2	2	1
17.	Arunachal Pradesh	13	5	0
18.	Chandigarh	1	1	0
19.	Dadra & Nagar Haveli	1	0	0
20.	Daman & Diu	2	0	0
21.	Delhi	1	0	0
22.	Goa	2	2	0
23.	Himachal Pradesh	12	7	0
24.	Jammu & Kashmir	14	11	1
25.	Lakshadweep	1	1	0
26.	Manipur	8	1	0
27.	Meghalaya	6*	4	1
28.	Mizoram	3	0	0
29.	Nagaland	7	2	0
30.	Pondicherry	4	4	0
31.	Sikkim	4	0	0
32.	Tripura	3	0	0
	TOTAL	503	124	6

The 124 districts with no child marriage are from the following states/ union territories: one each in Bihar, Chandigarh, Gujarat, Lakshadweep and Manipur; two each in Andaman & Nicobar, Goa, Nagaland and West Bengal; three each Madhya Pradesh, Punjab and Uttar Pradesh; four each in Meghalaya and Pondicherry; five in Arunachal Pradesh; six in Karnataka, seven in Himachal Pradesh; eight in Orissa; nine in Assam; ten each in Andhra Pradesh and Maharashtra; eleven in Jammu & Kashmir; and fourteen each in Kerala and Tamil Nadu. The names of these districts are given in Table 5.

Table 5
Districts with no child Marriage (Boys)

Sr. No.	*District (State)*	*Sr. No.*	*District (State)*	*Sr. No.*	*District (State)*
1.	Ahmadnagar(MAH)	43.	Jharsuguda(ORI)	85.	Prakasam(AP)
2.	Alappuzha(KER)	44.	Jorhat(ASM)	86.	Pudukottai(TN)
3.	Almora(UP)	45.	Kangra(HP)	87.	Purbi singhbhum(BIH)
4.	Amravali(MAH)	46.	Kanniyakumari(TN)	88.	Puri(ORI)
5.	Ananthapur(AP)	47.	Kannur(KER)	89.	Raigarh(MAH)
6.	Anantnag(J&K)	48.	Karaikal(PON)	90.	Raigarh(MP)
7.	Andaman(A&N)	49.	Karbi Anglong(ASM)	91.	Rajori(J&K)
8.	Balaghat(MP)	50.	Kasaragod(KER)	92.	Ramanathapuram(TN)
9.	Balasore(ORI)	51.	Kathua(J&K)	93.	Rangareddy(AP)
10.	Bangalore (KAR)	52.	Khordha(ORI)	94.	Ratnagari(MAH)
11.	Bangalore Rural(KAR)	53.	Kodagu(KAR)	95.	Salem(TN)
12.	Baramulla(J&K)	54.	Kollam(KER)	96.	Shivganganagar(TN)
13.	Barpeta(ASM)	55.	Kottayam(KER)	97.	Sibsagar(ASM)
14.	Betul(MP)	56.	Kozhikode(KER)	98.	Sindhudurg(MAH)
15.	Bhadrak(ORI)	57.	Kullu(HP)	99.	Sirmaur(HP)
16.	Bhandara(MAH)	58.	Kupuwada(J&K)	100.	Sonitpur(ASM)
17.	Bilaspur(HP)	59.	Lahul & Spiti(HP)	101.	South Goa(GOA)
18.	Buldana(MAH)	60.	Lakhimpur(ASM)	102.	Srikakulam(AP)
19.	Chamba(HP)	61.	Lakshadweep	103.	Srinagar(J&K)
20.	Chamoli(UP)	62.	Leh(J&K)	104.	Tawang(ARP)
21.	Chandigarh(CHN)	63.	Ludhiana(PUJ)	105.	Thanjavur(TN)
22.	Chengalpattu(TN)	64.	Mahe(PON)	106.	Thiruchirapalli(TN)
23.	Chennai(TN)	65.	Malappuram(KER)	107.	Thirunelveli(TN)
24.	Chittor(AP)	66.	Mandya(KAR)	108.	Thiruvanathapuram(KER)
25.	Churachandpur(MAN)	67.	Medak(AP)	109.	Thrissur(KER)
26.	Cuddapah(AP)	68.	Mokokchung(NAG)	110.	Tuensang(NAG)
27.	Dakshina Kannada(KAR)	69.	Nagpur(MAH)	111.	Tutikorin(TN)
28.	Debagarh(ORI)	70.	Nalbari(ASM)	112.	Udhampur(J&K)
29.	Dhubri(ASM)	71.	Namakkal(TN)	113.	Una(HP)
30.	Dindigul(TN)	72.	Nawanshahar(PUJ)	114.	Upper Siang(ARP)
31.	Doda(J&K)	73.	Nellore(AP)	115.	Uttar Kannada(KAR)
32.	East Kameng(ARP)	74.	Nicobar(A&N)	116.	Valsad(GUJ)
33.	East Khasi Hills(MEG)	75.	Nilgiris(TN)	117.	Wardha(MAH)

Contd....

Sr. No.	District (State)	Sr. No.	District (State)	Sr. No.	District (State)
34.	Ernakulam(KER)	76.	North 24 Parganas(WB)	118.	Wayanad(KER)
35.	Hoshiarpur(PUJ)	77.	North Cachar Hill(ASM)	119.	West Garo Hills(MEG)
36.	Hyderabad(AP)	78.	North Goa(GOA)	120.	West Godavari(AP)
37.	Idukki(KER)	79.	Palghat(KER)	121.	West Khasi Hills(MEG)
38.	Jagatsinghpur(ORI)	80.	Papumpare(ARP)	122.	West Siang(ARP)
39.	Jaintia Hill(MEG)	81.	Pathanamthitta(KER)	123.	Yanam(PON)
40.	Jajpur(ORI)	82.	Pauri Garhwal(UP)	124.	Yavatmal(MAH)
41.	Jalpaiguri(WB)	83.	Pondichery(PON)		
42.	Jammu(J&K)	84.	Poonch(J&K)		

The per cent of districts with at least one child marriage, with at least 25 per cent child marriages and at least 25 per cent marriages below legal minimum age at marriage based on actual reported ages at marriage is given in Table 6. This Table also gives the per cent of districts with child marriage and the per cent of districts with below legal minimum age at marriage, both based on median age.

Table 6
Per cent of Districts with Child and early Marriages based on Actual and Median Age at Marriage in each state/UT (Boys)

Sr. No.	State/UT	Total No. of districts	Per cent of districts with (Based on actual age at marriage)			Per cent of districts with	
			C M	At least 25% CM	At least 25% marriages below 21 years	Median age < 18 years	Median age 21 years
MAJOR STATES							
1.	Andhra Pradesh	23	56.5	0.0	65.2	0.0	0.0
2.	Assam	22	59.1	0.0	4.5	0.0	0.0
3.	Bihar	43	97.7	4.7	86.0	0.0	34.9
4.	Gujarat	19	94.7	0.0	78.9	0.0	10.5
5.	Haryana	17	100.0	0.0	64.7	0.0	0.0
6.	Karnataka	20	70.0	0.0	20.0	0.0	0.0
7.	Kerala	14	0.0	0.0	0.0	0.0	0.0
8.	Madhya Pradesh	45	93.3	15.6	84.4	0.0	46.7
9.	Maharashtra	30	66.7	0.0	16.7	0.0	0.0
10.	Orissa	30	73.3	0.0	30.0	0.0	3.3
11.	Punjab	17	82.4	0.0	41.2	0.0	0.0
12.	Rajasthan	30	100.0	16.7	100.0	0.0	70.0
13.	Tamil Nadu	23	39.1	0.0	0.0	0.0	0.0
14.	Uttar Pradesh	68	95.6	14.7	89.7	0.0	54.4
15.	West Bengal	18	88.9	0.0	33.3	0.0	0.0
SMALLER STATES/UNION TERRITORIES							
16.	Andaman & Nicobar	2	0.0	0.0	0.0	0.0	0.0
17.	Arunachal Pradesh	13	61.5	0.0	61.5	0.0	15.4
18.	Chandigarh	1	0.0	0.0	0.0	0.0	0.0

Contd...

Sr. No.	State/UT	Total No. of districts	Per cent of districts with (Based on actual age at marriage)			Per cent of districts with	
			C M	At least 25% CM	At least 25% marriages below 21 years	Median age < 18 years	Median age 21 years
19.	Dadra & Nagar Haveli	1	100.0	0.0	100.0	0.0	0.0
20.	Daman & Diu	2	100.0	0.0	0.0	0.0	0.0
21.	Delhi	1	100.0	0.0	0.0	0.0	0.0
22.	Goa	2	0.0	0.0	0.0	0.0	0.0
23.	Himachal Pradesh	12	41.7	0.0	0.0	0.0	0.0
24.	Jammu & Kashmir	14	21.4	0.0	14.3	0.0	0.0
25.	Lakshadweep	1	0.0	0.0	0.0	0.0	0.0
26.	Manipur	8	87.5	0.0	0.0	0.0	0.0
27.	Meghalaya	6	33.3	0.0	66.7	0.0	50.0
28.	Mizoram	3	100.0	0.0	33.3	0.0	0.0
29.	Nagaland	7	71.4	0.0	42.9	0.0	14.3
30.	Pondicherry	4	0.0	0.0	0.0	0.0	0.0
31.	Sikkim	4	100.0	0.0	0.0	0.0	0.0
32.	Tripura	3	100.0	0.0	66.7	0.0	0.0
	TOTAL	503	75.3	4.8	517	0.0	20.5

Of the 379 districts with at least one child marriage, 107 had only one or two stray cases of child marriages. But there are 24 districts with male child marriage forming at least 25 per cent of the total marriages. These districts are from Bihar (2), Madhya Pradesh (7), Rajasthan (5), and Uttar Pradesh (10) and their names are given below in Table 7. Seventy eight per cent of all the total child marriages are reported from Bihar (18.3%), Madhya Pradesh (17.1%), Rajasthan (16.9%) and Uttar Pradesh (25.8%). Similarly, 60 per cent of the total early marriages are also concentrated in these four states (16% in Bihar, 12 % in MP, 10% in Rajasthan and 22 % in UP).

Table 7
Districts with at least 25 per cent of Total Reported Marriages Falling in the Child Marriage category (Boys)

Sr. No.	District (State)	Sr. No.	District (State)	Sr. No.	District (State)
1.	Ambedkarnagar(UP)	9.	Gonda(UP)	17.	Nawada(BIH)
2.	Bahraich(UP)	10.	Gorakhpur(UP)	18.	Panna(MP)
3.	Basti(UP)	11.	Jhabua(MP)	19.	Rajgarh(MP)
4.	Bhadohi(UP)	12.	Jhalawar(RAJ)	20.	Rohtas(BIH)
5.	Bhilwara(RAJ)	13.	Lalitpur(UP)	21.	Sawaimadhopur(RAJ)
6.	Bundi(RAJ)	14.	Maharajganj(UP)	22.	Shajapur(MP)
7.	Chittorgarh(RAJ)	15.	Mandsaur(MP)	23.	Sidhart Nagar(UP)
8.	Faizabad(UP)	16.	Morena(MP)	24.	Sidhi(MP)

Except six districts, early marriages are found in all the districts with degrees of differences. The names of these six districts, along with the state to which they belong are given in Table 8.

Table 8
Districts with no Marriage below legal Minimum Age at Marriage of 21 years (Boys)

Sr. No.	*District (State)*	*Sr. No.*	*District (State)*
1.	Jainta Hills (Meghalaya)	4.	Nicobar (Andaman & Nicobar)
2.	Jammu (Jammu & Kashmir)	5.	Pathanamthitta (Kerala)
3.	Kannur (Kerala)	6.	Thirunelveli (Tamil Nadu)

The percentage distribution of districts with marriages below legal minimum is given in Figure M-2. Twenty two per cent of the districts had only less than 10 per cent of the total marriages below 21 years and another 17 per cent had only 10-20 per cent of the marriages in this category. At the other extreme, 2.4 per cent of the total districts (12 in number) reported more than 70 per cent of the marriages falling below legal minimum age. These districts are from three states- Madhya Pradesh (3), Rajasthan (1) and Uttar Pradesh (8) and their names are given in Table 9.

Fig. M-2: Percentage Distribution of Districts with Marriages below 21 years of Age based on Reported Marriages (Boys)

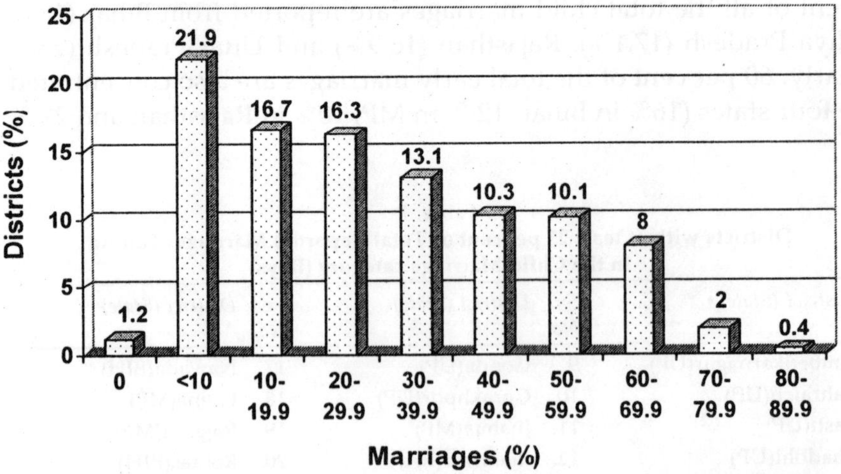

Of the total marriages, 50 per cent in Srinagar (Jammu & Kashmir) and 50.9 per cent in Karbi Anglong (Assam) are acceptable marriages which are the highest as far as this particular marriage category is concerned. In 263 districts, at least 50 per cent of their respective total marriages were preferred (155 districts with 50-74.9 per cent and the remaining 108 districts with at least 75 per cent of preferred marriages).

Table 9
Districts with at least Seventy per cent of Marriages below 21 years of age (Boys)

Sr. No.	*District (State)*	*Sr. No.*	*District (State)*	*Sr. No.*	*District (State)*
1.	Bahraich (UP)	5.	Gonda (UP)	9.	Panna (MP)
2.	Bhadohi (UP)	6.	Jhabua (MP)	10.	Pratapgarh (UP)
3.	Bundi (RAJ)	7.	Lalitpur (UP)	11.	Sidhart Nagar (UP)
4.	Deoria (UP)	8.	Maharajganj (UP)	12.	Tikamgarh (MP)

No district has fifty per cent or more of marriages in the preferred category in Rajasthan and Dadra and Nagar Haveli while all the districts in Kerala, Tamil Nadu, Andaman and Nicobar, Chandigarh, Daman and Diu, Delhi, Goa, Himachal Pradesh, Lakshadweep, Manipur, Mizoram, Pondicherry and Tripura have at least 50 per cent of marriages conducted after the boy attained 23 years of age.

In 243 districts at least 75 per cent of marriages were conducted only after the boy attained 21 years of age. Further, in 235 of these districts at least 50 per cent of marriages were effected only after the boy completed 23 years of age. The names of these 235 districts are given in Table 10.

Table 10
Districts with at least 75 per cent of Marriages after Completion of 21 years and at least 50 per cent of Marriages after Completion of age 23 years (Boys)

Sr. No.	*District (State)*	*Sr. No.*	*District (State)*	*Sr. No.*	*District (State)*
1.	Ahmadnagar(MAH)	79.	Idukki(KER)	157.	Pathanamthitta(KER)
2.	Aizwal(MIZ)	80.	Imphal(MAN)	158.	Patiala(PUJ)
3.	Akola(MAH)	81.	Jabalpur(MP)	159.	Pauri Garhwal(UP)
4.	Alappuzha(KER)	82.	Jagatsinghpur(ORI)	160.	Periyar(TN)
5.	Almora(UP)	83.	Jaintia Hill(MEG)	161.	Pondichery(PON)
6.	Ambala(HAR)	84.	Jajpur(ORI)	162.	Pudukottai(TN)
7.	Amravali(MAH)	85.	Jalandhar(PUJ)	163.	Pulawama(J&K)
8.	Amritsar(PUJ)	86.	Jalgaon(MAH)	164.	Punch(J&K)
9.	Ananthapur(AP)	87.	Jammu(J&K)	165.	Pune(MAH)
10.	Anantnag(J&K)	88.	Jharsuguda(ORI)	166.	Purbi Singhbhum(BIH)
11.	Andaman(A&N)	89.	Jorhat(ASM)	167.	Puri(ORI)
12.	Anghul(ORI)	90.	Junagadh(GUJ)	168.	Raigarh(MAH)
13.	Balaghat(MP)	91.	Kamrup(ASM)	169.	Raigarh(MP)
14.	Balasore(ORI)	92.	Kangra(HP)	170.	Rajauri(J&K)
15.	Bangalore (KAR)	93.	Kanniyakumari(TN)	171.	Rajkot(GUJ)
16.	Bangalore Rural(KAR)	94.	Kannur(KER)	172.	Ramanathapuram(TN)
17.	Bankura(WB)	95.	Kapurthala(PUJ)	173.	Ranchi(BIH)

Contd....

Sr. No.	District (State)	Sr. No.	District (State)	Sr. No.	District (State)
18.	Baramulla(J&K)	96.	Karaikal(PON)	174.	Rangareddy(AP)
19.	Bargarh(ORI)	97.	Kargil (J&K)	175.	Ratnagari(MAH)
20.	Barpeta(ASM)	98.	Karimganj(ASM)	176.	Rohtak(HAR)
21.	Belgaum(KAR)	99.	Kasaragod(KER)	177.	Rupnagar(PUJ)
22.	Bellary(KAR)	100.	Kathua(J&K)	178.	Salem(TN)
23.	Betul(MP)	101.	Kendrapara(ORI)	179.	Sambalpur(ORI)
24.	Bhadrak(ORI)	102.	Kendujhar(ORI)	180.	Sangli(MAH)
25.	Bhandara(MAH)	103.	Khordha(ORI)	181.	Satara(MAH)
26.	Bhopal(MP)	104.	Kinnaur(HP)	182.	Senapati(MAN)
27.	Bilaspur(HP)	105.	Kishanganj(BIH)	183.	Shimla(HP)
28.	Bishnupur(MAN)	106.	Koch Bihar(WB)	184.	Shimoga(KAR)
29.	Bongaigaon(ASM)	107.	Kodagu(KAR)	185.	Shivganganagar(TN)
30.	Buldana(MAH)	108.	Kolar(KAR)	186.	Sibsagar(ASM)
31.	Cachar(ASM)	109.	Kolhapur(MAH)	187.	Sindhudurg(MAH)
32.	Chamba(HP)	110.	Kolkata(WB)	188.	Sirmaur(HP)
33.	Chamoli(UP)	111.	Kollam(KER)	189.	Solan(HP)
34.	Chandel(MAN)	112.	Kottayam(KER)	190.	Solapur(MAH)
35.	Chandigarh(CHN)	113.	Kozhikode(KER)	191.	Sonepur(ORI)
36.	Chandrapur(MAH)	114.	Kullu(HP)	192.	Sonitpur(ASM)
37.	Chengalpattu(TN)	115.	Kupuwada(J&K)	193.	South 24 Parganas(WB)
38.	Chennai(TN)	116.	Kurnool(AP)	194.	South Arcot(TN)
39.	Chhindwara(MP)	117.	Lahul & Spiti(HP)	195.	South Goa(GOA)
40.	Chikmaglur(KAR)	118.	Lakhimpur(ASM)	196.	South Tripura(TRI)
41.	Chitradurga(KAR)	119.	Lakshadweep	197.	Srikakulam(AP)
42.	Chittor(AP)	120.	Latur(MAH)	198.	Sundergarh(ORI)
43.	Churachandpur(MAN)	121.	Leh(J&K)	199.	Surat(GUJ)
44.	Coimbatore(TN)	122.	Lohardaga(BIH)	200.	Tamenglong(MAN)
45.	Cuttak(ORI)	123.	Ludhiana(PUJ)	201.	Tawang(ARP)
46.	Dakshina Kannada(KAR)	124.	Lungeli(MIZ)	202.	Thane(MAH)
47.	Daman	125.	Madurai(TN)	203.	Thanjavur(TN)
48.	Darjeeling(WB)	126.	Mahe(PON)	204.	The Nilgiris(TN)
49.	Darrang(ASM)	127.	Malappuram(KER)	205.	Theni(TN)
50.	Debagarh(ORI)	128.	Maldah (WB)	206.	Thiruchirapalli(TN)
51.	Dehradun(UP)	129.	Mandi(HP)	207.	Thirunelveli(TN)
52.	Delhi	130.	Mandya(KAR)	208.	Thiruvanathapuram(KE)
53.	Dharmapuri(TN)	131.	Marigaon(ASM)	209.	Thoubal(MAN)
54.	Dharwad(KAR)	132.	Mayurbhanj(ORI)	210.	Thrissur(KER)
55.	Dhemaji(ASM)	133.	Medinipur(WB)	211.	Tinsukia(ASM)
56.	Dhenkanal(ORI)	134.	Mokokchung(NAG)	212.	Tirap (ARP)
57.	Dhubri(ASM)	135.	Mon(NAG)	213.	Tiruvannamalai(TN)
58.	Dhule(MAH)	136.	Mysore(KAR)	214.	Tuensang(NAG)
59.	Dindigul(TN)	137.	Nadia((WB)	215.	Tumkur(KAR)
60.	Diu	138.	Nagaon(ASM)	216.	Tutikorin(TN)
61.	Doda(J&K)	139.	Nagpur(MAH)	217.	Udhampur(J&K)
62.	East Sikkim(SIK)	140.	Nainital(UP)	218.	Ukhrul(MAN)
63.	Ernakulam(KER)	141.	Nalbari(ASM)	219.	Una(HP)
64.	Gadchiroli(MAH)	142.	Namakkal(TN)	220.	Upper Siang(ARP)
65.	Gajapati(ORI)	143.	Nashik(MAH)	221.	Upper Subansiri(ARP)
66.	Ganjam(ORI)	144.	Nawanshahar(PUJ)	222.	Uttar Dinajpur(WB)

Contd...

Sr. No.	*District (State)*	*Sr. No.*	*District (State)*	*Sr. No.*	*District (State)*
67.	Goalpara(ASM)	145.	Nayagarh(ORI)	223.	Uttar Kannada(KAR)
68.	Golaghat(ASM)	146.	Nellore(AP)	224.	Valsad(GUJ)
69.	Greater Bombay(MAH)	147.	Nicobar(A&N)	225.	Virudunagar(TN)
70.	Gulma(BIH)	148.	North 24 Parganas(WB)	226.	Wardha(MAH)
71.	Gurdaspur(PUJ)	149.	North Arcot(TN)	227.	Wayanad(KER)
72.	Hailakandi(ASM)	150.	North Cachar Hill(AS)	228.	West Godavari(AP)
73.	Hamirpur(HP)	151.	North Goa(GOA)	229.	West Siang(ARP)
74.	Haora(WB)	152.	North Tripura(TRI)	230.	West Sikkim(SIK)
75.	Hassan(KAR)	153.	Osmanabad(MAH)	231.	West Tripura(TRI)
76.	Hoshiarpur(PUJ)	154.	Palghat(KER)	232.	Wokha(NAG)
77.	Hugli(WB)	155.	Panchkula(HAR)	233.	Yamunanagar(HAR)
78.	Hyderabad(AP)	156.	Pashchmi Singhbhum(B)	234.	Yanam(PON)
				235.	Yavatmal(MAH)

Median Age at Marriage

On the whole there are 103 districts with a median age below legal minimum age at marriage and their names are given in Table 11. All these marriages were conducted after the boy attained 18 years of age but before completing 21 years of age.

Table 11
Districts with Median Age at Marriage below 21 years of age (Boys)

Sr. No.	*District (State)*	*Sr. No.*	*District (State)*	*Sr. No.*	*District (State)*
1.	Allahabad(UP)	36.	Ganganagar(RAJ)	71.	Nawada(BIH)
2.	Alwar(RAJ)	37.	Gaya(BIH)	72.	Palamu(BIH)
3.	Ambedkarnagar(UP)	38.	Ghazipur(UP)	73.	Panna(MP)
4.	Aurangabad(BIH)	39.	Giridih(BIH)	74.	Patna(BIH)
5.	Azamgarh(UP)	40.	Gonda(UP)	75.	Pilibhit(UP)
6.	Bahraich(UP)	41.	Gopalganj(BIH)	76.	Pratapgarh(UP)
7.	Banas Kantha(GUJ)	42.	Gorakhpur(UP)	77.	Raibareilly(UP)
8.	Banda(UP)	43.	Guna(MP)	78.	Rajgarh(MP)
9.	Banswara(RAJ)	44.	Hamirpur(UP)	79.	Rajsamand(RAJ)
10.	Barabanki(UP)	45.	Hanumangarh(RAJ)	80.	Rewa(MP)
11.	Barmer(RAJ)	46.	Hardoi(UP)	81.	Ri Bhoi (MEG)
12.	Basti(UP)	47.	Jalaun(UP)	82.	Rohtas(BIH)
13.	Bhadohi(UP)	48.	Jalore(RAJ)	83.	Sahibganj(BIH)
14.	Bharatpur(RAJ)	49.	Jaunpur(UP)	84.	Satna(MP)
15.	Bhilwara(RAJ)	50.	Jehanabad(BIH)	85.	Sawaimadhopur(RAJ)
16.	Bhind(MP)	51.	Jhabua(MP)	86.	Shahdol(MP)
17.	Bhojpur(BIH)	52.	Jhalawar(RAJ)	87.	Shajahanabad(UP)
18.	Bikaner(RAJ)	53.	Jhansi(UP)	88.	Shajapur(MP)
19.	Budaun(UP)	54.	Kheri(UP)	89.	Shivpuri(MP)
20.	Bundi(RAJ)	55.	Kohima(NAG)	90.	Sidhart Nagar(UP)
21.	Chattarpur(MP)	56.	Kota(RAJ)	91.	Sidhi(MP)
22.	Chittorgarh(RAJ)	57.	Lalitpur(UP)	92.	Sitapur(UP)

Contd....

Sr. No.	*District (State)*	*Sr. No.*	*District (State)*	*Sr. No.*	*District (State)*
23.	Churu(RAJ)	58.	Madhepura(BIH)	93.	Sonbhadra(UP)
24.	Damoh(MP)	59.	Madhubani(BIH)	94.	Sultanpur(UP)
25.	Datia(MP)	60.	Maharajganj(UP)	95.	Surguja(MP)
26.	Dausa(RAJ)	61.	Mahoba(UP)	96.	The Dangs(GUJ)
27.	Deoria(UP)	62.	Mainpuri(UP)	97.	Tikamgarh(MP)
28.	Dewas(MP)	63.	Malkangiri(ORI)	98.	Tonk(RAJ)
29.	Dhar(MP)	64.	Mandsaur(MP)	99.	Udaipur(RAJ)
30.	Dholpur(RAJ)	65.	Mau(UP)	100.	Unnao(UP)
31.	East Kameng(ARP)	66.	Mirzapur(UP)	101.	Varanasi(UP)
32.	East Khasi Hills(MEG)	67.	Morena(MP)	102.	Vidisha(MP)
33.	East Siang(ARP)	68.	Munger(BIH)	103.	West Khasi Hills(MEG)
34.	Faizabad(UP)	69.	Nagaur(RAJ)		
35.	Firozabad(UP)	70.	Nalanda(BIH)		

Based on median age, there is no male child marriage in any of the districts in the country. In Kerala, Tamil Nadu, Andaman & Nicobar, Chandigarh, Daman & Diu, Delhi, Goa, Himachal Pradesh, Lakshadweep, Manipur, Mizoram, Pondicherry and Tripura the median age at marriage in all districts fall in the preferred category, while in Dadra and Nagar Haveli and in Rajasthan there is no district with a median age at marriage that fall into the preferred category. Of the 84 districts belonging to the small states and Union territories, 93 per cent has median age at marriage of at least 21 years. The per centage distribution of the 103 districts with a median below 21 years is given in Figure M-3 below.

Fig. M-3: Percentage Distribution of the Districts with Median Age at Marriage below 21 years of Age (Boys)

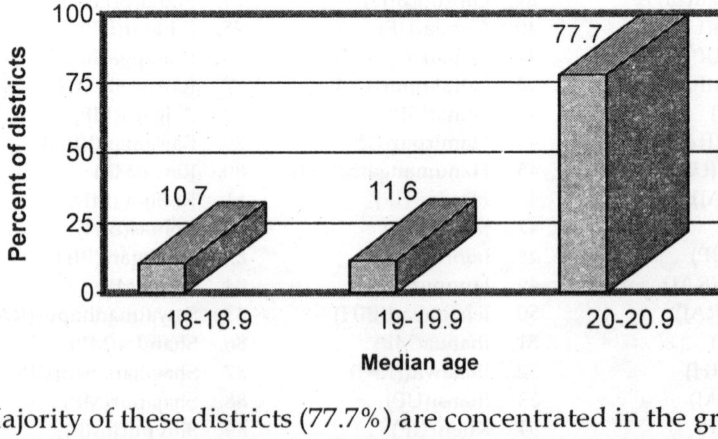

Majority of these districts (77.7%) are concentrated in the group where the median age at marriage is 20 years–just one year less than the legal minimum age at marriage. Of the total 103 districts with early marriages, 91.3 per cent are concentrated in Bihar (14.6%), Madhya Pradesh (20.4%), Rajasthan (20.4%) and Uttar Pradesh (35.9%) as can be seen from Figure

M-4. The remaining nine per cent are from Orissa and Nagaland (1% each), Gujarat and Arunachal Pradesh (1.9% each) and Meghalaya (2.9%) and they together constituted the "other" category in Figure M-4.

Fig. M-4: Percentage Distribution of Districts with Age at Marriage below 21 years in Selected States (Boys)

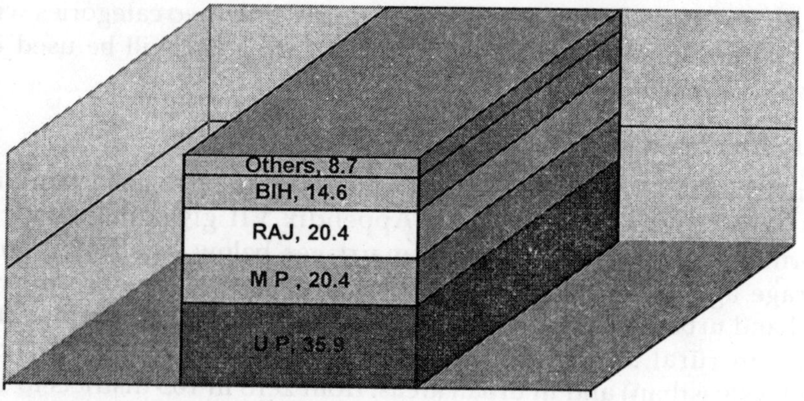

The per cent of districts in each state/union territory having a median age at marriage of at least 23 years for the boys (preferred marriage) is given in Figure M-5.

Fig. M-5: Per cent of Districts in each State/UT with a Median Age at Marriage of at least 23 years (Boys)

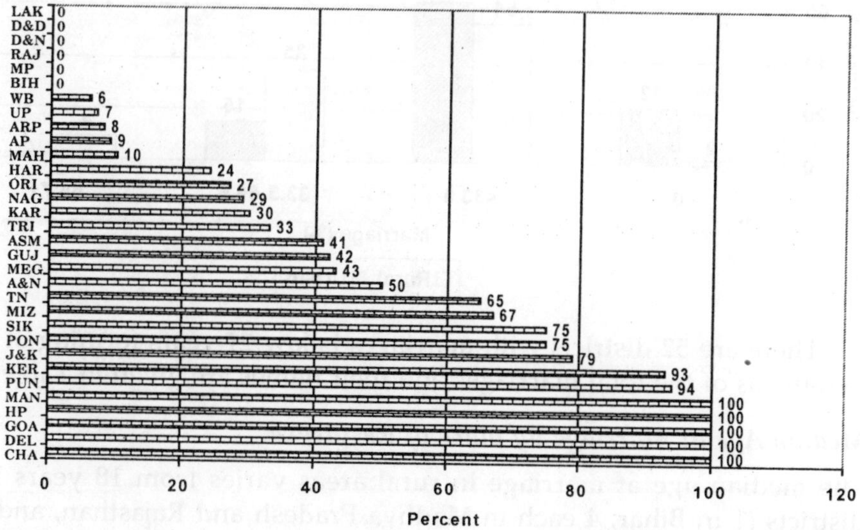

As pointed out earlier, in Kerala, Tamil Nadu, Andaman and Nicobar, Chandigarh, Daman & Diu, Delhi, Goa, Himachal Pradesh, Lakshadweep,

Manipur, Mizoram, Pondicherry and Tripura boys marrying after they attain at least 23 years of age have already became the norm as per median age at marriage. In Karnataka and Assam except in one district each late marriage has become the norm.

Age at Marriage by Characteristics

As in the case of age at marriage for girls, only two categories with the legal minimum age at marriage as the cut off point will be used in this part of the report also.

(a) Place of residence

No marriage of boys was reported from the rural areas of seven districts and urban areas of 21 districts. Appendix VII gives the district-wise information on per cent share of marriages below legal minimum age, average age at marriage and marriages reported from each district for rural and urban areas. The per cent share of the marriages below 21 years varies in rural areas from zero in eight districts to 84.3 per cent in Bundi (Rajasthan) and in urban areas, from zero in 105 districts to 100 per cent in Andaman of Andaman & Nicobar and West Ghasi Hills of Meghalaya and Nawada of Bihar[1]. The summary picture is provided in the Figure M-6.

Fig. M-6: Percentage Distribution of Districts by per cent Share of Marriages below 21 years of Age in Rural and Urban areas (Boys)

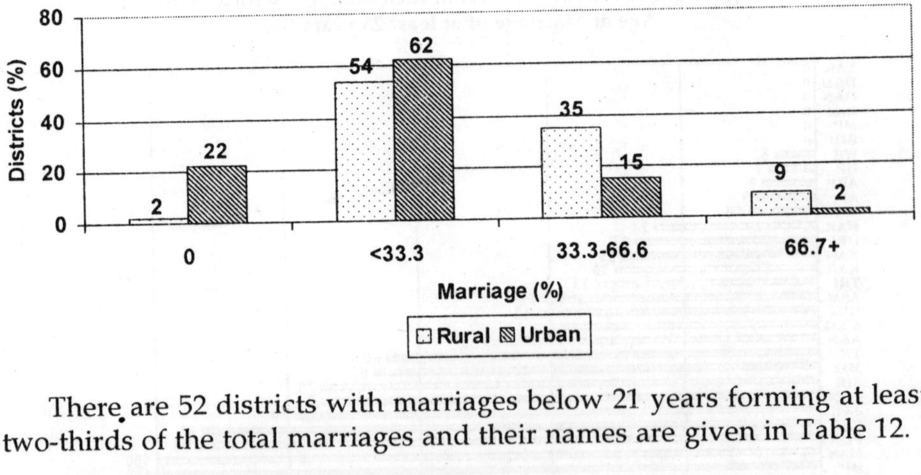

There are 52 districts with marriages below 21 years forming at least two-thirds of the total marriages and their names are given in Table 12.

Median Age at Marriage by place of Residence

The median age at marriage in rural areas varies from 18 years in 15 districts (1 in Bihar, 4 each in Madhya Pradesh and Rajasthan, and 6 in Uttar Pradesh) to 30 years in three districts (Cachar and Nalbari in Assam and North Goa). The corresponding variation observed in urban areas is from 18 years in Deoria[2] (Uttar Pradesh) to 34.5 years in Cachar (Assam).

Below legal minimum age at marriage is found in the rural areas of 130 districts and the urban areas of 18 districts.

Table 12
Districts with Marriages below 21 years of Age Forming at least two-thirds of the Total Marriages in Rural and Urban areas (Boys)

Sr. No.	Districts (State)	Sr. No.	Districts (State)	Sr. No.	Districts (State)
	RURAL		**RURAL**		**RURAL**
1.	Amreli(GUJ)	19.	Kheri(UP)	37.	Saharanpur(UP)
2.	Belgaum(KAR)	20.	Kolhapur(MAH)	38.	Sambalpur(ORI)
3.	Bulandshahr(UP)	21.	Kooch Bihar(WB)	39.	South 24 Parganas(WB)
4.	Buldana(MAH)	22.	Lower Subansiri(ARP)	40.	South Sikkim(SIK)
5.	Chhimtuipui(MIZ)	23.	Mandla(MP)	41.	Thane(MAH)
6.	Coimbatore(TN)	24.	Medinipur(WB)	42.	Tiruvannamalai(TN)
7.	Delhi	25.	Mon(NAG)	43.	Upper Subansiri(ARP)
8.	Dumka(BIH)	26.	Muradabad(UP)	44.	West Kameng(ARP)
9.	Gajapati(ORI)	27.	Muzaffarnagar(UP)		
10.	Golaghat(ASM)	28.	Nawapada(ORI)		**URBAN**
11.	Gulbarga(KAR)	29.	Nayagarh(ORI)	1.	Azamgarh(UP)
12.	Hamirpur(UP)	30.	Nizamabad(AP)	2.	Banda(UP)
13.	Hathras(UP)	31.	Panchmahal(GUJ)	3.	Deoria(UP)
14.	Jaisalmer(RAJ)	32.	Pithogarh(UP)	4.	East Garo Hill(MEG)
15.	Jamnagar(GUJ)	33.	Pulawama(J&K)	5.	Kohima(NAG)
16.	Junagadh(GUJ)	34.	Purnia(BIH)	6.	Maharajganj(UP)
17.	Kanpur Nagar(UP)	35.	Raisen(MP)	7.	Nawada(BIH)
18.	Karnal(HAR)	36.	Sagar(MP)	8.	West Khasi Hills(MEG)

The median age at marriage for all the marriages reported in rural areas works out to be 22 years as against the 25 years in urban marriages. The percentage distribution of districts by marriage category in rural and urban areas based on median age is given in Figure M-7. It is clear from the figure that districts with early marriages are high in rural and preferred marriages are high in urban areas, as one would expect.

Fig. M-7: Percentage Distribution of Districts by Marriage Category based on Median Age in Rural and Urban areas (Boys)

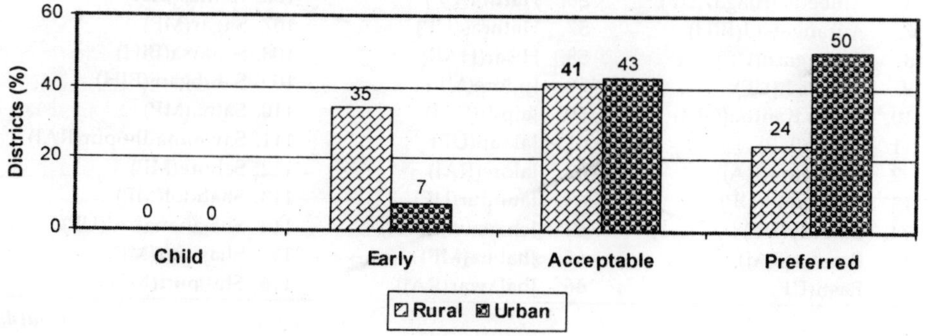

The per cent of districts in selected states with median age at marriage below legal minimum is given in Figure M-8 by place of residence.

Fig. M-8: Per cent Share of Selected States of Districts with Median Age at Marriage below 21 years by place of Residence (Boys)

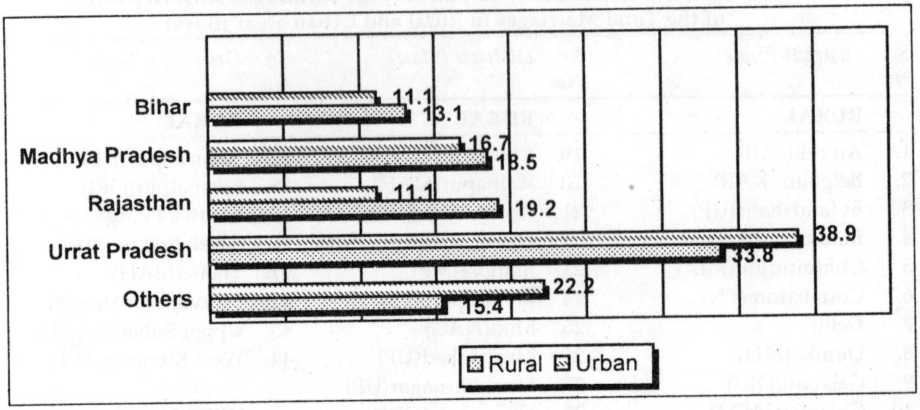

The four states, Bihar, Madhya Pradesh, Rajasthan and Uttar Pradesh, together accounts for eighty five per cent of the total number of districts with rural boys marrying below legal minimum age and the corresponding per cent of districts for urban areas is 78. The names of districts with below legal minimum median age at marriage for rural and urban areas are given below in Table 13.

Table 13

Districts with Median Age at Marriage below 21 years by place of Residence (Boys)

Sr. No.	*Districts (State)*	*Sr. No.*	*Districts (State)*	*Sr. No.*	*Districts (State)*
	RURAL AREAS		**RURAL AREAS**		**RURAL AREAS**
1.	Agra(UP)	51.	Gorakhpur(UP)	101.	Rajgarh(MP)
2.	Ahmadabad(GUJ)	52.	Guna(MP)	102.	Rajsamand(RAJ)
3.	Ajmer(RAJ)	53.	Gurgaon(HAR)	103.	Ratlam(MP)
4.	Allahabad(UP)	54.	Hamirpur(UP)	104.	Rewa(MP)
5.	Alwar(RAJ)	55.	Hanumangarh(RAJ)	105.	Ri Bhoi (MEG)
6.	Ambedkarnagar(UP)	56.	Hardoi(UP)	106.	Rohtas(BIH)
7.	Aurangabad(BIH)	57.	Hathras(UP)	107.	Sagar(MP)
8.	Azamgarh(UP)	58.	Hisar(HAR)	108.	Saharsa(BIH)
9.	Bahraich(UP)	59.	Indore(MP)	109.	Sahibganj(BIH)
10.	Banas Kantha(GUJ)	60.	Jaipur(RAJ)	110.	Satna(MP)
11.	Banda(UP)	61.	Jalaun(UP)	111.	Sawaimadhopur(RAJ)
12.	Banswara(RAJ)	62.	Jalore(RAJ)	112.	Sehore(MP)
13.	Barabanki(UP)	63.	Jaunpur(UP)	113.	Shahdol(MP)
14.	Bareilly(UP)	64.	Jehanabad(BIH)	114.	Shajahanabad(UP)
15.	Barmer(RAJ)	65.	Jhabua(MP)	115.	Shajapur(MP)
16.	Basti(UP)	66.	Jhalawar(RAJ)	116.	Shivpuri(MP)

Contd....

Sr. No.	Districts (State)	Sr. No.	Districts (State)	Sr. No.	Districts (State)
17.	Bhadohi(UP)	67.	Jhansi(UP)	117.	Sidhart Nagar(UP)
18.	Bharatpur(RAJ)	68.	Jodhpur(RAJ)	118.	Sidhi(MP)
19.	Bhilwara(RAJ)	69.	Kanpur Nagar(UP)	119.	Sitapur(UP)
20.	Bhind(MP)	70.	Kheri(UP)	120.	Sonbhadra(UP)
21.	Bhojpur(BIH)	71.	Kohima(NAG)	121.	Sultanpur(UP)
22.	Bhopal(MP)	72.	Koraput(ORI)	122.	Surguja(MP)
23.	Bikaner(RAJ)	73.	Kota(RAJ)	123.	The Dangs(GUJ)
24.	Budaun(UP)	74.	Krishna(AP)	124.	Tikamgarh(MP)
25.	Bundi(RAJ)	75.	Lalitpur(UP)	125.	Tonk(RAJ)
26.	Buxar(BIH)	76.	Lucknow(UP)	126.	Udaipur(RAJ)
27.	Chattarpur(MP)	77.	Madhepura(BIH)	127.	Unnao(UP)
28.	Chittorgarh(RAJ)	78.	Madhubani(BIH)	128.	Vadodara(GUJ)
29.	Churu(RAJ)	79.	Maharajganj(UP)	129.	Varanasi(UP)
30.	Dadra	80.	Mahoba(UP)	130.	Vidisha(MP)
31.	Damoh(MP)	81.	Mainpuri(UP)		
32.	Datia(MP)	82.	Malkangiri(ORI)		**URBAN AREAS**
33.	Dausa(RAJ)	83.	Mandsaur(MP)	1.	Azamgarh(UP)
34.	Deoghar(BIH)	84.	Mathura(UP)	2.	Banda(UP)
35.	Deoria(UP)	85.	Mau(UP)	3.	Bhadohi(UP)
36.	Dewas(MP)	86.	Mirzapur(UP)	4.	Bhojpur(BIH)
37.	Dhar(MP)	87.	Morena(MP)	5.	Deoria(UP)
38.	Dholpur(RAJ)	88.	Munger(BIH)	6.	Dholpur(RAJ)
39.	Dungarpur(RAJ)	89.	Muradabad(UP)	7.	East Garo Hill(MEG)
40.	East Kameng(ARP)	90.	Nagaur(RAJ)	8.	Kohima(NAG)
41.	East Khasi Hills(MEG)	91.	Nalanda(BIH)	9.	Lalitpur(UP)
42.	East Siang(ARP)	92.	Nawada(BIH)	10.	Maharajganj(UP)
43.	Faizabad(UP)	93.	Palamu(BIH)	11.	Mainpuri(UP)
44.	Firozabad(UP)	94.	Pali(RAJ)	12.	Morena(MP)
45.	Ganganagar(RAJ)	95.	Panchmahal(GUJ)	13.	Murshidabad(WB)
46.	Gaya(BIH)	96.	Panna(MP)	14.	Nawada(BIH)
47.	Ghazipur(UP)	97.	Patna(BIH)	15.	Raipur(MP)
48.	Giridih(BIH)	98.	Pilibhit(UP)	16.	Tikamgarh(MP)
49.	Gonda(UP)	99.	Pratapgarh(UP)	17.	Tonk(RAJ)
50.	Gopalganj(BIH)	100.	Raibareilly(UP)	18.	West Khasi Hills(MEG)

(b) Caste

When marriages are distributed by age at marriage in each caste group in each district, it is found that the percentage share of below legal marriages is high among the SC/ST/OBC group than the other group. Appendix VIII gives the district-wise picture. In 20 districts no marriage was reported among the castes other than SC/ST/OBC.

Of the total marriages, 51 per cent and 61 per cent are child marriages in Maharajganj and Sidhartnagar districts (both in Uttar Pradesh) respectively. Among SC/ST/OBC group, more than 25 per cent of total marriages are child marriages in 39 districts which belonged to Bihar (5), Gujarat (1), Madhya Pradesh (10), Rajasthan (9) and Uttar Pradesh (14). On the contrary among the "other caste" group there are just two districts with child marriage forming more than 25 per cent of their respective total marriages. These districts are Bundi (Rajasthan) with 26.5 per cent and Gondi (Uttar Pradesh) with 25.6 per cent.

The marriages below legal minimum age at marriage varied from none in 16 districts to 93.5 per cent in Mahesana (Gujarat) among SC/ST/OBC group and from none in 80 districts to 66 per cent in Gonda (Uttar Pradesh)[3]. The summary situation is shown in Figure M-9.

In eleven per cent of the districts, the per cent share of marriage below

Fig. M-9: Percentage Distribution of Districts by per cent Share of Marriages below 21 years of Age in each Caste Group (Boys)

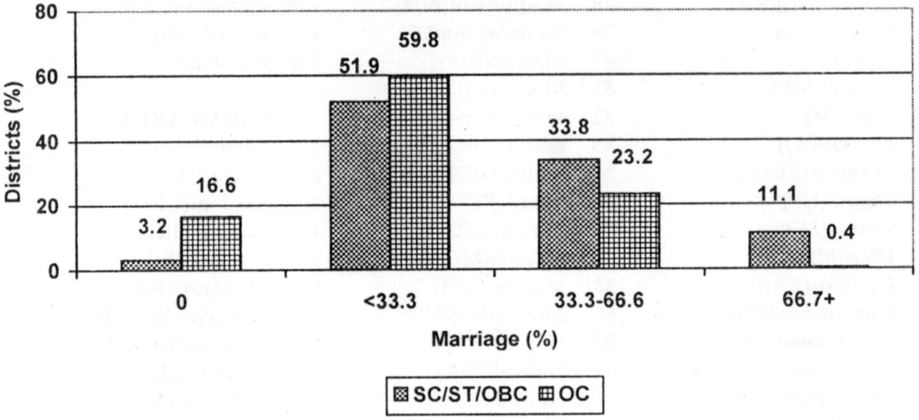

21 years among the SC/ST/OBC was at least two-thirds compared to a mere 0.4 per cent among the "other caste" group. The names of these districts are given below in Table 14.

Table 14
Districts with Marriages below 21 years of Age Forming at least two-thirds of the Total Marriages in each Caste Group (Boys)

Sr. No.	*District (State)*	*Sr. No.*	*District (State)*	*Sr. No.*	*District (State)*
	SC/ST/OBC		SC/ST/OBC		SC/ST/OBC
1.	Aligarh(UP)	21.	Jhansi(UP)	41.	Sawaimadhopur(RAJ)
2.	Ambedkarnagar(UP)	22.	Kangra(HP)	42.	Shajapur(MP)
3.	Amreli(GUJ)	23.	Kasaragod(KER)	43.	Shimoga(KAR)
4.	Amritsar(PUJ)	24.	Kathua(J&K)	44.	Shivganganagar(TN)
5.	Azamgarh(UP)	25.	Kollam(KER)	45.	Sidhart Nagar(UP)
6.	Bathinda(PUJ)	26.	Maharajganj(UP)	46.	Sikar(RAJ)
7.	Beed(MAH)	27.	Mahe(PON)	47.	Sindhudurg(MAH)
8.	Chittor(AP)	28.	Mahesana(GUJ)	48.	Theni(TN)
9.	Dakshina Kannada(KAR)	29.	Mandi(HP)	49.	Thrissur(KER)

Contd....

Sr. No.	District (State)	Sr. No.	District (State)	Sr. No.	District (State)
10.	Daman	30.	Morena(MP)	50.	Tuensang(NAG)
11.	Damoh(MP)	31.	Mysore(KAR)	51.	Udhamsingh Nagar (UP)
12.	Dausa(RAJ)	32.	Nalanda(BIH)	52.	Ujjain(MP)
13.	Deoghar(BIH)	33.	Nawapada(ORI)	53.	Una(HP)
14.	Dhenkanal(ORI)	34.	Nicobar(A&N)	54.	Uttar Dinajpur(WB)
15.	Dungarpur(RAJ)	35.	North 24 Parganas(WB)	55.	Vidisha(MP)
16.	East Khasi Hills(MEG)	36.	Palghat(KER)	56.	West Sikkim(SIK)
17.	Giridih(BIH)	37.	Purba Champaran(BIH)		
18.	Hisar(HAR)	38.	Sabar Kantha(GUJ)		OTHER CASTES
19.	Idukki(KER)	39.	Sagar(MP)	1.	Mandla(MP)*
20.	Jhalawar(RAJ)	40.	Sambalpur(ORI)	2.	Ukhrul(MAN)*

* Just one marriage each.

Median age at Marriage by Caste

On the whole the median age at marriage for SC/ST/OBC was less by one year (18 years) compared to the other castes (19 years).

The median age at marriage among the SC/ST/OBC ranged from 16 years in Sidhartnagar (Uttar Pradesh) to 31 years in Karimganj (Assam). Similar variation observed in the other caste group is from 18 years in Ukhrul (Manipur) to 32 years in Madurai (Tamil Nadu). Also in 21 districts, no marriage was reported from among the "other caste" group.

Figure M-10 gives the percentage distribution of districts by marriage category in each caste group which shows that the per cent of districts with child marriages are very negligible in the case of SC/ST/OBC group and is absolutely none in the case of the other caste group. For other caste group, the share of districts with early marriages is negligible and that of preferred marriages form two-thirds of the total districts.

Fig. M-10: Percentage Distribution of Districts by Marriage Category based on Median in each Caste Group (Boys)

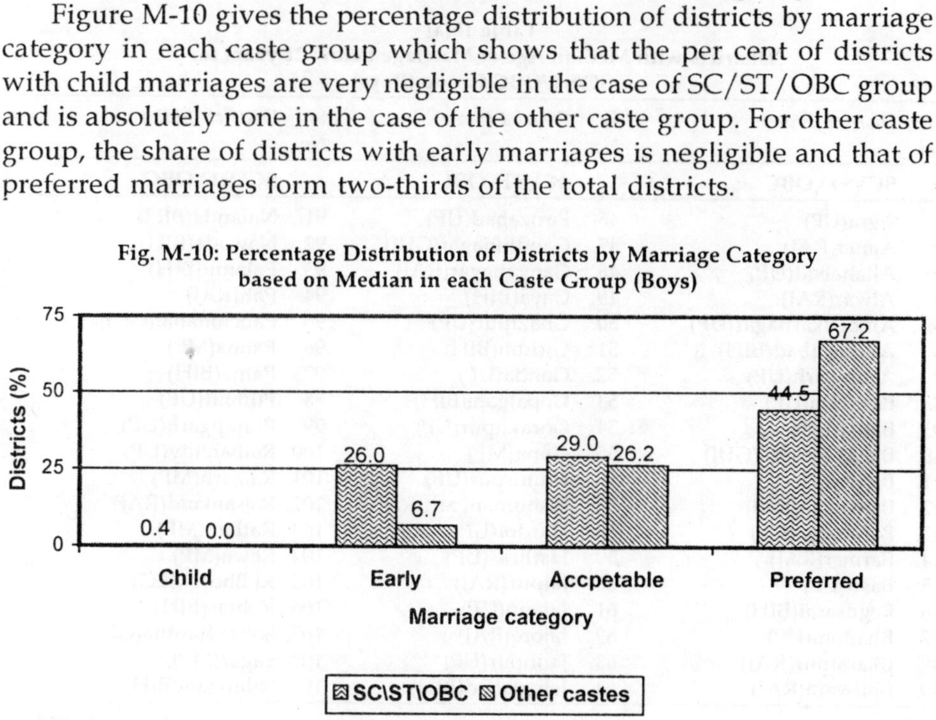

The per cent share of the selected states of the districts with median age at marriage below 21 years is given below in Figure M-11. Eighty eight per cent of districts with median age at marriage below legal minimum age are located in Bihar, Madhya Pradesh, Rajasthan and Uttar Pradesh for the SC\ST\OBC group. Similarly, for the "other caste" group, 91 per cent of the districts are located in the above mentioned states.

Fig. M-11: Per cent Share of Selected States of Districts with Median Age at Marriage below 21 years of Age by Caste (Boys)

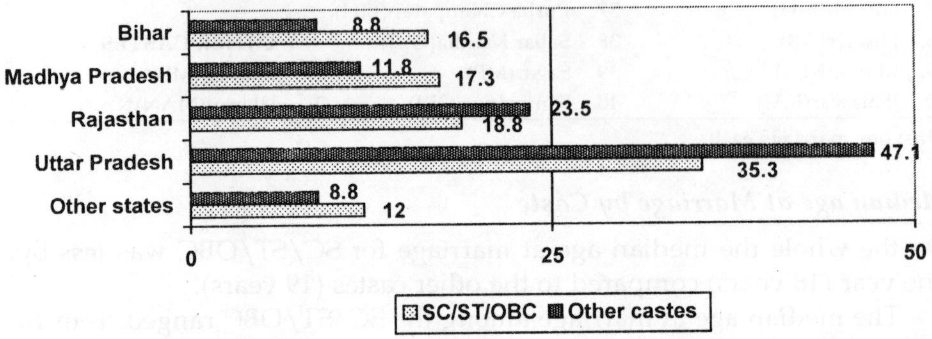

The names of districts with below legal minimum median age at marriage for the two caste groups are given below in Table 15 (a) and 15 (b).

Table 15(a)
Districts with Median Age at Marriage below 21 years for SC/ST/OBC Group (Boys)

Sr. No.	*District (State)*	*Sr. No.*	*District (State)*	*Sr. No.*	*District (State)*
	SC\ST\OBC		**SC\ST\OBC**		**SC\ST\OBC**
1.	Agra(UP)	46.	Firozabad(UP)	91.	Nalanda(BIH)
2.	Ajmer(RAJ)	47.	Gandhinagar(GUJ)	92.	Nawada(BIH)
3.	Allahabad(UP)	48.	Ganganagar(RAJ)	93.	Palamu(BIH)
4.	Alwar(RAJ)	49.	Gaya(BIH)	94.	Pali(RAJ)
5.	Ambedkarnagar(UP)	50.	Ghazipur(UP)	95.	Panchmahal(GUJ)
6.	Aurangabad(BIH)	51.	Giridih(BIH)	96.	Panna(MP)
7.	Azamgarh(UP)	52.	Gonda(UP)	97.	Patna(BIH)
8.	Bahraich(UP)	53.	Gopalganj(BIH)	98.	Pilibhit(UP)
9.	Ballia(UP)	54.	Gorakhpur(UP)	99.	Pratapgarh(UP)
10.	Banas Kantha(GUJ)	55.	Guna(MP)	100.	Raibareilly(UP)
11.	Banda(UP)	56.	Hamirpur(UP)	101.	Rajgarh(MP)
12.	Banswara(RAJ)	57.	Hanumangarh(RAJ)	102.	Rajsamand(RAJ)
13.	Barabanki(UP)	58.	Hardoi(UP)	103.	Ratlam(MP)
14.	Barmer(RAJ)	59.	Hathras(UP)	104.	Rewa(MP)
15.	Basti(UP)	60.	Jaipur(RAJ)	105.	Ri Bhoi (MEG)
16.	Begusarai(BIH)	61.	Jalaun(UP)	106.	Rohtas(BIH)
17.	Bhadohi(UP)	62.	Jalore(RAJ)	107.	Sabar Kantha(GUJ)
18.	Bharatpur(RAJ)	63.	Jaunpur(UP)	108.	Sagar(MP)
19.	Bhilwara(RAJ)	64.	Jehanabad(BIH)	109.	Sahibganj(BIH)

Contd....

Sr. No.	*District (State)*	*Sr. No.*	*District (State)*	*Sr. No.*	*District (State)*
20.	Bhind(MP)	65.	Jhabua(MP)	110.	Samastipur(BIH)
21.	Bhojpur(BIH)	66.	Jhalawar(RAJ)	111.	Satna(MP)
22.	Budaun(UP)	67.	Jhansi(UP)	112.	Sawaimadhopur(RAJ)
23.	Bulandshahr(UP)	68.	Jodhpur(RAJ)	113.	Shahdol(MP)
24.	Bundi(RAJ)	69.	Kanpur Dehat(UP)	114.	Shajahanabad(UP)
25.	Buxar(BIH)	70.	Kheri(UP)	115.	Shajapur(MP)
26.	Chattarpur(MP)	71.	Kohima(NAG)	116.	Shivpuri(MP)
27.	Chittorgarh(RAJ)	72.	Koraput(ORI)	117.	Sidhart Nagar(UP)
28.	Churu(RAJ)	73.	Kota(RAJ)	118.	Sidhi(MP)
29.	Dadra	74.	Lalitpur(UP)	119.	Sitamarhi(BIH)
30.	Damoh(MP)	75.	Lucknow(UP)	120.	Sitapur(UP)
31.	Darbhanga(BIH)	76.	Madhepura(BIH)	121.	Sonbhadra(UP)
32.	Datia(MP)	77.	Madhubani(BIH)	122.	Sultanpur(UP)
33.	Dausa(RAJ)	78.	Maharajganj(UP)	123.	Surguja(MP)
34.	Deoghar(BIH)	79.	Mahoba(UP)	124.	The Dangs(GUJ)
35.	Deoria(UP)	80.	Mainpuri(UP)	125.	Tikamgarh(MP)
36.	Dewas(MP)	81.	Malkangiri(ORI)	126.	Tonk(RAJ)
37.	Dhar(MP)	82.	Mandsaur(MP)	127.	Udaipur(RAJ)
38.	Dholpur(RAJ)	83.	Mathura(UP)	128.	Unnao(UP)
39.	Dungarpur(RAJ)	84.	Mau(UP)	129.	Vadodara(GUJ)
40.	East Kameng(ARP)	85.	Mirzapur(UP)	130.	Vaishali(BIH)
41.	East Khasi Hills(MEG)	86.	Morena(MP)	131.	Varanasi(UP)
42.	East Siang(ARP)	87.	Muktsar(PUJ)	132.	Vidisha(MP)
43.	Etah(UP)	88.	Munger(BIH)	133.	West Khasi Hills(MEG)
44.	Faizabad(UP)	89.	Muradabad(UP)		
45.	Fathepur(UP)	90.	Nagaur(RAJ)		

Table 15(b)
Districts with Median Age at Marriage below 21 years for Castes other than SC/ST/OBC (Boys)

Sr. No.	*District (State)*	*Sr. No.*	*District (State)*	*Sr. No.*	*District (State)*
	OTHER CASTES		**OTHER CASTES**		**OTHER CASTES**
1.	Allahabad(UP)	12.	Faizabad(UP)	23.	Mirzapur(UP)
2.	Bahraich(UP)	13.	Giridih(BIH)	24.	Morena(MP)
3.	Banas Kantha(GUJ)	14.	Gonda(UP)	25.	Nagaur(RAJ)
4.	Banda(UP)	15.	Gurgaon(HAR)	26.	Nawada(BIH)
5.	Bareilly(UP)	16.	Hanumangarh(RAJ)	27.	Pratapgarh(UP)
6.	Barmer(RAJ)	17.	Jalore(RAJ)	28.	Saharsa(BIH)
7.	Basti(UP)	18.	Jaunpur(UP)	29.	Shajahanabad(UP)
8.	Bhadohi(UP)	19.	Jhalawar(RAJ)	30.	Shajapur(MP)
9.	Bikaner(RAJ)	20.	Kheri(UP)	31.	Sidhart Nagar(UP)
10.	Churu(RAJ)	21.	Lalitpur(UP)	32.	Sidhi(MP)
11.	Dholpur(RAJ)	22.	Mandla(MP)	33.	Sultanpur(UP)
				34.	Ukhrul(MAN)

(c) Economic status

Economic status as assessed by the type of house they live in shows that there was no marriage was reported during the reference period among the well off persons in 12 districts. The corresponding number of districts among the medium group is one and among the poor group is five. Appendix IX provides the district-wise situation for the three categories of economic status.

The proportion of marriages below legal minimum age is much less among those who are well off than the poor group. The share of such marriages vary from none in the case of 114 districts to 86.7 per cent in Kohima in Nagaland among the economically well off persons. The corresponding situation among those who are in the medium category is 49 districts with no such marriages to 86.7 per cent in Dausa in Rajasthan. Similarly among the poor, the variation is from zero in the case of 42 districts to 100 per cent in Mansa (Punjab), Hisar and Gurgaon (both in Haryana)[4].

The summary situation is given in Figure M-12. There are only one per cent of districts with at least two-thirds of the marriages falling below 21 years among those who are economically well off compared to 7 per cent among the medium group and 19 per cent among the poor. The names of these districts are provided in Table 16(a) and 16(b) for the different economic status categories.

Table 16(a)

Fig. M-12: Percentage Distribution of Districts by per cent Share of Marriages below 21 years of Age by Economic Status (Boys)

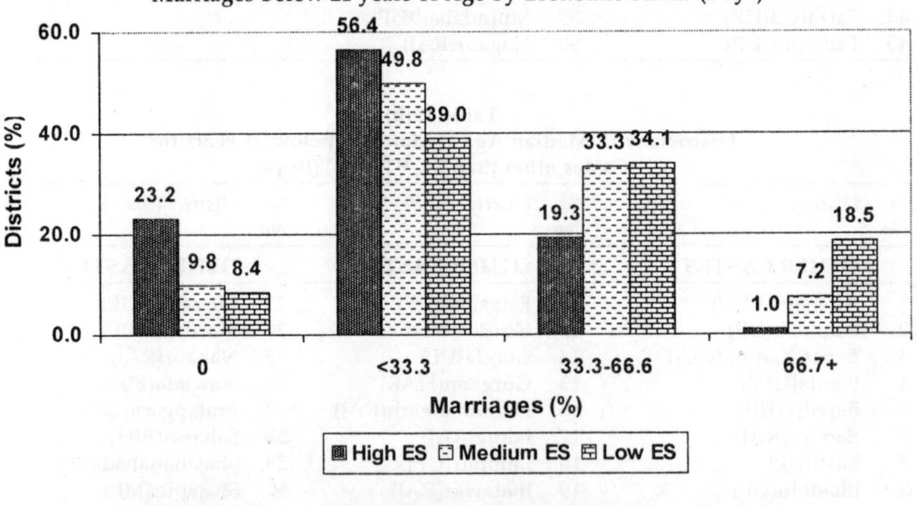

Districts with Marriages below 21 years of age Forming at least two-thirds of the Total Marriages in low Economic Status Category (Boys)

Sr. No.	*District (State)*	*Sr. No.*	*District (State)*	*Sr. No.*	*District (State)*
	Low ES		**Low ES**		**Low ES**
1.	Ahmadabad(GUJ)	34.	Gaya(BIH)	67.	Munger(BIH)
2.	Ajmer(RAJ)	35.	Gonda(UP)	68.	Nagaur(RAJ)
3.	Allahabad(UP)	36.	Gopalganj(BIH)	69.	Nawada(BIH)
4.	Alwar(RAJ)	37.	Guna(MP)	70.	Palamu(BIH)

Contd....

Sr. No.	*District (State)*	*Sr. No.*	*District (State)*	*Sr. No.*	*District (State)*
5.	Ambedkarnagar(UP)	38.	Gurgaon(HAR)	71.	Pali(RAJ)
6.	Aurangabad(BIH)	39.	Hamirpur(UP)	72.	Panna(MP)
7.	Azamgarh(UP)	40.	Hathras(UP)	73.	Pilibhit(UP)
8.	Bahraich(UP)	41.	Hisar(HAR)	74.	Pratapgarh(UP)
9.	Banda(UP)	42.	Jaintia Hill(MEG)	75.	Raibareilly(UP)
10.	Banswara(RAJ)	43.	Jalandhar(PUJ)	76.	Rajsamand(RAJ)
11.	Barabanki(UP)	44.	Jalaun(UP)	77.	Rewa(MP)
12.	Bareilly(UP)	45.	Jalore(RAJ)	78.	Ri Bhoi (MEG)
13.	Basti(UP)	46.	Jaunpur(UP)	79.	Rohtak(HAR)
14.	Bhadohi(UP)	47.	Jehanabad(BIH)	80.	Rohtas(BIH)
15.	Bharatpur(RAJ)	48.	Jhabua(MP)	81.	Satna(MP)
16.	Bhavnagar(GUJ)	49.	Jhalawar(RAJ)	82.	Sawaimadhopur(RAJ)
17.	Bhilwara(RAJ)	50.	Jhansi(UP)	83.	Shajahanabad(UP)
18.	Bhiwani(HAR)	51.	Kaithal(HAR)	84.	Shajapur(MP)
19.	Bhojpur(BIH)	52.	Kheri(UP)	85.	Shivpuri(MP)
20.	Bikaner(RAJ)	53.	Kohima(NAG)	86.	Sidhart Nagar(UP)
21.	Bundi(RAJ)	54.	Kota(RAJ)	87.	Sidhi(MP)
22.	Chattarpur(MP)	55.	Kupuwada(J&K)	88.	Sirsa(HAR)
23.	Chikmaglur(KAR)	56.	Lalitpur(UP)	89.	Sonbhadra(UP)
24.	Chittorgarh(RAJ)	57.	Lucknow(UP)	90.	Sonipat(HAR)
25.	Churu(RAJ)	58.	Maharajganj(UP)	91.	Sultanpur(UP)
26.	Datia(MP)	59.	Mahe(PON)	92.	Tikamgarh(MP)
27.	Dausa(RAJ)	60.	Mahendragarh(HAR)	93.	Tonk(RAJ)
28.	Delhi	61.	Mahoba(UP)	94.	Udaipur(RAJ)
29.	Deoria(UP)	62.	Mandsaur(MP)	95.	Vaishali(BIH)
30.	Faizabad(UP)	63.	Mansa(PUJ)	96.	Varanasi(UP)
31.	Firozabad(UP)	64.	Mau(UP)	97.	West Garo Hills(MEG)
32.	Gandhinagar(GUJ)	65.	Mirzapur(UP)	98.	Rohtas(BIH)
33.	Ganganagar(RAJ)	66.	Morena(MP)		

Table 16(b)

Districts with Marriages below 21 years of Age Forming at least two-thirds of the Total Marriages in Medium and High Economic Status Categories (Boys)

Sr. No.	District (State)	Sr. No.	District (State)	Sr. No.	District (State)
	Medium ES		**Medium ES**		**Medium ES**
1.	Alwar(RAJ)	15.	East Siang(ARP)	29.	Pratapgarh(UP)
2.	Ambedkarnagar(UP)	16.	Faizabad(UP)	30.	Rohtas(BIH)
3.	Banswara(RAJ)	17.	Firozabad(UP)	31.	Sidhart Nagar(UP)
4.	Bhadohi(UP)	18.	Ganganagar(RAJ)	32.	Sikar(RAJ)
5.	Bharatpur(RAJ)	19.	Gonda(UP)	33.	Sonbhadra(UP)
6.	Bhilwara(RAJ)	20.	Gorakhpur(UP)	34.	Sultanpur(UP)
7.	Bikaner(RAJ)	21.	Hanumangarh(RAJ)	35.	Tikamgarh(MP)
8.	Chattarpur(MP)	22.	Kheri(UP)	36.	Varanasi(UP)
9.	Chittorgarh(RAJ)	23.	Kota(RAJ)		**High ES**
10.	Churu(RAJ)	24.	Lalitpur(UP)	1.	Bahraich (UP)
11.	Dausa(RAJ)	25.	Lower Subansiri (ARP)	2.	Kohima (NAG)
12.	Deoria(UP)	26.	Maharajganj(UP)	3.	Maharajganj (UP)
13.	Dholpur(RAJ)	27.	Morena(MP)	4.	Sidhart Nagar (UP)
14.	East Khasi ills(MEG)	28.	Nawada(BIH)	5.	Tikamgarh (MP)

Median Age at Marriage by Economic Status

In general, there is one year difference in the median age at marriage among the three economic status categories. Whereas the median age at marriage for the low economic status category is 22 years, that of medium and high is found to be 23 and 24 years respectively. The variation in the median age at marriage in the low status category varied from 17 years in Bundi (Rajasthan), Maharajganj and Sidhartnagar (Uttar Pradesh) to 30 years in Allappuzha (Kerala)[5]. Among the medium class, the lowest median age of 16 years is found in Bhilwara (Rajasthan) and a maximum of 31 years is found in Cachar and Hailakandi (both in Assam). Among those with high economic status the lowest median age of 18 years is found in Maharajganj (Uttar Pradesh) to 34 years in West Tripura.

The percentage distribution of districts in each economic status group by category of marriage is given in Figure M-13.

Fig. M-13: Percentage Distribution of Districts in each Economic Status Group by Marriage Category based on median Age (Boys)

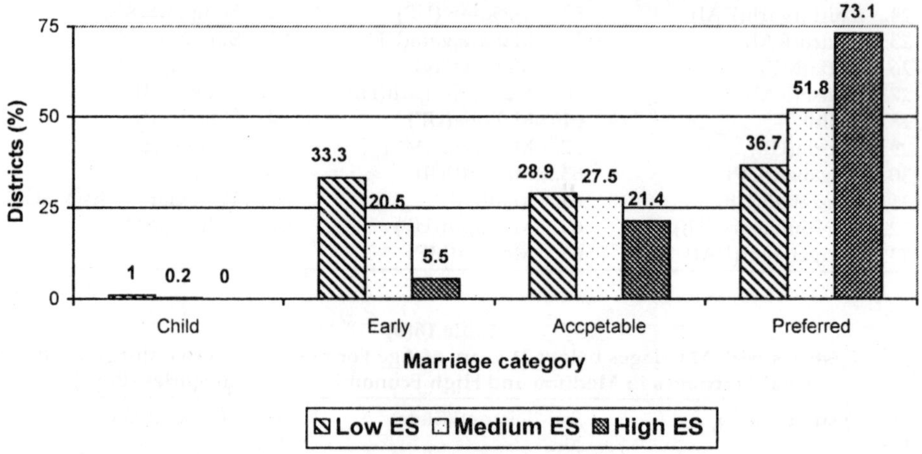

There are just six districts with a median age at marriage falling below 18 years of age and hence classified as child marriage, five from low status (Alwar and Bundi in Rajasthan, Maharajganj and Sidhartnagar in Uttar Pradesh and Gurgaon in Haryan a) and one from medium status (Bhilwara in Rajasthan). There is no child marriage among those who are in high economic condition and even the proportion of early marriage forms only about 6 per cent.

The number of districts with below legal minimum median age at marriage is 27, 104 and 171 respectively for high, medium and low economic status group. But unlike in the case of other variables, these districts failed to show any major concentration (except perhaps in the medium economic status group) in any state as can be seen from Figure M-14.

Fig. M-14: Per cent Share of Selected States of Districts with Median Age of Marriage below 21 years of Age by Economic Status (Boys)

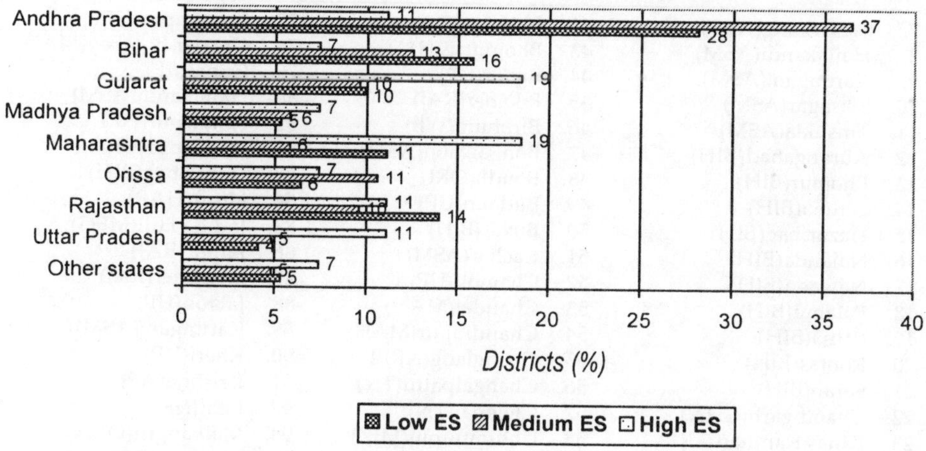

The names of districts with below legal minimum median age at marriage for each economic status group is given below in Tables 17(a), 17(b) and 17(c) respectively for high, medium and low economic status group.

Table 17(a)
Districts with Median Age at Marriage below 21 years of Age for High Economic Status Group (Boys)

Sr. No.	*District (State)*	*Sr. No.*	*District (State)*	*Sr. No.*	*District (State)*
1.	Adilabad(AP)	10.	Bankura(WB)	19.	Churu(RAJ)
2.	Amravali(MAH)	11.	Barabanki(UP)	20.	Dausa(RAJ)
3.	Anantnag(J&K)	12.	Baramulla(J&K)	21.	Deoria(UP)
4.	Andaman(A&N)	13.	Bhadohi(UP)	22.	Dholpur(RAJ)
5.	Anghul(ORI)	14.	Bhilwara(RAJ)	23.	Faizabad(UP)
6.	Azamgarh(UP)	15.	Bhojpur(BIH)	24.	Firozabad(UP)
7.	Bahraich(UP)	16.	Bilaspur(MP)	25.	Giridih(BIH)
8.	Banas Kantha(GUJ)	17.	Bolangir(ORI)	26.	Idukki(KER)
9.	Banda(UP)	18.	Bundi(RAJ)	27.	North 24 Parganas(WB)

Table 17(b)
Districts with Median Age at Marriage below 21 years of Age for Medium Economic Status Group (Boys)

Sr. No.	*District (State)*	*Sr. No.*	*District (State)*	*Sr. No.*	*District (State)*
1.	Agra(UP)	36.	Bhadrak(ORI)	71.	Fatehgarh Sahib(PUJ)
2.	Karimnagar(AP)	37.	Bhagalpur(BIH)	72.	Firozabad(UP)
3.	Krishna(AP)	38.	Bhandara(MAH)	73.	Gajapati(ORI)
4.	Medak(AP)	39.	Bharatpur(RAJ)	74.	Gandhinagar(GUJ)
5.	Nalgonda(AP)	40.	Bhavnagar(GUJ)	75.	Ghaziabad(UP)
6.	Rangareddy(AP)	41.	Bhilwara(RAJ)	76.	Gonda(UP)

Contd....

Sr. No.	District (State)	Sr. No.	District (State)	Sr. No.	District (State)
7.	West Siang(ARP)	42.	Bhind(MP)	77.	Gorakhpur(UP)
8.	Hailakandi(ASM)	43.	Bhojpur(BIH)	78.	Greater Bombay(MAH)
9.	Karimganj(ASM)	44.	Bijnor(UP)	79.	Guna(MP)
10.	Sibsagar(ASM)	45.	Bikaner(RAJ)	80.	Hailakandi(ASM)
11.	Tinsukia(ASM)	46.	Birbhum(WB)	81.	Hamirpur(HP)
12.	Aurangabad(BIH)	47.	Bongaigaon(ASM)	82.	Hamirpur(UP)
13.	Bhojpur(BIH)	48.	Boudh(ORI)	83.	Hazaribag(BIH)
14.	Gulma(BIH)	49.	Budaun(UP) ·	84.	Hisar(HAR)
15.	Hazaribag(BIH)	50.	Buxar(BIH)	85.	Jaintia Hill(MEG)
16.	Nalanda(BIH)	51.	Cachar(ASM)	86.	Jaipur(RAJ)
17.	Nawada(BIH)	52.	Chamoli(UP)	87.	Jaisalmer(RAJ)
18.	Palamu(BIH)	53.	Chandel(MAN)	88.	Jalaun(UP)
19.	Patna(BIH)	54.	Chandrapur(MAH)	89.	Karimganj(ASM)
20.	Rohtas(BIH)	55.	Changlang(ARP)	90.	Kheri(UP)
21.	Saran(BIH)	56.	Chengalpattu(TN)	91.	Krishna(AP)
22.	Chandigarh(CHN)	57.	Chennai(TN)	92.	Leh(J&K)
23.	Banas Kantha(GUJ	58.	Chhimtuipui(MIZ)	93.	Malkangiri(ORI)
24.	Bhavnagar(GUJ)	59.	Chhindwara(MP)	94.	Mirzapur(UP)
25.	Gandhinagar(GUJ)	60.	Churachandpur(MAN)	95.	Munger(BIH)
26.	Rajkot(GUJ)	61.	Churu(RAJ)	96.	Nainital(UP)
27.	The Dangs(GUJ)	62.	Coimbatore(TN)	97.	Nilgiris(TN)
28.	Gurgaon(HAR)	63.	Dadra	98.	Palghat(KER)
29.	Hisar(HAR)	64.	Datia(MP)	99.	Pali(RAJ)
30.	Karnal(HAR)	65.	Dausa(RAJ)	100.	Papumpare(ARP)
31.	Sonipat(HAR)	66.	Dewas(MP)	101.	Phek(NAG)
32.	Lahul & Spiti(HP)	67.	Dhar(MP)	102.	Purba Champaran(BIH)
33.	Sirmaur(HP)	68.	Dholpur(RAJ)	103.	The Dangs(GUJ)
34.	Kargil (J&K)	69.	East Nimar(MP)	104.	Tikamgarh(MP)
35.	Leh(J&K)	70.	East Sikkim(SIK)		

Table 17(c)

Districts with Median Age at Marriage below 21 years of Age for Low Economic Status Group (Boys)

Sr. No.	District (State)	Sr. No.	District (State)	Sr. No.	District (State)
1.	Adilabad(AP)	58.	Chamba(HP)	115.	Hamirpur(UP)
2.	Ahmadabad(GUJ)	59.	Chamoli(UP)	116.	Hanumangarh(RAJ)
3.	Ajmer(RAJ)	60.	Chandel(MAN)	117.	Hathras(UP)
4.	Akola(MAH)	61.	Chandigarh(CHN)	118.	Hugli(WB)
5.	Aligarh(UP)	62.	Chandrapur(MAH)	119.	Jagatsinghpur(ORI)
6.	Allahabad(UP)	63.	Changlang(ARP)	120.	Jajpur(ORI)
7.	Almora(UP)	64.	Chattarpur(MP)	121.	Jalna(MAH)
8.	Alwar(RAJ)	65.	Chennai(TN)	122.	Jalore(RAJ)
9.	Ambedkarnagar(UP)	66.	Chikmaglur(KAR)	123.	Jehanabad(BIH)
10.	Amravali(MAH)	67.	Chittor(AP)	124.	Jhabua(MP)
11.	Amreli(GUJ)	68.	Chittorgarh(RAJ)	125.	Jhalawar(RAJ)
12.	Amritsar(PUJ)	69.	Churu(RAJ)	126.	Jhunjhunu(RAJ)
13.	Ananthapur(AP)	70.	Coimbatore(TN)	127.	Jodhpur(RAJ)
14.	Andaman(A&N)	71.	Cuddapah(AP)	128.	Kachchh(GUJ)
15.	Anghul(ORI)	72.	Cuttak(ORI)	129.	Kangra(HP)
16.	Aurangabad(BIH)	73.	Dakshina Kannada(KAR)	130.	Kanpur Nagar(UP)
17.	Aurangabad(MAH)	74.	Darbhanga(BIH)	131.	Karimnagar(AP)

Contd....

Sr. No.	*District (State)*	*Sr. No.*	*District (State)*	*Sr. No.*	*District (State)*
18.	Bahraich(UP)	75.	Darjeeling(WB)	132.	Karnal(HAR)
19.	Balaghat(MP)	76.	Darrang(ASM)	133.	Katihar(BIH)
20.	Balasore(ORI)	77.	Datia(MP)	134.	Khagaria(BIH)
21.	Ballia(UP)	78.	Dausa(RAJ)	135.	Kheri(UP)
22.	Banas Kantha(GUJ)	79.	Deoghar(BIH)	136.	Kolar(KAR)
23.	Banda(UP)	80.	Dewas(MP)	137.	Kota(RAJ)
24.	Bangalore (KAR)	81.	Dhar(MP)	138.	Lalitpur(UP)
25.	Bangalore Rural(KAR)	82.	Dharwad(KAR)	139.	Leh(J&K)
26.	Banswara(RAJ)	83.	Dholpur(RAJ)	140.	Madhepura(BIH)
27.	Barabanki(UP)	84.	Dhubri(ASM)	141.	Madhubani(BIH)
28.	Baragarh(ORI)	85.	Dibrugarh(ASM)	142.	Mandsaur(MP)
29.	Baramulla(J&K)	86.	Dindigul(TN)	143.	Marigaon(ASM)
30.	Bareilly(UP)	87.	Diu	144.	Meerut(UP)
31.	Barmer(RAJ)	88.	Dungarpur(RAJ)	145.	Mokokchung(NAG)
32.	Barpeta(ASM)	89.	Durg(MP)	146.	Morena(MP)
33.	Bastar(MP)	90.	East Godavari(AP)	147.	Muktsar(PUJ)
34.	Basti(UP)	91.	East Kameng(ARP)	148.	Munger(BIH)
35.	Bathinda(PUJ)	92.	East Khasi Hills(MEG)	149.	Murshidabad(WB)
36.	Beed(MAH)	93.	East Siang(ARP)	150.	Nagpur(MAH)
37.	Begusarai(BIH)	94.	East Sikkim(SIK)	151.	Nawada(BIH)
38.	Bellary(KAR)	95.	Ernakulam(KER)	152.	Nawapada(ORI)
39.	Bhadohi(UP)	96.	Etah(UP)	153.	Nicobar(A&N)
40.	Bhandara(MAH)	97.	Etawah(UP)	154.	North Arcot(TN)
41.	Bharatpur(RAJ)	98.	Faizabad(UP)	155.	Panna(MP)
42.	Bharuch(GUJ)	99.	Faridabad(HAR)	156.	Patna(BIH)
43.	Bhavnagar(GUJ)	100.	Faridkot(PUJ)	157.	Pilibhit(UP)
44.	Bhilwara(RAJ)	101.	Fatehgarh Sahib(PUJ)	158.	Pratapgarh(UP)
45.	Bhind(MP)	102.	Fathepur(UP)	159.	Puri(ORI)
46.	Bhiwani(HAR)	103.	Firozabad(UP)	160.	Raigarh(MP)
47.	Bhojpur(BIH)	104.	Gandhinagar(GUJ)	161.	Raipur(MP)
48.	Bijnor(UP)	105.	Gaya(BIH)	162.	Rajgarh(MP)
49.	Bikaner(RAJ)	106.	Ghazipur(UP)	163.	Ranchi(BIH)
50.	Bilaspur(HP)	107.	Giridih(BIH)	164.	Rewa(MP)
51.	Bilaspur(MP)	108.	Golaghat(ASM)	165.	Saharsa(BIH)
52.	Bishnupur(MAN).	109.	Gopalganj(BIH)	166.	Sahibganj(BIH)
53.	Bongaigaon(ASM)	110.	Gulbarga(KAR)	167.	Shajapur(MP)
54.	Budaun(UP)	111.	Gulma(BIH)	168.	Sitapur(UP)
55.	Bulandshahr(UP)	112.	Guna(MP)	169.	Udaipur(RAJ)
56.	Bundi(RAJ)	113.	Guntur(AP)	170.	Vadodara(GUJ)
57.	Buxar(BIH)	114.	Gurgaon(HAR)	171.	Vaishali(BIH)

(d) Female Literacy Rate (FLR)

The district-wise situation of age at marriage of boys by female literacy rate group is given in Appendix X. Since female literacy rate is taken here as an indicator of development, the overall situation shows a negative relationship between development and age at marriage for boys.

The per cent of districts reporting child marriage among the boys in each category of FLR is 88.2, 82.7 and 42.4 respectively for low, medium and high. However, it should be noted that 79 per cent of districts reporting child marriage in the high FLR category have only 1 or 2 cases of such marriages. The corresponding per centage for the medium FLR category is 24 per cent and that for low FLR is 6 per cent. If these can be treated as stray cases, then the per cent of districts reporting child marriages works out to be 82.4, 62.6 and 9.1 respectively for low, medium and high category of FLR.

In districts with a low literacy rate, the variation in the share of child marriage is from zero in 6 districts to 44.3 in Maharajganj (Uttar Pradesh). Sixty one districts did not report any child marriage among the medium FLR group where the highest level of child marriage is only 36.3 per cent (in Bundi district of Rajasthan). The highest level of child marriage in the high literacy class turns out to be still less with just 6.5 per cent in Rajnandgaon in Madhya Pradesh and no child marriage was reported from 57 districts.

There are six districts with no marriage below legal minimum age of 21 years. Of them 3 are from medium FLR (Jaintia Hill of Meghalaya, Nicobar of Andaman and Nicobar Islands and Thirunelveli of Tamil Nadu) and the remaining three from high FLR category (Panchkula of Haryana, Kottayam of Kerala and Fatehgarh Sahib of Punjab). The percentage distribution of districts by their per cent share of marriages below 21 years in each literacy class is given in a summary form in Figure M-15.

Fig. M-15: Percentage Distribution of Districts by per cent Share of Marriages below 21 years of Age in each Category of Literacy (Boys)

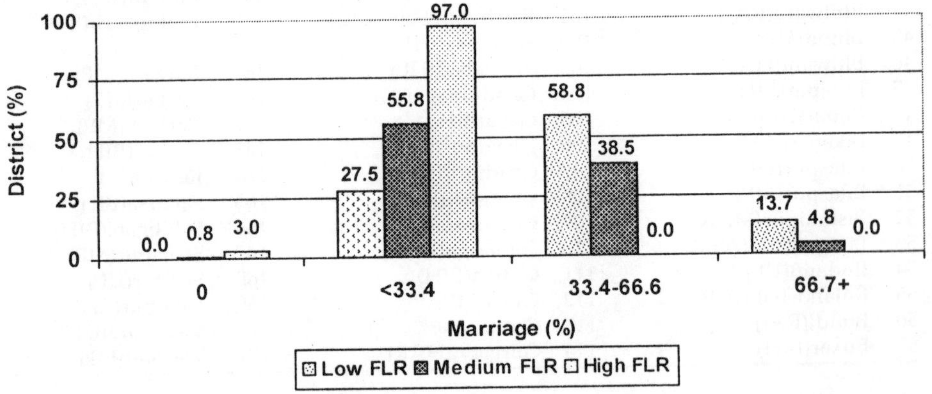

Note that the per cent share of marriages below legal minimum age in the high FLR category is less than one-third of reported marriages.

The names of districts with marriages below 21 years forming at least two-thirds of the total marriages in each category of FLR are given in Table 18.

Median Age at Marriage by Female Literacy Rate

On the whole the median age at marriage for districts with low FLR varies from a minimum of 18 years in Lalitpur, Maharajganj and Sidhartnagar districts of Uttar Pradesh to 26 in Doda of Jammu and Kashmir. The corresponding variation observed among the districts with medium FLR is 18 years in Rohtas (Bihar), Bhadohi, Faizabad (Uttar Pradesh), Morena, Tikamgarh (Madhya Pradesh) and Bundi (Rajasthan) to 30 years in Cachar and Nalbari (both in Assam). With high FLR reflecting comparatively high development, there is no median age at marriage below the legal minimum age of 21 years. Further only five per cent of the total districts (Rajnandgaon and Narsimhapur of Madhya Pradesh, Kanpur Nagar of Uttar Pradesh, Ahmedabad of Gujarat, Fatehgarh Sahib of Punjab) in this category have marriages less than 23 years, the preferred age at marriage. On the whole there is one year difference in median age at marriage between those who are living in districts with low FLR (21 years) and those living in districts with medium FLR (22 years). For the high FLR group the median age at marriage is 25 years, two years above even the preferred age at marriage.

Table 18

Districts with Marriages below 21 years of Age Forming at least two-thirds of the Total Marriages in low and Medium Category of Female Literacy Rate (Boys)

Sr. No.	*District (State)*	*Sr. No.*	*District (State)*	*Sr. No.*	*District (State)*
	Low FLR		**Medium FLR**		**Medium FLR**
1.	Bahraich(UP)	1.	Ambedkarnagar(UP)	10.	Morena(MP)
2.	Banswara(RAJ)	2.	Bhadohi(UP)	11.	Panna(MP)
3.	Gonda(UP)	3.	Bundi(RAJ)	12.	Pratapgarh(UP)
4.	Jhabua(MP)	4.	Chittorgarh(RAJ)	13.	Ri Bhoi (MEG)
5.	Lalitpur(UP)	5.	Dausa(RAJ)	14.	Rohtas(BIH)
6.	Maharajganj(UP)	6.	Deoria(UP)	15.	Sidhi(MP)
7.	Sidhart Nagar(UP)	7.	Faizabad(UP)	16.	Sultanpur(UP)
		8.	Kohima(NAG)	17.	Tikamgarh(MP)
		9.	Mirzapur(UP)		

Fig. M-16: Percentage Distribution of Districts in each Literacy Rate Group by Category of Marriage based on Median (Boys)

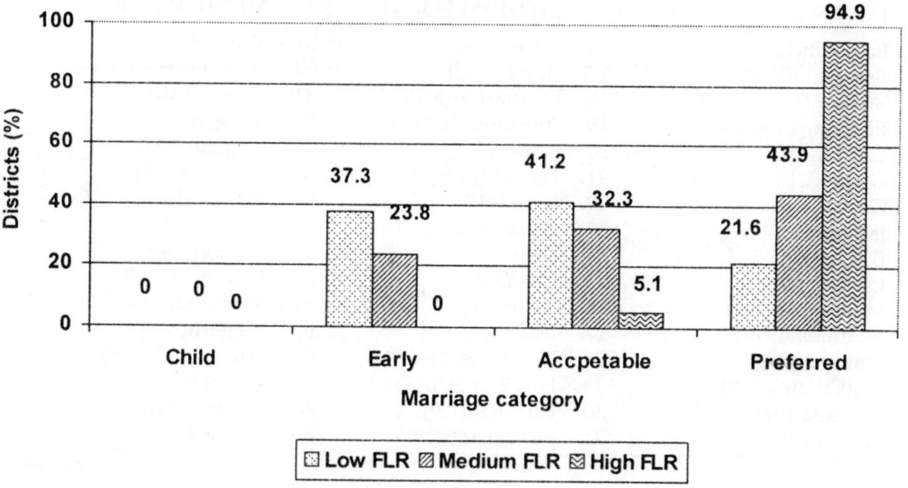

Percentage distribution of districts in each literacy rate group by age at marriage category is given below in Fig. M-16 which shows a direct relationship between development and age at marriage.

Of the 103 districts with a median age at marriage below legal minimum age of 21 years 71 per cent are located in Bihar (14.6%), Madhya Pradesh (19.4%), Rajasthan (12.6%) and Uttar Pradesh (24.3%). Their distribution by literacy rate is given in Figure M-17 and their names are given below in Table 19.

Fig. M-17: Per cent Share of Selected States of Districts with Median Age at Marriage below 21 years of Age by Female Literacy Rate (Boys)

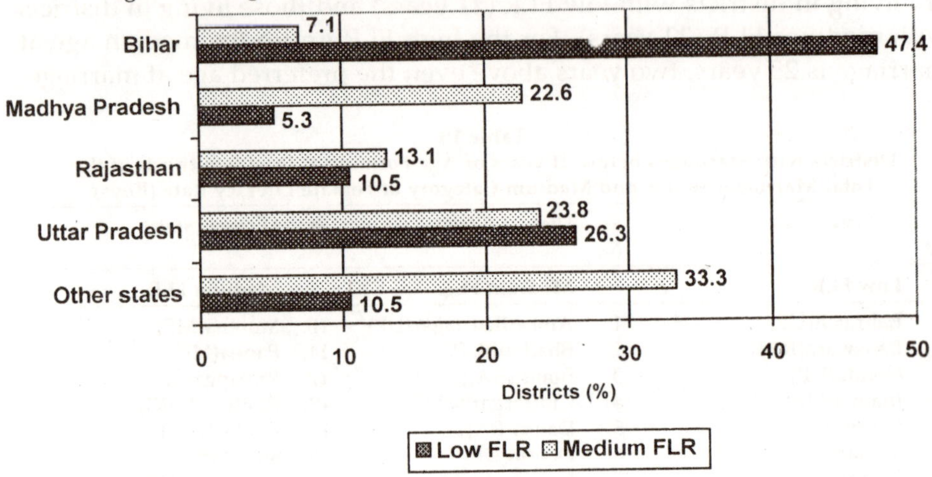

Table 19
Districts with Median Age at Marriage below 21 years of Age for Low and Medium Literacy Rate Groups (Boys)

Sr. No.	District (State)	Sr. No.	District (State)	Sr. No.	District (State)
	LOW FLR		**MEDIUM FLR**		**MEDIUM FLR**
1.	Bahraich(UP)	16.	Bikaner(RAJ)	51.	Mau(UP)
2.	Banswara(RAJ)	17.	Bundi(RAJ)	52.	Mirzapur(UP)
3.	Budaun(UP)	18.	Chattarpur(MP)	53.	Morena(MP)
4.	East Kameng(ARP)	19.	Chittorgarh(RAJ)	54.	Munger(BIH)
5.	Giridih(BIH)	20.	Churu(RAJ)	55.	Nagaur(RAJ)
6.	Gonda(UP)	21.	Damoh(MP)	56.	Nalanda(BIH)
7.	Gopalganj(BIH)	22.	Datia(MP)	57.	Panna(MP)
8.	Jalore(RAJ)	23.	Dausa(RAJ)	58.	Patna(BIH)
9.	Jhabua(MP)	24.	Deoria(UP)	59.	Pilibhit(UP)
10.	Lalitpur(UP)	25.	Dewas(MP)	60.	Pratapgarh(UP)
11.	Madhepura(BIH)	26.	Dhar(MP)	61.	Raibareilly(UP)
12.	Madhubani(BIH)	27.	Dholpur(RAJ)	62.	Rajgarh(MP)
13.	Maharajganj(UP)	28.	East Khasi Hills(MEG)	63.	Rajsamand(RAJ)
14.	Malkangiri(ORI)	29.	East Siang(ARP)	64.	Rewa(MP)
15.	Nawada(BIH)	30.	Faizabad(UP)	65.	Ri Bhoi (MEG)
16.	Palamu(BIH)	31.	Firozabad(UP)	66.	Rohtas(BIH)

Contd....

Sr. No.	*District (State)*	*Sr. No.*	*District (State)*	*Sr. No.*	*District (State)*
17.	Saharsa(BIH)	32.	Ganganagar(RAJ)	67.	Satna(MP)
18.	Sidhart Nagar(UP)	33.	Gaya(BIH)	68.	Sawaimadhopur(RAJ)
19.	Tonk(RAJ)	34.	Ghazipur(UP)	69.	Shahdol(MP)
	MEDIUM FLR	35.	Gorakhpur(UP)	70.	Shajahanabad(UP)
1.	Allahabad(UP)	36.	Guna(MP)	71.	Shajapur(MP)
2.	Alwar(RAJ)	37.	Hamirpur(UP)	72.	Shivpuri(MP)
3.	Ambedkarnagar(UP)	38.	Hanumangarh(RAJ)	73.	Sidhi(MP)
4.	Aurangabad(BIH)	39.	Hardoi(UP)	74.	Sitapur(UP)
5.	Azamgarh(UP)	40.	Jalaun(UP)	75.	Sonbhadra(UP)
6.	Banas Kantha(GUJ)	41.	Jaunpur(UP)	76.	Sultanpur(UP)
7.	Banda(UP)	42.	Jehanabad(BIH)	77.	Surguja(MP)
8.	Barabanki(UP)	43.	Jhalawar(RAJ)	78.	The Dangs(GUJ)
9.	Barmer(RAJ)	44.	Jhansi(UP)	79.	Tikamgarh(MP)
10.	Basti(UP)	45.	Kheri(UP)	80.	Udaipur(RAJ)
11.	Bhadohi(UP)	46.	Kohima(NAG)	81.	Unnao(UP)
12.	Bharatpur(RAJ)	47.	Kota(RAJ)	82.	Varanasi(UP)
13.	Bhilwara(RAJ)	48.	Mahoba(UP)	83.	Vidisha(MP)
14.	Bhind(MP)	49.	Mainpuri(UP)	84.	West Khasi Hills(MEG)
15.	Bhojpur(BIH)	50.	Mandsaur(MP)		

NOTES

1 Two marriages, one each at age 16 and 17 in Maharajganj district of Uttar Pradesh and at age 20 in East Garo Hills of Meghalaya are not considered.

2. Two marriages, one at age 16 and another at age 17 in Maharajganj district of Uttar Pradesh is not considered.

3. Not considering Mandla district in Uttar Pradesh and Ukhrul in Manipur with just one marriage each at age 20 and 18 years respectively.

4. The one marriage at age 19 in Jalandhar (Punjab) and at age 20 in Rohtak (Haryana) are not considered.

5. Ignoring the single marriage at age 36 in district Ernakulam in Kerala.

Chapter - 4

MAJOR FINDINGS AND CONCLUSIONS

MAJOR FINDINGS

This study was an attempt to find the timing of marriage of both boys and girls in India at the district level and thereby to identify the districts with a significant proportion of marriages below the legal minimum age at marriage of 18 years for girls and 21 years for boys. This will help to understand how far or near one is in attaining the cherished vision of India of getting the minimum age at marriage of girls raised to 20 years by 2010 or at least not getting any girl married before she completes 18 years of age.

For this purpose the data were taken from the district level Rapid Household Survey conducted by the Ministry of Health and Family Welfare, Government of India during 1997-99. A total of 53,410 marriages of girls who married at the age of ten years or later and 65,491 marriages of boys who married at the age of fourteen years or later from the selected 529,777 households of 504 districts were analysed. The marriages were grouped into four categories, child, early, acceptable and preferred, based on the reported age at marriage and also on the median age at marriage. Of the total marriages child marriage accounted for 9.1 per cent of girls (marriage at ages 10-14 years) and 6.3 per cent of boys (marriage at ages 14-18 years). However, a concentration of such marriages was noted in Bihar (17.6% of girls and 10.5% of boys), Madhya Pradesh (15.4% of girls and 13.3% of boys), Rajasthan (19.8% of girls and 17% boys) and Uttar Pradesh (14.3% of girls and 11.9% of boys). West Bengal also noted a concentration of child marriage of girls (14.8%).

There were 16 districts with at least 25 per cent of the reported marriages of *both* boys and girls falling in the child marriage category. These districts are Nawada and Rohtas from Bihar; Rajgarh, Shajapur and Sidhi from Madhya Pradesh; Bhilwara, Bundi and Jhalawar from Rajasthan; Ambedkarnagar, Bahraich, Basti, Faizabad, Gonda, Lalitpur,

Maharajganj and Sidhart Nagar from Uttar Pradesh. In all these districts the median age at marriage was below legal minimum age at marriage of 21 years for boys and 18 years for girls. These are the worst districts as far as age at marriage is concerned. It is also of interest to note that none of these districts were highly developed going by the development index of female literacy rate or type of house in which the household lived. Further, two-thirds of the marriages in these districts were among the SC/ST/OBC group.

Though not child marriage *per se,* there were 85 districts where at least 50 per cent of the reported marriages were conducted before the girl/boy reached the respective legal minimum age at marriage. Again these districts are concentrated mostly in Bihar (15), Madhya Pradesh (19), Rajasthan (17) and Uttar Pradesh (31). The names of these districts are given below in Table 4.1.

When viewed against the total number of districts in each of these four states, it shows the seriousness of the problem. Of the total districts in each of these states, the per cent of districts with marriages of both girls and boys below legal minimum age at marriage forming at least 50 per cent are: 34.9, 44.4, 53.3 and 45.6 respectively for Bihar, Madhya Pradesh, Rajasthan and Uttar Pradesh. That means, in a sizable number of districts in each of these states both boys and girls are getting married before they attain the legal minimum age at marriage of 18 years for girls and 21 years for boys.

The data also showed some satisfactory results. There were 124 districts with preferred age at marriage for *both* boys and girls forming at least 50 per cent of the total reported marriages (Table 4.2). Seventy seven per cent of these 124 districts are from ten states, namely Karnataka (4.0%), Gujarat (4.8%), Manipur (6.5%), Orissa (6.5%), Assam (7.3%), Jammu & Kashmir (7.3%), Punjab (8.1%), Himachal Pradesh (9.7%), Kerala (10.5%) and Tamil Nadu (12.1%).

Looking at the situation from the point of view of each state/UT, it is found that all the districts in Chandigarh, Delhi, Goa, Himachal Pradesh and Manipur had at least 50 per cent of marriages of both boys and girls after they attained the preferred age at marriage of 20 for girls and 23 for boys. In Kerala state 13 of the 14 districts fall into this category, the exception being Malappuram district where, although 71 per cent of boys got married after they completed 23 years of age, only 26 per cent of girls married after completing the preferred age of 20 years. In Tamil Nadu and Mizoram, 65-67 per cent of the districts fall into this category. Jammu & Kashmir and Punjab fallowed very closely with 64 and 59 per cent respectively.

As is well known, an average hides the true situation. The median age by district had shown the absence of child marriage in all but one district (Maharajganj of Uttar Pradesh) and that too only for girls. However, almost

Table 4.1
Districts with at least 50 per cent Marriages below legal Minimum Age at Marriage for both Girls and Boys

Sr. No.	*State/district*	*Sr. No.*	*State/district*	*Sr. No.*	*State/district*	*Sr. No.*	*State/district*
	Bihar (43)		**Madhya Pradesh**		**Rajasthan**		**Uttar Pradesh**
1.	Aurangabad	8.	Morena	10.	Dhaulpur	16.	Jalaun
2.	Bhojpur	9.	Panna	11.	Hanumangarh	17.	Jaunpur
3.	Gaya	10.	Rajgarh	12.	Jhalawar	18.	Kheri
4.	Giridih	11.	Rewa	13.	Kota	19.	Lalitpur
5.	Gopalganj	12.	Satna	14.	Nagaur	20.	Maharajganj
6.	Jehanabad	13.	Shahdol	15.	Tonk	21.	Mahoba
7.	Madhepura	14.	Shajapur	16.	Udaipur	22.	Mainpuri
8.	Madhubani	15.	Shivpuri		**Uttar Pradesh (68)**	23.	Mirzapur
9.	Munger	16.	Sidhi	1.	Allahabad	24.	Pilibhit
10.	Nalanda	17.	Surguja	2.	Ambedkarnagar	25.	Pratapgarh
11.	Nawada	18.	Tikamgarh	3.	Azamgarh	26.	Shajahanabad
12.	Palamu	19.	Vidisha	4.	Bahraich	27.	Siddharthnagar
13.	Patna			5.	Banda	28.	Sitapur
14.	Rohtas		**Rajasthan (30)**	6.	Barabanki	29.	Sonbhadra
15.	Saharsa	1.	Alwar	7.	Basti	30.	Sultanpur
	Madhya Pradesh (45)	2.	Banswara	8.	Bhadohi	31.	Varanasi
1.	Bhind	3.	Barmer	9.	Buduan		**Gujarat (19)**
2.	Chattarpur	4.	Bharatpur	10.	Deoria	1	Banas Kantha
3.	Damoh	5.	Bhilwara	11.	Faizabad		**Nagaland (7)**
4.	Dewas	6.	Bikaner	12.	Firozabad	1	Kohima
5.	Guna	7.	Bundi	13.	Ghazipur		**Orissa (30)**
6.	Jhabua	8.	Churu	14.	Gonda	1	Malkangiri
7.	Mandsaur	9.	Dausa	15.	Gorakhpur		

Note: Given in brackets are the total number of districts in the state

Table 4.2
Districts with at least 50 per cent Preferred Marriages for both Girls and Boys

Sr. No.	*State/District*	*Sr. No.*	*State/District*	*Sr. No.*	*State/District*
	Andaman & Nicobar (2)		**Jammu & Kashmir**		**Orissa**
1	Nicobar	4	Jammu	2	Bhadrak
	Andhra Pradesh (23)	5	Kathua	3	Cuttack
1	Chittoor	6	Kupwara	4	Jagatsinghapur
2	Hyderabad	7	Leh	5	Jajapur
	Arunachal Pradesh (13)	8	Pulwama	6	Kendrapara
1	Tawang	9	Punch	7	Khordha
2	Tirap		**Karnataka (20)**	8	Puri
	Assam (22)	1	Bangalore		**Pondicherry (4)**
1	Cachar	2	Chikmagalur	1	Karaikal
2	Dhemaji	3	Dakshina Kannada	2	Mahe
3	Hailakandi	4	Shimoga	3	Pondicherry
4	Jorhat	5	Uttara Kannada		**Punjab (17)**
5	Kamrup		**Kerala (14)**	1	Amritsar
6	Karimganj	1	Alappuzha	2	Gurdaspur
7	Nalbari	2	Ernakulam	3	Hoshiarpur
8	North Cachar Hills	3	Idukki	4	Jalandhar
9	Sibsagar	4	Kannur	5	Kapurthala
	Chandigarh (1)	5	Kasaragod	6	Ludhiana
	Delhi (1)	6	Kollam	7	Moga
	Goa (2)	7	Kottayam	8	Nawanshahr
1	North Goa	8	Kozhikode	9	Patiala
2	South Goa	9	Palakkad	10	Rupnagar
	Gujarat (19)	10	Pathanamthitta		**Sikkim (4)**
1	Bharuch	11	Thiruvananthapuram	1	East Sikkim
2	Jamnagar	12	Thrissur	2	North Sikkim
3	Junagadh	13	Wayanad		**Tamil Nadu (23)**
4	Rajkot		**Maharashtra (30)**	1	Chengalpattu
5	Surat	1	Greater Bombay (Mum	2	Chennai
6	Valsad	2	Sindhudurg	3	Coimbatore
	Haryana (17)		**Manipur (8)**	4	Kanniyakumari
1	Ambala	1	Bishnupur	5	Madurai
2	Yamunanagar	2	Chandel	6	Namakkal
	Himachal Pradesh (12)	3	Churachandpur	7	Periyar
1	Bilaspur(Pra.Him)	4	Imphal	8	Pudukkottai
2	Chamba	5	Senapati	9	Ramanathapuram
3	Hamirpur(HP)	6	Tamenglong	10	Sivaganganagar
4	Kangra	7	Thoubal	11	Thanjavur
5	Kinnaur	8	Ukhrul	12	The Nilgiris
6	Kullu		**Meghalaya (7)**	13	Tirunelveli
7	Lahul & Spiti	1	East Garo Hills	14	Tutikorin
8	Mandi	2	Jaintia Hills	15	Virudhunagar
9	Shimla		**Mizoram (3)**		**Tripura**
10	Sirmaur	1	Aizwal	1	West Tripura
11	Solan	2	Lunglei		**Uttar Pradesh (68)**
12	Una		**Nagaland (7)**	1	Chamoli
	Jammu & Kashmir (14)	1	Mokokchung	2	Dehradun
1	Anantanag	2	Tuensang		**West Bengal (18)**
2	Baramula		**Orissa (30)**	1	Darjiling
3	Doda	1	Balasore	2	Kolkata

Note: Given in brackets is the number of total districts in each state/Union Territory.

all districts in Bihar, Madhya Pradesh, Rajasthan and Uttar Pradesh had low median age at marriage. There was not even a single district with *both* girls and boys marrying after completing the preferred age at marriage of 20 years for girls and 23 years for boys in Bihar, Madhya Pradesh, Rajasthan, Dadra & Nagar Haveli, Daman & Diu and Lakshadweep.

An examination of a few available characteristics had revealed that, in general, the median age at marriage of residents of rural areas is lower compared to that in urban areas and that the proportion marrying below legal minimum age at marriage is high in the former than the latter. Similarly the comparatively low median age at marriage was found among those who belong to SC/ST/OBC when compared to the "other caste" category with a comparatively higher proportion of marriages below legal minimum age at marriage for the SC/ST/OBC group. Higher economic status was associated with higher age at marriage. Similarly, in the comparatively high literate districts[1] marriages were mostly after completion of the legal minimum age at marriage.

This study had clearly shown that there is concentration of districts with low age at marriage of boys and girls in the four major states, viz. Bihar, Madhya Pradesh, Rajasthan and Uttar Pradesh.

Since the Government's policy is mainly concerned with the age at marriage of girls, it should be pointed out here that this study found 42 districts with at least one in every four marriages of girls conducted before they completed 15 years of age. These districts are mainly from Bihar, Madhya Pradesh, Rajasthan and Uttar Pradesh (See Table 2.7 for their names). Further, there were 137 of the 504 districts with at least one in every two marriages conducted before the girl reached the legal minimum age at marriage of 18 years. (See Table 2.11 for their names).

Marriages before the boy reached the legal minimum age at marriage of 21 years is not as common as is the case with girls. Boy child marriage formed only 6 per cent of the reported marriages, though there were 24 districts with at least 25 per cent of marriages falling in the child marriage category (See Table 3.7 for their names). Marriages below legal minimum age at marriage formed almost one-third of the total and there were 103 districts with at least 50 per cent of marriages below 21 years of age (See Table 3.11 for their names).

While no marriage of girls were conducted before they attained the legal minimum age at marriage of 18 years in 16 districts, the corresponding number of districts for boys was only 6. (See Tables 2.8 and 3.8 respectively for their names). Besides these, there were 139 districts, forming 27.6 per cent of the total number of districts, which *need not be* a major concern at this point of time for the policy makers/administrators as at least 75 per cent of marriages among girls in these districts were conducted only after they attained 18 years of age (see Table 2.10 for their names). Also note that, of the total reported marriages in each of these districts, at least 50 per cent were preferred marriages. The corresponding number of districts for boys was 235 forming 46.7 per cent of the total number of districts (see Table 3.10 for their names).

This study has also underlined the importance of female education as a variable with 99 per cent of marriages of girls in the highly literate districts having marriages after completion of 18 years. Among these marriages three out of four were after completing the preferred age of 20 years. Similarly, its importance as a development variable is validated with 99 per cent of boys marrying only after completing the legal minimum age at marriage of 21 years and 94 per cent marrying only after they completed the preferred age of 23 years in the highly literate districts.

CONCLUSIONS

This study revealed that the achievement of Indian vision of having the girls married off only after they attain 20 years of age by 2010 is a far cry as two out of three marriages were conducted before the girl completed 20 years of age during the second half of 1990s. In 72 per cent of the total 504 districts, the median age at marriage of girls was also below 20 years. Even attaining a minimum age at marriage of 18 years (the legal minimum age at marriage) for all girls before 2010 is nothing short of wishful thinking.

Considering the diverse problems that face this country in social, economic and demographic front, perhaps age at marriage *per se* may not be seen as a major concern. But the education of girls cannot be ignored as a minor issue nor can the high fertility in some states. All these issues are interrelated and call for an integrated approach. Educated women tend to desire smaller family size and strive to achieve their desire. They have higher aspirations for their children. Other things remaining equal, they can get jobs and reduce their economic dependence on sons whereby reduce son preference to a certain extent. *Education will postpone age at marriage* and girls will be mentally and physically mature to have children of their own and to bring them up properly.

India has been trying very hard to bring down the fertility level ever since she became independent by promoting family planning and providing contraceptives to suit one and all. Her efforts have paid off as the total fertility rate has declined from 6 in 1971 to 3.4 in 1996. India being a big country with varying cultures, economic and social situation, the fertility level also varies from region to region. The TFR of Bihar (4.5), Madhya Pradesh (4.1), Rajasthan (4.2) and Uttar Pradesh (4.9) is a major concern. This study has shown that most of the districts in these states have a median below the legally acceptable age at marriage.

Further, past fertility levels have already created a rapid population growth momentum. As reducing the number of youths who have already entered the reproductive age is not desirable, the alternative is to postpone child bearing. In India child bearing out side wedlock is not appreciated and hence postponing the births and thereby reducing the duration of effective child bearing period can be achieved by postponing the marriage itself. As has already been pointed out at the outset of this study such a postponement will have many advantages to the mother, the child and the society at large. Moreover such a reduction in fertility will help to slow down the population momentum in future.

Thus, age at marriage is a very important factor that can play a vital role in raising the status of women, in reducing the fertility, in having healthy mother and children and in improving the inter-spouse communication and understanding. Creating laws and regulations, though by itself is very important, is not sufficient in raising the age at marriage. Further, having a vision puts forth the focus on line but moving towards its achievement needs strength and fortitude; a positive attitude and belief in its necessity. The Government cannot shy away from its responsibility of going beyond creating laws and regulations and has to accept the truth that India is way behind the goal she has set for herself in the filed of raising the age at marriage of girls and boys.

Though from another study, it has also been shown that even the correct knowledge of the legal minimum age at marriage is lacking in a vast majority of women in this country. As for the knowledge of men in this aspect, nothing is known so far directly, as no data were collected from them by any survey. If the actual age at marriage of boys and girls is any indication to the extent of their knowledge (as they are the decision makers in almost all families in India) it gives the impression that they too are fairly ignorant of the existence/provisions of the minimum age at marriage legislation.

Hence as a first step to raise the age at marriage, the Government should launch an awareness programme of the legal minimum age at marriage for the girls and boys and this should be directed not only to the women of the households but also to the men. Furthermore, efforts should be made to effectively implement the existing law relating to age at marriage so that the vision can be achieved sooner than later. Besides, it is of immense importance to impart knowledge about the distressing consequences of early age at marriage. The media can play a major role in this. To-day, one or the other mass media (radio, television, news papers or magazines) reach into almost every nook and corner of this country. They can carry essential messages like the importance of educating girls, the unwelcome consequences of early marriage like the denial of education, easy and increased subjugation of women. It should call attention to the fact that the girl's body or mind is not ready to take up the difficulties of bearing and rearing children and that pregnancy related deaths resulting mostly from obstructed labour, infection, hemmorrahage and abortion are the major causes of deaths among very young mothers. Having said all these, it should also be pointed out that the Government will be up against the deep rooted cultural and social values and norms and therefore, need careful handling of the subject under discussion.

NOTE

1. It is generally observed in India that boys are better educated than girls and as such high female literacy rate implies high male literacy rate as well.

REFERENCES

Agarwala, S.N. (1966), "Raising the Age at Marriage for Women-A Means to Lower the Birth Rate", *Economic and Political Weekly*, December 24.

Audinarayana, N. (1990), *Socio-cultural Dimensions of Marriage in Rural India,* Mittal Publications, New Delhi.

Bartz, K.W. and F.I. Nye (1970), "Early Marriage: A Propositional Formulation", Journal of Marriage and the Family, Vol. 32, pp. 258-268.

Bhagat, R.B. (2002), *Early Marriages in India: A Socio-geographical Study,* Rajat Publications, New Delhi.

Call, V.R.A and L.B. Otto (1977) "Age at Marriage as a Mobility Contingency: Estimates for the Nye-Berardo Model", *Journal of Marriage and the Family,* Vol. 39, pp. 67-79.

Coale, Ansley, J. (1965), "Factors Associated with the Development of Low Fertility: An historic Summary, Proceedings of the World Population Conference, Vol. 2, pp.

Coale, Ansley, J. (1973), *The Demographic Transition,* International Population Conference, Liege, 1973, Vol. I , pp. 53-72, Leige, IUSSP.

Davis, Kingsley and Judith Blake (1956), "Social Structure and Fertility: An Analytic Framework", *Economic Development and Cultural Change,* Vol. 4, April 1956 pp. 211-235.

Davis, Kingsley, (1973), *Human Society,* The Macmillan Company, New York.

Driver (1963), Education, Manpower and Development in South and Southeast Asia, Praeger Publishers, New York.

Freedman, Ronald (1979), "Theories of Fertility Decline: A Reappraisal", in P.M. Hauser, (ed.) World Population and Development, Syracuse, New York, Syracuse University Press.

French, Joan (2001), Quoted in UNICEF calls for Global Campaign to end Child Marriages, 9-3-2001.

Government of India (2000), *National Population Policy 2000*, New Delhi.

Goyal, R.P. (1964), "Birth Rate can be Reduced by a Third by late Marriage", *Yojana,* August, 30.

IIPS (International Institute for Population Sciences) (1995), *National Family Health Survey (MCH and Family Planning), India, 1992-93*. Bombay: IIPS.

IIPS (International Institute for Population Sciences) and ORC Macro (2000), *National Family Health Survey (NFHS-2), 1998-99: India.* Mumabi: IIPS.

IIPS (International Institute for Population Sciences) (2001), Reproductive and Child Health Project, Rapid Household Survey (Phase I & II), India, 1998-1999, Mumbai, IIPS.

Malhotra, Anju (1997), "Gender and the Timing of Marriage: Rural-Urban Differences in Java", Journal of Marriage and the Family, Vol. 59, pp. 434-450.

Malthus, Thomas Robert (1798), *An Essay on the Principle of Population*, Sixth Edition, John Murray, London, 1826.

McDonald, Peter F. (1981), "Social Change and Age at Marriage", *Proceedings of the International Population Conference*, Manila.

Population Reports (1979), *Age at Marriage and Fertility*, Series M, Number 4, Special Topic Monograph, Population Information Program, The Johns Hopkins University, Baltimore.

Radha Devi (1984), "Age at Marriage of Working and Non-working Women in Trivandrum District", *Bulletin of Gandhigram Institute of Rural Health and Family Welfare Trust*, 19 (3): 5-14.

Reddy, Krishna, (1998), *Marriage, Population and Society: Demographic Perspective of a Social Institution*, Kanishka Publishers, Distributors, New Delhi-110002.

Singh, R.P. and J. Richard (1989), "Socio-Economic and Demographic Correlates of Age at Marriage, *Demography India*, Vol. 18, 183-190.

Van de Valle, Etienne (1972), "Marriage and Marital Fertility" in D.V. Glass and Roger Revelle (eds.) *Population and Social Change*, Edward Arnold.

Westoff, Charles, F. and Norman B. Ryder (1977), *The Contraceptive Revolution*, Princeton, Princeton University Press.

APPENDIX - I

Percentage Distribution of Marriages by Category of Marriage, Average Age at Marriage and per cent Marrying before Attaining Age 18 in each District-GIRLS

Sr. No.	State/district	Category of marriage (percentages add to 100)				Total marri-ages	Average age at marraige		Percent of marri-ages <18 years
		CM	EM	AM	PM	#	Mean	Median	
1	**Andhra Pradesh**								
1.	Adilabad	7.9	40.4	36.0	15.7	89	17.4	18.0	48.3
2.	Anantapur	7.0	26.8	40.8	25.4	71	18.3	18.0	33.8
3.	Chittoor	6.5	16.1	22.6	54.8	31	19.9	20.0	22.6
4.	Cuddapah	6.8	26.2	40.8	26.2	103	18.2	18.0	33.0
5.	East Godavari	5.5	38.4	35.6	20.5	73	17.7	18.0	43.8
6.	Guntur	6.5	28.3	32.6	32.6	46	19.0	18.0	34.8
7.	Hyderabad	0.0	6.4	35.9	57.7	78	20.5	20.0	6.4
8.	Karimnagar	12.8	29.8	31.9	25.5	47	17.7	18.0	42.6
9.	Khammam	10.9	21.8	47.3	20.0	55	17.9	18.0	32.7
10.	Krishna	5.3	21.1	40.4	33.3	57	18.5	18.0	26.3
11.	Kurnool	9.3	29.1	37.2	24.4	86	18.1	18.0	38.4
12.	Mahbubnagar	14.5	26.1	37.7	21.7	69	17.7	18.0	40.6
13.	Medak	6.1	28.6	44.9	20.4	49	18.1	18.0	34.7
14.	Nalgonda	6.6	35.5	32.9	25.0	76	17.9	18.0	42.1
15.	Nellore	3.1	21.9	35.9	39.1	64	19.0	19.0	25.0
16.	Nizamabad	11.1	33.3	28.6	27.0	63	17.8	18.0	44.4
17.	Prakasam	9.4	31.3	34.4	25.0	64	18.2	18.0	40.6
18.	Rangareddi	7.7	29.7	30.8	31.9	91	18.7	18.0	37.4
19.	Srikakulam	6.6	42.5	36.8	14.2	106	17.4	18.0	49.1
20.	Vishkhapatanam	16.7	36.1	19.4	27.8	36	17.6	17.0	52.8
21.	Vizianagaram	13.1	27.4	32.1	27.4	84	17.9	18.0	40.5
22.	Warangal	12.5	35.9	29.7	21.9	64	17.7	18.0	48.4
23.	West Godavari	3.7	25.9	42.6	27.8	108	18.2	18.0	29.6
2	**Assam**								
1.	Barpeta	0.0	18.4	32.7	49.0	49	19.8	19.0	18.4
2.	Bongaigaon	9.5	31.1	20.9	38.5	148	19.3	18.0	40.5
3.	Cachar	3.0	17.2	24.2	55.6	99	20.4	20.0	20.2
4.	Darrang	12.3	21.1	21.1	45.6	57	18.9	19.0	33.3
5.	Dhemaji	0.0	3.9	37.3	58.8	51	20.3	20.0	3.9
6.	Dhubri	9.1	50.0	24.5	16.4	110	17.6	17.0	59.1
7.	Dibrugarh	0.0	23.3	36.7	40.0	30	20.7	19.0	23.3
8.	Goalpara	10.1	31.3	20.2	38.4	99	18.9	18.0	41.4
9.	Golaghat	3.3	26.1	23.9	46.7	92	19.5	19.0	29.3
10.	Hailakandi	1.4	6.9	33.1	58.6	145	21.5	20.0	8.3
11.	Jorhat	0.0	7.7	17.3	75.0	52	21.2	21.0	7.7
12.	Kamrup	2.2	17.2	20.4	60.2	93	20.8	21.0	19.4
13.	Karbi Anglong	0.0	4.8	50.8	44.4	63	19.7	19.0	4.8
14.	Karimganj	5.3	18.1	20.2	56.4	94	21.4	20.0	23.4
15.	Lakhimpur	4.0	32.0	20.0	44.0	25	19.6	18.0	36.0

Appendix - I (Continued)

Sr. No.	State/district	Category of marriage (percentages add to 100)				Total marriages	Average age at marraige		Percent of marriages <18 years
		CM	EM	AM	PM	#	Mean	Median	
16.	Marigaon	2.4	31.2	28.0	38.4	125	19.0	19.0	33.6
17.	Nagaon	7.3	33.6	15.5	43.6	110	18.8	18.0	40.9
18.	Nalbari	1.6	3.2	22.2	73.0	63	21.6	22.0	4.8
19.	North Cachar Hills	0.0	7.7	27.7	64.6	65	20.6	20.0	7.7
20.	Sibsagar	12.5	0.0	16.7	70.8	24	21.9	20.5	12.5
21.	Sonitpur	3.4	27.1	33.9	35.6	59	19.3	18.0	30.5
22.	Tinsukia	0.0	24.4	26.8	48.8	82	20.1	19.0	24.4
3	**Bihar**								
1.	Araria	8.3	43.2	27.3	21.2	132	17.5	17.0	51.5
2.	Aurangabad(Bih)	17.9	45.7	23.9	12.5	184	16.6	17.0	63.6
3.	Begusarai	15.0	43.7	27.5	13.8	167	16.7	17.0	58.7
4.	Bhagalpur	20.9	38.0	27.8	13.3	158	16.8	17.0	58.9
5.	Bhojpur	21.0	35.8	25.3	17.9	162	16.6	17.0	56.8
6.	Buxar	16.7	48.6	24.3	10.5	210	16.6	16.0	65.2
7.	Darbhanga	10.9	40.4	30.6	18.0	183	17.5	17.0	51.4
8.	Deoghar	35.2	31.3	21.1	12.5	128	16.0	16.0	66.4
9.	Dhanbad	8.2	34.1	35.3	22.4	85	18.0	18.0	42.4
10.	Dumka	8.6	40.5	31.9	19.0	116	17.5	18.0	49.1
11.	Gaya	31.4	30.2	25.0	13.4	172	16.2	16.0	61.6
12.	Giridih	16.8	42.0	25.2	16.0	119	16.9	17.0	58.8
13.	Godda	12.1	54.3	20.7	12.9	116	16.7	16.0	66.4
14.	Gopalganj	12.3	46.1	26.0	15.6	154	17.1	17.0	58.4
15.	Gulma	5.2	22.1	31.2	41.6	77	18.8	19.0	27.3
16.	Hazaribagh	21.7	45.0	20.2	13.2	129	16.4	16.0	66.7
17.	Jehanabad	19.5	34.9	28.2	17.4	195	16.9	17.0	54.4
18.	Katihar	8.5	39.3	27.4	24.8	117	17.5	18.0	47.9
19.	Khagaria	23.8	40.1	23.8	12.2	172	16.6	16.0	64.0
20.	Kishanganj	12.6	35.6	19.5	32.2	87	17.9	18.0	48.3
21.	Lohardaga	10.6	32.7	24.0	32.7	104	18.2	18.0	43.3
22.	Madhepura	17.8	48.6	22.6	11.0	146	16.4	16.0	66.4
23.	Madhubani	15.3	48.6	27.8	8.3	144	16.5	17.0	63.9
24.	Munger	24.4	36.2	26.8	12.6	127	16.4	16.0	60.6
25.	Muzaffarpur	13.3	39.9	24.3	22.5	173	17.5	17.0	53.2
26.	Nalanda	22.4	36.4	27.3	13.9	165	16.5	16.0	58.8
27.	Nawada	32.9	39.4	16.4	11.3	213	15.8	16.0	72.3
28.	Palamu	29.1	36.9	16.5	17.5	103	16.4	16.0	66.0
29.	Pashchim Champaran	9.1	31.7	32.9	26.2	164	18.0	18.0	40.9
30.	Pashchmi Singhbhum	3.6	25.0	45.2	26.2	84	18.9	18.0	28.6
31.	Patna	36.5	42.9	15.4	5.1	156	15.5	15.0	79.5
32.	Purba Champaran	22.8	40.2	17.4	19.6	184	16.8	16.0	63.0
33.	Purbi Singhbhum	6.6	26.4	23.6	43.4	106	19.5	19.0	33.0
34.	Purnia	10.6	37.7	23.8	27.8	151	18.1	18.0	48.3
35.	Ranchi	1.2	37.8	32.9	28.0	82	18.3	18.0	39.0
36.	Rohtas	25.0	43.9	18.2	12.9	132	16.4	16.0	68.9
37.	Saharsa	11.8	44.7	27.6	15.8	152	17.3	17.0	56.6
38.	Sahibganj	12.0	50.6	22.9	14.5	83	16.6	16.0	62.7
39.	Samastipur	30.8	33.3	23.3	12.6	159	16.2	16.0	64.2
40.	Saran	7.5	43.9	33.7	15.0	187	17.2	17.0	51.3

Appendix - I (Continued)

Sr. No.	State/district	Category of marriage (percentages add to 100)				Total marriages	Average age at marraige		Percent of marriages <18 years
		CM	EM	AM	PM	#	Mean	Median	
41.	Sitamarhi	20.3	44.4	21.6	13.7	153	16.5	16.0	64.7
42.	Siwan	9.3	34.3	28.5	27.9	172	17.8	18.0	43.6
43.	Vaishali	18.9	44.5	20.1	16.5	164	16.5	16.0	63.4
4	**Gujarat**								
1.	Ahmadabad	9.0	18.0	17.0	56.0	100	20.1	20.0	27.0
2.	Amreli	0.0	17.0	36.4	46.6	176	19.6	19.0	17.0
3.	Banas Kantha	18.1	33.9	26.0	22.0	127	17.2	17.0	52.0
4.	Bharuch	1.7	16.5	30.4	51.3	115	19.7	20.0	18.3
5.	Bhavnagar	4.6	23.7	37.5	34.2	152	18.6	18.0	28.3
6.	Gandhinagar	15.5	17.9	22.6	44.0	84	18.6	18.5	33.3
7.	Jamnagar	0.0	10.7	32.1	57.3	131	20.1	20.0	10.7
8.	Junagadh	0.6	11.1	30.9	57.4	162	20.2	20.0	11.7
9.	Kachchh	2.9	21.0	32.4	43.8	105	19.4	19.0	23.8
10.	Kheda	12.0	20.0	30.0	38.0	150	19.0	18.0	32.0
11.	Mahesana	9.0	23.9	29.1	38.1	134	18.6	18.5	32.8
12.	Panch Mahals	4.8	21.7	44.6	28.9	83	18.6	18.0	26.5
13.	Rajkot	1.4	12.5	25.7	60.4	144	19.8	20.0	13.9
14.	Sabar Kantha	2.3	28.2	35.1	34.4	131	18.7	19.0	30.5
15.	Surat	2.0	16.8	27.7	53.5	101	19.7	20.0	18.8
16.	Surendranagar	0.0	9.8	38.2	52.0	102	20.0	20.0	9.8
17.	The Dangs	7.6	39.7	37.4	15.3	131	17.6	18.0	47.3
18.	Vadodara	1.0	32.7	28.7	37.6	101	18.9	18.0	33.7
19.	Valsad	4.2	5.8	28.3	61.7	120	20.8	20.0	10.0
5	**Haryana**								
1.	Ambala	0.9	12.0	25.0	62.0	108	20.4	20.0	13.0
2.	Bhiwani	11.3	37.6	36.9	14.2	141	17.2	18.0	48.9
3.	Faridabad	2.2	28.1	36.7	33.1	139	18.8	18.0	30.2
4.	Gurgaon	7.7	28.8	34.6	28.8	104	17.9	18.0	36.5
5.	Hisar	4.3	38.5	41.0	16.2	117	17.5	18.0	42.7
6.	Jind	4.7	32.0	39.8	23.4	128	18.0	18.0	36.7
7.	Kaithal	7.6	25.3	41.8	25.3	79	18.3	18.0	32.9
8.	Karnal	1.4	14.9	35.1	48.6	148	19.5	19.0	16.2
9.	Kurukshetra	0.0	14.6	29.3	56.1	123	20.0	20.0	14.6
10.	Mahendragarh	12.6	33.7	32.6	21.1	175	17.6	18.0	46.3
11.	Panchkula	0.0	25.6	35.9	38.5	78	19.0	18.0	25.6
12.	Panipat	7.0	38.3	34.4	20.3	128	17.7	18.0	45.3
13.	Rewari	4.0	24.8	38.4	32.8	125	18.5	18.0	28.8
14.	Rohtak	4.3	29.8	35.5	30.5	141	18.7	18.0	34.0
15.	Sirsa	1.9	29.6	38.0	30.6	108	18.7	18.0	31.5
16.	Sonipat	0.8	5.5	28.9	64.8	128	20.5	20.0	6.3
17.	Yamunanagar	0.7	6.0	32.1	61.2	134	20.8	20.0	6.7
6	**Karnataka**								
1.	Bangalore	0.0	12.0	22.9	65.1	83	20.9	21.0	12.0
2.	Bangalore Rural	2.8	18.7	52.3	26.2	107	18.9	18.0	21.5
3.	Belgaum	16.0	39.5	21.8	22.7	119	17.4	17.0	55.5
4.	Bellary	11.5	32.8	26.0	29.8	131	18.5	18.0	44.3
5.	Bidar	31.3	36.4	18.2	14.2	176	16.3	16.0	67.6
6.	Bijapur	28.6	35.7	21.4	14.3	126	16.4	16.0	64.3
7.	Chikmagalur	3.4	10.2	32.0	54.4	147	20.5	20.0	13.6

Appendix - I (Continued)

Sr. No.	State/district	Category of marriage (percentages add to 100)				Total marri-ages	Average age at marraige		Percent of marri-ages <18 years
		CM	EM	AM	PM	#	Mean	Median	
8.	Chitradurga	6.8	23.7	35.6	33.9	118	18.6	18.0	30.5
9.	Dakshina Kannada	0.0	4.6	17.6	77.9	131	22.2	22.0	4.6
10.	Dharwad	8.7	27.8	20.0	43.5	115	19.5	19.0	36.5
11.	Gulbarga	20.4	27.4	22.1	30.1	113	17.7	18.0	47.8
12.	Hassan	0.8	14.5	38.2	46.6	131	19.9	19.0	15.3
13.	Kodagu	1.2	20.9	25.6	52.3	86	20.0	20.0	22.1
14.	Kolar	6.4	27.1	35.7	30.7	140	18.6	18.0	33.6
15.	Mandya	7.5	29.9	35.5	27.1	107	18.3	18.0	37.4
16.	Mysore	13.3	34.7	27.6	24.5	98	17.9	18.0	48.0
17.	Raichur	19.6	37.5	17.0	25.9	112	17.5	17.0	57.1
18.	Shimoga	1.2	15.3	21.5	62.0	163	20.6	20.0	16.6
19.	Tumkur	7.0	20.2	36.0	36.8	114	18.9	18.0	27.2
20.	Uttara Kannada	1.5	13.5	17.3	67.7	133	21.5	21.0	15.0
7	**Kerala**								
1.	Alappuzha	0.0	0.0	18.6	81.4	161	23.0	22.0	0.0
2.	Ernakulam	0.0	0.0	6.7	93.3	149	23.7	23.0	0.0
3.	Idukki	0.0	1.5	13.1	85.4	130	23.1	23.0	1.5
4.	Kannur	0.0	19.0	26.3	54.7	179	20.8	20.0	19.0
5.	Kasaragod	0.0	18.2	26.6	55.2	154	20.7	20.0	18.2
6.	Kollam	0.0	0.0	21.2	78.8	170	22.3	22.0	0.0
7.	Kottayam	0.0	0.0	4.9	95.1	163	24.4	24.0	0.0
8.	Kozhikode	0.0	13.6	34.7	51.7	147	20.7	20.0	13.6
9.	Malappuram	0.0	35.7	38.8	25.5	196	18.7	18.0	35.7
10.	Palakkad	0.0	10.4	34.1	55.5	164	21.0	20.0	10.4
11.	Pathanamthitta	0.0	0.0	10.4	89.6	115	23.3	23.0	0.0
12.	Thiruvananthapuram	0.0	0.0	20.0	80.0	135	22.8	23.0	0.0
13.	Thrissur	0.0	0.7	25.9	73.5	147	22.4	22.0	0.7
14.	Wayanad	0.0	7.1	36.2	56.7	141	20.8	20.0	7.1
8	**Madhya Pradesh**								
1.	Balaghat	2.9	29.4	52.9	14.7	34	18.2	19.0	32.4
2.	Bastar	3.6	30.4	33.9	32.1	56	18.6	18.0	33.9
3.	Betul	2.2	22.2	55.6	20.0	45	18.3	18.0	24.4
4.	Bhind	11.6	49.7	25.2	13.5	155	16.9	17.0	61.3
5.	Bhopal	10.1	18.8	36.2	34.8	69	19.1	18.0	29.0
6.	Bilaspur(MP)	8.4	31.9	30.3	29.4	119	18.2	18.0	40.3
7.	Chattarpur	25.0	48.1	15.4	11.5	52	16.6	16.0	73.1
8.	Chhindwara	2.4	28.5	43.1	26.0	123	18.4	18.0	30.9
9.	Damoh	11.6	43.2	27.4	17.9	95	17.3	17.0	54.7
10.	Datia	7.7	41.3	33.7	17.3	104	17.4	18.0	49.0
11.	Dewas	18.2	34.5	30.9	16.4	110	17.1	17.0	52.7
12.	Dhar	12.3	44.3	29.5	13.9	122	16.9	16.0	56.6
13.	Durg	2.9	29.0	31.9	36.2	69	19.0	19.0	31.9
14.	East Nimar	6.9	35.3	27.6	30.2	116	18.2	18.0	42.2
15.	Guna	17.4	51.4	13.8	17.4	109	16.9	16.0	68.8
16.	Gwalior	3.8	32.1	31.1	33.0	106	19.0	18.0	35.8
17.	Hoshangabad	5.8	34.6	30.8	28.8	52	17.9	18.0	40.4
18.	Indore	12.4	29.8	25.6	32.2	121	18.3	18.0	42.1
19.	Jabalpur	10.8	27.7	33.7	27.7	83	18.3	18.0	38.6
20.	Jhabua	13.2	45.3	22.6	18.9	106	17.2	17.0	58.5
21.	Mandla	2.5	35.0	50.0	12.5	40	17.6	18.0	37.5

Appendix - I (Continued)

Sr. No.	State/district	Category of marriage (percentages add to 100)				Total marriages	Average age at marraige		Percent of marriages <18 years
		CM	EM	AM	PM	#	Mean	Median	
22	Mandsaur	22.0	35.4	21.3	21.3	127	16.9	16.0	57.5
23.	Morena	22.9	48.2	19.3	9.6	83	16.1	16.0	71.1
24.	Narsimhapur	6.2	43.2	22.2	28.4	81	18.2	18.0	49.4
25.	Panna	16.3	40.8	24.5	18.4	49	17.0	16.0	57.1
26.	Raigarh(M P)	1.9	5.8	61.5	30.8	52	19.3	19.0	7.7
27.	Raipur	5.4	50.0	26.8	17.9	56	17.5	17.0	55.4
28.	Raisen	7.8	39.8	35.2	17.2	128	17.4	18.0	47.7
29.	Rajgarh	29.6	35.2	18.4	16.8	125	16.4	16.0	64.8
30.	Rajnandgaon	19.8	30.2	27.4	22.6	106	17.3	17.5	50.0
31.	Ratlam	25.3	20.5	27.7	26.5	83	17.3	18.0	45.8
32.	Rewa	19.5	40.7	29.3	10.6	123	16.5	16.0	60.2
33.	Sagar	23.2	36.8	14.7	25.3	95	17.0	17.0	60.0
34.	Satna	19.2	40.8	30.0	10.0	120	16.7	16.5	60.0
35.	Sehore	13.6	34.7	24.6	27.1	118	17.6	18.0	48.3
36.	Seoni	7.0	29.6	35.2	28.2	71	18.0	18.0	36.6
37.	Shahdol	25.6	41.0	20.5	12.8	39	16.4	16.0	66.7
38.	Shajapur	42.2	40.2	9.8	7.8	102	15.2	15.0	82.4
39.	Shivpuri	18.0	50.0	23.0	9.0	100	16.3	16.0	68.0
40.	Sidhi	33.7	33.7	23.3	9.3	86	15.7	16.0	67.4
41.	Surguja	19.7	36.8	27.6	15.8	76	16.7	17.0	56.6
42.	Tikamgarh	29.8	39.7	19.0	11.6	121	16.0	16.0	69.4
43.	Ujjain	19.7	19.7	31.1	29.5	132	17.9	18.0	39.4
44.	Vidisha	23.2	36.8	23.2	16.8	125	17.0	17.0	60.0
45.	West Nimar	12.7	29.4	40.2	17.6	102	17.6	18.0	42.2
9	**Maharashtra**								
1.	Ahmadnagar	12.8	28.0	40.0	19.2	125	17.6	18.0	40.8
2.	Akola	4.1	34.1	43.1	18.7	123	18.2	18.0	38.2
3.	Amravali	0.0	9.0	47.0	44.0	134	19.6	19.0	9.0
4.	Aurangabad(Mah)	10.8	39.2	37.8	12.2	148	17.2	17.5	50.0
5.	Bhandara	0.0	9.3	38.0	52.7	129	20.0	20.0	9.3
6.	Bid	13.8	45.0	28.4	12.8	109	16.9	17.0	58.7
7.	Buldana	2.1	31.4	40.7	25.7	140	18.4	18.0	33.6
8.	Chandrapur	2.0	23.8	38.6	35.6	101	18.8	18.0	25.7
9.	Dhule	6.7	33.3	38.1	21.9	105	18.2	18.0	40.0
10.	Gadchiroli	1.5	25.4	49.3	23.9	67	18.5	18.0	26.9
11.	Greater Bombay (Mumbai)	**	8.0	31.0	60.9	87	21.2	21.0	8.0
12.	Jalgaon	4.7	40.9	34.9	19.5	149	18.0	18.0	45.6
13.	Jalna	14.4	40.9	30.3	14.4	132	17.1	17.0	55.3
14.	Kolhapur	3.3	13.9	53.3	29.5	122	19.0	18.0	17.2
15.	Latur	14.9	43.3	23.4	18.4	141	17.2	17.0	58.2
16.	Nagpur	2.6	8.7	40.0	48.7	115	20.1	19.0	11.3
17.	Nanded	23.6	39.6	20.8	16.0	144	16.7	16.0	63.2
18.	Nashik	3.8	27.5	40.0	28.8	80	18.5	18.0	31.3
19.	Osmanabad	14.5	32.1	38.9	14.5	131	17.4	18.0	46.6
20.	Parbhani	13.5	33.1	36.1	17.3	133	17.5	18.0	46.6
21.	Pune	3.5	27.0	41.7	27.8	115	18.5	18.0	30.4
22.	Raigarh(MAH)	0.0	16.3	47.7	36.0	86	19.0	18.0	16.3
23.	Ratnagiri	0.8	12.2	42.3	44.7	123	19.9	19.0	13.0
24.	Sangli	2.4	23.2	45.6	28.8	125	18.6	18.0	25.6

Appendix - I (Continued)

Sr. No.	State/district	Category of marriage (percentages add to 100)				Total marri-ages	Average age at marraige		Percent of marri-ages <18 years
		CM	EM	AM	PM	#	Mean	Median	
25.	Satara	3.5	18.4	51.8	26.3	114	18.5	18.0	21.9
26.	Sindhudurg	0.0	3.9	24.5	71.6	102	21.5	21.0	3.9
27.	Solapur	9.0	32.8	30.3	27.9	122	18.2	18.0	41.8
28	Thane	1.2	18.5	37.0	43.2	81	19.8	19.0	19.8
29	Wardha	0.0	12.4	38.1	49.5	105	20.2	19.0	12.4
30	Yavatmal	2.6	24.0	47.4	26.0	154	18.4	18.0	26.6
10	**Orissa**								
1.	Anugul	2.7	37.3	20.9	39.1	110	18.8	18.0	40.0
2.	Balangir	2.8	54.9	18.3	23.9	71	18.3	17.0	57.7
3.	Balasore	1.4	27.1	20.1	51.4	144	19.8	20.0	28.5
4.	Bargarh	3.1	36.7	32.7	27.6	98	18.3	18.0	39.8
5.	Baudh	6.8	43.8	32.9	16.4	73	17.5	17.0	50.7
6.	Bhadrak	0.6	15.1	20.8	63.5	159	21.1	21.0	15.7
7.	Cuttack	0.0	10.6	24.2	65.2	132	20.9	20.0	10.6
8.	Debagarh	2.8	30.6	26.4	40.3	72	19.1	18.5	33.3
9.	Dhenkanal	5.3	31.3	19.8	43.5	131	19.0	19.0	36.6
10.	Gajapati	5.4	36.5	27.0	31.1	74	17.9	18.0	41.9
11.	Ganjam	8.2	42.5	27.6	21.6	134	17.9	17.0	50.7
12.	Jagatsinghapur	0.7	8.6	11.4	79.3	140	21.8	22.0	9.3
13.	Jajapur	0.7	14.1	19.0	66.2	142	20.7	21.0	14.8
14.	Jharsuguda	0.0	16.7	38.9	44.4	72	19.6	19.0	16.7
15.	Kalahandi	14.5	44.9	23.2	17.4	69	17.2	17.0	59.4
16.	Kendrapara	1.3	14.6	24.1	60.1	158	20.9	21.0	15.8
17.	Kendujhar	5.8	24.3	23.3	46.6	103	19.5	19.0	30.1
18.	Khordha	2.6	20.2	21.9	55.3	114	20.1	20.0	22.8
19.	Koraput	17.6	47.1	17.6	17.6	68	17.2	16.0	64.7
20.	Malkangiri	22.0	34.0	24.0	20.0	50	17.0	17.0	56.0
21.	Mayurbhanj	3.2	29.5	28.4	38.9	95	19.3	18.0	32.6
22.	Nabarangapur	28.3	41.3	10.9	19.6	46	16.8	16.0	69.6
23.	Nayagarh	5.7	47.9	25.7	20.7	140	17.8	17.0	53.6
24.	Nuapada	4.3	38.3	29.8	27.7	47	18.2	18.0	42.6
25.	Phulbani	11.7	30.0	36.7	21.7	60	17.7	18.0	41.7
26.	Puri	0.9	13.1	22.4	63.6	107	20.8	21.0	14.0
27.	Rayagada	2.9	35.7	25.7	35.7	70	18.6	18.0	38.6
28.	Sambalpur	0.0	29.3	31.0	39.7	58	19.3	19.0	29.3
29.	Sonapur	1.9	37.4	30.8	29.9	107	18.6	18.0	39.3
30.	Sundargarh	4.3	10.9	45.7	39.1	46	20.3	19.0	15.2
11	**Punjab**								
1.	Amritsar	0.9	10.3	31.6	57.3	117	20.1	20.0	11.1
2.	Bathinda	2.6	10.3	32.5	54.7	117	19.7	20.0	12.8
3.	Faridkot	1.6	11.0	28.3	59.1	127	20.1	20.0	12.6
4.	Fatehgarh Sahib	1.2	5.6	33.5	59.6	161	20.3	20.0	6.8
5.	Firozpur	2.6	22.4	34.5	40.5	116	19.4	19.0	25.0
6.	Gurdaspur	0.0	6.6	32.2	61.2	121	20.8	20.0	6.6
7.	Hoshiarpur	0.0	3.2	22.2	74.7	158	21.2	21.0	3.2
8.	Jalandhar	0.7	6.7	25.2	67.4	135	20.9	20.0	7.4
9.	Kapurthala	0.0	3.1	21.5	75.4	130	21.5	21.0	3.1
10.	Ludhiana	0.0	8.3	25.6	66.1	121	20.6	20.0	8.3
11.	Mansa	4.4	16.1	27.7	51.8	137	19.6	20.0	20.4
12.	Moga	0.6	12.4	31.8	55.3	170	20.1	20.0	12.9

Appendix - I (Continued)

Sr. No.	State/district	Category of marriage (percentages add to 100)				Total marri-ages	Average age at marraige		Percent of marri-ages <18 years
		CM	EM	AM	PM	#	Mean	Median	
13.	Muktsar	2.6	21.1	23.7	52.6	152	19.5	20.0	23.7
14.	Nawanshahr	0.0	2.1	23.4	74.5	141	21.3	21.0	2.1
15.	Patiala	3.4	6.9	24.1	65.5	87	20.3	20.0	10.3
16.	Rupnagar	0.0	6.0	26.1	67.9	134	21.0	21.0	6.0
17.	Sangrur	2.5	10.8	25.3	61.4	158	20.3	20.0	13.3
12	**Rajasthan**								
1.	Ajmer	25.0	23.0	15.0	37.0	100	17.8	18.0	48.0
2.	Alwar	13.9	38.9	26.4	20.8	144	17.2	17.0	52.8
3.	Banswara	10.4	44.2	35.1	10.4	77	16.9	17.0	54.5
4.	Barmer	16.3	33.7	35.6	14.4	104	16.9	17.5	50.0
5.	Bharatpur	17.3	38.3	25.6	18.8	133	17.1	17.0	55.6
6.	Bhilwara	36.4	34.1	11.4	18.2	132	15.8	15.5	70.5
7.	Bikaner	21.8	41.0	24.4	12.8	78	16.5	16.0	62.8
8.	Bundi	40.0	38.9	15.6	5.6	90	15.1	15.0	78.9
9.	Chittaurgarh	18.6	30.2	27.9	23.3	43	17.2	18.0	48.8
10.	Churu	21.8	46.0	21.8	10.5	124	16.3	17.0	67.7
11.	Dausa	25.2	45.8	20.6	8.4	131	15.9	16.0	71.0
12.	Dhaulpur	13.9	42.6	33.7	9.9	101	16.9	17.0	56.4
13.	Dungarpur	7.3	26.6	37.1	29.0	124	18.1	18.0	33.9
14.	Ganganagar	20.9	27.0	29.6	22.6	115	17.4	18.0	47.8
15.	Hanumangarh	13.2	38.4	30.5	17.9	151	17.2	17.0	51.7
16.	Jaipur	16.9	25.7	31.8	25.7	148	17.9	18.0	42.6
17.	Jaisalmer	13.5	36.5	33.8	16.2	74	17.2	17.5	50.0
18.	Jalor	10.3	35.3	31.6	22.8	136	17.4	18.0	45.6
19.	Jhalawar	38.9	31.0	18.6	11.5	113	15.7	15.0	69.9
20.	Jhunjhunun	14.0	32.9	32.2	21.0	143	17.3	18.0	46.9
21.	Jodhpur	17.5	36.8	15.8	29.8	57	17.8	17.0	54.4
22.	Kota	20.2	40.4	14.9	24.5	94	16.9	16.5	60.6
23.	Nagaur	25.0	41.1	18.8	15.2	112	16.2	16.0	66.1
24.	Pali	11.0	39.0	32.9	17.1	82	17.3	17.5	50.0
25.	Rajsamand	14.9	31.3	29.9	23.9	67	17.4	18.0	46.3
26.	Sawai Madhopur	18.9	30.0	26.7	24.4	90	17.2	18.0	48.9
27.	Sikar	12.6	29.3	31.1	26.9	167	17.7	18.0	41.9
28.	Sirohi	8.0	24.0	36.0	32.0	50	18.3	18.0	32.0
29.	Tonk	36.9	38.5	13.1	11.5	130	15.4	15.0	75.4
30.	Udaipur	26.9	33.7	23.1	16.3	104	16.5	16.0	60.6
13	**Tamil Nadu**								
1.	Chengalpattu	1.1	8.9	36.7	53.3	90	20.2	20.0	10.0
2.	Chennai	0.0	5.6	21.3	73.1	108	21.5	21.0	5.6
3.	Coimbatore	0.0	16.1	20.4	63.4	93	20.9	21.0	16.1
4.	Dharmapuri	3.8	30.0	39.2	26.9	130	18.6	18.0	33.8
5.	Dindigul	1.4	26.1	23.2	49.3	69	19.9	19.0	27.5
6.	Kanniyakumari	0.0	0.0	16.1	83.9	87	23.0	23.0	0.0
7.	Madurai	1.5	24.1	18.8	55.6	133	20.4	20.0	25.6
8.	Namakkal	0.0	12.8	31.4	55.8	86	20.3	20.0	12.8
9.	North Arcot	0.8	20.7	33.1	45.5	121	19.8	19.0	21.5
10.	Periyar	0.0	13.5	33.8	52.7	74	20.7	20.0	13.5
11.	Pudukkottai	0.8	10.2	28.1	60.9	128	20.9	20.0	10.9
12.	Ramanathapuram	0.0	13.4	35.7	50.9	112	20.0	20.0	13.4
13.	Salem	5.5	34.9	26.6	33.0	109	18.8	18.0	40.4

Appendix - I (Continued)

Sr. No.	State/district	Category of marriage (percentages add to 100)				Total marri-ages	Average age at marraige		Percent of marri-ages <18 years
		CM	EM	AM	PM	#	Mean	Median	
14.	Sivaganganagar	0.0	8.0	27.5	64.5	138	21.0	20.0	8.0
15.	South Arcot	3.8	23.8	30.0	42.3	130	19.3	19.0	27.7
16.	Thanjavur	0.0	12.9	24.2	62.9	62	21.1	20.0	12.9
17.	The Nilgiris	0.0	8.8	23.5	67.6	68	21.6	21.0	8.8
18.	Theni	4.7	24.4	29.1	41.9	86	19.2	19.0	29.1
19.	Tiruchirappalli	1.3	22.8	27.8	48.1	79	20.3	19.0	24.1
20.	Tirunelveli	0.0	6.8	28.4	64.8	88	21.4	21.0	6.8
21.	Tiruvanamalai	1.4	23.8	38.5	36.4	143	19.3	19.0	25.2
22.	Tutikorin	0.9	6.3	19.8	73.0	111	21.3	21.0	7.2
23.	Virudhunagar	0.9	12.7	31.8	54.5	110	19.8	20.0	13.6
14	**Uttar Pradesh**								
1.	Agra	3.9	34.4	33.6	28.1	128	18.2	18.0	38.3
2.	Aligarh	5.3	37.3	34.7	22.7	75	17.8	18.0	42.7
3.	Allahabad	11.3	41.1	29.8	17.7	124	17.3	17.0	52.4
4.	Almora	0.0	14.1	47.9	38.0	71	19.4	19.0	14.1
5.	Ambedkarnagar	27.8	41.7	22.6	7.8	115	16.1	16.0	69.6
6.	Azamgarh	24.5	39.6	17.0	18.9	106	16.4	16.0	64.2
7.	Bahraich	43.2	34.7	10.2	11.9	118	15.3	15.0	78.0
8.	Ballia	11.3	42.3	29.9	16.5	97	17.2	17.0	53.6
9.	Banda	33.6	37.3	18.2	10.9	110	15.9	16.0	70.9
10.	Barabanki	22.7	31.1	31.1	15.1	119	16.6	17.0	53.8
11.	Bareilly	7.8	21.9	32.8	37.5	64	18.7	18.0	29.7
12.	Basti	40.2	36.9	15.6	7.4	122	15.3	15.0	77.0
13.	Bhadohi	17.9	50.3	22.9	8.9	179	16.4	16.0	68.2
14.	Bijnor	0.0	15.6	44.0	40.4	109	19.4	19.0	15.6
15.	Budaun	9.7	40.9	30.1	19.4	93	17.5	17.0	50.5
16.	Bulandshahar	1.3	26.0	35.1	37.7	77	18.8	18.0	27.3
17.	Chamoli	2.6	5.3	32.9	59.2	76	20.0	20.0	7.9
18.	Dehradun	1.2	13.1	17.9	67.9	84	20.6	20.0	14.3
19.	Deoria	20.4	36.1	26.9	16.7	108	17.1	17.0	56.5
20.	Etah	8.2	49.3	26.0	16.4	73	17.3	17.0	57.5
21.	Etawah	13.2	31.6	34.2	21.1	114	17.6	18.0	44.7
22.	Faizabad	30.2	32.6	21.7	15.5	129	16.2	16.0	62.8
23.	Farrukhabad	4.5	32.7	44.5	18.2	110	17.8	18.0	37.3
24.	Fatehpur	9.1	37.5	30.1	23.3	176	17.6	18.0	46.6
25.	Firozabad	9.2	42.3	29.6	19.0	142	17.6	17.0	51.4
26.	Ghaziabad	1.7	16.9	39.8	41.5	118	19.4	19.0	18.6
27.	Ghazipur	17.6	43.5	21.4	17.6	131	16.9	17.0	61.1
28.	Gonda	37.8	31.6	17.3	13.3	98	15.4	15.0	69.4
29.	Gorakhpur	21.1	44.7	13.2	21.1	76	16.7	16.0	65.8
30.	Hamirpur(UP)	6.8	42.9	34.0	16.3	147	17.3	18.0	49.7
31.	Hardoi	4.3	40.0	31.4	24.3	70	17.7	18.0	44.3
32.	Hardwar	1.1	11.4	35.2	52.3	88	20.0	20.0	12.5
33.	Hathras	11.4	36.0	31.6	21.1	114	17.9	18.0	47.4
34.	Jalaun	12.4	48.1	32.6	7.0	129	16.8	17.0	60.5
35.	Jaunpur	16.4	39.8	26.9	17.0	171	17.0	17.0	56.1
36.	Jhansi	10.1	32.3	30.3	27.3	99	17.9	18.0	42.4
37.	Kanpur Dehat	6.0	28.6	35.3	30.1	133	18.3	18.0	34.6
38.	Kanpur Nagar	0.0	5.7	30.7	63.6	88	21.0	20.5	5.7
39.	Kheri	8.1	45.6	32.2	14.1	149	17.2	17.0	53.7

Appendix - I (Continued)

Sr. No.	*State/district*	*Category of marriage (percentages add to 100)*				*Total marri-ages*	*Average age at marraige*		*Percent of marri-ages <18 years*
		CM	*EM*	*AM*	*PM*	*#*	*Mean*	*Median*	
40.	Lalitpur	45.2	38.7	9.7	6.5	93	15.2	15.0	83.9
41.	Lucknow	8.2	26.8	24.7	40.2	97	19.0	18.0	35.1
42.	Maharajganj	50.0	31.1	10.8	8.1	74	14.8	14.5	81.1
43.	Mahoba	19.1	46.1	23.5	11.3	115	16.6	16.0	65.2
44.	Mainpuri	7.8	42.2	32.8	17.2	116	17.5	17.5	50.0
45.	Mathura	4.7	37.5	37.5	20.3	64	17.7	18.0	42.2
46.	Mau	8.4	30.1	33.7	27.7	166	18.0	18.0	38.6
47.	Meerut	0.0	14.5	34.8	50.7	69	19.8	20.0	14.5
48.	Mirzapur	20.0	37.2	30.3	12.4	145	16.9	17.0	57.2
49.	Muradabad	2.9	26.7	38.1	32.4	105	18.7	18.0	29.5
50.	Muzaffarnagar	5.1	15.3	37.8	41.8	98	19.4	19.0	20.4
51.	Nainital	1.4	8.2	46.6	43.8	73	19.7	19.0	9.6
52.	Pauri Garhwal	0.0	6.7	51.7	41.6	89	19.5	19.0	6.7
53.	Pilibhit	13.9	41.8	26.6	17.7	79	17.2	17.0	55.7
54.	Pithoragarh	3.6	19.3	44.6	32.5	83	18.9	18.0	22.9
55.	Pratapgarh	13.4	41.8	35.1	9.7	134	16.9	17.0	55.2
56.	Rae Bareli	14.6	29.9	37.5	18.1	144	17.2	18.0	44.4
57.	Rampur	5.2	26.0	53.2	15.6	77	18.0	18.0	31.2
58.	Saharanpur	3.1	15.3	41.8	39.8	98	19.2	19.0	18.4
59.	Shajahanabad	24.7	39.8	24.7	10.8	93	16.3	16.0	64.5
60.	Siddharthnagar	43.1	22.5	21.6	12.7	102	15.3	15.0	65.7
61.	Sitapur	21.5	42.1	19.6	16.8	107	16.7	16.0	63.6
62.	Sonbhadra	26.8	39.0	25.6	8.5	82	16.0	16.0	65.9
63.	Sultanpur	25.2	38.7	25.2	10.8	111	16.1	16.0	64.0
64.	Tehri Garhwal	0.0	13.1	54.8	32.1	84	18.9	19.0	13.1
65.	Udhamsingh Nagar	4.3	23.9	34.8	37.0	92	18.8	18.0	28.3
66.	Unnao	7.8	37.9	32.0	22.3	103	17.7	18.0	45.6
67.	Uttarkashi	0.0	17.1	42.9	40.0	70	19.4	19.0	17.1
68.	Varanasi	31.6	40.1	17.8	10.5	152	16.2	16.0	71.7
15	**West Bengal**								
1.	Bankura	18.0	32.0	23.3	26.7	150	17.9	17.5	50.0
2.	Barddhaman	18.5	36.3	18.5	26.8	157	17.8	17.0	54.8
3.	Birbhum	20.5	38.6	20.5	20.5	127	17.0	16.0	59.1
4.	Dakshin Dinajpur	21.9	43.7	20.5	13.9	151	16.7	16.0	65.6
5.	Darjiling	1.0	24.0	25.0	50.0	104	20.1	19.5	25.0
6.	Haora	5.5	32.3	19.7	42.5	127	19.2	18.0	37.8
7.	Hugli	4.4	29.2	27.4	38.9	113	19.6	19.0	33.6
8.	Jalpaiguri	10.0	25.5	22.7	41.8	110	19.3	18.0	35.5
9.	Koch Bihar	17.1	35.0	26.4	21.4	140	17.8	17.0	52.1
10.	Kolkata	1.1	17.6	28.6	52.7	91	20.6	20.0	18.7
11.	Maldah	18.6	38.1	27.8	15.5	97	17.1	17.0	56.7
12.	Medinipur	9.6	30.4	30.4	29.6	125	18.7	18.0	40.0
13.	Murshidabad	31.6	47.5	13.3	7.6	158	16.0	16.0	79.1
14.	Nadia	5.0	36.6	32.7	25.7	101	18.6	18.0	41.6
15.	North 24 Parganas	11.0	37.0	26.0	26.0	100	18.2	18.0	48.0
16.	Puruliya	30.5	44.0	12.1	13.5	141	16.1	16.0	74.5
17.	South 24 Parganas	3.7	45.0	32.1	19.3	109	17.9	18.0	48.6
18.	Uttar Dinajpur	17.5	41.6	24.1	16.8	137	17.1	17.0	59.1
16	**Andaman & Nicobar**								
1.	Andaman	0.0	15.9	41.3	42.9	63	20.3	19.0	15.9
2.	Nicobar	0.0	3.4	10.3	86.2	58	22.5	22.0	3.4

Appendix - I (Continued)

Sr. No.	State/district	Category of marriage (percentages add to 100)				Total marri-ages	Average age at marraige		Percent of marri-ages <18 years
		CM	EM	AM	PM	#	Mean	Median	
17	**Arunachal Pradesh**								
1.	Changlang	10.5	22.8	28.1	38.6	57	19.2	19.0	33.3
2.	Dibang Valley	7.3	26.8	34.1	31.7	41	19.0	18.0	34.1
3.	East Kameng	1.4	42.5	46.6	9.6	73	17.5	18.0	43.8
4.	East Siang	0.0	34.0	17.0	48.9	47	19.1	19.0	34.0
5.	Lohit	0.0	11.6	55.8	32.6	43	19.2	19.0	11.6
6.	Lower Subansiri	8.2	24.5	38.8	28.6	49	18.8	18.0	32.7
7.	Papum Pare	0.0	23.7	31.6	44.7	38	19.6	19.0	23.7
8.	Tawang	0.0	0.0	41.2	58.8	17	21.2	20.0	0.0
9.	Tirap	0.0	38.9	11.1	50.0	18	19.5	19.5	38.9
10.	Upper Siang	0.0	8.3	45.8	45.8	24	19.3	19.0	8.3
11.	Upper Subansiri	5.8	34.6	32.7	26.9	52	18.3	18.0	40.4
12.	West Kameng	0.0	38.1	38.1	23.8	42	18.8	18.0	38.1
13.	West Siang	0.0	35.5	45.2	19.4	31	18.7	18.0	35.5
18	**Chandigarh**								
1.	Chandigarh	0.0	0.0	16.3	83.7	43	22.7	22.0	0.0
19	**Dadra & Nagar Haveli**								
1.	Dadra & Nagar Haveli	14.8	35.8	27.2	22.2	81	17.5	17.0	50.6
20	**Daman & Diu**								
1.	Daman	0.7	16.7	37.0	45.7	138	19.7	19.0	17.4
2.	Diu	0.0	15.6	35.4	49.0	96	19.8	19.0	15.6
21	**DELHI**								
1.	Delhi	0.0	6.7	25.2	68.1	119	20.7	21.0	6.7
22	**GOA**								
1.	North Goa	1.4	2.8	9.7	86.1	72	23.6	24.0	4.2
2.	South Goa	0.0	2.2	4.5	93.3	89	24.0	24.0	2.2
23	**Himachal Pradesh**								
1.	Bilaspur (Pra. Him.)	0.0	4.6	30.8	64.6	65	20.7	20.0	4.6
2.	Chamba	0.0	2.4	24.8	72.8	125	21.5	21.0	2.4
3.	Hamirpur (HP)	0.0	0.9	36.4	62.7	110	20.4	20.0	0.9
4.	Kangra	0.0	3.5	21.2	75.3	85	21.1	21.0	3.5
5.	Kinnaur	1.8	14.3	16.1	67.9	56	20.8	21.0	16.1
6.	Kullu	0.0	1.6	38.1	60.3	63	20.5	20.0	1.6
7.	Lahul & Spiti	0.0	0.0	13.6	86.4	22	23.0	22.0	0.0
8.	Mandi	0.0	4.2	34.5	61.3	119	20.6	20.0	4.2
9.	Shimla	0.0	1.9	25.0	73.1	52	21.3	21.0	1.9
10.	Sirmaur	0.0	6.9	32.8	60.3	58	20.5	20.0	6.9
11.	Solan	0.0	1.4	25.7	73.0	74	20.9	20.0	1.4
12.	Una	0.0	0.9	21.3	77.8	108	21.2	21.0	0.9
24	**Jammu & Kashmir**								
1.	Anantanag	0.0	2.0	6.0	92.0	50	22.4	22.0	2.0
2.	Badgam	0.0	3.2	22.6	74.2	31	21.2	20.0	3.2
3.	Baramula	0.0	7.5	17.0	75.5	53	21.5	20.0	7.5
4.	Doda	0.0	0.0	36.3	63.7	215	20.5	20.0	0.0

Appendix - I (Continued)

Sr. No.	State/district	Category of marriage (percentages add to 100) CM	EM	AM	PM	Total marri-ages #	Average age at marraige Mean	Median	Percent of marri-ages <18 years
5.	Jammu	0.0	1.1	23.4	75.5	184	21.1	22.0	1.1
6.	Kargil	2.2	25.3	42.9	29.7	91	18.7	18.0	27.5
7.	Kathua	0.0	0.0	16.9	83.1	148	21.8	22.0	0.0
8.	Kupwara	0.0	0.0	20.8	79.2	24	20.2	20.0	0.0
9.	Leh	1.5	0.0	25.0	73.5	68	20.8	20.0	1.5
10.	Pulwama	0.0	0.0	11.1	88.9	18	22.8	23.0	0.0
11.	Punch	0.0	3.5	26.3	70.2	114	20.7	20.0	3.5
12.	Rajauri	0.0	0.2	80.9	18.9	461	18.9	19.0	0.2
13.	Srinagar	3.0	6.1	30.3	60.6	33	19.4	20.0	9.1
14.	Udhampur	0.0	1.3	54.3	44.4	151	19.4	19.0	1.3
25	**Lakshadweep**								
1.	Lakshadweep	0.0	18.2	33.3	48.4	159	19.9	19.0	18.2
26	**Manipur**								
1.	Bishnupur	0.0	16.2	21.2	62.6	99	22.2	21.0	16.2
2.	Chandel	2.6	17.9	23.1	56.4	78	21.9	20.0	20.5
3.	Churachandpur	2.1	8.5	19.1	70.2	47	22.3	21.0	10.6
4.	Imphal	1.4	3.4	8.2	87.1	147	25.6	25.0	4.8
5.	Senapati	0.0	18.2	12.1	69.7	33	21.8	22.0	18.2
6.	Tamenglong	1.2	19.5	25.6	53.7	82	21.0	20.0	20.7
7.	Thoubal	1.8	13.8	22.0	62.4	109	21.3	20.0	15.6
8.	Ukhrul	0.0	18.2	12.1	69.7	33	23.1	21.0	18.2
27	**Meghalaya**								
1.	East Garo Hills	0.0	0.0	44.4	55.6	27	20.4	20.0	0.0
2.	East Khasi Hills	4.5	9.1	45.5	40.9	22	19.5	19.0	13.6
3.	Jaintia Hills	0.4	0.4	42.5	56.7	261	20.3	20.0	0.8
4.	Ri Bhoi	0.0	2.3	55.8	41.9	43	19.5	19.0	2.3
5.	South Garo Hills	0.0	0.0	60.0	40.0	5	21.0	18.0	0.0
6.	West Garo Hills	0.0	12.5	50.0	37.5	16	21.1	19.0	12.5
7.	West Khasi Hills	0.0	2.0	45.1	52.9	51	20.0	20.0	2.0
28	**Mizoram**								
1.	Aizwal	0.0	7.1	35.7	57.1	84	21.8	20.0	7.1
2.	Chhimtuipui	0.0	25.3	32.0	42.7	75	19.5	19.0	25.3
3.	Lunglei	0.0	6.8	27.3	65.9	44	20.9	20.0	6.8
29	**Nagaland**								
1.	Kohima	0.0	55.8	31.4	12.8	86	17.6	17.0	55.8
2.	Mokokchung	0.0	14.0	18.0	68.0	50	20.7	20.5	14.0
3.	Mon	0.0	11.2	51.3	37.5	152	19.3	19.0	11.2
4.	Phek	0.0	36.8	47.4	15.8	19	18.1	18.0	36.8
5.	Tuensang	0.0	8.6	40.7	50.6	81	19.8	20.0	8.6
6.	Wokha	0.0	25.4	30.3	44.3	122	19.4	19.0	25.4
7.	Zunheboto	0.7	23.3	29.3	46.7	150	19.0	19.0	24.0
30	**Pondicherry**								
1.	Karaikal	0.7	4.9	24.6	69.7	142	21.2	21.0	5.6
2.	Mahe	0.0	2.6	23.6	73.8	191	22.4	21.0	2.6
3.	Pondicherry	0.0	4.5	30.4	65.2	112	21.6	21.0	4.5
4.	Yanam	1.2	22.0	41.5	35.4	82	18.9	19.0	23.2

Appendix - I (Continued)

Sr. No.	State/district	Category of marriage (percentages add to 100)				Total marri-ages	Average age at marraige		Percent of marri-ages <18 years
		CM	EM	AM	PM	#	Mean	Median	
31	**Sikkim**								
1.	East Sikkim	1.8	10.9	20.0	67.3	55	21.8	22.0	12.7
2.	North Sikkim	0.0	13.6	31.8	54.5	22	21.2	20.5	13.6
3.	South Sikkim	0.0	13.0	26.1	60.9	23	21.1	20.0	13.0
4.	West Sikkim	0.0	17.1	34.3	48.6	70	20.4	19.0	17.1
32	**Tripura**								
1.	North Tripura	1.4	33.3	31.9	33.3	72	18.8	18.0	34.7
2.	South Tripura	8.2	37.8	22.4	31.6	98	19.2	18.0	45.9
3.	West Tripura	2.5	12.3	24.7	60.5	81	21.5	20.0	14.8

Note: (1) In the column showing percent of marriages below legal minimum age, 0.0 indicates no marriage below 18 years.
(2) CM = Child Marriage; EM = Early marriage; AM = acceptable marriage; PM = Preferred Marriage.

APPENDIX - II

Percent of Marriages below Legal Minimum Age of 18 years and Average Age at Marriage in each District by place of Residence-GIRLS

Sr. No.	*State/District*	*Age at Marriage*						*Total Number of marriages*	
		<18 years (%)		*Mean*		*Median*			
		Rural	*Urban*	*Rural*	*Urban*	*Rural*	*Urban*	*Rural*	*Urban*
1	**Andhra Pradesh**								
1.	Adilabad	49.3	45.0	17.1	18.3	18.0	18.0	69	20
2.	Anantapur	37.3	25.0	18.0	19.0	18.0	18.0	51	20
3.	Chittoor	26.9	0.0	19.8	20.2	20.0	20.0	26	5
4.	Cuddapah	32.5	34.8	18.1	18.7	18.0	18.0	80	23
5.	East Godavari	55.4	5.9	17.0	19.9	17.0	19.0	56	17
6.	Guntur	36.7	31.3	18.5	19.9	18.0	19.0	30	16
7.	Hyderabad	**	6.4	NA	20.5	NA	20.0	**	78
8.	Karimnagar	42.6	**	17.7	NA	18.0	NA	47	**
9.	Khammam	27.9	50.0	18.0	17.3	18.0	17.5	43	12
10.	Krishna	33.3	18.5	17.7	19.5	18.0	20.0	30	27
11.	Kurnool	40.8	26.7	17.8	19.5	18.0	18.0	71	15
12.	Mahbubnagar	43.5	14.3	17.4	20.1	18.0	19.0	62	7
13.	Medak	37.2	16.7	17.9	19.3	18.0	18.5	43	6
14.	Nalgonda	42.3	40.0	17.8	19.6	18.0	18.0	71	5
15.	Nellore	24.4	26.3	18.7	19.8	18.0	19.0	45	19
16.	Nizamabad	49.0	25.0	17.6	18.8	18.0	18.0	51	12
17.	Prakasam	39.6	45.5	18.3	18.1	18.0	18.0	53	11
18.	Rangareddi	60.0	15.2	16.7	20.6	17.0	20.0	45	46
19.	Srikakulam	52.0	12.5	17.3	19.6	17.0	20.0	98	8
20.	Vishkhapatanam	56.0	45.5	17.1	18.8	17.0	18.0	25	11
21.	Vizianagaram	44.3	21.4	17.6	19.3	18.0	19.0	70	14
22.	Warangal	51.9	33.3	17.0	20.8	17.0	20.5	52	12
23.	West Godavari	30.8	23.5	18.1	18.4	18.0	18.0	91	17
2	**Assam**								
1.	Barpeta	17.8	25.0	19.9	18.3	20.0	18.5	45	4
2.	Bongaigaon	43.5	0.0	19.0	23.6	18.0	23.0	138	10
3.	Cachar	21.3	0.0	20.4	21.4	20.0	21.0	94	5
4.	Darrang	34.7	25.0	18.7	20.3	19.0	20.0	49	8
5.	Dhemaji	3.9	**	20.3	NA	20.0	NA	51	**
6.	Dhubri	62.5	35.7	17.5	18.6	17.0	18.0	96	14
7.	Dibrugarh	28.0	0.0	19.6	26.2	19.0	26.0	25	5
8.	Goalpara	43.0	16.7	18.8	20.3	18.0	20.0	93	6
9.	Golaghat	28.9	50.0	19.5	20.0	19.0	20.0	90	2
10.	Hailakandi	8.9	0.0	21.2	24.5	20.0	24.5	135	10
11.	Jorhat	9.8	0.0	21.0	21.8	21.0	21.0	41	11
12	Kamrup	24.6	4.2	20.0	23.1	20.0	24.0	69	24
13	Karbi Anglong	4.8	**	19.7	NA	19.0	NA	63	**
14	Karimganj	25.0	0.0	21.2	24.8	20.0	24.0	88	6
15	Lakhimpur	39.1	0.0	19.3	22.5	18.0	22.5	23	2

Appendix - II (Continued)

Sr. No.	State/District	Age at Marriage						Total Number of marriages	
		<18 years (%)		Mean		Median			
		Rural	Urban	Rural	Urban	Rural	Urban	Rural	Urban
16.	Marigaon	34.1	0.0	19.0	22.0	19.0	22.0	123	2
17.	Nagaon	42.6	22.2	18.4	23.6	18.0	25.0	101	9
18.	Nalbari	3.3	50.0	21.5	26.0	22.0	26.0	61	2
19.	North Cachar Hills	7.8	7.1	20.5	21.1	20.0	21.0	51	14
20.	Sibsagar	13.0	0.0	21.9	22.0	20.0	22.0	23	1
21.	Sonitpur	31.6	0.0	19.3	18.5	18.0	18.5	57	2
22.	Tinsukia	27.5	7.7	19.4	23.8	18.0	23.0	69	13
3	**Bihar**								
1.	Araria	55.5	15.4	17.4	18.5	17.0	18.0	119	13
2.	Aurangabad(Bih)	64.0	58.3	16.5	17.3	17.0	16.5	172	12
3.	Begusarai	58.3	63.6	16.7	16.5	16.5	17.0	156	11
4.	Bhagalpur	63.9	32.0	16.6	18.0	16.0	18.0	133	25
5.	Bhojpur	58.3	36.4	16.5	18.3	16.0	19.0	151	11
6.	Buxar	65.5	61.5	16.5	17.2	16.0	16.0	197	13
7.	Darbhanga	54.9	21.1	17.2	20.2	17.0	20.0	164	19
8.	Deoghar	69.0	41.7	15.7	18.6	15.5	18.5	116	12
9.	Dhanbad	48.7	37.0	17.3	18.7	18.0	18.0	39	46
10.	Dumka	49.0	50.0	17.4	17.8	18.0	17.5	104	12
11.	Gaya	66.0	26.3	15.8	18.9	16.0	18.0	153	19
12.	Giridih	59.4	55.6	16.8	17.4	17.0	17.0	101	18
13.	Godda	66.1	100.0	16.7	17.0	16.0	17.0	115	1
14.	Gopalganj	60.1	36.4	16.9	18.5	17.0	18.0	143	11
15.	Gulma	27.5	25.0	18.8	18.8	18.0	19.5	69	8
16.	Hazaribagh	68.2	57.9	16.2	17.8	16.0	17.0	110	19
17.	Jehanabad	55.8	35.7	16.9	17.9	17.0	18.5	181	14
18.	Katihar	51.0	23.1	17.4	18.3	17.0	19.0	104	13
19.	Khagaria	65.9	25.0	16.5	19.0	16.0	18.0	164	8
20.	Kishanganj	51.3	27.3	17.7	19.3	17.0	19.0	76	11
21.	Lohardaga	47.4	0.0	17.8	22.2	18.0	22.0	95	9
22.	Madhepura	66.9	60.0	16.5	15.8	16.0	16.0	136	10
23.	Madhubani	63.4	100.0	16.5	16.0	17.0	16.0	142	2
24.	Munger	66.1	27.8	16.1	18.6	16.0	18.0	109	18
25.	Muzaffarpur	59.7	12.5	17.0	20.3	17.0	20.0	149	24
26.	Nalanda	59.7	52.4	16.5	16.7	16.0	17.0	144	21
27.	Nawada	72.9	64.3	15.7	16.6	16.0	15.0	199	14
28.	Palamu	67.3	40.0	16.3	18.2	16.0	18.0	98	5
29.	Pashchim champaran	54.5	19.0	17.2	19.4	17.0	19.0	101	63
30.	Pashchmi Singhbhum	30.6	16.7	18.7	19.9	18.0	18.0	72	12
31.	Patna	78.7	86.7	15.5	15.3	15.0	15.0	141	15
32.	Purba Champaran	63.5	50.0	16.7	20.0	16.0	19.5	178	6
33.	Purbi Singhbhum	44.6	20.0	17.9	21.2	18.0	21.0	56	50
34.	Purnia	49.6	33.3	18.0	18.5	18.0	18.0	139	12
35.	Ranchi	43.9	18.8	17.8	20.5	18.0	20.0	66	16
36.	Rohtas	68.8	75.0	16.4	17.0	16.0	15.0	128	4
37.	Saharsa	58.6	14.3	17.1	20.3	17.0	20.0	145	7
38.	Sahibganj	67.1	14.3	16.5	18.0	16.0	18.0	76	7
39.	Samastipur	65.6	37.5	16.2	16.6	16.0	18.0	151	8
40.	Saran	53.0	38.1	17.1	18.0	17.0	18.0	166	21
41.	Sitamarhi	65.1	57.1	16.5	16.6	16.0	16.0	146	7
42.	Siwan	44.3	20.0	17.8	19.4	18.0	18.0	167	5
43.	Vaishali	61.6	84.6	16.5	16.2	16.0	17.0	151	13

Appendix - II (Continued)

Sr. No.	State/District	Age at Marriage						Total Number of marriages	
		<18 years (%)		Mean		Median			
		Rural	*Urban*	*Rural*	*Urban*	*Rural*	*Urban*	*Rural*	*Urban*
4	**Gujarat**								
1.	Ahmadabad	79.2	10.5	15.8	21.5	16.0	21.0	24	76
2.	Amreli	13.6	27.3	19.7	19.4	19.0	19.0	132	44
3.	Banas Kantha	54.2	22.2	17.1	19.1	17.0	20.0	118	9
4.	Bharuch	19.6	7.7	19.5	21.5	19.0	21.0	102	13
5.	Bhavnagar	35.2	11.4	18.1	19.8	18.0	19.5	108	44
6.	Gandhinagar	37.3	17.6	17.8	21.8	18.0	21.0	67	17
7.	Jamnagar	10.0	12.2	19.8	20.7	20.0	20.0	90	41
8.	Junagadh	12.1	10.5	20.0	20.9	20.0	20.0	124	38
9.	Kachchh	27.0	16.1	18.9	20.7	19.0	20.0	74	31
10.	Kheda	36.0	12.0	18.7	20.3	18.0	20.0	125	25
11.	Mahesana	36.5	20.0	18.1	20.1	18.0	20.0	104	30
12.	Panch Mahals	28.8	10.0	18.6	18.9	18.0	18.0	73	10
13.	Rajkot	19.0	6.7	19.5	20.3	20.0	20.0	84	60
14.	Sabar Kantha	29.7	38.5	18.6	19.3	18.5	20.0	118	13
15.	Surat	30.0	7.8	18.9	20.5	19.0	20.0	50	51
16.	Surendranagar	13.9	0.0	19.3	21.8	19.0	21.0	72	30
17.	The Dangs	49.6	12.5	17.5	19.3	18.0	18.5	123	8
18.	Vadodara	44.3	17.5	18.0	20.4	18.0	20.0	61	40
19.	Valsad	12.0	0.0	20.4	22.7	20.0	22.5	100	20
5	**Haryana**								
1.	Ambala	16.3	3.6	19.8	22.1	20.0	22.0	80	28
2.	Bhiwani	51.2	35.0	17.0	18.4	17.0	18.0	121	20
3.	Faridabad	45.3	5.7	17.7	20.6	18.0	20.0	86	53
4.	Gurgaon	38.8	26.3	17.6	19.3	18.0	20.0	85	19
5.	Hisar	48.0	15.8	17.2	18.9	18.0	18.0	98	19
6.	Jind	39.3	23.8	17.8	19.0	18.0	18.0	107	21
7.	Kaithal	40.6	0.0	17.7	21.3	18.0	20.0	64	15
8.	Karnal	17.4	12.1	19.3	20.4	19.0	20.0	115	33
9.	Kurukshetra	18.0	0.0	19.8	21.0	20.0	21.0	100	23
10.	Mahendragarh	51.9	4.8	17.2	20.5	17.0	20.0	154	21
11.	Panchkula	37.0	0.0	17.9	21.5	18.0	21.0	54	24
12.	Panipat	47.3	31.3	17.5	19.4	18.0	20.0	112	16
13.	Rewari	33.0	9.1	18.1	20.5	18.0	21.0	103	22
14.	Rohtak	38.1	17.9	18.5	19.3	18.0	19.0	113	28
15.	Sirsa	35.5	6.7	18.2	22.2	18.0	21.0	93	15
16.	Sonipat	8.4	0.0	20.1	21.7	20.0	22.0	95	33
17.	Yamunanagar	7.8	3.1	20.0	23.3	20.0	23.0	102	32
6	**Karnataka**								
1.	Bangalore	35.7	7.2	18.2	21.5	18.0	21.0	14	69
2.	Bangalore Rural	23.6	11.1	18.8	19.4	18.0	19.5	89	18
3.	Belgaum	60.0	41.4	16.9	19.0	17.0	19.0	90	29
4.	Bellary	54.4	22.0	17.8	20.1	17.0	19.0	90	41
5.	Bidar	69.7	52.4	16.1	18.2	16.0	17.0	155	21
6.	Bijapur	69.0	46.2	15.9	18.2	16.0	18.0	100	26
7.	Chikmagalur	15.1	4.8	20.5	20.7	20.0	20.0	126	21
8.	Chitradurga	32.6	21.7	18.4	19.7	18.0	19.0	95	23
9.	Dakshina Kannada	5.0	3.2	21.9	23.2	21.0	23.0	100	31
10.	Dharwad	46.3	22.9	18.1	21.4	18.0	21.5	67	48
11.	Gulbarga	58.8	14.3	16.7	20.6	16.0	20.0	85	28

Appendix - II (Continued)

Sr. No.	State/District	Age at Marriage						Total Number of marriages	
		<18 years (%)		Mean		Median			
		Rural	Urban	Rural	Urban	Rural	Urban	Rural	Urban
12.	Hassan	15.9	12.5	19.4	21.9	19.0	22.0	107	24
13.	Kodagu	22.9	18.8	19.8	20.6	19.5	21.5	70	16
14.	Kolar	37.3	20.0	18.0	20.7	18.0	19.0	110	30
15.	Mandya	38.9	29.4	18.0	20.1	18.0	19.0	90	17
16.	Mysore	54.4	33.3	17.4	19.2	17.0	18.0	68	30
17.	Raichur	59.3	47.6	17.1	19.1	17.0	18.0	91	21
18.	Shimoga	19.0	9.5	20.3	21.4	20.0	21.0	121	42
19.	Tumkur	29.2	0.0	18.6	23.9	18.0	23.5	106	8
20.	Uttara Kannada	15.1	14.8	21.3	22.3	21.0	22.0	106	27
7	**Kerala**								
1.	Alappuzha	0.0	0.0	23.0	22.9	22.0	22.0	119	42
2.	Ernakulam	0.0	0.0	23.7	23.8	23.5	23.0	80	69
3.	Idukki	1.7	0.0	23.2	21.0	23.0	20.0	121	9
4.	Kannur	25.3	12.5	19.9	21.7	19.0	21.0	91	88
5.	Kasaragod	16.2	29.2	21.0	19.2	20.0	18.0	130	24
6.	Kollam	0.0	0.0	22.3	21.7	22.0	21.0	150	20
7.	Kottayam	0.0	0.0	24.4	24.4	24.0	24.0	146	17
8.	Kozhikode	16.9	9.4	20.5	20.9	20.0	19.0	83	64
9.	Malappuram	35.7	36.4	18.7	19.9	18.0	18.0	185	11
10.	Palakkad	11.5	4.0	21.0	21.1	20.0	20.0	139	25
11.	Pathanamthitta	0.0	0.0	23.2	23.6	23.0	24.0	92	23
12.	Thiruvananthapuram	0.0	0.0	22.4	23.7	22.0	24.0	90	45
13.	Thrissur	0.9	0.0	22.6	22.0	22.0	22.0	110	37
14.	Wayanad	6.6	25.0	20.8	20.8	20.0	20.0	137	4
8	**Madhya Pradesh**								
1.	Balaghat	40.7	0.0	17.8	20.0	18.0	19.0	27	7
2.	Bastar	36.5	0.0	18.4	21.0	18.0	21.0	52	4
3.	Betul	26.5	18.2	17.9	19.6	18.0	19.0	34	11
4.	Bhind	64.8	44.4	16.7	17.9	16.0	18.0	128	27
5.	Bhopal	66.7	18.5	16.5	19.8	16.0	19.0	15	54
6.	Bilaspur(MP)	44.4	27.6	17.8	19.3	18.0	19.0	90	29
7.	Chattarpur	81.0	40.0	15.6	20.7	15.0	20.0	42	10
8.	Chhindwara	37.8	4.0	17.7	21.2	18.0	20.0	98	25
9.	Damoh	60.3	29.4	16.9	19.2	16.0	18.0	78	17
10.	Datia	58.2	20.0	16.8	19.1	16.0	18.0	79	25
11.	Dewas	59.1	27.3	16.7	18.8	17.0	18.0	88	22
12.	Dhar	60.4	18.2	16.7	18.9	16.0	20.0	111	11
13.	Durg	33.3	27.8	18.5	20.3	18.0	19.5	51	18
14.	East Nimar	50.0	21.9	17.7	19.5	17.5	19.0	84	32
15.	Guna	77.4	18.8	16.2	20.8	16.0	20.5	93	16
16.	Gwalior	62.5	19.7	17.0	20.3	17.0	19.5	40	66
17.	Hoshangabad	42.6	20.0	17.8	19.2	18.0	19.0	47	5
18.	Indore	80.4	14.3	15.8	20.2	16.0	20.0	51	70
19.	Jabalpur	55.3	16.7	16.7	20.2	17.0	19.0	47	36
20.	Jhabua	61.2	25.0	16.8	21.4	17.0	22.0	98	8
21.	Mandla	38.5	0.0	17.5	23.0	18.0	23.0	39	1
22.	Mandsaur	65.4	21.7	16.2	20.1	16.0	20.0	104	23
23.	Morena	74.6	50.0	15.9	17.4	16.0	17.0	71	12
24.	Narsimhapur	56.5	8.3	17.7	21.0	17.0	21.5	69	12
25.	Panna	65.6	41.2	16.3	18.4	16.0	18.0	32	17
26.	Raigarh	8.2	0.0	19.3	20.0	19.0	18.0	49	3

Appendix - II (Continued)

Sr. No.	State/District	Age at Marriage						Total Number of marriages	
		<18 years (%)		Mean		Median			
		Rural	Urban	Rural	Urban	Rural	Urban	Rural	Urban
27.	Raipur	61.2	14.3	17.3	19.0	17.0	19.0	49	7
28.	Raisen	48.7	40.0	17.5	17.3	18.0	18.0	113	15
29.	Rajgarh	69.0	48.0	15.8	19.0	16.0	19.0	100	25
30.	Rajnandgaon	53.3	31.3	16.8	20.4	17.0	18.5	90	16
31.	Ratlam	58.8	25.0	16.0	19.4	17.0	19.0	51	32
32.	Rewa	63.1	33.3	16.4	17.6	16.0	18.0	111	12
33.	Sagar	83.1	10.0	15.5	20.3	15.0	20.0	65	30
34.	Satna	68.3	42.1	16.2	17.8	16.0	18.0	82	38
35.	Sehore	60.0	10.7	16.9	20.1	17.0	20.0	90	28
36.	Seoni	41.0	10.0	17.5	20.9	18.0	20.5	61	10
37.	Shahdol	79.3	30.0	15.5	18.8	16.0	18.0	29	10
38.	Shajapur	84.4	66.7	14.9	17.2	15.0	16.5	90	12
39.	Shivpuri	71.4	50.0	16.2	17.2	16.0	17.5	84	16
40.	Sidhi	69.0	0.0	15.6	19.0	16.0	19.0	84	2
41.	Surguja	59.7	42.9	16.4	18.0	16.5	18.0	62	14
42.	Tikamgarh	74.3	37.5	15.7	18.0	15.0	18.0	105	16
43.	Ujjain	53.2	20.0	16.8	19.4	17.0	19.0	77	55
44.	Vidisha	71.9	20.7	15.9	20.5	16.0	20.0	96	29
45.	West Nimar	45.8	26.3	17.4	18.3	18.0	18.0	83	19
9	**Maharashtra**								
1.	Ahmadnagar	45.0	12.5	17.3	19.8	18.0	20.5	109	16
2.	Akola	43.7	25.0	17.7	19.3	18.0	18.0	87	36
3.	Amravali	10.1	6.7	19.3	20.2	19.0	20.0	89	45
4.	Aurangabad	54.7	32.3	16.7	19.1	17.0	18.0	117	31
5.	Bhandara	11.1	0.0	19.5	22.2	19.0	22.0	108	21
6.	Bid	64.4	31.6	16.6	18.0	17.0	18.0	90	19
7.	Buldana	38.4	14.3	18.1	19.8	18.0	18.5	112	28
8.	Chandrapur	30.6	13.8	18.5	19.7	18.0	20.0	72	29
9.	Dhule	45.5	11.8	17.7	20.8	18.0	20.0	88	17
10.	Gadchiroli	30.2	14.3	18.1	20.1	18.0	19.5	53	14
11.	Greater Bombay (Mumbai)	**	8.0	NA	21.2	NA	21.0	**	87
12.	Jalgaon	51.3	27.8	17.7	18.9	17.0	18.5	113	36
13.	Jalna	56.8	47.6	17.0	17.8	17.0	18.0	111	21
14.	Kolhapur	18.6	10.0	18.4	21.8	18.0	21.0	102	20
15.	Latur	64.3	34.5	16.7	19.1	16.5	19.0	112	29
16.	Nagpur	15.4	7.9	18.9	21.2	19.0	21.0	52	63
17.	Nanded	68.3	37.5	16.4	18.3	16.0	18.0	120	24
18.	Nashik	32.7	28.6	18.3	19.0	18.0	19.0	52	28
19.	Osmanabad	49.6	25.0	17.3	18.6	18.0	18.0	115	16
20.	Parbhani	54.3	29.3	17.0	18.6	17.0	18.0	92	41
21.	Pune	35.7	22.2	18.1	19.0	18.0	18.0	70	45
22.	Raigarh	16.9	11.1	18.9	19.8	18.0	18.0	77	9
23.	Ratnagiri	13.7	0.0	19.7	24.2	19.0	25.0	117	6
24.	Sangli	26.9	21.9	18.2	19.8	18.0	20.0	93	32
25.	Satara	23.2	13.3	18.4	18.9	18.0	19.0	99	15
26.	Sindhudurg	4.1	0.0	21.4	23.0	21.0	25.0	97	5
27.	Solapur	47.8	23.3	17.5	20.3	18.0	19.0	92	30
28.	Thane	28.6	15.1	18.7	20.3	18.0	20.0	28	53
29.	Wardha	14.3	4.8	19.8	21.6	19.0	21.0	84	21
30.	Yavatmal	24.8	36.0	18.4	18.5	18.0	18.0	129	25

Appendix - II (Continued)

Sr. No.	State/District	Age at Marriage						Total Number of marriages	
		<18 years (%)		Mean		Median			
		Rural	Urban	Rural	Urban	Rural	Urban	Rural	Urban
10	**Orissa**								
1.	Anugul	42.7	0.0	18.4	23.9	18.0	24.0	103	7
2.	Balangir	63.3	27.3	17.5	22.7	17.0	24.0	60	11
3.	Balasore	30.6	0.0	19.6	23.2	19.0	23.0	134	10
4.	Bargarh	44.3	0.0	18.1	20.1	18.0	18.5	88	10
5.	Baudh	52.2	33.3	17.5	18.2	17.0	18.0	67	6
6.	Bhadrak	17.0	0.0	21.0	22.6	21.0	22.5	147	12
7.	Cuttack	12.4	3.7	20.6	22.2	20.0	22.0	105	27
8.	Debagarh	34.3	0.0	19.0	20.0	18.0	20.0	70	2
9.	Dhenkanal	37.8	25.0	18.8	20.4	18.0	21.5	119	12
10.	Gajapati	42.4	37.5	17.7	19.8	18.0	19.0	66	8
11.	Ganjam	53.1	38.1	17.5	19.8	17.0	19.0	113	21
12.	Jagatsinghapur	9.0	14.3	21.8	21.6	22.0	21.0	133	7
13.	Jajapur	14.1	28.6	20.6	21.6	21.0	21.0	135	7
14.	Jharsuguda	14.9	20.0	19.9	19.0	19.0	19.0	47	25
15.	Kalahandi	59.7	50.0	17.2	19.5	17.0	19.5	67	2
16.	Kendrapara	15.8	16.7	20.8	22.1	21.0	22.5	146	12
17.	Kendujhar	31.9	16.7	19.3	21.8	19.0	23.0	91	12
18.	Khordha	29.1	3.6	19.4	22.1	19.0	21.5	86	28
19.	Koraput	69.1	46.2	16.7	19.1	16.0	18.0	55	13
20.	Malkangiri	56.0	**	17.0	NA	17.0	NA	50	**
21.	Mayurbhanj	38.3	0.0	18.8	22.1	18.0	22.5	81	14
22.	Nabarangapur	69.6	**	16.8	NA	16.0	NA	46	**
23.	Nayagarh	53.6	**	17.8	NA	17.0	NA	140	**
24.	Nuapada	45.5	0.0	18.2	18.0	18.0	18.0	44	3
25.	Phulbani	42.9	25.0	17.6	18.5	18.0	19.0	56	4
26.	Puri	15.4	6.3	20.5	22.3	20.0	23.0	91	16
27.	Rayagada	45.7	25.0	18.1	19.6	18.0	19.5	46	24
28.	Sambalpur	37.5	11.1	18.5	21.3	18.0	21.0	40	18
29.	Sonapur	41.9	21.4	18.5	19.6	18.0	18.5	93	14
30.	Sundargarh	16.2	11.1	20.1	21.0	19.0	21.0	37	9
11	**Punjab**								
1.	Amritsar	11.8	9.4	19.7	21.2	20.0	21.0	85	32
2.	Bathinda	13.5	9.5	19.4	21.0	20.0	21.0	96	21
3.	Faridkot	12.1	14.3	19.9	20.9	20.0	21.0	99	28
4.	Fatehgarh Sahib	8.0	0.0	20.1	21.2	20.0	21.0	138	23
5.	Firozpur	32.1	10.5	19.0	20.3	18.5	20.0	78	38
6.	Gurdaspur	8.0	0.0	20.4	22.9	20.0	22.0	100	21
7.	Hoshiarpur	3.8	0.0	21.0	22.4	21.0	22.0	133	25
8.	Jalandhar	8.4	5.0	20.6	21.6	20.0	21.0	95	40
9.	Kapurthala	3.2	2.7	21.3	21.9	21.0	21.0	93	37
10.	Ludhiana	11.0	4.2	20.2	21.2	20.0	21.0	73	48
11.	Mansa	23.4	7.7	19.3	20.7	20.0	20.5	111	26
12.	Moga	15.3	0.0	19.8	22.1	19.5	22.0	144	26
13.	Muktsar	25.8	14.3	19.4	20.0	20.0	20.0	124	28
14.	Nawanshahr	2.3	0.0	21.2	22.9	21.0	22.5	131	10
15.	Patiala	11.8	5.3	20.2	20.5	20.0	21.0	68	19
16.	Rupnagar	7.1	0.0	20.7	22.5	20.0	22.0	113	21
17.	Sangrur	14.9	9.1	20.2	20.6	20.0	20.0	114	44
12	**Rajasthan**								
1.	Ajmer	80.7	4.7	14.7	22.0	15.0	22.0	57	43
2.	Alwar	58.2	22.7	16.8	19.5	17.0	19.0	122	22

Appendix - II (Continued)

Sr. No.	State/District	Age at Marriage						Total Number of marriages	
		<18 years (%)		Mean		Median			
		Rural	Urban	Rural	Urban	Rural	Urban	Rural	Urban
3.	Banswara	56.8	0.0	16.8	19.3	17.0	18.0	74	3
4.	Barmer	56.0	7.7	16.6	18.9	17.0	18.0	91	13
5.	Bharatpur	61.5	29.2	16.7	18.8	17.0	19.0	109	24
6.	Bhilwara	77.7	30.0	15.2	19.6	15.0	19.0	112	20
7.	Bikaner	70.4	45.8	15.8	18.0	16.0	18.0	54	24
8.	Bundi	83.1	28.6	14.7	20.7	15.0	22.0	83	7
9.	Chittaurgarh	56.8	0.0	16.8	20.0	17.0	18.5	37	6
10.	Churu	73.9	50.0	16.0	17.3	16.0	17.5	92	32
11.	Dausa	73.7	46.2	15.8	17.7	16.0	18.0	118	13
12.	Dhaulpur	57.6	50.0	16.7	17.6	16.0	17.5	85	16
13.	Dungarpur	35.9	0.0	18.0	19.7	18.0	20.0	117	7
14.	Ganganagar	49.0	38.5	17.2	18.9	18.0	18.0	102	13
15.	Hanumangarh	57.0	6.3	16.8	20.3	17.0	20.0	135	16
16.	Jaipur	58.2	12.0	16.6	20.5	17.0	20.0	98	50
17.	Jaisalmer	56.4	31.6	16.6	18.8	17.0	18.0	55	19
18.	Jalor	48.4	16.7	17.2	20.3	18.0	19.5	124	12
19.	Jhalawar	76.8	33.3	15.1	18.7	15.0	18.5	95	18
20.	Jhunjhunun	49.1	37.9	17.2	17.7	18.0	18.0	114	29
21.	Jodhpur	76.7	29.6	15.4	20.5	15.0	20.0	30	27
22.	Kota	77.6	33.3	15.6	19.1	16.0	19.5	58	36
23.	Nagaur	71.1	33.3	16.0	17.5	16.0	18.0	97	15
24.	Pali	54.2	39.1	17.1	17.9	17.0	18.0	59	23
25.	Rajsamand	50.0	14.3	17.2	19.0	17.5	18.0	60	7
26.	Sawai Madhopur	54.4	31.8	16.6	19.0	17.0	18.0	68	22
27.	Sikar	45.4	23.1	17.5	19.0	18.0	20.0	141	26
28.	Sirohi	42.4	11.8	17.7	19.4	18.0	19.0	33	17
29.	Tonk	80.7	47.6	14.9	18.5	15.0	18.0	109	21
30.	Udaipur	69.8	16.7	15.9	19.3	16.0	19.0	86	18
13	**Tamil Nadu**								
1.	Chengalpattu	16.7	0.0	19.4	21.4	19.0	21.0	54	36
2.	Chennai	**	5.6	NA	21.5	NA	21.0	**	108
3.	Coimbatore	13.0	19.1	20.3	21.4	20.0	21.0	46	47
4.	Dharmapuri	36.2	14.3	18.4	20.9	18.0	21.0	116	14
5.	Dindigul	29.8	16.7	19.8	20.3	19.0	20.5	57	12
6.	Kanniyakumari	0.0	0.0	23.0	23.0	23.0	23.0	76	11
7.	Madurai	34.4	18.1	19.3	21.3	19.0	21.0	61	72
8.	Namakkal	13.8	9.5	19.9	21.3	20.0	20.0	65	21
9.	North Arcot	24.7	15.9	19.2	20.8	19.0	20.0	77	44
10.	Periyar	14.5	10.5	20.8	20.6	19.0	21.0	55	19
11.	Pudukkottai	10.4	13.6	20.7	22.4	20.0	22.5	106	22
12.	Ramanathapuram	11.6	19.2	20.0	20.1	19.5	20.0	86	26
13.	Salem	47.2	27.0	18.2	19.9	18.0	19.0	72	37
14.	Sivaganganagar	9.2	5.0	21.0	21.1	20.0	21.0	98	40
15.	South Arcot	29.8	12.5	19.1	20.6	18.0	19.5	114	16
16.	Thanjavur	14.9	6.7	20.8	22.3	20.0	21.0	47	15
17.	The Nilgiris	10.3	6.9	21.2	22.1	20.0	22.0	39	29
18.	Theni	32.7	22.6	18.7	20.0	18.0	20.0	55	31
19.	Tiruchirappalli	28.6	13.0	19.6	21.9	19.0	21.0	56	23
20.	Tirunelveli	10.9	2.4	21.7	21.2	21.0	20.5	46	42
21.	Tiruvanamalai	27.2	11.1	19.1	20.5	19.0	19.0	125	18
22.	Tutikorin	8.3	5.9	21.4	21.2	21.0	21.0	60	51
23.	Virudhunagar	18.3	8.0	19.3	20.4	19.0	20.0	60	50

Appendix - II (Continued)

Sr. No.	State/District	Age at Marriage						Total Number of marriages	
		<18 years (%)		Mean		Median			
		Rural	Urban	Rural	Urban	Rural	Urban	Rural	Urban
14	**Uttar Pradesh**								
1.	Agra	45.9	23.3	17.5	19.6	18.0	19.0	85	43
2.	Aligarh	48.3	20.0	17.5	18.8	18.0	19.0	60	15
3.	Allahabad	59.4	11.1	16.9	19.7	17.0	19.0	106	18
4.	Almora	14.7	0.0	19.2	23.0	19.0	24.0	68	3
5.	Ambedkarnagar	72.7	0.0	16.0	18.2	16.0	18.0	110	5
6.	Azamgarh	64.0	66.7	16.4	16.8	16.0	16.0	100	6
7.	Bahraich	79.5	50.0	15.0	20.3	15.0	18.5	112	6
8.	Ballia	55.6	28.6	17.1	18.9	17.0	18.0	90	7
9.	Banda	76.8	33.3	15.2	19.9	15.0	19.0	95	15
10.	Barabanki	55.8	16.7	16.6	18.0	17.0	18.0	113	6
11.	Bareilly	32.6	23.8	18.0	20.0	18.0	20.0	43	21
12.	Basti	79.0	0.0	15.2	19.7	15.0	18.0	119	3
13.	Bhadohi	69.5	50.0	16.2	17.8	16.0	17.5	167	12
14.	Bijnor	12.3	22.2	19.1	20.0	19.0	19.5	73	36
15.	Budaun	54.8	35.0	17.3	18.3	17.0	18.0	73	20
16.	Bulandshahar	29.7	15.4	18.5	20.0	18.0	20.0	64	13
17.	Chamoli	8.6	0.0	19.9	21.0	20.0	21.5	70	6
18.	Dehradun	20.4	5.7	19.9	21.5	20.0	21.0	49	35
19.	Deoria	58.6	33.3	16.8	19.4	17.0	18.0	99	9
20.	Etah	63.1	12.5	17.0	20.1	17.0	18.5	65	8
21.	Etawah	46.7	22.2	17.4	20.4	18.0	20.0	105	9
22.	Faizabad	66.1	12.5	16.0	20.1	16.0	20.0	121	8
23.	Farrukhabad	37.5	35.7	17.8	17.7	18.0	18.0	96	14
24.	Fatehpur	50.0	20.0	17.4	18.8	17.5	18.0	156	20
25.	Firozabad	58.7	27.3	17.1	19.3	17.0	19.0	109	33
26.	Ghaziabad	26.5	0.0	18.7	21.2	18.0	21.0	83	35
27.	Ghazipur	61.2	60.0	17.0	16.9	17.0	15.5	121	10
28.	Gonda	70.7	50.0	15.3	16.0	15.0	17.0	92	6
29.	Gorakhpur	71.9	33.3	16.1	19.8	16.0	20.5	64	12
30.	Hamirpur	52.8	33.3	17.2	18.0	17.0	18.0	123	24
31.	Hardoi	46.2	20.0	17.6	19.6	18.0	20.0	65	5
32.	Hardwar	19.3	0.0	19.0	21.8	19.0	21.0	57	31
33.	Hathras	54.7	10.5	17.3	20.7	17.0	21.0	95	19
34.	Jalaun	66.3	36.0	16.5	18.0	17.0	18.0	104	25
35.	Jaunpur	57.7	25.0	16.9	19.1	17.0	18.5	163	8
36.	Jhansi	58.5	11.8	16.7	20.2	17.0	20.0	65	34
37.	Kanpur Dehat	35.2	20.0	18.3	19.2	18.0	20.0	128	5
38.	Kanpur Nagar	18.2	3.9	19.1	21.3	20.0	21.0	11	77
39.	Kheri	53.5	57.1	17.2	18.0	17.0	16.0	142	7
40.	Lalitpur	86.6	63.6	15.0	16.4	15.0	16.0	82	11
41.	Lucknow	48.3	15.4	17.4	21.4	18.0	20.0	58	39
42.	Maharajganj	82.2	0.0	14.7	19.0	14.0	19.0	73	1
43.	Mahoba	68.1	52.4	16.4	17.4	16.0	17.0	94	21
44.	Mainpuri	50.5	40.0	17.4	19.4	17.0	18.0	111	5
45.	Mathura	48.1	16.7	17.5	18.8	18.0	19.0	52	12
46.	Mau	43.7	8.3	17.5	20.3	18.0	20.0	142	24
47.	Meerut	15.2	13.9	19.1	20.4	19.0	20.0	33	36
48.	Mirzapur	60.3	28.6	16.6	19.4	17.0	18.0	131	14
49.	Muradabad	41.4	5.7	17.8	20.5	18.0	20.0	70	35
50.	Muzaffarnagar	23.4	9.5	18.9	21.2	18.0	22.0	77	21
51.	Nainital	8.5	14.3	19.6	20.2	19.0	20.0	59	14

Appendix - II (Continued)

Sr. No.	State/District	Age at Marriage						Total Number of marriages	
		<18 years (%)		Mean		Median			
		Rural	Urban	Rural	Urban	Rural	Urban	Rural	Urban
52.	Pauri Garhwal	7.4	0.0	19.4	20.0	19.0	19.5	81	8
53.	Pilibhit	61.3	35.3	16.9	18.4	16.0	18.0	62	17
54.	Pithoragarh	24.7	0.0	18.7	21.0	18.0	20.5	77	6
55.	Pratapgarh	56.3	37.5	16.8	19.1	17.0	18.0	126	8
56.	Rae Bareli	46.0	14.3	17.1	20.9	18.0	21.0	137	7
57.	Rampur	41.1	4.8	17.7	19.0	18.0	18.0	56	21
58.	Saharanpur	24.0	0.0	18.6	20.9	18.0	21.0	75	23
59.	Shajahanabad	65.7	60.9	16.2	16.8	15.0	16.0	70	23
60.	Siddharthnagar	66.3	50.0	15.2	17.5	15.0	17.5	98	4
61.	Sitapur	66.7	42.9	16.4	18.3	16.0	18.0	93	14
62.	Sonbhadra	72.2	20.0	15.6	18.7	16.0	18.5	72	10
63.	Sultanpur	64.8	33.3	16.0	17.7	16.0	18.0	108	3
64.	Tehri Garhwal	13.4	0.0	18.9	20.5	19.0	20.5	82	2
65.	Udhamsingh Nagar	33.3	17.2	18.4	19.5	18.0	19.0	63	29
66.	Unnao	46.7	38.5	17.6	18.6	18.0	18.0	90	13
67.	Uttarkashi	18.2	0.0	19.4	20.3	19.0	19.0	66	4
68.	Varanasi	80.6	32.1	15.4	19.5	15.0	19.0	124	28
15	**West Bengal**								
1.	Bankura	53.2	0.0	17.7	21.2	17.0	21.0	141	9
2.	Barddhaman	62.0	42.1	17.1	19.2	17.0	19.0	100	57
3.	Birbhum	60.2	25.0	16.9	19.5	16.0	19.5	123	4
4.	Dakshin Dinajpur	67.9	42.9	16.5	18.8	16.0	18.0	137	14
5.	Darjiling	29.6	15.2	19.1	22.1	19.0	22.0	71	33
6.	Haora	45.6	25.0	18.5	20.5	18.0	20.0	79	48
7.	Hugli	36.0	25.0	19.4	20.1	19.0	19.0	89	24
8.	Jalpaiguri	37.5	21.4	19.0	21.8	18.0	20.0	96	14
9.	Koch Bihar	55.5	16.7	17.4	22.3	17.0	20.0	128	12
10.	Kolkata	**	18.7	NA	20.6	NA	20.0	**	91
11.	Maldah	59.3	16.7	16.8	21.2	16.0	21.0	91	6
12.	Medinipur	40.9	30.0	18.5	20.0	18.0	20.0	115	10
13.	Murshidabad	78.9	81.3	15.8	17.4	16.0	16.0	142	16
14.	Nadia	46.8	22.7	17.9	20.8	18.0	19.0	79	22
15.	North 24 Parganas	58.1	31.6	16.7	20.6	17.0	20.0	62	38
16.	Puruliya	79.5	28.6	15.7	19.6	15.0	19.0	127	14
17.	South 24 Parganas	51.0	22.2	17.7	20.3	17.0	19.0	100	9
18.	Uttar Dinajpur	65.3	21.1	16.7	19.9	17.0	19.0	118	19
16	**Andaman & Nicobar**								
1.	Andaman	18.9	0.0	20.0	22.1	19.0	21.5	53	10
2.	Nicobar	3.4	**	22.5	NA	22.0	NA	58	**
17	**Arunachal Pradesh**								
1.	Changlang	32.7	40.0	19.3	18.4	18.5	19.0	52	5
2.	Dibang Valley	36.1	20.0	19.2	17.6	18.0	18.0	36	5
3.	East Kameng	46.9	22.2	17.2	20.2	18.0	20.0	64	9
4.	East Siang	35.1	30.0	19.1	19.2	19.0	19.0	37	10
5.	Lohit	6.3	27.3	19.4	18.5	19.0	18.0	32	11
6.	Lower Subansiri	30.8	40.0	18.2	20.9	18.0	18.5	39	10
7.	Papum Pare	21.1	26.3	20.0	19.2	19.0	19.0	19	19
8.	Tawang	0.0	**	21.2	NA	20.0	NA	17	**
9.	Tirap	35.3	100.0	19.7	16.0	20.0	16.0	17	1
10.	Upper Siang	5.9	14.3	18.9	20.3	19.0	20.0	17	7

Appendix - II (Continued)

Sr. No.	State/District	Age at Marriage						Total Number of marriages	
		<18 years (%)		Mean		Median			
		Rural	Urban	Rural	Urban	Rural	Urban	Rural	Urban
11.	Upper Subansiri	43.3	36.4	17.9	18.8	18.0	18.0	30	22
12.	West Kameng	38.7	36.4	19.0	18.3	18.0	18.0	31	11
13.	West Siang	40.7	0.0	18.4	20.3	18.0	18.5	27	4
18	**Chandigarh**								
1.	Chandigarh	0.0	0.0	18.0	22.8	18.0	22.5	1	42
19	**Dadra & Nagar Haveli**								
1.	Dadra & Nagar Haveli	54.7	0.0	17.1	21.7	17.0	22.5	75	6
20	**Daman & Diu**								
1.	Daman	21.8	9.8	19.3	20.3	19.0	20.0	87	51
2.	Diu	20.8	10.4	19.3	20.3	19.0	20.0	48	48
21	**Delhi**								
1.	Delhi	14.3	4.4	19.4	21.1	19.0	21.0	28	91
22	**Goa**								
1.	North Goa	2.3	6.9	23.7	23.6	24.0	24.0	43	29
2.	South Goa	2.8	1.9	23.5	24.2	24.0	24.0	36	53
23	**Himachal Pradesh**								
1.	Bilaspur(Pra.Him)	5.1	0.0	20.7	20.8	20.0	21.0	59	6
2.	Chamba	2.6	0.0	21.3	23.8	21.0	24.0	114	11
3.	Hamirpur(HP)	0.9	0.0	20.3	23.7	20.0	23.0	107	3
4.	Kangra	3.8	0.0	21.0	23.8	21.0	24.0	80	5
5.	Kinnaur	16.1	**	20.8	NA	21.0	NA	56	**
6.	Kullu	1.6	**	20.5	NA	20.0	NA	63	**
7.	Lahul & Spiti	0.0	**	23.0	NA	22.0	NA	22	**
8.	Mandi	4.2	0.0	20.6	22.0	20.0	22.0	118	1
9.	Shimla	2.2	0.0	21.2	22.7	21.0	22.5	46	6
10.	Sirmaur	7.5	0.0	20.3	21.8	20.0	20.0	53	5
11.	Solan	1.5	0.0	20.5	25.0	20.0	25.0	68	6
12.	Una	1.0	0.0	21.2	21.8	21.0	21.0	103	5
24	**Jammu & Kashmir**								
1.	Anantanag	2.0	**	22.4	NA	22.0	NA	50	**
2.	Badgam	3.2	**	21.2	NA	20.0	NA	31	**
3.	Baramula	7.5	**	21.5	NA	20.0	NA	53	**
4.	Doda	0.0	**	20.5	NA	20.0	NA	215	**
5.	Jammu	1.1	**	21.1	NA	22.0	NA	184	**
6.	Kargil	27.5	**	18.7	NA	18.0	NA	91	**
7.	Kathua	0.0	**	21.8	NA	22.0	NA	148	**
8.	Kupwara	0.0	**	20.2	NA	20.0	NA	24	**
9.	Leh	1.5	**	20.8	NA	20.0	NA	68	**
10.	Pulwama	0.0	**	22.8	NA	23.0	NA	18	**
11.	Punch	3.5	**	20.7	NA	20.0	NA	114	**
12.	Rajauri	0.2	0.0	18.9	18.0	19.0	18.0	460	1
13.	Srinagar	9.1	**	19.4	NA	20.0	NA	33	**
14.	Udhampur	1.3	**	19.4	NA	19.0	NA	151	**
25	**Lakshadweep**								
1.	Lakshadweep	16.2	20.0	20.1	19.8	20.0	19.0	74	85
26	**Manipur**								
1.	Bishnupur	18.5	5.6	21.9	23.2	21.0	22.5	81	18
2.	Chandel	20.0	25.0	21.9	21.9	20.0	20.0	70	8

Appendix - II (Continued)

Sr. No.	State/District	Age at Marriage						Total Number of marriages	
		<18 years (%)		Mean		Median			
		Rural	Urban	Rural	Urban	Rural	Urban	Rural	Urban
3.	Churachandpur	13.9	0.0	21.8	23.7	20.0	24.0	36	11
4.	Imphal	6.6	0.0	24.6	28.2	24.0	27.0	106	41
5.	Senapati	19.4	0.0	22.1	18.0	22.0	18.0	31	2
6.	Tamenglong	21.3	0.0	20.8	27.5	20.0	27.5	80	2
7.	Thoubal	14.3	20.0	21.2	21.8	20.0	21.0	84	25
8.	Ukhrul	18.8	0.0	23.2	20.0	21.0	20.0	32	1
27	**Meghalaya**								
1.	East Garo Hills	0.0	0.0	20.5	19.0	20.0	19.0	26	1
2.	East Khasi Hills	10.5	33.3	19.2	21.3	19.0	24.0	19	3
3.	Jaintia Hills	0.8	0.0	20.1	22.3	20.0	22.0	241	20
4.	Ri Bhoi	2.3	**	19.5	NA	19.0	NA	43	**
5.	South Garp Hills	0.0	0.0	22.0	19.5	18.0	19.5	3	2
6.	West Garo Hills	15.4	0.0	19.2	29.3	19.0	32.0	13	3
7.	West Khasi Hills	2.0	0.0	20.0	20.0	20.0	20.0	49	2
28	**Mizoram**								
1.	Aizwal	4.5	10.0	21.8	21.8	21.0	19.0	44	40
2.	Chhimtuipui	24.1	29.4	19.3	19.9	19.0	19.0	58	17
3.	Lunglei	9.1	4.5	20.4	21.5	20.0	21.0	22	22
29	**Nagaland**								
1.	Kohima	57.7	52.9	17.3	17.9	17.0	17.0	52	34
2.	Mokokchung	14.9	0.0	20.7	19.3	21.0	19.0	47	3
3.	Mon	12.0	0.0	19.2	20.3	19.0	20.0	142	10
4.	Phek	35.3	50.0	18.2	17.0	18.0	17.0	17	2
5.	Tuensang	8.9	0.0	19.9	18.0	20.0	18.0	79	2
6.	Wokha	24.8	29.4	19.4	19.1	19.0	19.0	105	17
7.	Zunheboto	24.3	23.3	19.0	19.0	19.0	19.0	107	43
30	**Pondicherry**								
1.	Karaikal	9.1	1.5	21.4	21.0	21.0	20.0	77	65
2.	Mahe	**	2.6	NA	22.4	NA	21.0	**	191
3.	Pondicherry	7.7	2.7	20.5	22.2	20.0	22.0	39	73
4.	Yanam	**	23.2	NA	18.9	NA	19.0	**	82
31	**Sikkim**								
1.	East Sikkim	10.6	25.0	22.0	20.6	22.0	21.5	47	8
2.	North Sikkim	14.3	0.0	20.8	29.0	20.0	29.0	21	1
3.	South Sikkim	13.0	20.0	21.1	20.4	20.0	21.0	23	5
4.	West Sikkim	16.9	**	20.4	NA	19.0	NA	65	**
32	**Tripura**								
1.	North Tripura	35.5	30.0	18.6	19.8	18.0	18.5	62	10
2.	South Tripura	47.3	20.0	19.1	22.4	18.0	24.0	93	5
3.	West Tripura	15.6	0.0	21.5	21.5	20.0	21.5	77	4

Note: In the column showing percent of marriages below legal minimum age, 0.0 indicates no marriage below 18 years.

** No marriage is reported in that category of characteristic/district.

NA Not applicable.

APPENDIX - III

Percent of Marriages below legal Minimum Age of 18 years and Average Age at Marriage in each District by Caste-GIRLS

Sr. No.	State/District	Age at Marriage <18 years (%) SC/ST/OBC	<18 years (%) OC	Mean SC/ST	Mean OC	Median SC/ST OBC	Median OC	Total Number of marriages SC/ST OBC	Total Number of marriages OC
1	**Andhra Pradesh**								
1.	Adilabad	47.9	42.9	17.4	18.3	18.0	18.0	71	7
2.	Anantapur	40.7	12.5	17.8	19.8	18.0	18.5	54	16
3.	Chittoor	23.5	23.1	19.4	20.3	20.0	20.0	17	13
4.	Cuddapah	40.0	25.0	17.6	19.3	18.0	19.0	60	40
5.	East Godavari	44.2	42.1	17.9	17.4	18.0	18.0	52	19
6.	Guntur	40.0	30.0	19.0	19.0	18.0	18.0	25	20
7.	Hyderabad	9.1	4.9	19.9	21.1	19.5	20.0	22	41
8.	Karimnagar	43.9	33.3	17.6	18.0	18.0	18.5	41	6
9.	Khammam	35.0	21.4	17.6	18.8	18.0	19.0	40	14
10.	Krishna	35.3	13.0	18.3	19.0	18.0	18.0	34	23
11.	Kurnool	47.5	10.5	17.4	20.5	18.0	20.0	61	19
12.	Mahbubnagar	42.9	34.6	17.6	17.9	18.0	18.0	42	26
13.	Medak	38.2	27.3	18.1	17.7	18.0	18.0	34	11
14.	Nalgonda	45.8	29.4	17.8	18.4	18.0	18.0	59	17
15.	Nellore	23.4	29.4	19.1	18.9	19.0	18.0	47	17
16.	Nizamabad	50.0	33.3	17.4	18.7	17.5	18.0	44	18
17.	Prakasam	42.5	37.5	18.0	18.6	18.0	18.0	40	24
18.	Rangareddi	40.3	20.0	18.4	20.4	18.0	20.0	62	20
19.	Srikakulam	55.1	40.7	17.0	18.4	17.0	18.0	69	27
20.	Vishkhapatanam	66.7	35.7	16.9	18.3	16.0	18.0	21	14
21.	Vizianagaram	45.1	16.7	17.5	19.6	18.0	19.0	71	12
22.	Warangal	50.0	37.5	17.4	19.6	17.5	18.0	56	8
23.	West Godavari	31.9	27.3	18.0	18.3	18.0	18.0	69	33
2	**Assam**								
1.	Barpeta	0.0	24.3	21.7	19.1	21.5	19.0	12	37
2.	Bongaigaon	26.8	48.9	19.7	19.0	19.0	18.0	56	92
3.	Cachar	20.0	19.7	21.1	20.0	21.0	20.0	35	61
4.	Darrang	23.8	38.9	20.0	18.3	20.0	19.0	21	36
5.	Dhemaji	4.2	0.0	20.3	21.7	20.0	20.0	48	3
6.	Dhubri	50.0	60.4	17.4	17.7	17.5	17.0	14	96
7.	Dibrugarh	16.7	40.0	21.0	20.2	19.0	19.0	18	10
8.	Goalpara	30.8	53.2	19.8	17.9	19.5	17.0	52	47
9.	Golaghat	27.3	31.3	19.7	19.4	19.5	19.0	44	48
10.	Hailakandi	9.0	8.0	22.3	20.6	20.0	20.0	67	75
11.	Jorhat	12.1	0.0	20.5	22.3	21.0	22.0	33	19
12.	Kamrup	13.2	16.0	20.4	21.5	20.0	22.0	38	50
13.	Karbi Anglong	4.8	**	19.7	NA	19.0	NA	63	**
14.	Karimganj	13.5	29.8	22.7	20.6	22.0	19.0	37	57

Appendix - III (Continued)

Sr. No.	State/District	Age at Marriage <18 years (%) SC/ST/OBC	OC	Mean SC/ST OBC	OC	Median SC/ST OBC	OC	Total Number of marriages SC/ST OBC	OC
15.	Lakhimpur	41.2	25.0	19.1	20.6	18.0	19.0	17	8
16.	Marigaon	15.5	49.3	20.0	18.2	20.0	18.0	58	67
17.	Nagaon	24.2	49.3	20.5	18.0	20.0	18.0	33	75
18.	Nalbari	0.0	7.5	21.7	21.6	22.0	22.0	23	40
19.	North Cachar Hills	7.8	0.0	20.6	21.0	20.0	21.0	64	1
20.	Sibsagar	0.0	18.8	23.8	20.9	21.5	20.0	8	16
21.	Sonitpur	31.6	28.6	18.9	19.9	18.0	19.0	38	21
22.	Tinsukia	15.0	26.2	21.1	19.9	21.5	19.0	20	61
3	**Bihar**								
1.	Araria	54.3	40.7	17.3	18.2	17.0	18.0	105	27
2.	Aurangabad (Bih)	67.7	38.5	16.3	18.2	16.0	18.0	158	26
3.	Begusarai	67.8	33.3	16.1	18.2	16.0	18.0	121	45
4.	Bhagalpur	65.3	35.3	16.3	18.6	16.0	18.0	124	34
5.	Bhojpur	68.0	22.5	15.9	18.7	16.0	19.0	122	40
6.	Buxar	76.7	39.1	16.0	17.9	16.0	18.0	146	64
7.	Darbhanga	70.0	23.3	16.6	18.8	16.0	18.0	110	73
8.	Deoghar	70.3	41.2	15.7	17.8	15.0	18.0	111	17
9.	Dhanbad	53.8	24.2	17.2	19.4	17.0	19.0	52	33
10.	Dumka	49.0	50.0	17.4	18.3	18.0	17.5	102	12
11.	Gaya	68.3	27.6	15.8	18.1	16.0	18.0	142	29
12.	Giridih	62.1	45.5	16.6	18.2	16.0	18.0	95	22
13.	Godda	67.0	60.0	16.6	17.6	16.0	16.5	106	10
14.	Gopalganj	65.1	28.6	16.6	19.1	17.0	18.5	126	28
15.	Gulma	30.0	17.6	18.7	19.2	18.0	20.0	60	17
16.	Hazaribagh	71.3	42.9	16.1	18.4	16.0	18.0	108	21
17.	Jehanabad	62.8	27.7	16.4	18.5	16.0	18.0	148	47
18.	Katihar	52.9	34.4	17.4	18.0	17.0	18.0	85	32
19.	Khagaria	70.6	31.0	16.1	19.0	16.0	20.0	143	29
20.	Kishanganj	46.7	50.0	17.6	18.1	18.0	17.5	45	42
21.	Lohardaga	42.0	50.0	18.2	18.4	18.0	18.0	88	16
22.	Madhepura	74.6	15.0	16.1	18.7	16.0	18.5	126	20
23.	Madhubani	76.9	25.0	15.9	18.2	16.0	18.0	108	36
24.	Munger	63.5	47.8	16.0	18.3	16.0	18.0	104	23
25.	Muzaffarpur	64.9	17.5	16.6	20.2	16.0	20.0	131	40
26.	Nalanda	65.6	28.1	16.1	18.3	16.0	18.0	131	32
27.	Nawada	79.4	47.9	15.2	17.6	15.0	18.0	165	48
28.	Palamu	78.8	22.7	15.5	19.3	15.0	19.5	80	22
29.	Pashchim Champaran	45.0	24.2	17.5	20.1	18.0	20.0	131	33
30.	Pashchmi Singhbhum	29.2	25.0	19.0	18.3	18.0	18.0	72	12
31.	Patna	84.3	62.9	15.1	16.7	15.0	17.0	121	35
32.	Purba Champaran	68.2	41.7	16.5	18.1	16.0	18.0	148	36
33.	Purbi Singhbhum	42.9	13.9	18.4	21.6	18.0	21.0	70	36
34.	Purnia	57.7	22.5	17.1	20.7	17.0	20.5	111	40
35.	Ranchi	43.1	10.0	17.9	21.1	18.0	20.5	72	10
36.	Rohtas	76.7	42.9	15.9	18.2	16.0	18.0	103	28
37.	Saharsa	63.2	34.3	16.5	19.6	16.0	18.0	117	35
38.	Sahibganj	65.2	52.9	16.5	17.1	16.0	16.0	66	17
39.	Samastipur	71.3	33.3	15.9	17.8	16.0	18.0	129	30
40.	Saran	54.7	42.0	17.0	17.9	17.0	18.0	137	50
41.	Sitamarhi	75.5	37.2	16.1	17.7	16.0	18.0	110	43

Appendix - III (Continued)

Sr. No.	State/District	Age at Marriage <18 years (%) SC/ST/OBC	OC	Mean SC/ST OBC	OC	Median SC/ST OBC	OC	Total Number of marriages SC/ST OBC	OC
42.	Siwan	55.0	25.7	17.2	18.9	17.0	19.0	100	70
43.	Vaishali	73.6	30.8	15.9	18.5	16.0	18.0	125	39
4	**Gujarat**								
1.	Ahmadabad	46.8	9.4	18.4	21.6	18.0	22.0	47	53
2.	Amreli	26.8	7.3	19.0	20.3	18.5	20.0	82	82
3.	Banas Kantha	55.1	47.9	17.1	17.4	17.0	18.0	78	48
4.	Bharuch	21.4	11.9	19.2	20.8	19.0	20.0	70	42
5.	Bhavnagar	34.7	17.5	18.0	19.6	18.0	19.0	95	57
6.	Gandhinagar	51.1	6.1	17.4	20.7	17.0	21.0	47	33
7.	Jamnagar	16.4	3.5	19.6	20.8	20.0	21.0	73	57
8.	Junagadh	13.9	6.5	20.2	20.3	20.0	20.0	115	46
9.	Kachchh	28.1	15.2	18.6	20.5	19.0	20.0	57	46
10.	Kheda	30.3	14.9	18.6	19.9	18.0	20.0	33	47
11.	Mahesana	44.3	20.3	17.8	19.4	18.0	19.5	70	64
12.	Panch Mahals	34.0	15.4	18.2	19.2	18.0	19.0	53	26
13.	Rajkot	17.9	10.4	19.3	20.3	19.0	20.0	67	77
14.	Sabar Kantha	34.1	24.5	18.3	19.2	18.0	19.0	82	49
15.	Surat	20.3	16.2	19.5	20.0	20.0	20.0	64	37
16.	Surendranagar	13.3	7.0	19.2	20.8	19.0	20.0	45	43
17.	The Dangs	47.2	50.0	17.7	18.0	18.0	19.0	125	4
18.	Vadodara	40.0	17.6	18.1	20.7	18.0	21.0	65	34
19.	Valsad	7.4	7.1	20.6	21.9	20.0	21.5	81	14
5	**Haryana**								
1.	Ambala	15.7	10.9	19.6	21.1	20.0	21.0	51	55
2.	Bhiwani	54.7	44.2	16.9	17.5	17.0	18.0	64	77
3.	Faridabad	36.8	25.6	18.2	19.3	18.0	19.0	57	82
4.	Gurgaon	36.8	36.4	17.7	18.0	18.0	18.0	38	66
5.	Hisar	47.3	38.7	17.4	17.6	18.0	18.0	55	62
6.	Jind	36.2	37.0	17.7	18.1	18.0	18.0	47	81
7.	Kaithal	40.0	29.2	17.8	18.7	18.0	18.0	30	48
8.	Karnal	15.1	17.3	19.2	19.9	19.0	20.0	73	75
9.	Kurukshetra	24.4	9.8	19.0	20.5	19.0	20.0	41	82
10.	Mahendragarh	53.0	33.3	17.2	18.5	17.0	18.0	115	60
11.	Panchkula	42.4	13.6	17.6	20.0	18.0	20.0	33	44
12.	Panipat	48.3	38.5	17.6	18.1	18.0	18.0	89	39
13.	Rewari	34.3	26.7	18.1	18.7	18.0	19.0	35	90
14.	Rohtak	38.8	29.7	18.5	18.8	18.0	18.0	67	74
15.	Sirsa	38.5	27.5	17.8	19.2	18.0	19.0	39	69
16.	Sonipat	9.5	1.9	19.9	21.4	19.5	21.0	74	54
17.	Yamunanagar	8.5	5.3	20.5	21.1	20.0	20.0	59	75
6	**Karnataka**								
1.	Bangalore	18.2	8.6	20.3	21.7	20.0	21.0	33	35
2.	Bangalore Rural	27.7	0.0	18.6	20.4	18.0	19.0	83	17
3.	Belgaum	68.6	43.5	16.5	18.2	16.0	18.0	51	46
4.	Bellary	59.5	28.1	17.1	20.3	17.0	20.0	74	32
5.	Bidar	81.6	64.7	15.6	16.6	16.0	16.0	49	102
6.	Bijapur	75.8	50.0	15.3	17.3	15.0	17.5	66	40
7.	Chikmagalur	18.2	12.6	19.8	21.1	20.0	20.0	33	87
8.	Chitradurga	39.7	9.4	18.0	20.2	18.0	20.0	78	32
9.	Dakshina Kannada	11.1	3.1	21.6	23.2	21.0	23.0	27	65

Appendix - III (Continued)

Sr. No.	State/District	Age at Marriage <18 years (%) SC/ST/OBC	OC	Mean SC/ST OBC	OC	Median SC/ST OBC	OC	Total Number of marriages SC/ST OBC	OC
10.	Dharwad	50.0	29.4	18.4	20.3	17.5	19.0	40	51
11.	Gulbarga	68.9	33.3	15.8	18.7	15.0	19.0	45	45
12.	Hassan	19.4	5.3	19.6	20.7	19.0	20.0	93	38
13.	Kodagu	18.5	5.7	20.0	21.1	20.0	21.0	27	35
14.	Kolar	36.5	10.0	18.2	21.1	18.0	22.0	115	10
15.	Mandya	40.4	39.6	17.8	18.4	18.0	18.0	52	48
16.	Mysore	55.2	31.6	17.4	18.9	17.0	18.0	67	19
17.	Raichur	73.3	45.9	15.9	18.6	16.0	18.0	45	61
18.	Shimoga	16.5	13.2	20.3	21.5	20.0	21.0	91	53
19.	Tumkur	39.6	20.3	17.9	19.5	18.0	18.0	48	59
20.	Uttara Kannada	18.1	2.8	21.0	23.1	20.0	23.0	83	36
7	**Kerala**								
1.	Alappuzha	0.0	0.0	22.7	23.8	22.0	23.0	101	43
2.	Ernakulam	0.0	0.0	23.9	24.2	23.0	24.0	34	31
3.	Idukki	1.7	2.1	22.7	23.8	23.0	23.5	58	48
4.	Kannur	8.6	0.0	22.5	23.1	22.0	24.0	81	11
5.	Kasaragod	19.6	6.1	20.5	22.8	20.0	22.0	102	33
6.	Kollam	0.0	0.0	21.9	23.4	21.0	23.0	78	41
7.	Kottayam	0.0	0.0	23.8	24.3	23.0	24.0	62	30
8.	Kozhikode	12.8	0.0	20.9	23.4	20.0	23.0	109	17
9.	Malappuram	22.9	14.3	19.4	21.3	18.0	19.0	35	7
10.	Palakkad	11.1	0.0	20.6	23.9	20.0	23.0	117	30
11.	Pathanamthitta	0.0	0.0	22.9	23.5	23.0	23.0	55	39
12.	Thiruvananthapuram	0.0	0.0	22.8	23.8	23.0	24.0	52	47
13.	Thrissur	0.0	0.0	22.6	22.2	21.0	22.0	85	39
14.	Wayanad	13.0	5.0	20.6	22.5	20.0	21.5	46	20
8	**Madhya Pradesh**								
1.	Balaghat	34.5	0.0	18.0	20.7	18.0	19.0	29	3
2.	Bastar	32.6	28.6	18.4	19.7	18.0	20.0	46	7
3.	Betul	26.2	0.0	18.2	19.7	18.0	19.0	42	3
4.	Bhind	73.5	46.5	16.4	17.5	16.0	18.0	83	71
5.	Bhopal	36.7	23.1	17.5	20.3	18.0	19.0	30	39
6.	Bilaspur(MP)	43.0	18.2	17.9	21.1	18.0	22.0	107	11
7.	Chattarpur	80.0	50.0	16.3	17.8	16.0	17.5	40	12
8.	Chhindwara	34.9	5.9	18.2	19.8	18.0	19.0	106	17
9.	Damoh	63.8	6.7	16.8	20.1	16.0	20.0	80	15
10.	Datia	55.8	29.6	17.0	18.5	17.0	19.0	77	27
11.	Dewas	60.8	32.3	16.6	18.5	17.0	18.0	79	31
12.	Dhar	58.5	50.0	16.7	17.5	16.0	17.5	94	28
13.	Durg	39.2	5.9	18.6	20.2	18.0	20.0	51	17
14.	East Nimar	45.5	26.9	17.8	19.7	18.0	19.0	88	26
15.	Guna	76.7	31.6	16.4	19.1	16.0	19.0	90	19
16.	Gwalior	50.9	18.4	17.9	20.4	17.0	19.0	55	49
17.	Hoshangabad	43.8	35.3	17.3	18.9	18.0	20.0	32	17
18.	Indore	44.4	35.9	17.9	19.3	18.0	20.0	81	39
19.	Jabalpur	48.3	19.0	17.4	20.1	18.0	18.0	58	21
20.	Jhabua	61.2	14.3	17.0	20.1	17.0	20.0	98	7
21.	Mandla	38.5	**	17.6	NA	18.0	NA	39	**
22.	Mandsaur	71.1	31.0	15.9	18.8	16.0	18.0	83	42
23.	Morena	88.1	50.0	15.0	17.2	15.0	17.5	42	32

Appendix - III (Continued)

Sr. No.	State/District	Age at Marriage <18 years (%) SC/ST/OBC	OC	Mean SC/ST OBC	OC	Median SC/ST OBC	OC	Total Number of marriages SC/ST OBC	OC
24.	Narsimhapur	56.1	27.3	17.8	19.5	17.0	20.0	57	22
25.	Panna	61.5	47.6	16.8	17.7	16.0	18.0	26	21
26.	Raigarh(M P)	8.7	0.0	19.2	20.3	18.0	20.0	46	6
27.	Raipur	56.5	42.9	17.4	18.0	17.0	18.0	46	7
28.	Raisen	52.0	26.9	17.2	18.5	17.0	18.5	100	26
29.	Rajgarh	72.6	47.5	15.5	18.5	15.0	18.0	84	40
30.	Rajnandgaon	49.5	25.0	17.5	17.3	18.0	18.0	99	4
31.	Ratlam	52.3	30.3	16.6	18.7	17.0	19.0	44	33
32.	Rewa	69.0	50.8	15.8	17.2	15.5	17.0	58	63
33.	Sagar	74.6	13.0	16.1	20.0	16.0	20.0	71	23
34.	Satna	67.7	51.7	16.1	17.4	16.0	17.0	62	58
35.	Sehore	50.0	31.0	17.5	18.9	17.5	19.0	76	29
36.	Seoni	42.4	8.3	17.4	21.0	18.0	20.0	59	12
37.	Shahdol	87.5	40.0	15.1	18.0	16.0	18.0	16	15
38.	Shajapur	84.4	78.9	15.2	15.2	15.0	15.0	64	38
39.	Shivpuri	73.5	46.2	15.9	17.8	16.0	18.0	68	26
40.	Sidhi	76.8	48.3	14.9	17.1	15.0	18.0	56	29
41.	Surguja	64.3	21.4	16.1	19.1	16.0	18.5	56	14
42.	Tikamgarh	78.4	21.1	15.4	19.1	15.0	18.0	102	19
43.	Ujjain	53.2	14.6	16.9	19.5	17.0	19.0	79	48
44.	Vidisha	68.4	45.7	16.0	18.7	16.0	18.0	79	46
45.	West Nimar	44.9	31.8	17.2	19.1	18.0	18.0	78	22
9	**Maharashtra**								
1.	Ahmadnagar	54.5	29.0	16.7	18.4	17.0	18.0	55	69
2.	Akola	37.9	33.3	18.1	18.6	18.0	18.0	87	33
3.	Amravali	9.9	6.3	19.5	19.9	19.0	19.5	101	32
4.	Aurangabad(Mah)	52.9	46.0	17.2	17.4	17.0	18.0	51	87
5.	Bhandara	9.8	0.0	20.0	20.3	20.0	20.0	122	6
6.	Bid	64.1	50.0	16.8	17.2	17.0	17.5	39	58
7.	Buldana	39.2	20.9	18.0	19.5	18.0	19.0	97	43
8.	Chandrapur	28.4	9.1	18.7	20.2	18.0	20.0	88	11
9.	Dhule	33.9	46.3	18.4	18.0	18.0	18.0	62	41
10.	Gadchiroli	27.9	16.7	18.4	20.3	18.0	20.0	61	6
11.	Greater Bombay (Mumbai)	19.2	3.4	20.3	21.6	19.0	21.0	26	59
12.	Jalgaon	47.7	41.1	17.7	18.3	18.0	18.0	88	56
13.	Jalna	55.2	55.4	17.1	17.2	17.0	17.0	67	65
14.	Kolhapur	23.8	12.7	18.3	19.4	18.0	18.0	42	79
15.	Latur	70.4	50.0	16.4	17.7	16.0	17.5	54	86
16.	Nagpur	13.8	3.6	19.8	21.2	19.0	20.0	87	28
17.	Nanded	67.0	56.6	16.6	16.9	16.0	17.0	91	53
18.	Nashik	35.3	28.6	18.2	18.7	18.0	18.0	34	42
19.	Osmanabad	47.8	45.9	17.2	17.6	18.0	18.0	46	85
20.	Parbhani	60.0	34.8	17.1	18.0	16.0	18.0	55	66
21.	Pune	26.9	33.9	18.3	18.5	18.0	18.0	52	62
22.	Raigarh(MAH)	17.3	14.7	19.2	18.6	19.0	18.0	52	34
23.	Ratnagiri	16.2	8.2	19.7	20.3	19.0	19.0	74	49
24.	Sangli	26.8	23.5	18.8	18.5	18.0	18.0	56	68
25.	Satara	26.7	20.2	18.7	18.4	18.0	18.0	30	84
26.	Sindhudurg	3.1	4.3	21.3	21.6	20.0	21.0	32	70

Appendix - III (Continued)

Sr. No.	State/District	Age at Marriage <18 years (%) SC/ST/ OBC	OC	Mean SC/ST OBC	OC	Median SC/ST OBC	OC	Total Number of marriages SC/ST OBC	OC
27.	Solapur	51.1	37.0	17.3	18.8	17.0	18.0	47	73
28.	Thane	29.8	5.9	18.7	21.3	18.0	21.0	47	34
29.	Wardha	13.8	0.0	20.0	21.5	19.0	20.0	94	11
30.	Yavatmal	27.7	20.0	18.4	19.0	18.0	19.0	137	15
10	**Orissa**								
1.	Anugul	42.4	37.2	18.3	19.6	18.0	19.0	66	43
2.	Balangir	62.9	22.2	17.6	23.0	17.0	21.0	62	9
3.	Balasore	32.9	22.4	19.5	20.3	19.0	20.0	85	58
4.	Bargarh	41.8	14.3	18.2	20.7	18.0	22.0	91	7
5.	Baudh	57.1	10.0	17.2	19.6	17.0	18.0	63	10
6.	Bhadrak	20.0	10.1	20.5	21.9	20.0	22.0	90	69
7.	Cuttack	17.2	4.4	19.8	22.0	20.0	22.0	64	68
8.	Debagarh	34.9	22.2	18.9	20.3	18.0	20.0	63	9
9.	Dhenkanal	51.2	8.9	18.0	20.8	17.0	20.0	86	45
10.	Gajapati	46.0	18.2	17.6	19.7	18.0	20.0	63	11
11.	Ganjam	52.5	45.5	17.7	18.3	17.0	18.0	101	33
12.	Jagatsinghapur	13.4	5.5	21.4	22.2	21.0	23.0	67	73
13.	Jajapur	17.3	7.0	20.4	21.6	20.0	22.0	98	43
14.	Jharsuguda	18.6	7.7	19.3	20.6	19.0	20.0	59	13
15.	Kalahandi	67.9	23.1	16.6	20.2	16.5	21.0	56	13
16.	Kendrapara	20.0	8.6	20.1	22.2	20.0	23.0	100	58
17.	Kendujhar	33.7	0.0	19.2	22.1	19.0	23.0	89	12
18.	Khordha	25.9	20.0	19.6	20.6	19.0	21.0	58	55
19.	Koraput	68.9	28.6	16.8	20.7	16.0	21.0	61	7
20.	Malkangiri	55.6	60.0	17.0	17.0	17.0	17.0	45	5
21.	Mayurbhanj	38.9	13.0	18.8	20.9	18.0	21.0	72	23
22.	Nabarangapur	78.0	0.0	16.3	21.2	16.0	20.0	41	5
23.	Nayagarh	56.1	41.4	17.5	19.0	17.0	18.0	107	29
24.	Nuapada	48.8	0.0	17.8	21.2	18.0	20.5	41	6
25.	Phulbani	36.7	63.6	17.8	17.0	18.0	17.0	49	11
26.	Puri	16.7	12.7	20.7	20.8	20.5	21.0	36	71
27.	Rayagada	43.9	16.7	18.2	20.6	18.0	20.0	57	12
28.	Sambalpur	35.4	0.0	18.8	21.7	18.0	21.0	48	10
29.	Sonapur	41.5	23.1	18.6	19.2	18.0	18.0	94	13
30.	Sundargarh	13.9	20.0	20.3	20.1	19.0	18.5	36	10
11	**Punjab**								
1.	Amritsar	9.3	12.2	20.8	19.7	20.0	20.0	43	74
2.	Bathinda	26.1	4.2	18.9	20.3	19.0	20.0	46	71
3.	Faridkot	19.0	6.3	19.5	20.8	19.0	20.0	63	64
4.	Fatehgarh Sahib	10.8	3.4	19.8	20.7	19.0	21.0	74	87
5.	Firozpur	31.5	19.4	18.3	20.4	18.0	20.0	54	62
6.	Gurdaspur	6.1	5.6	20.9	20.8	20.0	20.0	49	71
7.	Hoshiarpur	3.1	3.2	21.0	21.6	20.5	22.0	96	62
8.	Jalandhar	3.0	11.8	21.2	20.6	20.0	21.0	67	68
9.	Kapurthala	3.9	2.5	21.4	21.5	22.0	21.0	51	79
10.	Ludhiana	15.6	3.9	20.2	20.9	20.0	21.0	45	76
11.	Mansa	29.7	12.3	18.6	20.4	19.0	20.0	64	73
12.	Moga	22.5	2.5	19.2	21.2	19.0	20.0	89	81
13.	Muktsar	36.1	8.7	18.5	20.6	18.0	20.0	83	69
14.	Nawanshahr	2.9	0.0	20.9	22.7	20.0	23.0	105	36

Appendix - III (Continued)

Sr. No.	State/District	Age at Marriage <18 years (%) SC/ST/OBC	OC	Mean SC/ST OBC	OC	Median SC/ST OBC	OC	Total Number of marriages SC/ST OBC	OC
15.	Patiala	13.2	8.2	19.7	20.7	20.0	21.0	38	49
16	Rupnagar	8.2	4.1	20.4	21.4	20.0	22.0	61	73
17	Sangrur	17.9	9.9	19.3	21.1	19.0	21.0	67	91
12	**Rajasthan**								
1.	Ajmer	64.4	34.5	15.8	19.4	16.0	20.0	45	55
2.	Alwar	68.0	36.2	16.2	18.4	16.0	18.0	75	69
3.	Banswara	61.5	16.7	16.6	18.6	17.0	19.0	65	12
4.	Barmer	54.7	45.1	16.8	17.0	17.0	18.0	53	51
5.	Bharatpur	65.0	47.9	16.3	17.8	16.0	18.0	60	73
6.	Bhilwara	78.9	58.9	14.6	17.5	15.0	17.0	76	56
7.	Bikaner	67.6	59.1	16.4	16.5	16.0	16.5	34	44
8.	Bundi	88.6	45.0	14.4	17.7	15.0	18.0	70	20
9.	Chittaurgarh	58.3	36.8	16.3	18.4	17.0	19.0	24	19
10.	Churu	75.5	62.0	15.6	16.9	16.0	17.0	53	71
11.	Dausa	79.6	30.4	15.4	18.4	15.0	18.0	108	23
12.	Dhaulpur	70.8	43.4	16.1	17.5	16.0	18.0	48	53
13.	Dungarpur	37.7	29.1	17.8	18.5	18.0	18.0	69	55
14.	Ganganagar	60.0	38.5	16.4	18.1	17.0	18.0	50	65
15.	Hanumangarh	54.5	49.4	17.0	17.3	17.0	18.0	66	85
16.	Jaipur	59.0	24.3	16.6	19.4	17.0	19.0	78	70
17.	Jaisalmer	55.9	45.0	16.7	17.5	17.0	18.0	34	40
18.	Jalor	55.0	32.1	16.9	18.3	17.0	18.0	80	56
19.	Jhalawar	87.3	48.0	14.6	17.1	15.0	18.0	63	50
20.	Jhunjhunun	53.2	39.1	16.9	17.9	17.0	18.0	79	64
21.	Jodhpur	75.0	46.3	15.9	18.6	16.0	18.0	16	41
22.	Kota	73.8	31.0	15.9	19.3	16.0	20.0	65	29
23.	Nagaur	73.5	60.3	15.4	16.8	15.0	17.0	49	63
24.	Pali	52.3	47.4	17.1	17.5	17.0	18.0	44	38
25.	Rajsamand	55.2	39.5	16.8	17.9	17.0	18.0	29	38
26.	Sawai Madhopur	61.2	32.5	16.4	18.4	16.0	18.0	49	40
27.	Sikar	45.5	39.6	17.2	18.1	18.0	18.0	66	101
28.	Sirohi	41.9	15.8	17.7	19.1	18.0	19.0	31	19
29.	Tonk	80.2	61.8	14.8	17.3	15.0	17.0	96	34
30.	Udaipur	70.4	50.0	15.8	17.3	16.0	17.5	54	50
13	**Tamil Nadu**								
1.	Chengalpattu	10.6	0.0	20.2	20.6	20.0	19.0	85	5
2.	Chennai	6.1	0.0	21.3	23.1	21.0	23.0	98	10
3.	Coimbatore	14.6	33.3	21.0	19.7	21.0	18.0	82	9
4.	Dharmapuri	34.9	0.0	18.5	22.0	18.0	21.5	126	4
5.	Dindigul	26.5	100.0	19.9	16.0	19.5	16.0	68	1
6.	Kanniyakumari	0.0	0.0	23.1	22.6	23.0	22.5	71	16
7.	Madurai	26.2	0.0	20.4	22.3	20.0	23.0	130	3
8.	Namakkal	13.1	0.0	20.2	22.5	20.0	22.5	84	2
9.	North Arcot	21.1	25.0	19.7	20.6	19.0	19.5	109	12
10.	Periyar	13.7	0.0	20.8	18.0	20.0	18.0	73	1
11.	Pudukkottai	11.2	0.0	20.9	23.0	20.0	22.0	125	3
12.	Ramanathapuram	12.7	50.0	20.0	17.0	20.0	17.0	110	2
13.	Salem	42.3	0.0	18.6	21.6	18.0	21.0	104	5
14.	Sivaganganagar	8.1	0.0	21.0	24.7	20.0	25.0	135	3
15.	South Arcot	28.1	0.0	19.2	24.5	19.0	24.5	128	2

Appendix - III (Continued)

Sr. No.	State/District	Age at Marriage <18 years (%) SC/ST/ OBC	OC	Mean SC/ST OBC	OC	Median SC/ST OBC	OC	Total Number of marriages SC/ST OBC	OC
16.	Thanjavur	11.9	33.3	21.1	21.3	20.0	22.0	59	3
17.	The Nilgiris	9.0	0.0	21.5	29.0	21.0	29.0	67	1
18.	Theni	29.1	**	19.2	NA	19.0	NA	86	**
19.	Tiruchirappalli	24.3	20.0	20.2	21.2	19.0	21.0	74	5
20.	Tirunelveli	6.9	0.0	21.4	24.0	21.0	24.0	87	1
21.	Tiruvanamalai	25.9	0.0	19.2	21.3	19.0	21.0	139	4
22.	Tutikorin	7.5	0.0	21.2	23.6	21.0	22.0	106	5
23.	Virudhunagar	12.8	100.0	19.8	16.0	20.0	16.0	109	1
14	**Uttar Pradesh**								
1.	Agra	46.9	23.4	17.7	19.2	18.0	19.0	81	47
2.	Aligarh	54.3	32.5	17.1	18.4	17.0	18.0	35	40
3.	Allahabad	59.3	36.8	17.0	17.9	17.0	18.0	86	38
4.	Almora	22.2	11.8	19.0	19.4	18.0	19.0	18	51
5.	Ambedkarnagar	71.7	56.3	15.9	17.1	16.0	17.0	99	16
6.	Azamgarh	74.0	41.9	15.6	18.5	15.0	18.0	73	31
7.	Bahraich	88.0	60.5	14.4	16.9	14.0	16.0	75	43
8.	Ballia	69.4	25.7	16.4	18.7	16.0	18.0	62	35
9.	Banda	82.3	56.3	15.0	17.0	15.0	16.5	62	48
10.	Barabanki	64.7	26.5	15.8	18.6	16.0	18.0	85	34
11.	Bareilly	32.0	25.0	17.7	19.5	18.0	19.0	25	36
12.	Basti	82.1	59.3	14.7	17.4	15.0	17.0	95	27
13.	Bhadohi	69.6	63.4	16.3	16.4	16.0	16.0	138	41
14.	Bijnor	15.5	16.3	19.0	19.8	18.0	19.0	58	49
15.	Budaun	50.0	52.9	17.3	17.9	17.5	17.0	58	34
16.	Bulandshahar	38.5	21.6	18.0	19.2	18.0	19.0	26	51
17.	Chamoli	25.0	3.4	18.7	20.4	19.0	20.0	16	59
18.	Dehradun	29.0	5.7	18.9	21.6	19.0	21.0	31	53
19.	Deoria	60.5	40.9	16.6	19.0	16.0	18.0	86	22
20.	Etah	66.7	48.6	16.7	17.9	16.0	18.0	36	37
21.	Etawah	54.2	19.4	16.8	19.7	17.0	19.0	83	31
22.	Faizabad	62.7	62.3	15.9	16.7	16.0	17.0	75	53
23.	Farrukhabad	40.8	30.8	17.5	18.2	18.0	18.0	71	39
24.	Fatehpur	48.1	42.5	17.5	17.8	18.0	18.0	135	40
25.	Firozabad	58.6	34.9	16.9	19.1	17.0	19.0	99	43
26.	Ghaziabad	24.6	11.3	18.7	20.3	18.0	19.0	65	53
27.	Ghazipur	74.5	21.2	16.2	19.1	16.0	19.0	98	33
28.	Gonda	80.0	55.8	14.2	16.9	14.0	17.0	55	43
29.	Gorakhpur	79.2	34.8	15.7	19.0	16.0	20.0	53	23
30.	Hamirpur(UP)	55.9	30.6	17.0	18.4	17.0	18.0	111	36
31.	Hardoi	47.4	40.6	17.4	18.1	18.0	18.0	38	32
32.	Hardwar	21.7	2.4	18.7	21.5	18.0	21.0	46	42
33.	Hathras	55.7	37.7	17.1	18.9	17.0	18.0	61	53
34.	Jalaun	60.2	61.1	16.7	17.2	16.0	17.0	93	36
35.	Jaunpur	61.8	45.9	16.8	17.5	17.0	18.0	110	61
36.	Jhansi	50.8	27.8	17.3	19.1	17.0	18.0	63	36
37.	Kanpur Dehat	40.0	23.3	18.1	18.8	18.0	19.0	90	43
38.	Kanpur Nagar	6.7	4.7	20.2	21.8	20.0	22.0	45	43
39.	Kheri	56.5	46.3	16.9	18.2	17.0	18.0	108	41
40.	Lalitpur	95.7	42.9	14.3	18.1	14.0	18.0	70	21
41.	Lucknow	43.5	14.3	18.0	21.6	18.0	21.5	69	28
42.	Maharajganj	87.7	62.5	14.1	17.0	14.0	16.0	57	16

Appendix - III (Continued)

Sr. No.	State/District	Age at Marriage <18 years (%) SC/ST/OBC	OC	Mean SC/ST OBC	OC	Median SC/ST OBC	OC	Total Number of marriages SC/ST OBC	OC
43.	Mahoba	72.4	42.9	16.2	17.7	16.0	18.0	87	28
44.	Mainpuri	51.5	42.1	17.4	18.1	17.0	18.0	97	19
45.	Mathura	50.0	39.1	17.3	17.9	17.5	18.0	18	46
46.	Mau	42.3	23.1	17.5	19.6	18.0	20.0	123	39
47.	Meerut	13.3	15.8	19.6	19.8	20.0	19.0	30	38
3.	Mirzapur	63.3	44.7	16.5	17.8	16.5	18.0	98	47
49.	Muradabad	31.3	24.0	18.5	19.4	18.0	19.0	80	25
50.	Muzaffarnagar	37.5	8.6	18.1	20.3	18.0	20.0	40	58
51.	Nainital	9.5	9.6	19.0	20.0	18.0	19.0	21	52
52.	Pauri Garhwal	5.0	5.9	19.3	19.6	19.0	19.0	20	68
53.	Pilibhit	69.0	19.0	16.6	19.0	16.0	19.0	58	21
54.	Pithoragarh	27.8	21.5	18.3	19.0	18.0	19.0	18	65
55.	Pratapgarh	54.1	57.1	17.0	16.8	17.0	17.0	85	49
56.	Rae Bareli	47.6	40.0	16.8	17.9	18.0	18.0	84	60
57.	Rampur	37.0	22.6	17.7	18.5	18.0	18.0	46	31
58.	Saharanpur	22.9	14.6	18.8	19.6	18.0	19.0	48	48
59.	Shajahanabad	69.0	57.1	16.1	16.8	15.0	16.0	58	35
60.	Siddharthnagar	84.4	34.2	13.8	17.8	14.0	18.0	64	38
61.	Sitapur	70.1	46.7	16.2	17.8	16.0	18.0	77	30
62.	Sonbhadra	69.2	52.9	15.7	17.0	16.0	15.0	65	17
63.	Sultanpur	67.6	57.5	15.6	16.9	16.0	16.5	71	40
64.	Tehri Garhwal	13.3	13.0	17.9	19.1	18.0	19.0	15	69
65.	Udhamsingh Nagar	32.8	18.8	18.1	20.0	18.0	20.0	58	32
66.	Unnao	51.3	26.9	17.3	18.9	17.0	18.0	76	26
67.	Uttarkashi	0.0	18.2	18.3	19.5	18.0	19.0	4	66
68.	Varanasi	78.6	52.5	15.6	17.7	15.5	17.0	112	40
15	**West Bengal**								
1.	Bankura	56.3	41.4	17.0	18.8	17.0	18.0	64	70
2.	Barddhaman	71.4	42.4	16.8	18.7	16.0	18.0	63	92
3.	Birbhum	73.2	50.6	15.8	17.8	16.0	17.0	41	79
4.	Dakshin Dinajpur	64.9	64.7	16.5	17.0	16.0	17.0	57	85
5.	Darjiling	38.6	15.0	19.0	20.9	18.0	21.0	44	60
6.	Haora	39.1	39.6	19.4	19.1	19.0	18.0	23	91
7.	Hugli	32.4	34.7	19.3	19.6	18.0	19.0	37	75
8.	Jalpaiguri	35.1	39.3	19.2	20.3	18.0	19.5	74	28
9.	Koch Bihar	60.6	42.3	16.8	19.0	17.0	18.0	66	71
10.	Kolkata	33.3	16.9	21.4	20.6	21.5	20.0	12	71
11.	Maldah	61.2	51.2	17.0	17.3	17.0	16.0	49	43
12.	Medinipur	45.9	38.0	17.9	19.0	18.0	18.0	37	79
13.	Murshidabad	84.0	77.0	15.4	16.1	15.0	16.0	25	126
14.	Nadia	43.9	39.0	18.4	18.7	18.0	18.0	41	59
15.	North 24 Parganas	50.0	47.9	17.9	18.3	17.5	18.0	26	73
16.	Puruliya	82.6	58.7	15.6	17.1	16.0	16.0	92	46
17.	South 24 Parganas	62.5	37.3	17.2	18.6	17.0	18.0	48	59
18.	Uttar Dinajpur	63.2	51.6	17.2	17.4	17.0	17.0	57	62
16	**Andaman & Nicobar**								
1.	Andaman	20.0	16.1	20.3	20.8	20.0	19.0	15	31
2.	Nicobar	2.1	11.1	23.0	20.1	23.0	20.0	47	9
17	**Arunachal Pradesh**								
1.	Changlang	29.2	33.3	19.6	17.0	19.0	18.0	48	3
2.	Dibang Valley	33.3	100.0	19.1	14.0	18.0	14.0	39	1

Appendix - III (Continued)

Sr. No.	State/District	Age at Marriage <18 years (%) SC/ST/OBC	OC	Mean SC/ST OBC	OC	Median SC/ST OBC	OC	Total Number of marriages SC/ST OBC	OC
3.	East Kameng	44.1	40.0	17.4	19.0	18.0	19.0	68	5
4.	East Siang	36.4	0.0	18.9	24.0	19.0	24.0	44	2
5.	Lohit	7.9	40.0	19.4	17.8	19.0	18.0	38	5
6.	Lower Subansiri	31.8	40.0	18.7	19.0	18.0	18.0	44	5
7.	Papum Pare	22.2	50.0	19.6	20.5	19.0	20.5	36	2
8.	Tawang	0.0	0.0	21.5	19.5	20.0	19.5	15	2
9.	Tirap	38.9	0.0	19.5	20.5	19.5	20.5	18	2
10.	Upper Siang	8.3	37.5	19.3	19.0	19.0	18.5	24	8
11.	Upper Subansiri	42.0	42.9	18.2	17.4	18.0	18.0	50	7
12.	West Kameng	38.2	**	18.7	NA	18.0	NA	34	**
13.	West Siang	33.3	**	19.0	NA	18.0	NA	24	**
18	**Chandigarh**								
1.	Chandigarh	0.0	0.0	19.0	23.1	18.0	23.0	5	38
19	**Dadra & Nagar Haveli**								
1.	Dadra & Nagar Haveli	55.6	11.1	17.1	20.6	17.0	21.0	72	9
20	**Daman & Diu**								
1.	Daman	15.6	22.2	19.7	19.4	19.0	18.0	96	18
2.	Diu	16.2	14.3	19.7	20.2	19.0	19.5	68	28
21	**Delhi**								
1.	Delhi	23.8	3.1	19.2	21.0	18.0	21.0	21	98
22	**Goa**								
1.	North Goa	20.0	2.2	19.9	24.2	21.0	24.0	10	46
2.	South Goa	0.0	0.0	22.8	24.5	22.0	24.0	4	47
23	**Himachal Pradesh**								
1.	Bilaspur(Pra.Him)	14.3	2.0	19.9	20.9	19.5	20.0	14	51
2.	Chamba	2.0	2.6	20.9	21.9	20.0	22.0	49	76
3.	Hamirpur(HP)	3.7	0.0	19.3	20.8	18.0	20.0	27	83
4.	Kangra	0.0	5.0	21.3	21.1	21.0	21.0	25	60
5.	Kinnaur	26.5	0.0	20.1	21.9	20.0	21.5	34	22
6.	Kullu	0.0	2.0	19.2	20.8	19.0	21.0	12	51
7.	Lahul & Spiti	0.0	0.0	23.6	20.5	23.5	20.0	18	4
8.	Mandi	7.5	2.5	19.8	21.0	19.0	20.0	40	79
9.	Shimla	0.0	2.4	20.4	21.5	19.5	21.5	10	42
10.	Sirmaur	0.0	9.1	20.5	20.5	21.0	20.0	14	44
11.	Solan	6.7	0.0	20.7	21.0	20.0	20.0	15	59
12.	Una	2.3	0.0	20.8	21.5	20.5	21.0	44	64
24	**Jammu & Kashmir**								
1.	Anantanag	2.8	0.0	22.5	22.0	22.5	22.0	36	14
2.	Badgam	10.0	0.0	21.8	20.7	22.5	20.0	10	16
3.	Baramula	8.7	6.7	22.7	20.6	23.0	20.0	23	30
4.	Doda	0.0	0.0	20.5	20.6	20.0	20.0	142	73
5.	Jammu	0.9	1.3	21.3	20.8	22.0	21.0	109	75
6.	Kargil	27.5	**	18.7	NA	18.0	NA	91	**
7.	Kathua	0.0	0.0	21.3	22.0	21.5	22.0	50	98
8.	Kupwara	0.0	0.0	20.1	20.4	20.0	20.0	14	10
9.	Leh	1.5	**	20.8	NA	20.0	NA	68	**
10.	Pulwama	0.0	0.0	25.7	22.3	24.0	22.0	3	15
11.	Punch	4.2	3.3	20.6	20.7	20.0	20.0	24	90
12.	Rajauri	0.3	0.0	18.9	18.8	19.0	19.0	384	77

Appendix - III (Continued)

Sr. No.	State/District	Age at Marriage <18 years (%) SC/ST/OBC	OC	Mean SC/ST OBC	OC	Median SC/ST OBC	OC	Total Number of marriages SC/ST OBC	OC
13.	Srinagar	16.7	7.4	18.0	19.7	19.0	20.0	6	27
14.	Udhampur	0.9	2.7	19.1	20.2	19.0	20.0	114	37
25	**Lakshadweep**								
1.	Lakshadweep	18.2	**	19.9	NA	19.0	NA	159	**
26	**Manipur**								
1.	Bishnupur	10.7	13.4	22.9	22.2	22.0	21.0	28	67
2.	Chandel	20.8	0.0	21.9	18.0	20.0	18.0	77	1
3.	Churachandpur	11.4	0.0	22.4	19.0	21.0	19.0	44	2
4.	Imphal	6.9	4.2	25.0	25.8	24.0	25.5	29	118
5.	Senapati	17.2	25.0	22.1	20.0	22.0	20.5	29	4
6.	Tamenglong	20.7	**	21.0	NA	20.0	NA	82	**
7.	Thoubal	6.3	17.2	21.5	21.3	20.5	20.0	16	93
8.	Ukhrul	18.8	0.0	23.3	18.0	21.0	18.0	32	1
27	**Meghalaya**								
1.	East Garo Hills	0.0	**	20.4	NA	20.0	NA	27	**
2.	East Khasi Hills	5.3	50.0	20.0	16.0	19.0	16.0	19	2
3.	Jaintia Hills	0.8	**	20.3	NA	20.0	NA	259	**
4.	Ri Bhoi	2.4	**	19.5	NA	19.0	NA	42	**
5.	South Garp Hills	0.0	**	21.0	NA	18.0	NA	5	**
6.	West Garo Hills	7.1	50.0	21.6	17.0	19.0	17.0	14	2
7.	West Khasi Hills	2.0	**	20.1	NA	20.0	NA	50	**
28	**Mizoram**								
1.	Aizwal	7.1	**	21.8	NA	20.0	NA	84	**
2.	Chhimtuipui	25.7	0.0	19.5	19.0	19.0	19.0	74	1
3.	Lunglei	6.8	**	20.9	NA	20.0	NA	44	**
29	**Nagaland**								
1.	Kohima	56.5	0.0	17.5	24.0	17.0	24.0	85	1
2.	Mokokchung	14.0	**	20.7	NA	20.5	NA	50	**
3.	Mon	11.3	0.0	19.3	23.0	19.0	23.0	151	1
4.	Phek	36.8	**	18.1	NA	18.0	NA	19	**
5.	Tuensang	9.5	**	19.8	NA	19.0	NA	74	**
6.	Wokha	25.4	**	19.4	NA	19.0	NA	122	**
7.	Zunheboto	24.0	**	19.0	NA	19.0	NA	150	**
30	**Pondicherry**								
1.	Karaikal	5.7	0.0	21.2	20.0	21.0	20.0	141	1
2.	Mahe	2.9	0.0	22.2	24.8	21.0	24.0	175	16
3.	Pondicherry	4.5	0.0	21.6	24.5	21.0	24.5	110	2
4.	Yanam	19.0	36.8	19.1	18.2	19.0	18.0	63	19
31	**Sikkim**								
1.	East Sikkim	16.7	9.7	22.1	21.5	22.0	21.0	24	31
2.	North Sikkim	16.7	0.0	21.2	21.0	20.0	21.0	18	4
3.	South Sikkim	6.7	33.3	21.5	21.2	20.0	21.0	15	6
4.	West Sikkim	16.7	19.0	20.6	19.9	19.0	19.0	48	21
32	**Tripura**								
1.	North Tripura	38.6	28.6	18.5	19.3	18.0	18.0	44	28
2.	South Tripura	61.9	33.9	18.3	19.9	17.0	19.0	42	56
3.	West Tripura	14.7	14.9	20.6	22.2	20.5	20.0	34	47

Note: In the column showing percent of marriages below legal minimum age, 0.0 indicates no marriage below 18 years.

** No marriage is reported in that category of characteristic/district

NA Not applicable

APPENDIX - IV

Percent of Marriages below legal Minimum Age of 18 years and Average Age at marriage in each District by Economic Status - GIRLS

Sr. No.	State/District	Age at marriage									Total number of marriages		
		< 18 years (%) Economic status			Mean Economic status			Median Economic status			Economic status		
		Low	Medium	High	Low	Medium	High	Low	Medium	High	Low	Medium	High
1	**Andhra Pradesh**												
1.	Adilabad	51.5	45.5	50.0	17.1	17.5	18.0	17.0	18.0	17.0	33	44	12
2.	Anantapur	46.7	38.5	23.3	17.3	18.1	18.9	18.0	18.0	18.0	15	26	30
3.	Chittoor	40.0	33.3	6.7	19.8	19.0	20.3	20.0	19.0	20.0	10	6	15
4.	Cuddapah	47.8	27.8	17.9	17.3	17.9	19.5	18.0	18.5	19.0	46	18	39
5.	East Godavari	60.0	45.7	22.2	16.8	17.7	18.7	16.5	18.0	19.0	20	35	18
6.	Guntur	43.8	43.8	14.3	18.3	17.3	21.6	18.0	18.0	19.5	16	16	14
7.	Hyderabad	**	8.3	6.1	NA	19.0	20.8	NA	18.0	20.0	**	12	66
8.	Karimnagar	33.3	39.3	53.8	17.3	17.9	17.3	18.0	18.0	17.0	6	28	13
9.	Khammam	40.7	29.4	18.2	17.2	18.6	18.4	18.0	19.0	18.0	27	17	11
10.	Krishna	39.3	7.7	18.8	17.5	20.1	19.1	18.0	20.0	19.5	28	13	16
11.	Kurnool	35.3	57.1	31.3	18.0	17.7	18.4	18.0	17.0	18.0	17	21	48
12.	Mahbubnagar	75.0	28.1	33.3	15.8	18.0	18.8	16.0	18.0	18.0	16	32	21
13.	Medak	25.0	40.9	30.4	19.5	17.9	18.0	18.5	18.0	18.0	4	22	23
14.	Nalgonda	42.9	38.2	47.6	18.2	17.8	17.8	18.0	18.0	18.0	21	34	21
15.	Nellore	40.0	22.2	15.4	17.8	19.5	19.7	18.0	20.0	19.0	20	18	26
16.	Nizamabad	50.0	39.1	47.1	17.2	17.9	17.9	17.0	18.0	18.0	6	23	34
17.	Prakasam	56.3	20.0	46.4	16.9	19.5	18.1	17.0	18.0	18.0	16	20	28
18.	Rangareddi	75.0	45.2	22.0	16.0	17.6	20.3	15.0	18.0	20.0	8	42	41
19.	Srikakulam	52.2	42.4	51.9	17.4	17.6	17.3	17.0	18.0	16.0	46	33	27
20.	Vishkhapatanam	72.7	50.0	36.4	16.4	17.1	19.6	16.0	17.0	20.0	11	14	11
21.	Vizianagaram	52.5	31.3	25.0	17.0	18.6	19.1	17.0	18.0	19.5	40	32	12
22.	Warangal	61.5	50.0	39.1	15.9	17.8	18.7	16.0	17.5	18.0	13	28	23
23.	West Godavari	37.5	31.7	5.3	17.8	18.2	18.9	18.0	18.0	19.0	48	41	19

Appendix - IV (Continued)

Sr. No.	State/District	Age at marriage: < 18 years (%) Economic status: Low	Medium	High	Mean Economic status: Low	Medium	High	Median Economic status: Low	Medium	High	Total number of marriages Economic status: Low	Medium	High
2	**Assam**												
1.	Barpeta	25.0	5.9		18.9	21.4		19.0	20.0		32	17	
2.	Bongaigaon	44.1	54.5	12.5	19.0	18.7	20.8	18.0	17.0	22.0	102	22	24
3.	Cachar	27.5	4.2	0.0	19.6	21.9	23.7	18.0	21.5	21.0	69	24	6
4.	Darrang	43.6	15.4	0.0	18.2	20.1	21.8	18.0	20.0	20.0	39	13	5
5.	Dhemaji	2.6	8.3	**	20.5	19.8	NA	20.0	20.0	NA	39	12	**
6.	Dhubri	65.1	53.8	18.2	17.0	18.5	21.3	17.0	17.0	20.0	86	13	11
7.	Dibrugarh	35.7	11.1	14.3	20.2	20.2	22.4	19.0	19.0	23.0	14	9	7
8.	Goalpara	49.4	25.0	0.0	18.5	19.1	21.5	18.0	18.0	20.5	77	12	10
9.	Golaghat	32.9	12.5	18.2	19.1	21.9	20.7	19.0	22.5	20.0	73	8	11
10.	Hailakandi	10.5	0.0	0.0	20.8	24.2	21.0	20.0	24.0	21.0	114	29	2
11.	Jorhat	17.4	0.0	0.0	20.4	21.5	23.0	21.0	21.0	24.0	23	25	4
12.	Kamrup	31.6	16.7	6.5	19.3	20.1	23.0	18.0	20.0	23.0	38	24	31
13.	Karbi Anglong	5.7	0.0	**	19.6	20.4	NA	19.0	19.5	NA	53	10	**
14.	Karimganj	29.4	15.4	0.0	20.3	23.4	25.3	19.0	22.0	24.0	68	13	13
15.	Lakhimpur	33.3	50.0	37.5	18.9	16.5	21.8	18.0	16.5	21.5	15	2	8
16.	Marigaon	43.5	15.2	0.0	18.5	19.3	24.1	18.0	19.0	25.0	85	33	7
17.	Nagaon	50.0	11.8	11.1	18.0	20.2	23.0	17.5	20.0	25.0	84	17	9
18.	Nalbari	5.6	4.8	0.0	20.6	22.0	26.3	20.5	22.0	25.0	36	21	6
19.	North Cachar Hills	10.7	3.1	20.0	20.1	20.9	21.6	20.0	20.5	22.0	28	32	5
20.	Sibsagar	18.8	0.0	0.0	20.8	27.8	20.5	20.0	27.0	19.5	16	4	4
21.	Sonitpur	36.2	25.0	0.0	18.7	21.3	21.4	18.0	22.0	20.0	47	4	8
22.	Tinsukia	31.6	18.2	0.0	19.3	20.5	23.3	18.0	21.0	22.0	57	11	14
3	**Bihar**												
1.	Araria	54.4	37.5	30.0	17.4	18.3	18.3	17.0	18.0	18.0	114	8	10
2.	Aurangabad(Bih)	70.7	54.1	41.7	16.1	17.5	17.9	16.0	17.0	18.0	123	37	24
3.	Begusarai	69.6	55.4	42.4	16.3	16.7	17.5	16.0	17.0	18.0	69	65	33
4.	Bhagalpur	76.8	40.0	38.7	15.8	18.0	17.9	16.0	18.0	18.0	82	45	31

Appendix - IV (Continued)

Sr. No.	State/District	Age at marriage									Total number of marriages		
		< 18 years (%) Economic status			Mean Economic status			Median Economic status			Economic status		
		Low	Medium	High	Low	Medium	High	Low	Medium	High	Low	Medium	High
5.	Bhojpur	78.5	40.0	33.3	15.3	17.2	18.2	15.0	18.0	19.0	79	35	48
6.	Buxar	80.2	61.2	45.5	15.7	16.9	17.6	16.0	16.0	18.0	81	85	44
7.	Darbhanga	70.2	36.9	32.4	16.8	17.8	18.9	16.0	18.0	18.5	84	65	34
8.	Deoghar	78.4	50.0	31.8	15.2	17.5	18.0	15.0	17.5	18.0	88	18	22
9.	Dhanbad	56.8	71.4	24.4	16.9	16.4	19.3	16.0	16.0	19.0	37	7	41
10.	Dumka	49.5	50.0	42.9	17.4	17.9	18.0	18.0	17.5	18.0	101	8	7
11.	Gaya	74.2	59.1	25.8	15.3	16.5	18.6	15.0	16.0	18.0	97	44	31
12.	Giridih	57.1	71.4	52.4	16.6	16.7	18.4	17.0	17.0	17.0	77	21	21
13.	Godda	73.9	46.2	40.0	16.3	17.1	18.7	16.0	18.0	19.0	88	13	15
14.	Gopalganj	80.0	45.7	40.7	15.8	17.7	18.1	16.0	18.0	18.0	65	35	54
15.	Gulma	28.1	22.2	25.0	18.9	18.6	18.8	18.0	19.0	19.0	64	9	4
16.	Hazaribagh	73.1	60.9	30.8	15.9	17.4	18.2	16.0	16.0	18.0	93	23	13
17.	Jehanabad	69.8	50.8	32.0	15.9	17.2	18.4	16.0	17.0	18.0	86	59	50
18.	Katihar	55.3	30.0	7.7	17.2	18.7	19.2	17.0	19.0	20.0	94	10	13
19.	Khagaria	72.7	59.4	40.0	15.8	17.2	17.9	16.0	17.0	18.0	88	64	20
20.	Kishanganj	51.4	57.1	12.5	17.6	17.9	20.5	17.0	17.0	20.0	72	7	8
21.	Lohardaga	46.5	33.3	0.0	18.1	18.3	21.3	18.0	18.0	22.0	86	15	3
22.	Madhepura	73.4	51.9	30.0	15.9	17.5	18.8	16.0	17.0	19.5	109	27	10
23.	Madhubani	72.2	42.1	35.3	16.2	17.1	17.5	16.0	18.0	18.0	108	19	17
24.	Munger	73.9	43.9	47.1	15.5	17.4	17.9	15.0	18.0	18.0	69	41	17
25.	Muzaffarpur	66.3	53.8	20.0	16.7	17.3	19.6	16.0	17.0	20.0	86	52	35
26.	Nalanda	68.5	49.0	44.0	15.7	17.6	17.5	16.0	18.0	18.0	89	51	25
27.	Nawada	84.2	66.7	47.9	14.8	16.3	17.6	15.0	16.0	18.0	120	45	48
28.	Palamu	67.4	70.0	42.9	16.2	16.0	19.9	16.0	16.0	18.0	86	10	7
29.	Pashchim Champaran	66.7	55.8	22.4	16.3	17.3	19.1	16.5	17.0	19.0	36	43	85
30.	Pashchmi Singhbhum	31.4	20.0	11.1	18.7	20.6	19.4	18.0	20.0	19.0	70	5	9
31.	Patna	86.2	58.8	76.9	15.2	16.4	15.5	15.0	16.0	15.0	109	34	13
32.	Purba Champaran	66.7	60.0	50.0	16.5	17.1	18.1	16.0	17.0	17.5	117	45	22
33.	Purbi Singhbhum	59.2	30.8	4.5	17.3	18.6	22.1	17.0	18.0	21.5	49	13	44

Appendix - IV (Continued)

Sr. No.	State/District	Age at marriage									Total number of marriages		
		< 18 years (%) Economic status			Mean Economic status			Median Economic status			Economic status		
		Low	Medium	High	Low	Medium	High	Low	Medium	High	Low	Medium	High
34.	Purnia	50.7	33.3	0.0	17.9	18.7	21.4	17.0	18.0	20.0	140	6	5
35.	Ranchi	45.8	30.8	10.0	17.8	19.3	20.3	18.0	20.0	19.5	59	13	10
36.	Rohtas	88.7	79.1	7.4	15.3	15.6	20.0	16.0	16.0	20.0	62	43	27
37.	Saharsa	64.7	28.6	25.0	16.7	18.4	20.7	16.0	18.0	18.5	119	21	12
38.	Sahibganj	70.4	20.0	14.3	16.3	18.6	18.7	16.0	18.0	19.0	71	5	7
39.	Samastipur	80.4	44.0	35.3	15.5	17.1	17.4	15.0	18.0	18.0	92	50	17
40.	Saran	52.9	57.3	34.3	16.7	17.3	18.2	17.0	17.0	18.0	70	82	35
41.	Sitamarhi	73.0	52.6	40.0	16.1	17.2	17.7	16.0	17.0	18.0	100	38	15
42.	Siwan	62.1	54.1	24.6	16.7	17.4	18.8	16.0	17.0	19.0	29	74	69
43.	Vaishali	72.1	63.8	40.7	15.8	16.5	18.1	16.0	16.0	18.0	68	69	27
4	**Gujarat**												
1.	Ahmadabad	33.3	58.3	16.4	16.7	17.0	21.3	18.0	16.5	21.0	3	24	73
2.	Amreli	26.2	17.9	8.9	18.7	19.7	20.2	18.0	20.0	20.0	42	78	56
3.	Banas Kantha	66.7	68.3	32.1	16.8	16.3	18.1	16.0	16.0	19.0	30	41	56
4.	Bharuch	29.6	6.7	12.5	18.8	20.2	21.6	18.0	20.0	21.5	54	45	16
5.	Bhavnagar	40.0	34.6	19.7	17.8	18.3	19.0	18.0	18.0	19.0	5	81	66
6.	Gandhinagar	100.0	44.1	14.0	15.6	17.1	20.3	16.0	18.0	21.0	7	34	43
7.	Jamnagar	25.0	12.8	7.5	18.2	19.5	20.7	18.0	19.0	21.0	12	39	80
8.	Junagadh	10.0	17.2	0.0	20.0	19.7	21.6	20.0	19.0	21.0	30	93	39
9.	Kachchh	7.7	25.7	26.3	20.2	19.1	19.4	20.0	18.0	19.0	13	35	57
10.	Kheda	58.7	33.9	4.2	16.9	19.1	20.8	17.0	18.0	20.0	46	56	48
11.	Mahesana	66.7	53.3	25.7	16.7	16.9	19.1	17.0	17.0	19.0	3	30	101
12.	Panch Mahals	31.6	29.0	7.1	18.6	18.2	19.6	18.0	18.0	19.0	38	31	14
13.	Rajkot	28.6	33.3	8.9	19.0	18.7	20.1	19.5	19.0	20.0	14	18	112
14.	Sabar Kantha	36.4	25.5	30.0	18.1	18.7	19.3	18.0	19.0	19.0	44	47	40
15.	Surat	63.6	23.1	9.4	17.1	19.0	20.4	16.0	19.5	20.0	11	26	64
16.	Surendranagar	10.5	9.8	9.4	19.2	19.3	21.7	19.0	19.0	21.0	19	51	32
17.	The Dangs	50.0	48.1	0.0	17.4	17.5	22.5	17.5	18.0	22.0	50	77	4

Appendix - IV (Continued)

Sr. No.	State/District	Age at marriage: < 18 years (%) Economic status			Mean Economic status			Median Economic status			Total number of marriages Economic status		
		Low	Medium	High	Low	Medium	High	Low	Medium	High	Low	Medium	High
18.	Vadodara	68.0	40.0	10.9	17.0	18.3	20.4	17.0	18.0	20.0	25	30	46
19.	Valsad	14.6	16.1	0.0	19.6	21.0	21.9	19.5	20.0	21.0	48	31	41
5	**Haryana**												
1.	Ambala	0.0	12.3	15.9	22.9	19.4	21.3	24.0	19.0	21.0	7	57	44
2.	Bhiwani	66.7	58.1	30.6	16.0	16.8	18.1	16.5	17.0	18.0	6	86	49
3.	Faridabad	66.7	43.5	20.7	16.3	17.8	19.5	16.5	18.0	19.0	6	46	87
4.	Gurgaon	33.3	49.1	21.4	17.8	17.2	18.8	18.0	18.0	18.5	9	53	42
5.	Hisar	42.9	50.0	26.5	17.3	17.2	18.2	18.0	17.5	18.0	7	76	34
6.	Jind	0.0	42.3	23.1	18.8	17.6	19.3	18.0	18.0	19.0	5	97	26
7.	Kaithal	100.0	40.0	17.9	16.0	17.6	19.8	16.0	18.0	19.0	1	50	28
8.	Karnal	0.0	22.2	10.5	19.1	19.0	20.4	18.5	19.0	20.0	10	81	57
9.	Kurukshetra	14.3	23.1	3.9	18.9	19.2	21.1	19.0	19.0	21.0	7	65	51
10.	Mahendragarh	63.6	52.2	36.5	16.5	17.2	18.3	17.0	17.0	18.0	11	90	74
11.	Panchkula	**	37.0	9.4	NA	18.0	20.3	NA	18.0	20.0	**	46	32
12.	Panipat	42.9	59.6	34.8	18.4	17.0	18.2	18.0	17.0	18.0	7	52	69
13.	Rewari	**	46.8	11.1	NA	17.6	19.4	NA	18.0	19.0	**	62	63
14.	Rohtak	61.1	37.3	21.4	17.9	18.4	19.2	17.0	18.0	19.0	18	67	56
15.	Sirsa	50.0	41.0	17.8	17.0	17.9	20.0	17.0	18.0	19.0	2	61	45
16.	Sonipat	17.4	6.7	0.0	19.5	20.2	21.5	19.0	20.0	21.0	23	60	45
17.	Yamunanagar	12.5	14.5	0.0	18.5	19.3	22.2	18.0	19.0	22.0	8	55	71
6	**Karnataka**												
1.	Bangalore	**	36.4	3.3	NA	18.4	21.9	NA	18.5	22.0	**	22	61
2.	Bangalore Rural	16.7	23.3	18.2	18.3	19.0	19.1	18.0	18.0	19.0	12	73	22
3.	Belgaum	81.0	55.6	23.5	15.1	17.5	19.7	15.0	17.0	20.0	21	81	17
4.	Bellary	61.5	40.0	0.0	17.1	18.5	23.5	17.0	18.0	24.5	52	65	14
5.	Bidar	84.8	64.1	38.5	15.5	16.3	19.5	15.0	16.0	18.0	46	117	13
6.	Bijapur	70.8	65.5	46.7	16.3	16.3	17.1	16.0	16.0	18.0	24	87	15
7.	Chikmagalur	14.3	14.5	0.0	19.4	20.6	20.0	18.0	20.0	20.0	7	131	9

Appendix - IV (Continued)

Sr. No.	State/District	Age at marriage: < 18 years (%) Economic status			Mean Economic status			Median Economic status			Total number of marriages Economic status		
		Low	Medium	High	Low	Medium	High	Low	Medium	High	Low	Medium	High
8.	Chitradurga	33.3	33.7	0.0	17.7	18.3	22.5	18.0	18.0	23.0	9	98	11
9.	Dakshina Kannada	4.2	5.5	0.0	21.5	22.2	23.4	21.0	22.0	23.0	24	91	16
10.	Dharwad	75.0	40.9	13.0	16.0	18.9	22.5	16.0	19.0	22.0	4	88	23
11.	Gulbarga	61.3	37.8	14.3	16.5	18.6	20.6	16.0	18.0	20.0	62	37	14
12.	Hassan	27.3	16.8	0.0	19.5	19.7	21.1	20.0	19.0	20.0	11	101	19
13.	Kodagu	75.0	20.8	17.6	15.8	20.1	20.3	15.0	19.5	20.0	4	48	34
14.	Kolar	35.3	30.9	41.4	18.2	18.6	19.0	18.0	18.0	18.0	17	94	29
15.	Mandya	56.5	34.5	26.9	17.1	18.6	18.8	17.0	18.0	18.0	23	58	26
16.	Mysore	83.3	45.3	27.3	14.8	18.1	19.9	14.0	18.0	20.0	12	75	11
17.	Raichur	79.2	56.5	38.5	15.8	17.2	19.7	16.0	16.0	18.5	24	62	26
18.	Shimoga	21.4	22.0	6.9	19.8	20.0	21.6	19.0	20.0	21.0	14	91	58
19.	Tumkur	75.0	26.9	0.0	16.8	18.9	21.8	17.0	18.0	20.0	4	104	6
20.	Uttara Kannada	14.3	18.6	3.4	19.4	21.3	22.6	18.0	21.0	22.0	7	97	29
7	**Kerala**												
1.	Alappuzha	0.0	0.0	0.0	22.9	23.3	22.9	21.5	22.0	22.0	16	41	104
2.	Ernakulam	0.0	0.0	0.0	20.6	23.2	24.0	20.0	22.0	24.0	5	26	118
3.	Idukki	0.0	6.3	0.0	19.0	22.7	23.5	18.5	22.5	23.0	6	32	92
4.	Kannur	16.7	8.0	28.3	20.4	22.2	19.7	19.5	22.0	19.0	12	75	92
5.	Kasaragod	50.0	11.9	21.7	18.0	20.9	20.7	17.5	20.0	20.0	4	67	83
6.	Kollam	0.0	0.0	0.0	22.2	22.3	22.2	21.0	22.0	22.0	22	104	44
7.	Kottayam	0.0	0.0	0.0	24.6	24.1	24.8	24.0	23.0	24.0	16	70	77
8.	Kozhikode	0.0	10.5	14.5	19.0	19.5	20.9	18.0	19.0	20.0	4	19	124
9.	Malappuram	19.4	36.1	40.9	19.0	18.8	18.6	19.0	18.0	18.0	31	72	93
10.	Palakkad	12.5	10.5	10.2	19.5	21.3	21.0	18.5	21.0	20.0	8	38	118
11.	Pathanamthitta	0.0	0.0	0.0	25.2	22.9	23.6	26.0	23.0	23.0	5	61	49
12.	Thiruvananthapuram	**	0.0	0.0	NA	22.3	23.1	NA	22.0	23.0	**	45	90
13.	Thrissur	0.0	0.0	0.9	19.6	21.6	22.9	20.0	20.0	22.0	11	24	112
14.	Wayanad	16.7	7.7	4.8	20.4	20.0	21.2	20.0	19.0	20.0	18	39	84

Appendix - IV (Continued)

Sr. No.	State/District	Age at marriage									Total number of marriages		
		< 18 years (%) Economic status			Mean Economic status			Median Economic status			Economic status		
		Low	Medium	High	Low	Medium	High	Low	Medium	High	Low	Medium	High
8	**Madhya Pradesh**												
1.	Balaghat	37.5	33.3	0.0	17.8	18.7	20.5	18.0	19.0	20.0	24	6	4
2.	Bastar	41.9	11.1	0.0	18.1	19.7	21.3	18.0	20.0	21.5	43	9	4
3.	Betul	29.4	14.3	0.0	17.7	20.6	19.5	18.0	20.0	19.5	34	7	4
4.	Bhind	65.9	65.0	53.7	16.3	16.8	17.4	17.0	16.0	17.0	41	60	54
5.	Bhopal	41.9	25.0	13.6	17.7	18.6	21.4	18.0	18.5	20.5	31	16	22
6.	Bilaspur(MP)	51.2	11.1	17.6	17.3	19.4	20.9	17.0	18.5	21.0	84	18	17
7.	Chattarpur	86.5	40.0	40.0	15.7	16.2	20.0	15.0	18.0	18.0	37	5	10
8.	Chhindwara	39.1	13.6	7.1	17.6	20.0	21.1	18.0	20.0	20.0	87	22	14
9.	Damoh	60.8	60.0	9.1	16.8	16.6	21.5	16.5	16.0	22.0	74	10	11
10.	Datia	61.1	59.5	22.6	16.8	17.0	18.6	17.0	16.0	18.0	36	37	31
11.	Dewas	55.4	60.9	36.4	16.9	16.9	18.0	17.0	17.0	18.0	65	23	22
12.	Dhar	63.6	63.2	30.8	16.4	16.7	18.5	16.0	16.0	18.0	77	19	26
13.	Durg	36.7	22.2	18.2	18.4	19.3	21.4	18.0	18.0	21.0	49	9	11
14.	East Nimar	57.7	28.6	8.3	17.1	18.8	20.8	16.0	19.0	20.5	71	21	24
15.	Guna	81.6	50.0	29.4	15.9	18.2	20.2	15.5	17.5	20.0	76	16	17
16.	Gwalior	72.7	60.0	26.3	16.5	17.1	19.8	16.0	16.0	19.0	11	15	80
17.	Hoshangabad	41.9	57.1	0.0	17.5	17.8	19.9	18.0	17.0	20.0	31	14	7
18.	Indore	68.4	37.8	23.9	16.2	18.5	20.0	16.0	18.0	20.0	38	37	46
19.	Jabalpur	49.1	35.3	0.0	17.3	18.8	21.2	18.0	19.0	20.0	53	17	13
20.	Jhabua	62.6	40.0	20.0	16.8	18.7	21.0	17.0	18.5	22.0	91	10	5
21.	Mandla	40.6	33.3	20.0	17.5	18.3	18.0	18.0	19.0	18.0	32	3	5
22.	Mandsaur	77.6	50.0	12.9	15.4	17.7	19.9	15.0	17.5	20.0	76	20	31
23.	Morena	91.2	76.9	50.0	15.0	15.7	17.3	15.0	15.0	17.5	34	13	36
24.	Narsimhapur	59.6	40.0	11.1	17.6	18.3	21.2	17.0	18.0	22.0	52	20	9
25.	Panna	62.2	57.1	20.0	16.6	17.4	20.0	16.0	17.0	18.0	37	7	5
26.	Raigarh (M P)	9.1	0.0	0.0	19.4	19.2	19.0	18.0	19.0	19.0	44	5	3
27.	Raipur	70.0	23.1	0.0	16.8	19.5	18.0	17.0	19.0	18.0	40	13	3
28.	Raisen	52.3	40.7	30.8	17.2	18.1	18.0	17.0	18.0	18.0	88	27	13

Appendix - IV (Continued)

Sr. No.	State/District	Age at marriage: < 18 years (%) Economic status			Mean Economic status			Median Economic status			Total number of marriages Economic status		
		Low	Medium	High	Low	Medium	High	Low	Medium	High	Low	Medium	High
29.	Rajgarh	73.2	67.6	30.0	15.4	16.7	19.7	15.0	16.0	20.0	71	34	20
30.	Rajnandgaon	57.1	26.7	14.3	16.6	19.5	21.7	16.0	18.0	20.0	84	15	7
31.	Ratlam	70.6	28.6	28.6	15.5	17.5	19.1	16.0	18.5	19.0	34	14	35
32.	Rewa	65.3	52.6	22.2	16.2	16.9	18.9	16.0	17.0	18.0	95	19	9
33.	Sagar	77.2	52.9	19.0	15.9	17.2	20.0	16.0	16.0	20.0	57	17	21
34.	Satna	69.5	52.2	20.0	16.2	17.3	18.9	16.0	17.0	18.0	82	23	15
35.	Sehore	54.9	53.8	19.0	17.1	17.5	19.6	17.0	17.0	20.0	71	26	21
36.	Seoni	44.0	27.3	10.0	17.5	17.2	21.4	18.0	18.0	20.5	50	11	10
37.	Shahdol	70.0	50.0	66.7	15.9	18.0	17.3	16.0	17.0	17.0	30	6	3
38.	Shajapur	87.5	81.8	37.5	14.9	14.7	18.9	15.0	15.0	19.5	72	22	8
39.	Shivpuri	82.2	59.1	54.5	15.6	16.5	17.2	15.0	16.0	17.0	45	22	33
40.	Sidhi	74.6	42.9	25.0	15.3	17.3	18.0	15.0	18.0	18.5	71	7	8
41.	Surguja	62.1	25.0	16.7	16.3	18.3	19.3	16.0	18.5	19.0	66	4	6
42.	Tikamgarh	75.4	64.7	59.1	15.3	16.4	17.5	15.0	16.5	17.0	65	34	22
43.	Ujjain	55.9	24.2	27.5	16.6	18.5	19.3	17.0	18.0	19.0	59	33	40
44.	Vidisha	75.9	35.3	14.3	15.9	18.8	20.1	16.0	18.0	18.0	87	17	21
45.	West Nimar	55.6	21.4	18.2	16.8	18.4	20.3	17.0	18.0	19.0	63	28	11
9	**Maharashtra**												
1.	Ahmadnagar	48.7	47.5	28.3	16.9	17.4	18.4	18.0	18.0	18.0	39	40	46
2.	Akola	48.1	33.3	20.0	17.2	18.7	19.6	18.0	18.0	20.0	54	54	15
3.	Amravali	16.9	3.6	0.0	18.8	20.1	20.8	18.0	20.0	22.0	59	56	19
4.	Aurangabad(Mah)	59.1	52.4	36.6	16.4	17.4	17.9	16.0	17.0	18.0	44	63	41
5.	Bhandara	15.0	6.4	0.0	19.3	20.3	21.1	19.0	20.0	21.0	60	47	22
6.	Bid	64.1	48.1	55.6	16.5	17.6	17.3	16.0	18.0	17.0	64	27	18
7.	Buldana	41.8	28.3	22.2	17.7	18.6	20.0	18.0	18.0	20.0	67	46	27
8.	Chandrapur	41.7	22.4	0.0	18.1	19.1	19.7	18.0	18.0	19.5	36	49	16
9.	Dhule	53.8	40.4	25.9	17.0	18.1	19.6	17.0	18.0	19.0	26	52	27
10.	Gadchiroli	28.1	20.7	50.0	18.3	18.7	19.3	18.0	18.0	17.5	32	29	6

Appendix - IV (Continued)

Sr. No.	State/District	Age at marriage < 18 years (%) Economic status			Mean Economic status			Median Economic status			Total number of marriages Economic status		
		Low	Medium	High	Low	Medium	High	Low	Medium	High	Low	Medium	High
11.	Greater Bombay (Mumbai)	50.0	7.5	0.0	18.3	20.8	22.4	18.0	20.0	21.0	6	53	28
12.	Jalgaon	74.5	36.2	22.5	16.9	17.9	19.4	17.0	18.0	19.0	51	58	40
13.	Jalna	68.2	51.0	13.3	16.3	17.5	19.8	16.0	17.0	19.0	66	51	15
14.	Kolhapur	21.7	21.1	9.5	17.8	18.8	19.8	18.0	18.0	19.0	23	57	42
15.	Latur	71.4	69.0	35.4	16.4	16.4	18.7	16.0	16.5	18.0	35	58	48
16.	Nagpur	27.3	10.3	2.9	17.8	19.8	22.1	18.0	19.0	22.0	22	58	35
17.	Nanded	74.2	62.7	26.3	15.9	16.6	20.2	16.0	16.0	20.0	66	59	19
18.	Nashik	38.9	34.0	13.3	18.1	18.3	19.9	18.0	18.0	20.0	18	47	15
19.	Osmanabad	54.5	50.8	20.8	17.3	17.1	18.6	17.0	17.0	18.5	44	63	24
20.	Parbhani	64.4	45.0	21.4	16.7	17.3	19.2	16.0	18.0	19.5	45	60	28
21.	Pune	51.6	26.8	18.6	17.5	18.6	19.0	17.0	18.0	18.0	31	41	43
22.	Raigarh(MAH)	33.3	16.3	0.0	18.4	19.3	18.9	18.0	19.0	18.0	21	43	22
23.	Ratnagiri	0.0	15.2	10.7	18.0	19.9	20.0	18.0	19.0	19.0	1	66	56
24.	Sangli	33.3	26.8	13.3	17.8	18.6	19.5	18.0	18.0	19.0	39	56	30
25.	Satara	31.8	16.7	25.0	17.7	18.7	18.5	18.0	18.0	18.0	22	60	32
26.	Sindhudurg	18.8	1.4	0.0	20.3	21.6	22.5	20.0	21.0	23.0	16	71	15
27.	Solapur	60.8	23.1	34.4	17.1	18.5	19.6	17.0	18.0	19.0	51	39	32
28.	Thane	30.0	26.1	10.5	18.3	19.7	20.6	18.0	18.0	20.0	20	23	38
29.	Wardha	18.2	8.5	7.1	19.0	20.5	22.8	18.0	20.0	23.0	44	47	14
30.	Yavatmal	33.3	23.1	19.2	17.8	18.5	19.6	18.0	19.0	19.0	63	65	26
10	**Orissa**												
1.	Anugul	49.3	34.8	11.1	18.0	19.2	21.4	18.0	19.0	22.0	69	23	18
2.	Balangir	64.2	54.5	14.3	17.5	19.0	23.4	17.0	17.0	26.0	53	11	7
3.	Balasore	26.4	41.9	0.0	19.9	18.8	23.0	20.0	18.0	22.0	106	31	7
4.	Bargarh	48.6	16.7	14.3	17.8	18.3	21.3	18.0	18.0	20.0	72	12	14
5.	Baudh	55.0	28.6	33.3	17.3	18.3	18.8	17.0	18.0	18.0	60	7	6
6.	Bhadrak	18.0	0.0	0.0	20.9	22.2	22.4	20.0	21.0	23.0	139	9	11
7.	Cuttack	15.5	7.1	3.0	20.3	20.7	22.5	20.0	20.0	22.0	71	28	33
8.	Debagarh	35.2	33.3	0.0	18.6	20.1	21.7	18.0	20.0	20.0	54	15	3

Appendix - IV (Continued)

Sr. No.	State/District	Age at marriage: < 18 years (%) Economic status			Mean Economic status			Median Economic status			Total number of marriages Economic status		
		Low	Medium	High	Low	Medium	High	Low	Medium	High	Low	Medium	High
9.	Dhenkanal	46.1	23.8	9.5	18.3	20.0	20.7	18.0	20.0	20.0	89	21	21
10.	Gajapati	43.8	36.4	40.0	17.6	18.4	18.5	18.0	18.0	18.0	48	11	15
11.	Ganjam	59.0	37.9	47.7	17.0	18.8	18.4	17.0	18.0	18.0	61	29	44
12.	Jagatsinghapur	13.6	0.0	2.6	21.2	22.4	23.0	21.0	23.5	23.0	88	14	38
13.	Jajapur	20.8	0.0	3.7	20.2	21.9	21.4	20.0	22.0	21.0	96	19	27
14.	Jharsuguda	16.0	22.9	0.0	20.1	18.8	20.7	20.0	18.0	20.0	25	35	12
15.	Kalahandi	69.4	37.5	25.0	16.6	18.6	20.3	16.0	18.0	20.0	49	16	4
16.	Kendrapara	17.6	0.0	5.9	20.4	22.6	23.7	20.0	23.0	23.0	136	5	17
17.	Kendujhar	38.5	5.9	0.0	18.8	21.4	22.5	18.0	20.0	23.5	78	17	8
18.	Khordha	37.8	20.0	7.7	18.4	20.7	21.5	18.0	21.0	21.0	45	30	39
19.	Koraput	76.7	52.6	16.7	16.0	18.5	21.2	16.0	17.0	20.5	43	19	6
20.	Malkangiri	55.3	66.7	**	17.0	16.3	NA	17.0	16.0	NA	47	3	**
21.	Mayurbhanj	41.2	16.7	0.0	18.6	20.2	22.4	18.0	20.0	23.0	68	18	9
22.	Nabarangapur	78.9	28.6	0.0	16.2	19.7	21.0	16.0	18.0	21.0	38	7	1
23.	Nayagarh	57.1	61.5	37.9	17.6	17.9	18.5	17.0	17.0	18.0	98	13	29
24.	Nuapada	46.2	28.6	0.0	18.1	18.1	22.0	18.0	18.0	22.0	39	7	1
25.	Phulbani	44.2	30.8	50.0	17.4	17.9	19.5	18.0	18.0	19.0	43	13	4
26.	Puri	15.5	12.5	11.8	20.2	20.9	22.8	20.0	20.0	23.0	58	32	17
27.	Rayagada	48.8	44.4	11.1	17.5	18.2	21.5	18.0	18.0	22.0	43	9	18
28.	Sambalpur	38.1	8.3	0.0	18.6	20.8	22.8	18.0	20.5	24.0	42	12	4
29.	Sonapur	43.5	33.3	10.0	18.6	18.2	19.7	18.0	18.0	19.5	85	12	10
30.	Sundargarh	14.7	25.0	12.5	19.9	20.5	21.6	19.0	18.5	23.0	34	4	8
11	**Punjab**												
1.	Amritsar	0.0	13.6	9.5	20.1	19.6	21.0	20.0	19.0	21.0	9	66	42
2.	Bathinda	0.0	16.7	5.6	19.0	19.2	20.9	19.0	19.0	20.0	3	78	36
3.	Faridkot	100.0	13.8	8.7	15.0	19.6	21.2	15.0	20.0	21.0	1	80	46
4.	Fatehgarh Sahib	0.0	11.8	2.4	20.0	19.3	21.1	18.0	19.0	21.0	3	76	82
5.	Firozpur	52.9	24.6	11.8	17.4	19.3	20.8	17.0	19.0	21.0	17	65	34
6.	Gurdaspur	0.0	12.1	0.0	19.5	19.7	22.4	19.5	19.0	22.0	6	66	49

Appendix - IV (Continued)

Sr. No.	State/District	Age at marriage									Total number of marriages		
		< 18 years (%) Economic status			Mean Economic status			Median Economic status			Economic status		
		Low	Medium	High	Low	Medium	High	Low	Medium	High	Low	Medium	High
7.	Hoshiarpur	0.0	5.4	1.2	24.0	20.2	22.1	24.0	20.0	22.0	1	74	83
8.	Jalandhar	0.0	11.7	4.2	20.7	20.2	21.5	20.0	20.0	21.0	3	60	72
9.	Kapurthala	0.0	5.5	1.4	21.0	21.3	21.6	21.0	21.0	21.0	2	55	73
10.	Ludhiana	0.0	11.4	6.8	19.7	19.8	21.1	20.0	20.0	21.0	3	44	74
11.	Mansa	40.0	22.1	16.4	17.8	19.3	20.1	19.0	19.0	20.0	5	77	55
12.	Moga	25.0	18.8	0.0	18.6	19.7	21.2	18.5	19.0	20.0	12	101	57
13.	Muktsar	50.0	28.1	9.8	17.8	19.0	20.7	17.5	19.0	20.0	12	89	51
14.	Nawanshahr	**	3.0	1.4	NA	21.0	21.7	NA	20.0	21.0	**	67	74
15.	Patiala	33.3	14.9	2.7	18.7	19.7	21.1	19.0	20.0	21.0	3	47	37
16.	Rupnagar	22.2	8.5	2.6	18.9	20.7	21.3	19.0	20.0	21.0	9	47	78
17.	Sangrur	0.0	20.2	3.6	19.3	19.7	21.5	19.0	20.0	22.0	8	94	56
12	**Rajasthan**												
1.	Ajmer	80.0	82.4	28.6	14.8	14.8	19.6	15.5	15.0	20.0	20	17	63
2.	Alwar	81.0	73.2	35.4	15.3	15.9	18.4	16.0	16.0	18.0	21	41	82
3.	Banswara	61.8	40.0	33.3	16.6	17.4	17.8	17.0	18.0	18.0	55	10	12
4.	Barmer	60.3	64.3	9.1	16.3	16.8	18.7	17.0	17.0	18.0	68	14	22
5.	Bharatpur	63.6	55.3	53.4	16.0	17.1	17.5	16.0	17.0	17.0	22	38	73
6.	Bhilwara	91.4	92.9	50.7	13.8	13.9	17.6	14.0	14.0	17.0	35	28	69
7.	Bikaner	88.2	69.2	52.1	14.5	16.2	17.3	15.0	16.0	17.0	17	13	48
8.	Bundi	92.2	87.5	43.5	14.0	14.2	18.2	15.0	14.0	18.0	51	16	23
9.	Chittaurgarh	56.7	66.7	0.0	16.9	15.2	20.1	17.0	15.5	19.0	30	6	7
10.	Churu	81.8	76.2	64.1	15.1	15.2	16.8	15.0	15.0	17.0	11	21	92
11.	Dausa	90.9	72.7	64.5	14.4	15.5	16.6	15.0	16.0	16.0	22	33	76
12.	Dhaulpur	60.0	69.4	44.4	16.2	16.6	17.4	16.0	16.0	18.0	20	36	45
13.	Dungarpur	41.1	21.4	24.3	17.9	18.4	18.4	18.0	18.0	19.0	73	14	37
14.	Ganganagar	52.4	48.0	37.0	16.9	17.8	18.1	17.0	18.0	18.0	63	25	27
15.	Hanumangarh	65.4	60.0	28.6	16.4	16.8	18.4	16.0	17.0	18.0	52	50	49
16.	Jaipur	82.1	54.5	28.6	15.1	17.0	18.9	15.0	17.0	18.0	28	22	98
17.	Jaisalmer	59.3	50.0	41.4	16.4	17.2	17.9	17.0	17.5	18.0	27	18	29

Appendix - IV (Continued)

Sr. No.	State/District	Age at marriage: < 18 years (%) Economic status			Mean Economic status			Median Economic status			Total number of marriages Economic status		
		Low	Medium	High	Low	Medium	High	Low	Medium	High	Low	Medium	High
18.	Jalor	55.4	41.4	27.3	16.6	17.6	19.1	17.0	18.0	19.0	74	29	33
19.	Jhalawar	82.0	81.8	36.7	14.8	15.3	17.9	15.0	14.5	18.0	61	22	30
20.	Jhunjhunun	100.0	66.7	38.2	13.6	16.1	17.9	14.0	16.0	18.0	9	24	110
21.	Jodhpur	88.2	57.1	36.4	14.7	16.9	19.6	15.0	17.0	18.0	17	7	33
22.	Kota	75.7	92.3	38.6	16.2	13.5	18.6	15.0	14.0	18.0	37	13	44
23.	Nagaur	89.7	66.7	57.1	14.5	17.0	16.8	15.0	16.5	17.0	29	6	77
24.	Pali	70.8	53.8	37.8	16.8	16.7	17.7	16.0	17.0	18.0	24	13	45
25.	Rajsamand	86.7	38.5	33.3	15.1	17.2	18.4	15.0	18.0	18.0	15	13	39
26.	Sawai Madhopur	60.7	47.4	41.9	16.3	17.3	17.8	16.5	18.0	18.0	28	19	43
27.	Sikar	58.3	41.2	40.6	16.6	17.0	17.9	17.0	18.0	18.0	12	17	138
28.	Sirohi	57.9	30.0	9.5	16.8	18.8	19.3	16.0	18.5	19.0	19	10	21
29.	Tonk	85.5	76.9	60.4	14.6	15.2	16.7	15.0	16.0	16.0	69	13	48
30.	Udaipur	79.1	82.4	34.1	15.2	15.8	18.2	15.0	16.0	18.0	43	17	44
13	**Tamil Nadu**												
1.	Chengalpattu	14.8	7.1	8.6	19.5	20.4	20.7	19.0	19.0	20.0	27	28	35
2.	Chennai	16.7	9.1	2.7	20.0	21.0	21.9	20.0	20.0	22.0	12	22	74
3.	Coimbatore	44.4	12.3	18.2	18.4	21.0	22.0	18.0	21.0	22.0	9	73	11
4.	Dharmapuri	56.3	34.9	17.9	17.6	18.6	19.5	17.0	18.0	19.0	16	86	28
5.	Dindigul	38.5	25.0	25.0	19.8	19.9	19.8	18.0	19.5	19.0	13	44	12
6.	Kanniyakumari	0.0	0.0	0.0	24.0	22.5	23.4	23.0	22.0	23.0	10	48	29
7.	Madurai	18.2	35.4	15.8	20.7	19.2	21.7	20.0	19.0	22.0	11	65	57
8.	Namakkal	28.6	10.5	6.7	18.6	20.5	21.1	19.0	20.0	21.0	14	57	15
9.	North Arcot	37.9	17.1	15.8	18.2	20.1	20.4	18.0	19.0	20.0	29	35	57
10.	Periyar	10.0	14.3	12.5	20.0	20.8	21.1	18.5	20.5	20.0	10	56	8
11.	Pudukkottai	12.9	9.7	12.0	20.8	20.9	21.1	21.0	20.0	20.0	31	72	25
12.	Ramanathapuram	14.3	13.3	12.9	19.7	20.0	20.2	19.0	19.0	20.0	21	60	31
13.	Salem	63.6	44.0	17.4	17.5	18.4	20.5	16.0	18.0	19.0	11	75	23
14.	Sivaganganagar	0.0	9.7	4.2	21.8	20.9	21.3	22.0	20.0	20.5	11	103	24

Appendix - IV (Continued)

Sr. No.	State/District	Age at marriage									Total number of marriages		
		< 18 years (%) Economic status			Mean Economic status			Median Economic status			Economic status		
		Low	Medium	High	Low	Medium	High	Low	Medium	High	Low	Medium	High
15.	South Arcot	24.7	46.2	15.8	19.1	18.3	21.3	18.0	18.0	21.0	85	26	19
16.	Thanjavur	23.8	4.0	12.5	19.6	22.2	21.5	19.0	21.0	21.5	21	25	16
17.	The Nilgiris	25.0	8.7	5.6	20.5	21.8	21.2	20.0	21.0	20.5	4	46	18
18.	Theni	80.0	31.7	9.5	16.4	19.1	20.2	17.0	19.0	21.0	5	60	21
19.	Tiruchirappalli	29.2	26.8	7.1	19.2	19.8	23.5	19.0	19.0	23.0	24	41	14
20.	Tirunelveli	14.3	7.5	4.9	20.4	21.6	21.4	20.0	21.0	21.0	7	40	41
21.	Tiruvanamalai	28.2	23.9	24.3	18.7	19.5	19.5	19.0	19.0	19.0	39	67	37
22.	Tutikorin	0.0	8.5	7.0	22.3	21.1	21.3	21.0	21.0	21.0	9	59	43
23.	Virudhunagar	12.5	14.6	13.0	19.1	19.5	20.1	19.5	20.0	20.0	8	48	54
14	**Uttar Pradesh**												
1.	Agra	75.0	33.3	26.8	16.3	18.0	19.3	16.0	18.0	19.0	24	48	56
2.	Aligarh	80.0	57.9	28.3	16.4	16.8	18.5	16.0	17.0	18.0	10	19	46
3.	Allahabad	66.7	43.5	38.6	16.8	17.9	17.6	17.0	18.0	18.0	57	23	44
4.	Almora	14.3	21.9	6.3	18.7	19.0	19.9	18.0	19.0	19.0	7	32	32
5.	Ambedkarnagar	70.6	76.5	38.5	15.7	15.6	19.5	16.0	15.0	18.0	51	51	13
6.	Azamgarh	73.2	64.7	35.7	16.0	16.2	18.7	16.0	16.0	20.0	41	51	14
7.	Bahraich	83.8	78.6	50.0	14.7	14.9	18.8	14.0	15.0	17.5	74	28	16
8.	Ballia	71.0	43.8	50.0	16.0	17.6	18.1	16.0	18.0	17.5	31	48	18
9.	Banda	76.6	70.8	22.2	15.4	15.9	20.2	15.0	16.0	20.0	77	24	9
10.	Barabanki	61.2	54.1	11.1	15.7	16.9	19.9	16.0	17.0	18.0	49	61	9
11.	Bareilly	27.3	33.3	26.9	18.5	18.5	18.9	19.0	18.0	18.0	11	27	26
12.	Basti	84.2	81.9	25.0	14.3	15.4	18.4	14.0	15.0	18.0	38	72	12
13.	Bhadohi	80.0	70.0	48.1	15.9	16.6	16.9	16.0	16.0	18.0	85	40	54
14.	Bijnor	8.8	19.4	17.9	19.2	19.1	19.9	19.0	18.0	20.0	34	36	39
15.	Budaun	60.0	56.8	21.1	17.0	17.0	19.5	16.0	16.5	20.0	30	44	19
16.	Bulandshahar	0.0	32.0	25.5	20.0	18.0	19.1	20.0	18.0	18.0	1	25	51
17.	Chamoli	21.4	3.2	6.5	19.5	19.7	20.5	20.0	20.0	21.0	14	31	31
18.	Dehradun	44.4	17.6	2.0	18.2	20.1	21.6	18.0	20.0	21.0	18	17	49
19.	Deoria	59.5	62.9	47.2	17.0	16.7	17.5	17.0	16.0	18.0	37	35	36

Appendix - IV (Continued)

Sr. No.	State/District	Age at marriage: < 18 years (%) Economic status			Mean Economic status			Median Economic status			Total number of marriages Economic status		
		Low	Medium	High	Low	Medium	High	Low	Medium	High	Low	Medium	High
20.	Etah	85.0	56.0	39.3	15.8	17.6	18.3	16.0	17.0	18.0	20	25	28
21.	Etawah	57.1	43.1	23.8	16.4	17.6	19.9	16.0	18.0	20.0	42	51	21
22.	Faizabad	74.3	55.6	28.6	15.4	16.7	18.6	15.0	17.0	18.0	70	45	14
23.	Farrukhabad	51.2	35.2	6.7	17.0	18.1	18.5	17.0	18.0	18.0	41	54	15
24.	Fatehpur	54.9	41.8	30.0	17.1	17.8	18.6	17.0	18.0	18.0	91	55	30
25.	Firozabad	71.4	60.6	19.5	16.7	16.9	19.6	16.0	17.0	19.0	35	66	41
26.	Ghaziabad	45.5	24.3	11.4	17.6	18.2	20.3	18.0	18.0	20.0	11	37	70
27.	Ghazipur	78.0	65.8	26.5	16.0	17.1	18.4	15.0	17.0	18.0	59	38	34
28.	Gonda	76.0	67.7	63.6	14.5	15.7	15.7	14.0	16.0	16.0	25	62	11
29.	Gorakhpur	89.7	41.2	56.7	15.3	17.2	17.8	16.0	18.0	17.0	29	17	30
30.	Hamirpur(UP)	60.3	46.3	25.0	16.8	17.3	18.7	16.5	18.0	18.0	78	41	28
31.	Hardoi	48.4	43.3	33.3	17.2	18.0	18.7	18.0	18.0	19.0	31	30	9
32.	Hardwar	25.0	21.6	2.3	17.5	18.9	21.4	18.0	18.0	21.0	8	37	43
33.	Hathras	63.6	54.4	25.7	17.0	17.3	19.5	17.0	17.0	19.0	22	57	35
34.	Jalaun	67.7	52.9	54.5	16.5	16.9	17.2	17.0	17.0	17.0	62	34	33
35.	Jaunpur	61.1	58.7	41.7	16.6	17.1	17.6	17.0	17.0	18.0	72	63	36
36.	Jhansi	68.8	54.1	23.9	15.6	17.7	19.0	15.0	17.0	19.0	16	37	46
37.	Kanpur Dehat	50.0	32.5	9.1	17.3	18.6	20.0	17.5	18.0	20.0	60	40	33
38.	Kanpur Nagar	25.0	8.3	1.6	18.5	20.8	21.5	18.0	20.5	21.0	12	12	64
39.	Kheri	55.4	58.2	18.2	17.0	16.9	20.9	17.0	17.0	20.0	83	55	11
40.	Lalitpur	86.8	96.0	53.3	14.6	14.5	18.5	14.0	14.0	17.0	53	25	15
41.	Lucknow	42.9	42.4	22.2	17.6	18.3	20.8	18.0	18.0	20.0	28	33	36
42.	Maharajganj	79.3	87.0	77.3	14.7	14.4	15.3	15.0	14.0	15.0	29	23	22
43.	Mahoba	80.3	55.6	33.3	15.8	17.0	18.3	16.0	17.0	18.0	61	36	18
44.	Mainpuri	60.4	52.0	16.7	16.8	17.4	19.8	17.0	17.0	20.0	48	50	18
45.	Mathura	71.4	52.9	24.2	16.5	17.2	18.5	16.5	17.0	18.0	14	17	33
46.	Mau	38.7	46.7	17.2	17.5	17.6	20.0	18.0	18.0	20.0	62	75	29
47.	Meerut	45.5	4.0	12.1	17.8	20.2	20.1	18.0	20.0	20.0	11	25	33
48.	Mirzapur	65.4	63.9	29.0	16.5	16.6	18.2	16.0	17.0	18.0	78	36	31

Appendix - IV (Continued)

Sr. No.	State/District	Age at marriage									Total number of marriages		
		< 18 years (%) Economic status			Mean Economic status			Median Economic status			Economic status		
		Low	Medium	High	Low	Medium	High	Low	Medium	High	Low	Medium	High
49.	Muradabad	40.0	45.1	9.1	17.9	17.5	20.3	18.0	18.0	20.0	10	51	44
50.	Muzaffarnagar	14.3	34.8	6.7	18.0	18.6	20.4	19.0	18.0	20.0	7	46	45
51.	Nainital	11.8	13.6	5.9	18.8	18.8	20.7	18.0	19.0	20.0	17	22	34
52.	Pauri Garhwal	4.8	11.8	5.9	19.2	19.2	19.7	19.0	19.0	19.0	21	17	51
53.	Pilibhit	66.7	64.5	13.3	16.3	16.8	20.1	16.0	16.0	20.0	33	31	15
54.	Pithoragarh	20.0	26.8	18.8	18.4	18.5	19.5	18.0	18.0	19.0	10	41	32
55.	Pratapgarh	55.7	51.7	58.8	16.8	16.9	17.8	17.0	17.0	17.0	88	29	17
56.	Rae Bareli	54.9	34.2	25.0	16.7	17.4	19.0	17.0	18.0	19.0	82	38	24
57.	Rampur	38.9	41.2	12.0	17.4	17.7	18.8	18.0	18.0	18.0	18	34	25
58.	Saharanpur	21.4	32.3	5.1	18.3	18.6	20.2	18.0	19.0	20.0	28	31	39
59.	Shajahanabad	84.6	53.5	36.4	15.3	16.7	18.6	15.0	17.0	19.0	39	43	11
60.	Siddharthnagar	87.1	61.5	50.0	13.2	15.8	16.8	13.0	16.0	17.5	31	39	32
61.	Sitapur	65.8	57.1	60.0	16.6	16.7	16.9	16.0	16.0	17.0	76	21	10
62.	Sonbhadra	70.8	85.7	20.0	15.6	14.9	19.0	16.0	16.0	19.0	65	7	10
63.	Sultanpur	71.4	54.2	71.4	15.5	16.6	17.0	16.0	17.0	15.0	56	48	7
64.	Tehri Garhwal	26.7	15.6	0.0	18.1	18.6	20.0	18.0	18.0	20.0	15	45	24
65.	Udhamsingh Nagar	40.9	40.7	14.0	17.4	18.1	19.9	18.0	18.0	20.0	22	27	43
66.	Unnao	50.7	44.4	25.0	17.1	17.6	20.4	17.0	18.0	21.0	69	18	16
67.	Uttarkashi	21.4	20.0	12.9	19.1	19.0	19.9	19.0	19.0	19.0	14	25	31
68.	Varanasi	76.9	76.7	63.2	15.5	15.8	17.0	15.0	16.0	16.0	52	43	57
15	**West Bengal**												
1.	Bankura	59.8	28.6	11.5	17.3	18.9	20.5	17.0	18.0	20.0	117	7	26
2.	Barddhaman	69.3	66.7	29.1	16.5	16.6	20.2	16.0	16.0	19.0	75	27	55
3.	Birbhum	68.0	44.4	16.7	16.3	17.3	20.8	16.0	18.0	21.0	100	9	18
4.	Dakshin Dinajpur	70.2	35.7	33.3	16.3	19.0	20.8	16.0	18.5	21.5	131	14	6
5.	Darjiling	36.7	18.4	5.9	18.4	21.3	21.9	18.0	21.0	22.0	49	38	17
6.	Haora	47.6	29.6	27.0	18.2	18.7	21.4	18.0	19.0	21.0	63	27	37
7.	Hugli	40.0	40.6	16.1	18.6	19.3	21.4	18.0	18.0	21.0	50	32	31
8.	Jalpaiguri	41.0	20.8	0.0	18.7	21.3	20.7	18.0	20.0	20.0	83	24	3

Appendix - IV (Continued)

Sr. No.	State/District	< 18 years (%) Economic status			Age at marriage: Mean Economic status			Median Economic status			Total number of marriages Economic status		
		Low	Medium	High	Low	Medium	High	Low	Medium	High	Low	Medium	High
9.	Koch Bihar	58.9	0.0	0.0	17.0	24.6	21.0	17.0	24.0	20.0	124	13	3
10.	Kolkata	57.1	22.7	7.5	17.6	19.8	22.0	17.0	19.0	21.0	7	44	40
11.	Maldah	63.8	68.8	0.0	16.4	16.4	21.8	16.0	16.0	22.0	69	16	12
12.	Medinipur	47.1	6.3	14.3	18.0	22.7	18.7	18.0	22.0	18.0	102	16	7
13.	Murshidabad	83.7	78.6	67.5	15.5	16.0	17.2	15.0	15.5	17.0	104	14	40
14.	Nadia	52.3	25.0	20.0	17.4	20.3	21.1	17.0	19.5	22.0	65	16	20
15.	North 24 Parganas	61.2	48.0	23.1	16.7	17.9	21.2	17.0	18.0	21.0	49	25	26
16.	Puruliya	77.9	55.6	63.2	15.7	17.7	18.1	15.0	17.0	16.0	113	9	19
17.	South 24 Parganas	66.2	29.0	7.7	16.9	18.6	21.7	17.0	18.0	20.0	65	31	13
18.	Uttar Dinajpur	65.0	37.5	16.7	16.8	18.3	19.7	17.0	18.5	19.5	117	8	12
16	**Andaman & Nicobar**												
1.	Andaman	14.8	17.9	12.5	19.3	20.6	23.0	19.0	19.0	24.0	27	28	8
2.	Nicobar	0.0	7.1	0.0	22.9	22.0	23.0	22.0	22.0	20.0	24	28	6
17	**Arunachal Pradesh**												
1.	Changlang	37.0	0.0	33.3	18.9	21.4	19.3	18.0	22.0	19.5	46	5	6
2.	Dibang Valley	32.4	42.9	**	18.8	20.0	NA	18.0	18.0	NA	34	7	**
3.	East Kameng	45.2	30.0	100.0	17.4	18.4	16.0	18.0	18.0	16.0	62	10	1
4.	East Siang	29.4	71.4	16.7	19.0	17.4	21.3	19.5	16.0	22.0	34	7	6
5.	Lohit	14.3	6.7	**	18.8	19.9	NA	18.0	19.0	NA	28	15	**
6.	Lower Subansiri	35.0	22.2	**	18.6	19.7	NA	18.0	18.0	NA	40	9	**
7.	Papum Pare	22.7	50.0	10.0	19.3	20.2	20.0	18.0	18.5	19.5	22	6	10
8.	Tawang	0.0	0.0	0.0	18.7	21.9	20.0	19.0	21.0	20.0	3	13	1
9.	Tirap	37.5	100.0	0.0	19.8	16.0	18.0	20.0	16.0	18.0	16	1	1
10.	Upper Siang	4.8	0.0	50.0	19.5	21.0	16.5	19.0	21.0	16.5	21	1	2
11.	Upper Subansiri	43.2	40.0	25.0	17.9	18.5	20.4	18.0	18.0	20.0	44	15	8
12.	West Kameng	38.5	50.0	0.0	18.9	21.5	20.0	18.0	21.5	20.0	26	2	1
13.	West Siang	39.1	**	16.7	18.2	NA	19.5	18.0	NA	18.0	23	**	6

Appendix - IV (Continued)

Sr. No.	State/District	Age at marriage									Total number of marriages		
		< 18 years (%) Economic status			Mean Economic status			Median Economic status			Economic status		
		Low	Medium	High	Low	Medium	High	Low	Medium	High	Low	Medium	High
18	**Chandigarh**												
1.	Chandigarh	0.0	0.0	0.0	18.0	21.0	22.8	18.0	21.0	23.0	1	1	41
19	**Dadra & Nagar Haveli**												
1.	Dadra & Nagar Haveli	57.8	56.3	30.0	16.7	17.1	19.6	16.0	16.5	19.0	45	16	20
20	**Daman & Diu**												
1.	Daman	27.3	20.0	12.7	19.3	18.8	20.3	19.0	19.0	20.0	22	45	71
2.	Diu	**	30.0	14.0	NA	20.1	19.8	NA	19.5	19.0	**	10	86
21	**Delhi**												
1.	Delhi	0.0	28.6	2.1	18.0	18.4	21.2	18.0	18.0	21.0	1	21	97
22	**Goa**												
1.	North Goa	0.0	3.8	5.3	29.0	23.5	23.7	29.0	23.0	24.0	1	52	19
2.	South Goa	33.3	1.6	0.0	20.3	24.1	23.9	18.0	24.0	24.0	3	61	25
23	**Himachal Pradesh**												
1.	Bilaspur(Pra.Him)	0.0	4.8	5.7	20.0	20.2	21.2	19.0	20.0	20.0	9	21	35
2.	Chamba	6.1	2.1	0.0	19.8	21.3	23.1	19.0	21.0	23.0	33	48	44
3.	Hamirpur(HP)	0.0	2.8	0.0	19.6	20.5	20.9	19.0	20.0	20.0	29	36	45
4.	Kangra	9.1	2.6	0.0	20.5	21.2	21.6	20.5	21.0	21.5	22	39	24
5.	Kinnaur	18.2	13.6	0.0	20.8	20.8	22.0	20.0	21.0	22.0	33	22	1
6.	Kullu	0.0	2.9	0.0	20.8	20.2	20.9	21.5	20.0	21.0	14	34	15
7.	Lahul & Spiti	0.0	0.0	0.0	22.4	21.0	24.8	21.0	20.0	24.0	5	7	10
8.	Mandi	6.1	7.3	0.0	19.9	20.2	21.4	20.0	20.0	20.0	33	41	45
9.	Shimla	5.6	0.0	0.0	20.3	21.5	22.7	20.0	21.0	22.0	18	23	11
10.	Sirmaur	12.5	6.7	3.7	19.5	20.1	21.3	19.0	18.0	21.0	16	15	27
11.	Solan	0.0	0.0	1.9	19.4	20.9	21.1	20.0	21.0	20.0	5	17	52
12.	Una	0.0	0.0	1.6	20.3	21.2	21.4	20.0	21.0	22.0	11	33	64
24	**Jammu & Kashmir**												
1.	Anantanag	0.0	7.1	0.0	22.1	22.4	22.6	22.0	22.5	23.0	15	14	21
2.	Badgam	0.0	12.5	0.0	22.3	20.6	21.3	23.0	20.0	20.0	3	8	20

Appendix - IV (Continued)

Sr. No.	State/District	Age at marriage									Total number of marriages		
		< 18 years (%) Economic status			Mean Economic status			Median Economic status			Economic status		
		Low	*Medium*	*High*	*Low*	*Medium*	*High*	*Low*	*Medium*	*High*	*Low*	*Medium*	*High*
3.	Baramula	13.3	0.0	0.0	20.8	22.4	22.5	20.0	22.0	23.0	30	8	15
4.	Doda	0.0	0.0	0.0	20.4	20.7	21.4	20.0	20.0	21.5	154	51	10
5.	Jammu	0.0	1.9	2.0	20.9	21.0	21.4	21.0	22.0	22.0	81	53	50
6.	Kargil	25.7	35.3	**	18.5	19.5	NA	18.0	18.0	NA	74	17	**
7.	Kathua	0.0	0.0	0.0	21.4	21.6	22.2	22.0	22.0	22.0	48	44	56
8.	Kupwara	0.0	0.0	0.0	20.0	20.0	20.2	20.0	20.0	20.0	1	1	22
9.	Leh	1.7	0.0	**	20.4	22.5	NA	20.0	22.0	NA	58	10	**
10.	Pulwama	0.0	0.0	0.0	22.3	20.4	24.2	24.0	20.0	24.5	3	5	10
11.	Punch	4.8	2.6	0.0	20.3	21.2	20.8	20.0	21.0	20.0	63	38	13
12.	Rajauri	0.2	0.0	**	18.9	18.8	NA	19.0	19.0	NA	433	28	**
13.	Srinagar	0.0	14.3	5.6	20.0	18.6	19.9	20.0	19.0	20.0	1	14	18
14.	Udhampur	0.8	4.5	0.0	19.1	20.5	20.7	19.0	20.0	21.0	126	22	3
25	**Lakshadweep**												
1.	Lakshadweep	**	0.0	19.1	NA	21.1	19.9	NA	20.0	19.0	**	7	152
26	**Manipur**												
1.	Bishnupur	28.3	4.1	25.0	20.6	23.7	20.5	19.5	23.0	20.5	46	49	4
2.	Chandel	25.6	16.2	0.0	21.8	21.8	27.0	20.0	21.0	27.0	39	37	2
3.	Churachandpur	11.8	10.7	0.0	20.4	23.1	27.0	20.0	22.0	27.0	17	28	2
4.	Imphal	5.7	0.0	6.7	24.9	27.9	26.7	24.0	27.0	27.0	105	27	15
5.	Senapati	27.8	7.1	0.0	21.6	22.4	18.0	21.5	23.0	18.0	18	14	1
6.	Tamenglong	21.4	20.0	0.0	20.5	21.8	27.0	20.0	20.0	27.0	56	25	1
7.	Thoubal	15.2	16.9	0.0	19.6	21.9	23.4	20.0	22.0	24.0	33	71	5
8.	Ukhrul	18.5	16.7	**	23.0	23.5	NA	21.0	23.0	NA	27	6	**
27	**Meghalaya**												
1.	East Garo Hills	0.0	0.0	0.0	19.9	23.7	21.0	20.0	24.0	20.0	21	3	3
2.	East Khasi Hills	33.3	7.1	0.0	19.3	18.8	25.0	19.5	18.0	25.0	6	14	2
3.	Jaintia Hills	**	0.6	1.1	NA	20.0	20.8	NA	19.0	20.5	**	167	94

Appendix - IV (Continued)

Sr. No.	State/District	Age at marriage									Total number of marriages		
		< 18 years (%) Economic status			Mean Economic status			Median Economic status			Economic status		
		Low	Medium	High	Low	Medium	High	Low	Medium	High	Low	Medium	High
4.	Ri Bhoi	3.1	0.0	0.0	19.3	20.3	21.0	19.0	20.0	21.0	32	10	1
5.	South Garp Hills	0.0	**	0.0	22.0	NA	19.5	18.0	NA	19.5	3	**	2
6.	West Garo Hills	20.0	0.0	0.0	18.5	26.7	24.0	19.0	27.0	19.0	10	3	3
7.	West Khasi Hills	0.0	2.7	0.0	20.8	19.8	18.0	21.0	19.0	18.0	13	37	1
28	**Mizoram**												
1.	Aizwal	15.4	6.5	0.0	20.9	21.8	22.8	20.0	20.0	19.0	13	62	9
2.	Chhimtuipui	24.4	27.3	0.0	19.4	19.5	22.0	18.0	19.0	22.0	41	33	1
3.	Lunglei	0.0	10.3	0.0	21.1	20.8	21.6	20.5	20.0	20.0	10	29	5
29	**Nagaland**												
1.	Kohima	52.2	50.0	65.5	18.2	17.6	17.0	17.0	17.5	17.0	23	34	29
2.	Mokokchung	9.1	18.5	0.0	20.6	20.4	27.0	21.0	20.0	27.0	22	27	1
3.	Mon	13.0	10.1	0.0	19.0	19.5	20.5	19.0	19.0	20.0	69	79	4
4.	Phek	30.8	50.0	**	18.2	17.7	NA	18.0	17.0	NA	13	6	**
5.	Tuensang	10.4	6.5	0.0	19.6	20.0	22.0	19.0	20.0	22.0	48	31	2
6.	Wokha	32.7	20.0	**	19.5	19.3	NA	19.0	19.0	NA	52	70	**
7.	Zunheboto	22.4	28.6	50.0	19.2	18.5	17.5	20.0	19.0	17.5	125	21	4
30	**Pondicherry**												
1.	Karaikal	7.5	2.8	5.1	20.9	20.9	22.1	20.0	20.0	23.0	67	36	39
2.	Mahe	0.0	12.5	2.2	19.0	20.4	22.5	19.0	20.0	21.0	1	8	182
3.	Pondicherry	15.4	0.0	2.2	21.0	21.0	22.5	20.0	20.0	22.0	26	40	46
4.	Yanam	33.3	5.3	26.7	18.1	19.4	19.0	18.0	19.0	19.0	18	19	45
31	**Sikkim**												
1.	East Sikkim	15.0	10.0	13.3	21.8	22.5	20.9	22.5	21.5	21.0	20	20	15
2.	North Sikkim	11.1	22.2	0.0	22.1	18.8	24.5	21.0	19.0	23.5	9	9	4
3.	South Sikkim	15.8	0.0	**	20.4	24.8	NA	20.0	25.5	NA	19	4	**
4.	West Sikkim	23.1	17.1	0.0	19.0	21.1	21.6	19.0	20.0	22.0	26	35	9

Appendix - IV (Continued)

Sr. No.	State/District	Age at marriage									Total number of marriages		
		< 18 years (%) Economic status			Mean Economic status			Median Economic status			Economic status		
		Low	Medium	High	Low	Medium	High	Low	Medium	High	Low	Medium	High
32	**Tripura**												
1.	North Tripura	35.9	50.0	16.7	18.6	20.0	20.7	18.0	20.0	20.0	64	2	6
2.	South Tripura	48.2	33.3	33.3	18.9	21.2	19.3	18.0	20.5	19.0	83	12	3
3.	West Tripura	18.2	12.5	5.6	20.9	22.4	23.2	20.0	21.5	23.0	55	8	18

Note: In the column showing percent of marriages below legal minimum age, 0.0 indicates no marriage below 18 years.

** No marriage is reported in that category of characteristic/district.

NA Not applicable

APPENDIX - V

Percent of Marriages below Legal Minimum Age of 18 years and Average Age at Marriage in each District by level of Female Literacy Rate-GIRLS

Sr. No.	*State/district*	*Level of FLR*	*Age at marriage*			*Total Marriages (#)*
			<18 years (%)	*Mean*	*Median*	
1	**Andhra Pradesh**					
1.	Mahbubnagar	Low	40.6	17.7	18.0	69
2.	Adilabad	Medium	48.3	17.4	18.0	89
3.	Anantapur	"	33.8	18.3	18.0	71
4.	Chittoor	"	22.6	19.9	20.0	31
5.	Cuddapah	"	33.0	18.2	18.0	103
6.	East Godavari	"	43.8	17.7	18.0	73
7.	Guntur	"	34.8	19.0	18.0	46
8.	Karimnagar	"	42.6	17.7	18.0	47
9.	Khammam	"	32.7	17.9	18.0	55
10.	Krishna	"	26.3	18.5	18.0	57
11.	Kurnool	"	38.4	18.1	18.0	86
12.	Medak	"	34.7	18.1	18.0	49
13.	Nalgonda	"	42.1	17.9	18.0	76
14.	Nellore	"	25.0	19.0	19.0	64
15.	Nizamabad	"	44.4	17.8	18.0	63
16.	Prakasam	"	40.6	18.2	18.0	64
17.	Rangareddi	"	37.4	18.7	18.0	91
18.	Srikakulam	"	49.1	17.4	18.0	106
19.	Vishkhapatanam	"	52.8	17.6	17.0	36
20.	Vizianagaram	"	40.5	17.9	18.0	84
21.	Warangal	"	48.4	17.7	18.0	64
22.	Hyderabad	High	6.4	20.5	20.0	78
23.	West Godavari	"	29.6	18.2	18.0	108
2	**Assam**					
1.	Barpeta	Medium	18.4	19.8	19.0	49
2.	Bongaigaon	"	40.5	19.3	18.0	148
3.	Cachar	"	20.2	20.4	20.0	99
4.	Darrang	"	33.3	18.9	19.0	57
5.	Dhemaji	"	3.9	20.3	20.0	51
6.	Dhubri	"	59.1	17.6	17.0	110
7.	Dibrugarh	"	23.3	20.7	19.0	30
8.	Goalpara	"	41.4	18.9	18.0	99
9.	Golaghat	"	29.3	19.5	19.0	92
10.	Hailakandi	"	8.3	21.5	20.0	145
11.	Karbi Anglong	"	4.8	19.7	19.0	63
12.	Karimganj	"	23.4	21.4	20.0	94
13.	Lakhimpur	"	36.0	19.6	18.0	25
14.	Marigaon	"	33.6	19.0	19.0	125
15.	Nagaon	"	40.9	18.8	18.0	110
16.	Nalbari	Medium	4.8	21.6	22.0	63

Appendix - V (Continued)

Sr. No.	State/district	Level of FLR	Age at marriage <18 years (%)	Mean	Median	Total Marriages (#)
17.	North Cachar Hills	"	7.7	20.6	20.0	65
18.	Sonitpur	"	30.5	19.3	18.0	59
19.	Tinsukia	"	24.4	20.1	19.0	82
20.	Jorhat	High	7.7	21.2	21.0	52
21.	Kamrup	"	19.4	20.8	21.0	93
22.	Sibsagar	"	12.5	21.9	20.5	24
3	**Bihar**					
1.	Araria	Low	51.5	17.5	17.0	132
2.	Darbhanga	"	51.4	17.5	17.0	183
3.	Deoghar	"	66.4	16.0	16.0	128
4.	Dumka	"	49.1	17.5	18.0	116
5.	Giridih	"	58.8	16.9	17.0	119
6.	Godda	"	66.4	16.7	16.0	116
7.	Gopalganj	"	58.4	17.1	17.0	154
8.	Katihar	"	47.9	17.5	18.0	117
9.	Khagaria	"	64.0	16.6	16.0	172
10.	Kishanganj	"	48.3	17.9	18.0	87
11.	Madhepura	"	66.4	16.4	16.0	146
12.	Madhubani	"	63.9	16.5	17.0	144
13.	Nawada	"	72.3	15.8	16.0	213
14.	Palamu	"	66.0	16.4	16.0	103
15.	Pashchmi Singhbhum	"	28.6	18.9	18.0	84
16.	Purba Champaran	"	63.0	16.8	16.0	184
17.	Purnia	"	48.3	18.1	18.0	151
18.	Saharsa	"	56.6	17.3	17.0	152
19.	Sahibganj	"	62.7	16.6	16.0	83
20.	Samastipur	"	64.2	16.2	16.0	159
21.	Sitamarhi	"	64.7	16.5	16.0	153
22.	Aurangabad(Bih)	Medium	63.6	16.6	17.0	184
23.	Begusarai	"	58.7	16.7	17.0	167
24.	Bhagalpur	"	58.9	16.8	17.0	158
25.	Bhojpur	"	56.8	16.6	17.0	162
26.	Buxar-	"	65.2	16.6	16.0	210
27.	Dhanbad	"	42.4	18.0	18.0	85
28.	Gaya	"	61.6	16.2	16.0	172
29.	Gulma	"	27.3	18.8	19.0	77
30.	Hazaribagh	"	66.7	16.4	16.0	129
31.	Jehanabad	"	54.4	16.9	17.0	195
32.	Lohardaga	"	43.3	18.2	18.0	104
33.	Munger	Medium	60.6	16.4	16.0	127
34.	Muzaffarpur	"	53.2	17.5	17.0	173
35.	Nalanda	"	58.8	16.5	16.0	165
36.	Pashchim Champaran	"	40.9	18.0	18.0	164
37.	Patna	"	79.5	15.5	15.0	156
38.	Purbi Singhbhum	"	33.0	19.5	19.0	106
39.	Ranchi	"	39.0	18.3	18.0	82
40.	Rohtas	"	68.9	16.4	16.0	132
41.	Saran	"	51.3	17.2	17.0	187
42.	Siwan	"	43.6	17.8	18.0	172
43.	Vaishali	"	63.4	16.5	16.0	164

Appendix - V (Continued)

Sr. No.	State/district	Level of FLR	Age at marriage <18 years (%)	Mean	Median	Total Marriages (#)
4	**Gujarat**					
1.	Amreli	Medium	17.0	19.6	19.0	176
2.	Banas Kantha	"	52.0	17.2	17.0	127
3.	Bharuch	"	18.3	19.7	20.0	115
4.	Bhavnagar	"	28.3	18.6	18.0	152
5.	Gandhinagar	"	33.3	18.6	18.5	84
6.	Jamnagar	"	10.7	20.1	20.0	131
7.	Junagadh	"	11.7	20.2	20.0	162
8.	Kachchh	"	23.8	19.4	19.0	105
9.	Kheda	"	32.0	19.0	18.0	150
10.	Mahesana	"	32.8	18.6	18.5	134
11.	Panch Mahals	"	26.5	18.6	18.0	83
12.	Sabar Kantha	"	30.5	18.7	19.0	131
13.	Surendranagar	"	9.8	20.0	20.0	102
14.	The Dangs	"	47.3	17.6	18.0	131
15.	Vadodara	"	33.7	18.9	18.0	101
16.	Valsad	"	10.0	20.8	20.0	120
17.	Ahmadabad	High	27.0	20.1	20.0	100
18.	Rajkot	"	13.9	19.8	20.0	144
19.	Surat	"	18.8	19.7	20.0	101
5	**Haryana**					
1.	Bhiwani	Medium	48.9	17.2	18.0	141
2.	Faridabad	"	30.2	18.8	18.0	139
3.	Gurgaon	"	36.5	17.9	18.0	104
4.	Hisar	"	42.7	17.5	18.0	117
5.	Jind	"	36.7	18.0	18.0	128
6.	Kaithal	"	32.9	18.3	18.0	79
7.	Karnal	"	16.2	19.5	19.0	148
8.	Kurukshetra	"	14.6	20.0	20.0	123
9.	Mahendragarh	Medium	46.3	17.6	18.0	175
10.	Panchkula	"	25.6	19.0	18.0	78
11.	Panipat	"	45.3	17.7	18.0	128
12.	Rewari	"	28.8	18.5	18.0	125
13.	Rohtak	"	34.0	18.7	18.0	141
14.	Sirsa	"	31.5	18.7	18.0	108
15.	Sonipat	"	6.3	20.5	20.0	128
16.	Ambala	High	13.0	20.4	20.0	108
17.	Yamunanagar	"	6.7	20.8	20.0	134
6	**Karnataka**					
1.	Bangalore Rural	Medium	21.5	18.9	18.0	107
2.	Belgaum	"	55.5	17.4	17.0	119
3.	Bellary	"	44.3	18.5	18.0	131
4.	Bidar	"	67.6	16.3	16.0	176
5.	Bijapur	"	64.3	16.4	16.0	126
6.	Chikmagalur	"	13.6	20.5	20.0	147
7.	Chitradurga	"	30.5	18.6	18.0	118
8.	Dharwad	"	36.5	19.5	19.0	115
9.	Gulbarga	"	47.8	17.7	18.0	113
10.	Hassan	"	15.3	19.9	19.0	131
11.	Kolar	"	33.6	18.6	18.0	140
12.	Mandya	"	37.4	18.3	18.0	107
13.	Mysore	"	48.0	17.9	18.0	98

Appendix - V (Continued)

Sr. No.	State/district	Level of FLR	Age at marriage <18 years (%)	Mean	Median	Total Marriages (#)
14.	Raichur	"	57.1	17.5	17.0	112
15.	Tumkur	"	27.2	18.9	18.0	114
16.	Bangalore	High	12.0	20.9	21.0	83
17.	Dakshina Kannada	"	4.6	22.2	22.0	131
18.	Kodagu	"	22.1	20.0	20.0	86
19.	Shimoga	"	16.6	20.6	20.0	163
20.	Uttara Kannada	"	15.0	21.5	21.0	133
7	**Kerala**					
1.	Alappuzha	High		23.0	22.0	161
2.	Ernakulam	"		23.7	23.0	149
3.	Idukki	"	1.5	23.1	23.0	130
4.	Kannur	"	19.0	20.8	20.0	179
5.	Kasaragod	"	18.2	20.7	20.0	154
6.	Kollam	"		22.3	22.0	170
7.	Kottayam	"		24.4	24.0	163
8.	Kozhikode	"	13.6	20.7	20.0	147
9.	Malappuram	"	35.7	18.7	18.0	196
10.	Palakkad	High	10.4	21.0	20.0	164
11.	Pathanamthitta	"		23.3	23.0	115
12.	Thiruvananthapuram	"	22.8	23.0	135	
13.	Thrissur	"	0.7	22.4	22.0	147
14.	Wayanad	"	7.1	20.8	20.0	141
8	**Madhya Pradesh**					
1.	Jhabua	Low	58.5	17.2	17.0	106
2.	Balaghat	Medium	32.4	18.2	19.0	34
3.	Bastar	"	33.9	18.6	18.0	56
4.	Betul	"	24.4	18.3	18.0	45
5.	Bhind	"	61.3	16.9	17.0	155
6.	Bilaspur(MP)	"	40.3	18.2	18.0	119
7.	Chattarpur	"	73.1	16.6	16.0	52
8.	Chhindwara	"	30.9	18.4	18.0	123
9.	Damoh	"	54.7	17.3	17.0	95
10.	Datia	"	49.0	17.4	18.0	104
11.	Dewas	"	52.7	17.1	17.0	110
12.	Dhar	"	56.6	16.9	16.0	122
13.	Durg	"	31.9	19.0	19.0	69
14.	East Nimar	"	42.2	18.2	18.0	116
15.	Guna	"	68.8	16.9	16.0	109
16.	Gwalior	"	35.8	19.0	18.0	106
17.	Hoshangabad	"	40.4	17.9	18.0	52
18.	Indore	"	42.1	18.3	18.0	121
19.	Jabalpur	"	38.6	18.3	18.0	83
20.	Mandla	"	37.5	17.6	18.0	40
21.	Mandsaur	"	57.5	16.9	16.0	127
22.	Morena	"	71.1	16.1	16.0	83
23.	Panna	"	57.1	17.0	16.0	49
24.	Raigarh (MP)	"	7.7	19.3	19.0	52
25.	Raipur	"	55.4	17.5	17.0	56
26.	Raisen	"	47.7	17.4	18.0	128
27.	Rajgarh	"	64.8	16.4	16.0	125
28.	Ratlam	"	45.8	17.3	18.0	83

Appendix - V (Continued)

Sr. No.	State/district	Level of FLR	Age at marriage <18 years (%)	Mean	Median	Total Marriages (#)
29.	Rewa	"	60.2	16.5	16.0	123
30.	Sagar	"	60.0	17.0	17.0	95
31.	Satna	"	60.0	16.7	16.5	120
32.	Sehore	"	48.3	17.6	18.0	118
33.	Seoni	"	36.6	18.0	18.0	71
34.	Shahdol	"	66.7	16.4	16.0	39
35.	Shajapur	Medium	82.4	15.2	15.0	102
36.	Shivpuri	"	68.0	16.3	16.0	100
37.	Sidhi	"	67.4	15.7	16.0	86
38.	Surguja	"	56.6	16.7	17.0	76
39.	Tikamgarh	"	69.4	16.0	16.0	121
40.	Ujjain	"	39.4	17.9	18.0	132
41.	Vidisha	"	60.0	17.0	17.0	125
42.	West Nimar	"	42.2	17.6	18.0	102
43.	Bhopal	High	29.0	19.1	18.0	69
44.	Narsimhapur	"	49.4	18.2	18.0	81
45.	Rajnandgaon	"	50.0	17.3	17.5	106
9	**Maharashtra**					
1.	Ahmadnagar	Medium	40.8	17.6	18.0	125
2.	Aurangabad(Mah)	"	50.0	17.2	17.5	148
3.	Bid	"	58.7	16.9	17.0	109
4.	Buldana	"	33.6	18.4	18.0	140
5.	Chandrapur	"	25.7	18.8	18.0	101
6.	Dhule	"	40.0	18.2	18.0	105
7.	Gadchiroli	"	26.9	18.5	18.0	67
8.	Jalgaon	"	45.6	18.0	18.0	149
9.	Jalna	"	55.3	17.1	17.0	132
10.	Kolhapur	"	17.2	19.0	18.0	122
11.	Latur	"	58.2	17.2	17.0	141
12.	Nanded	"	63.2	16.7	16.0	144
13.	Nashik	"	31.3	18.5	18.0	80
14.	Osmanabad	"	46.6	17.4	18.0	131
15.	Parbhani	"	46.6	17.5	18.0	133
16.	Ratnagiri	"	13.0	19.9	19.0	123
17.	Solapur	"	41.8	18.2	18.0	122
18.	Yavatmal	"	26.6	18.4	18.0	154
19.	Akola	High	38.2	18.2	18.0	123
20.	Amravali	"	9.0	19.6	19.0	134
21.	Bhandara	"	9.3	20.0	20.0	129
22.	Greater Bombay (Mumbai)	"	8.0	21.2	21.0	87
23.	Nagpur	"	11.3	20.1	19.0	115
24.	Pune	"	30.4	18.5	18.0	115
25.	Raigarh(MAH)	"	16.3	19.0	18.0	86
26.	Sangli	"	25.6	18.6	18.0	125
27.	Satara	"	21.9	18.5	18.0	114
28.	Sindhudurg	"	3.9	21.5	21.0	102
29.	Thane	High	19.8	19.8	19.0	81
30.	Wardha	"	12.4	20.2	19.0	105
10	**Orissa**					
1.	Gajapati	Low	41.9	17.9	18.0	74
2.	Kalahandi	"	59.4	17.2	17.0	69
3.	Koraput	"	64.7	17.2	16.0	68

Appendix - V (Continued)

Sr. No.	State/district	Level of FLR	Age at marriage <18 years (%)	Mean	Median	Total Marriages (#)
4.	Malkangiri	"	56.0	17.0	17.0	50
5.	Nabarangapur	"	69.6	16.8	16.0	46
6.	Nuapada	"	42.6	18.2	18.0	47
7.	Rayagada	"	38.6	18.6	18.0	70
8.	Anugul	Medium	40.0	18.8	18.0	110
9.	Balangir	"	57.7	18.3	17.0	71
10.	Balasore	"	28.5	19.8	20.0	144
11.	Bargarh	"	39.8	18.3	18.0	98
12.	Baudh	"	50.7	17.5	17.0	73
13.	Bhadrak	"	15.7	21.1	21.0	159
14.	Cuttack	"	10.6	20.9	20.0	132
15.	Debagarh	"	33.3	19.1	18.5	72
16.	Dhenkanal	"	36.6	19.0	19.0	131
17.	Ganjam	"	50.7	17.9	17.0	134
18.	Jajapur	"	14.8	20.7	21.0	142
19.	Jharsuguda	"	16.7	19.6	19.0	72
20.	Kendujhar	"	30.1	19.5	19.0	103
21.	Mayurbhanj	"	32.6	19.3	18.0	95
22.	Nayagarh	"	53.6	17.8	17.0	140
23.	Phulbani	"	41.7	17.7	18.0	60
24.	Sambalpur	"	29.3	19.3	19.0	58
25.	Sonapur	"	39.3	18.6	18.0	107
26.	Sundargarh	"	15.2	20.3	19.0	46
27.	Jagatsinghapur	High	9.3	21.8	22.0	140
28.	Kendrapara	"	15.8	20.9	21.0	158
29.	Khordha	"	22.8	20.1	20.0	114
30.	Puri	"	14.0	20.8	21.0	107
11	**Punjab**					
1.	Amritsar	Medium	11.1	20.1	20.0	117
2.	Bathinda	"	12.8	19.7	20.0	117
3.	Faridkot	"	12.6	20.1	20.0	127
4.	Firozpur	"	25.0	19.4	19.0	116
5.	Mansa	"	20.4	19.6	20.0	137
6.	Moga	"	12.9	20.1	20.0	170
7.	Muktsar	Medium	23.7	19.5	20.0	152
8.	Patiala	"	10.3	20.3	20.0	87
9.	Sangrur	"	13.3	20.3	20.0	158
10.	Fatehgarh Sahib	High	6.8	20.3	20.0	161
11.	Gurdaspur	"	6.6	20.8	20.0	121
12.	Hoshiarpur	"	3.2	21.2	21.0	158
13.	Jalandhar	"	7.4	20.9	20.0	135
14.	Kapurthala	"	3.1	21.5	21.0	130
15.	Ludhiana	"	8.3	20.6	20.0	121
16.	Nawanshahr	"	2.1	21.3	21.0	141
17.	Rupnagar	"	6.0	21.0	21.0	134
12	**Rajasthan**					
1.	Banswara	Low	54.5	16.9	17.0	77
2.	Dungarpur	"	33.9	18.1	18.0	124
3.	Jaisalmer	"	50.0	17.2	17.5	74
4.	Jalor	"	45.6	17.4	18.0	136
5.	Tonk	"	75.4	15.4	15.0	130

Appendix - V (Continued)

Sr. No.	State/district	Level of FLR	Age at marriage <18 years (%)	Mean	Median	Total Marriages (#)
6.	Ajmer	Medium	48.0	17.8	18.0	100
7.	Alwar	"	52.8	17.2	17.0	144
8.	Barmer	"	50.0	16.9	17.5	104
9.	Bharatpur	"	55.6	17.1	17.0	133
10.	Bhilwara	"	70.5	15.8	15.5	132
11.	Bikaner	"	62.8	16.5	16.0	78
12.	Bundi	"	78.9	15.1	15.0	90
13.	Chittaurgarh	"	48.8	17.2	18.0	43
14.	Churu	"	67.7	16.3	17.0	124
15.	Dausa	"	71.0	15.9	16.0	131
16.	Dhaulpur	"	56.4	16.9	17.0	101
17.	Ganganagar	"	47.8	17.4	18.0	115
18.	Hanumangarh	"	51.7	17.2	17.0	151
19.	Jaipur	"	42.6	17.9	18.0	148
20.	Jhalawar	"	69.9	15.7	15.0	113
21.	Jhunjhunun	"	46.9	17.3	18.0	143
22.	Jodhpur	"	54.4	17.8	17.0	57
23.	Kota	"	60.6	16.9	16.5	94
24.	Nagaur	"	66.1	16.2	16.0	112
25.	Pali	"	50.0	17.3	17.5	82
26.	Rajsamand	"	46.3	17.4	18.0	67
27.	Sawai Madhopur	"	48.9	17.2	18.0	90
28.	Sikar	"	41.9	17.7	18.0	167
29.	Sirohi	Medium	32.0	18.3	18.0	50
30.	Udaipur	"	60.6	16.5	16.0	104
13	**Tamil Nadu**					
1.	Dharmapuri	Medium	33.8	18.6	18.0	130
2.	Dindigul	"	27.5	19.9	19.0	69
3.	Namakkal	"	12.8	20.3	20.0	86
4.	North Arcot	"	21.5	19.8	19.0	121
5.	Periyar	"	13.5	20.7	20.0	74
6.	Pudukkottai	"	10.9	20.9	20.0	128
7.	Ramanathapuram	"	13.4	20.0	20.0	112
8.	Salem	"	40.4	18.8	18.0	109
9.	Sivaganganagar	"	8.0	21.0	20.0	138
10.	South Arcot	"	27.7	19.3	19.0	130
11.	Theni	"	29.1	19.2	19.0	86
12.	Tirunelveli	"	6.8	21.4	21.0	88
13.	Virudhunagar	"	13.6	19.8	20.0	110
14.	Chengalpattu	High	10.0	20.2	20.0	90
15.	Chennai	"	5.6	21.5	21.0	108
16.	Coimbatore	"	16.1	20.9	21.0	93
17.	Kanniyakumari	"		23.0	23.0	87
18.	Madurai	"	25.6	20.4	20.0	133
19.	Thanjavur	"	12.9	21.1	20.0	62
20.	The Nilgiris	"	8.8	21.6	21.0	68
21.	Tiruchirappalli	"	24.1	20.3	19.0	79
22.	Tiruvanamalai	"	25.2	19.3	19.0	143
23.	Tutikorin	"	7.2	21.3	21.0	111
14	**Uttar Pradesh**					
1.	Bahraich	Low	78.0	15.3	15.0	118
2.	Budaun	"	50.5	17.5	17.0	93

Appendix - V (Continued)

Sr. No.	State/district	Level of FLR	Age at marriage <18 years (%)	Mean	Median	Total Marriages (#)
3.	Gonda	"	69.4	15.4	15.0	98
4.	Lalitpur	'	83.9	15.2	15.0	93
5.	Maharajganj	"	81.1	14.8	14.5	74
6.	Muradabad	"	29.5	18.7	18.0	105
7.	Rampur	"	31.2	18.0	18.0	77
8.	Siddharthnagar	"	65.7	15.3	15.0	102
9.	Agra	Medium	38.3	18.2	18.0	128
10.	Aligarh	"	42.7	17.8	18.0	75
11.	Allahabad	"	52.4	17.3	17.0	124
12.	Almora	"	14.1	19.4	19.0	71
13.	Ambedkarnagar	"	69.6	16.1	16.0	115
14.	Azamgarh	Medium	64.2	16.4	16.0	106
15.	Ballia	"	53.6	17.2	17.0	97
16.	Banda	"	70.9	15.9	16.0	110
17.	Barabanki	"	53.8	16.6	17.0	119
18.	Bareilly	"	29.7	18.7	18.0	64
19.	Basti	"	77.0	15.3	15.0	122
20.	Bhadohi	"	68.2	16.4	16.0	179
21.	Bijnor	"	15.6	19.4	19.0	109
22.	Bulandshahar	"	27.3	18.8	18.0	77
23.	Chamoli	"	7.9	20.0	20.0	76
24.	Deoria	"	56.5	17.1	17.0	108
25.	Etah	"	57.5	17.3	17.0	73
26.	Etawah	"	44.7	17.6	18.0	114
27.	Faizabad	"	62.8	16.2	16.0	129
29.	Fatehpur	"	46.6	17.6	18.0	176
30.	Firozabad	"	51.4	17.6	17.0	142
31.	Ghaziabad	"	18.6	19.4	19.0	118
32.	Ghazipur	"	61.1	16.9	17.0	131
33.	Gorakhpur	"	65.8	16.7	16.0	76
34.	Hamirpur(UP)	"	49.7	17.3	18.0	147
35.	Hardoi	"	44.3	17.7	18.0	70
36.	Hardwar	"	12.5	20.0	20.0	88
37.	Hathras	"	47.4	17.9	18.0	114
38.	Jalaun	"	60.5	16.8	17.0	129
39.	Jaunpur	"	56.1	17.0	17.0	171
40.	Jhansi	"	42.4	17.9	18.0	99
41.	Kanpur Dehat	"	34.6	18.3	18.0	133
42.	Kheri	"	53.7	17.2	17.0	149
43.	Lucknow	"	35.1	19.0	18.0	97
44.	Mahoba	"	65.2	16.6	16.0	115
45.	Mainpuri	"	50.0	17.5	17.5	116
46.	Mathura	"	42.2	17.7	18.0	64
47.	Mau	"	38.6	18.0	18.0	166
48.	Meerut	"	14.5	19.8	20.0	69
49.	Mirzapur	"	57.2	16.9	17.0	145
50.	Muzaffarnagar	"	20.4	19.4	19.0	98
51.	Pauri Garhwal	"	6.7	19.5	19.0	89
52.	Pilibhit	"	55.7	17.2	17.0	79
53.	Pithoragarh	"	22.9	18.9	18.0	83
54.	Pratapgarh	Medium	55.2	16.9	17.0	134
55.	Rae Bareli	"	44.4	17.2	18.0	144

Appendix - V (Continued)

Sr. No.	State/district	Level of FLR	Age at marriage <18 years (%)	Mean	Median	Total Marriages (#)
56.	Saharanpur	"	18.4	19.2	19.0	98
57.	Shajahanabad	"	64.5	16.3	16.0	93
58.	Sitapur	"	63.6	16.7	16.0	107
59.	Sonbhadra	"	65.9	16.0	16.0	82
60.	Sultanpur	"	64.0	16.1	16.0	111
61.	Tehri Garhwal	"	13.1	18.9	19.0	84
62.	Udhamsingh Nagar	"	28.3	18.8	18.0	92
63.	Unnao	"	45.6	17.7	18.0	103
64.	Uttarkashi	"	17.1	19.4	19.0	70
65.	Varanasi	"	71.7	16.2	16.0	152
66.	Dehradun	High	14.3	20.6	20.0	84
67.	Kanpur Nagar	"	5.7	21.0	20.5	88
68.	Nainital	"	9.6	19.7	19.0	73
15	**West Bengal**					
1.	Bankura	Medium	50.0	17.9	17.5	150
2.	Barddhaman	"	54.8	17.8	17.0	157
3.	Birbhum	"	59.1	17.0	16.0	127
4.	Dakshin Dinajpur	"	65.6	16.7	16.0	151
5.	Darjiling	"	25.0	20.1	19.5	104
6.	Jalpaiguri	"	35.5	19.3	18.0	110
7.	Koch Bihar	"	52.1	17.8	17.0	140
8.	Maldah	"	56.7	17.1	17.0	97
9.	Medinipur	"	40.0	18.7	18.0	125
10.	Murshidabad	"	79.1	16.0	16.0	158
11.	Nadia	"	41.6	18.6	18.0	101
12.	Puruliya	"	74.5	16.1	16.0	141
13.	South 24 Parganas	"	48.6	17.9	18.0	109
14.	Uttar Dinajpur	"	59.1	17.1	17.0	137
15.	Haora	High	37.8	19.2	18.0	127
16.	Hugli	"	33.6	19.6	19.0	113
17.	Kolkata	"	18.7	20.6	20.0	91
18.	North 24 Parganas	"	48.0	18.2	18.0	100
16	**Andman & Nicobar**					
1.	Nicobar	Medium	3.4	22.5	22.0	58
2.	Andaman	High	15.9	20.3	19.0	63
17	**Arunachal Pradesh**					
1.	East Kameng	Low	43.8	17.5	18.0	73
2.	Tawang	"		21.2	20.0	17
3.	Tirap	Low	38.9	19.5	19.5	18
4.	Changlang	Medium	33.3	19.2	19.0	57
5.	Dibang Valley	"	34.1	19.0	18.0	41
6.	East Siang	"	34.0	19.1	19.0	47
7.	Lohit	"	11.6	19.2	19.0	43
8.	Lower Subansiri	"	32.7	18.8	18.0	49
9.	Papum Pare	"	23.7	19.6	19.0	38
10.	Upper Siang	"	8.3	19.3	19.0	24
11.	Upper Subansiri	"	40.4	18.3	18.0	52
12.	West Kameng	"	38.1	18.8	18.0	42
13.	West Siang	"	35.5	18.7	18.0	31
18	**Chandigarh**					
1.	Chandigarh	High		22.7	22.0	43

Appendix - V (Continued)

Sr. No.	State/district	Level of FLR	Age at marriage <18 years (%)	Mean	Median	Total Marriages (#)
19	**Dadra & Nagar Haveli**					
1.	Dadra & Nagar Haveli	Medium	50.6	17.5	17.0	81
20	**Daman & Diu**					
1.	Daman	Medium	17.4	19.7	19.0	138
2.	Diu	High	15.6	19.8	19.0	96
21	**Delhi**					
1.	Delhi	High	6.7	20.7	21.0	119
22	**Goa**					
1.	North Goa	High	4.2	23.6	24.0	72
2.	South Goa	"	2.2	24.0	24.0	89
23	**Himachal Pradesh**					
1.	Chamba	Medium	2.4	21.5	21.0	125
2.	Kinnaur	"	16.1	20.8	21.0	56
3.	Kullu	"	1.6	20.5	20.0	63
4.	Lahul & Spiti	"		23.0	22.0	22
5.	Mandi	"	4.2	20.6	20.0	119
6.	Sirmaur	"	6.9	20.5	20.0	58
7.	Bilaspur	High	4.6	20.7	20.0	65
8.	Hamirpur	"	0.9	20.4	20.0	110
9.	Kangra	"	3.5	21.1	21.0	85
10.	Shimla	"	1.9	21.3	21.0	52
11.	Solan	"	1.4	20.9	20.0	74
12.	Una	"	0.9	21.2	21.0	108
24	**Jammu & Kashmir**					
1.	Anantanag	Low	2.0	22.4	22.0	50
2.	Badgam	"	3.2	21.2	20.0	31
3.	Baramula	"	7.5	21.5	20.0	53
4.	Doda	Low		20.5	20.0	215
5.	Kupwara	"		20.2	20.0	24
6.	Kargil	Medium	27.5	18.7	18.0	91
7.	Kathua	"		21.8	22.0	148
8.	Leh	"	1.5	20.8	20.0	68
9.	Pulwama	"		22.8	23.0	18
10.	Punch	"	3.5	20.7	20.0	114
11.	Rajauri	"	0.2	18.9	19.0	461
12.	Srinagar	"	9.1	19.4	20.0	33
13.	Udhampur	"	1.3	19.4	19.0	151
14.	Jammu	High	1.1	21.1	22.0	184
25	**Lakshadweep**					
1.	Lakshadweep	High	18.2	19.9	19.0	159
26	**Manipur**					
1.	Bishnupur	Medium	16.2	22.2	21.0	99
2.	Chandel	"	20.5	21.9	20.0	78
3.	Churachandpur	"	10.6	22.3	21.0	47
4.	Senapati	"	18.2	21.8	22.0	33
5.	Tamenglong	"	20.7	21.0	20.0	82
6.	Thoubal	"	15.6	21.3	20.0	109
7.	Ukhrul	"	18.2	23.1	21.0	33
8.	Imphal	High	4.8	25.6	25.0	147

Appendix - V (Continued)

Sr. No.	State/district	Level of FLR	Age at marriage <18 years (%)	Mean	Median	Total Marriages (#)
27	**Meghalaya**					
1.	East Garo Hills	Medium	0.0	20.4	20.0	27
2.	Jaintia Hills	"	0.8	20.3	20.0	261
3.	Ri Bhoi	"	2.3	19.5	19.0	43
4.	South Garp Hills	"	0.0	21.0	18.0	5
5.	West Khasi Hills	"	2.0	20.0	20.0	51
6.	West Garo Hills	"	12.5	21.1	19.0	16
7.	East Khasi Hills	High	13.6	19.5	19.0	22
28	**Mizoram**					
1.	Chhimtuipui	Medium	25.3	19.5	19.0	75
2.	Aizwal	High	7.1	21.8	20.0	84
3.	Lunglei	"	6.8	20.9	20.0	44
29	**Nagaland**					
1.	Kohima	Medium	55.8	17.6	17.0	86
2.	Mon	"	11.2	19.3	19.0	152
3.	Phek	"	36.8	18.1	18.0	19
4.	Tuensang	"	8.6	19.8	20.0	81
5.	Zunheboto	"	24.0	19.0	19.0	150
6.	Mokokchung	High	14.0	20.7	20.5	50
7.	Wokha	"	25.4	19.4	19.0	122
30	**Pondicherry**					
1.	Karaikal	High	5.6	21.2	21.0	142
2.	Mahe	"	2.6	22.4	21.0	191
3.	Pondicherry	"	4.5	21.6	21.0	112
4.	Yanam	"	23.2	18.9	19.0	82
31	**Sikkim**					
1.	North Sikkim	Medium	13.6	21.2	20.5	22
2.	South Sikkim	"	13.0	21.1	20.0	23
3.	West Sikkim	"	17.1	20.4	19.0	70
4.	East Sikkim	High	12.7	21.8	22.0	55
32	**Tripura**					
1.	North Tripura	Medium	34.7	18.8	18.0	72
2.	South Tripura	"	45.9	19.2	18.0	98
3.	West Tripura	High	14.8	21.5	20.0	81

Note: In the column showing percent of marriages below legal minimum age, 0.0 indicates no marriage below 18 years.

FLR= Female literacy rate.

APPENDIX - VI

Percentage Distribution of Marriages by Category of Marriage, Average Age at Marriage and percent Marrying before Attaining Age 21 in each District-BOYS

Sr. No.	State/district	Category of marriage (percentages add to 100)				Total marri-ages	Average age at marraige		Percent of marri-ages < 21 years
		CM	EM	AM	PM	#	Mean	Median	
1	**Andhra Pradesh**								
1.	Adilabad	2.8	28.7	20.4	48.1	108	22.5	22.0	31.5
2.	Anantapur	0.0	21.0	17.3	61.7	81	24.1	24.0	21.0
3.	Chittoor	0.0	17.2	17.2	65.5	58	25.1	25.0	17.2
4.	Cuddapah	0.0	20.8	29.9	49.4	77	23.4	22.0	20.8
5.	East Godavari	1.2	26.8	26.8	45.1	82	22.5	22.0	28.0
6.	Guntur	3.7	25.9	33.3	37.0	81	22.3	22.0	29.6
7.	Hyderabad	0.0	0.9	14.8	84.3	115	26.5	26.0	0.9
8.	Karimnagar	4.9	32.8	27.9	34.4	61	22.1	22.0	37.7
9.	Khammam	1.5	28.8	15.2	54.5	66	22.6	23.0	30.3
10.	Krishna	9.8	32.7	15.0	42.5	153	22.4	22.0	42.5
11.	Kurnool	1.0	21.0	15.0	63.0	100	23.7	24.5	22.0
12.	Mahbubnagar	6.8	37.0	13.7	42.5	73	22.0	22.0	43.8
13.	Medak	0.0	26.1	22.6	51.3	115	23.1	23.0	26.1
14.	Nalgonda	7.2	33.6	17.1	42.1	152	22.0	22.0	40.8
15.	Nellore	0.0	21.4	23.8	54.8	84	23.3	23.0	21.4
16.	Nizamabad	8.9	29.7	17.8	43.6	101	22.2	22.0	38.6
17.	Prakasam	0.0	26.1	23.2	50.7	69	23.1	23.0	26.1
18.	Rangareddi	0.0	17.1	20.7	62.1	140	23.9	24.0	17.1
19.	Srikakulam	0.0	23.0	21.3	55.7	122	23.4	23.0	23.0
20.	Vishkhapatanam	10.2	22.4	8.2	59.2	98	23.1	23.0	32.7
21.	Vizianagaram	4.5	25.8	21.3	48.3	89	22.6	22.0	30.3
22.	Warangal	9.4	30.2	24.0	36.5	96	21.6	22.0	39.6
23.	West Godavari	0.0	25.0	23.3	51.7	120	23.0	23.0	25.0
2	**Assam**								
1.	Barpeta	0.0	3.7	6.8	89.5	162	27.5	28.0	3.7
2.	Bongaigaon	3.8	10.4	10.4	75.5	106	25.9	26.0	14.2
3.	Cachar	1.0	3.1	5.1	90.8	98	28.9	30.0	4.1
4.	Darrang	2.1	4.2	8.3	85.4	96	27.8	28.0	6.3
5.	Dhemaji	0.3	1.2	2.5	96.0	322	27.7	28.0	1.6
6.	Dhubri	0.0	3.4	8.1	88.5	148	26.3	26.0	3.4
7.	Dibrugarh	5.0	27.5	5.0	62.5	40	25.0	26.0	32.5
8.	Goalpara	0.8	11.5	8.4	79.4	131	26.8	27.0	12.2
9.	Golaghat	2.1	10.4	15.3	72.2	144	26.1	25.5	12.5
10.	Hailakandi	1.2	3.5	4.7	90.7	86	29.3	29.0	4.7
11.	Jorhat	0.0	2.1	3.3	94.6	239	28.0	28.0	2.1
12.	Kamrup	0.6	4.6	4.0	90.8	173	28.1	29.0	5.2
13.	Karbi Anglong	0.0	15.5	50.9	33.6	110	22.4	21.0	15.5
14.	Karimganj	0.7	2.8	4.2	92.3	143	29.8	29.0	3.5
15.	Lakhimpur	0.0	7.0	9.3	83.7	43	28.1	28.0	7.0

Appendix - VI (Continued)

Sr. No.	State/district	Category of marriage (percentages add to 100)				Total marri-ages	Average age at marraige		Percent of marri-ages < 21 years
		CM	EM	AM	PM	#	Mean	Median	
16.	Marigaon	0.9	7.2	11.3	80.6	222	26.7	27.0	8.1
17.	Nagaon	1.0	11.4	13.5	74.1	193	25.3	25.0	12.4
18.	Nalbari	0.0	2.4	3.2	94.4	124	28.9	30.0	2.4
19.	North Cachar Hills	0.0	13.9	9.7	76.4	72	24.5	25.0	13.9
20.	Sibsagar	0.0	10.0	1.7	88.3	60	27.7	28.0	10.0
21.	Sonitpur	0.0	11.4	13.8	74.8	123	26.1	26.0	11.4
22.	Tinsukia	3.1	18.6	14.0	64.3	129	25.0	25.0	21.7
3	**Bihar**								
1.	Araria	7.7	27.1	17.4	47.7	155	22.5	22.0	34.8
2.	Aurangabad(Bih)	15.6	48.2	12.9	23.2	224	20.4	20.0	63.8
3.	Begusarai	12.1	34.9	24.7	28.4	215	21.1	21.0	47.0
4.	Bhagalpur	4.8	29.3	16.2	49.7	167	23.2	22.0	34.1
5.	Bhojpur	19.6	42.2	14.1	24.1	199	20.4	20.0	61.8
6.	Buxar	7.5	42.3	20.4	29.9	201	21.1	21.0	49.8
7.	Darbhanga	3.7	36.9	23.4	36.0	214	21.8	21.0	40.7
8.	Deoghar	12.6	35.1	19.9	32.5	151	21.5	21.0	47.7
9.	Dhanbad	3.7	33.6	23.4	39.3	107	22.1	21.0	37.4
10.	Dumka	2.1	26.6	24.5	46.9	143	22.9	22.0	28.7
11.	Gaya	22.4	32.3	22.4	23.0	161	20.3	20.0	54.7
12.	Giridih	12.6	40.7	21.4	25.3	182	21.1	20.0	53.3
13.	Godda	2.5	23.3	26.7	47.5	120	23.1	22.0	25.8
14.	Gopalganj	18.1	38.6	16.3	27.0	215	20.7	20.0	56.7
15.	Gulma	3.3	16.3	20.3	60.2	123	23.8	24.0	19.5
16.	Hazaribagh	7.1	30.8	32.5	29.6	169	21.8	22.0	37.9
17.	Jehanabad	15.3	42.4	17.2	25.1	203	20.7	20.0	57.6
18.	Katihar	8.3	27.8	19.5	44.4	133	22.7	22.0	36.1
19.	Khagaria	4.3	39.5	22.2	34.0	162	21.8	21.0	43.8
20.	Kishanganj	2.0	19.7	17.8	60.5	152	24.0	24.0	21.7
21.	Lohardaga	3.4	16.8	28.6	51.3	119	23.2	23.0	20.2
22.	Madhepura	8.2	44.2	17.7	29.9	147	21.3	20.0	52.4
23.	Madhubani	12.6	41.5	17.5	28.4	183	21.0	20.0	54.1
24.	Munger	24.1	37.9	15.9	22.1	145	20.4	20.0	62.1
25.	Muzaffarpur	7.1	32.9	29.4	30.6	170	21.9	21.5	40.0
26.	Nalanda	15.6	37.7	21.0	25.7	167	21.1	20.0	53.3
27.	Nawada	27.4	38.6	14.7	19.3	197	19.8	20.0	66.0
28.	Palamu	15.4	45.5	17.9	21.2	156	20.6	20.0	60.9
29.	Pashchim Champaran	7.8	33.5	20.4	38.3	167	22.1	22.0	41.3
30.	Pashchmi Singhbhum	3.1	20.4	17.3	59.2	98	23.7	25.0	23.5
31.	Patna	8.3	45.0	16.0	30.8	169	21.3	20.0	53.3
32.	Purba Champaran	10.0	34.2	17.4	38.4	190	22.0	22.0	44.2
33.	Purbi Singhbhum	0.0	9.3	15.0	75.7	140	26.1	26.0	9.3
34.	Purnia	2.4	25.6	25.6	46.3	164	22.9	22.0	28.0
35.	Ranchi	0.9	20.4	14.8	63.9	108	23.7	24.0	21.3
36.	Rohtas	34.0	35.9	17.0	13.1	153	19.3	18.0	69.9
37.	Saharsa	11.5	38.5	17.0	33.0	182	21.6	20.5	50.0
38.	Sahibganj	13.2	36.4	18.5	31.8	151	21.5	21.0	49.7
39.	Samastipur	10.9	37.0	22.7	29.4	211	21.5	21.0	47.9
40.	Saran	8.2	29.7	20.1	42.0	219	22.4	22.0	37.9
41.	Sitamarhi	9.3	38.5	22.4	29.8	161	21.4	21.0	47.8
42.	Siwan	5.2	31.4	22.0	41.4	191	22.4	22.0	36.6
43.	Vaishali	8.3	37.8	25.3	28.6	217	21.2	21.0	46.1

Appendix - VI (Continued)

Sr. No.	State/district	Category of marriage (percentages add to 100) CM	EM	AM	PM	Total marriages #	Average age at marraige Mean	Median	Percent of marriages < 21 years
4	**Gujarat**								
1.	Ahmadabad	5.6	25.9	19.8	48.8	162	22.9	22.0	31.5
2.	Amreli	1.3	28.8	27.1	42.8	236	22.3	22.0	30.1
3.	Banas Kantha	19.6	36.7	25.3	18.4	158	20.0	20.0	56.3
4.	Bharuch	2.1	25.7	19.8	52.4	187	23.5	23.0	27.8
5.	Bhavnagar	6.5	31.8	29.4	32.4	170	21.5	21.0	38.2
6.	Gandhinagar	16.4	25.7	15.8	42.1	152	21.7	21.0	42.1
7.	Jamnagar	3.5	22.8	22.8	50.9	171	23.0	23.0	26.3
8.	Junagadh	2.8	18.3	26.4	52.4	246	23.0	23.0	21.1
9.	Kachchh	1.5	26.3	27.8	44.4	133	22.6	22.0	27.8
10.	Kheda	9.8	25.7	28.0	36.4	214	22.0	22.0	35.5
11.	Mahesana	11.3	28.2	27.4	33.1	124	21.4	21.0	39.5
12.	Panch Mahals	11.2	37.1	25.9	25.9	197	21.1	21.0	48.2
13.	Rajkot	1.8	17.2	29.0	52.1	169	23.3	23.0	18.9
14.	Sabar Kantha	8.5	38.0	29.1	24.4	213	21.1	21.0	46.5
15.	Surat	3.2	16.7	18.3	61.9	126	23.2	23.0	19.8
16.	Surendranagar	0.6	27.7	31.2	40.5	173	22.6	22.0	28.3
17.	The Dangs	6.1	54.5	22.7	16.7	132	20.5	20.0	60.6
18.	Vadodara	9.9	35.5	17.4	37.2	172	21.9	21.0	45.3
19.	Valsad	0.0	8.9	26.8	64.3	157	24.6	24.0	8.9
5	**Haryana**								
1.	Ambala	2.7	19.7	21.1	56.5	147	23.4	23.0	22.4
2.	Bhiwani	11.3	32.5	21.1	35.1	194	21.5	21.0	43.8
3.	Faridabad	5.4	26.0	18.1	50.5	204	22.6	23.0	31.4
4.	Gurgaon	12.2	33.1	19.2	35.5	172	21.5	21.0	45.3
5.	Hisar	6.0	39.6	21.6	32.8	134	21.7	21.0	45.5
6.	Jind	5.3	28.8	28.8	37.1	170	21.8	21.0	34.1
7.	Kaithal	3.7	24.1	29.0	43.2	162	22.3	22.0	27.8
8.	Karnal	1.2	16.5	40.2	42.1	164	22.7	22.0	17.7
9.	Kurukshetra	2.7	21.2	29.5	46.6	146	22.8	22.0	24.0
10.	Mahendragarh	5.5	37.4	29.1	28.0	182	21.1	21.0	42.9
11.	Panchkula	0.6	14.4	24.1	60.9	174	23.5	23.0	14.9
12.	Panipat	8.2	29.7	22.2	39.9	158	21.7	22.0	38.0
13.	Rewari	6.2	34.8	27.1	31.9	210	21.4	21.0	41.0
14.	Rohtak	3.2	17.2	24.8	54.8	157	23.0	23.0	20.4
15.	Sirsa	4.8	32.7	21.2	41.2	165	22.2	22.0	37.6
16.	Sonipat	1.7	30.9	23.2	44.2	181	22.3	22.0	32.6
17.	Yamunanagar	1.8	15.5	28.6	54.2	168	23.3	23.0	17.3
6	**Karnataka**								
1.	Bangalore	0.0	4.2	15.8	80.0	95	26.0	25.0	4.2
2.	Bangalore Rural	0.0	1.0	8.3	90.6	96	26.1	25.5	1.0
3.	Belgaum	5.1	15.9	18.1	60.9	138	24.1	23.0	21.0
4.	Bellary	2.5	11.4	19.0	67.1	158	24.7	24.0	13.9
5.	Bidar	5.7	24.6	23.4	46.3	175	22.6	22.0	30.3
6.	Bijapur	6.2	19.2	13.0	61.6	177	23.8	24.0	25.4
7.	Chikmagalur	0.5	8.6	8.6	82.2	185	26.5	27.0	9.2
8.	Chitradurga	2.1	11.2	15.5	71.1	187	25.3	25.0	13.4
9.	Dakshina Kannada	0.0	3.5	8.3	88.2	144	27.8	27.0	3.5
10.	Dharwad	1.4	10.8	15.1	72.7	139	24.9	25.0	12.2
11.	Gulbarga	8.8	20.6	15.4	55.1	136	23.0	23.0	29.4

Appendix - VI (Continued)

Sr. No.	*State/district*	*Category of marriage (percentages add to 100)*				*Total marri-ages*	*Average age at marraige*		*Percent of marri-ages < 21 years*
		CM	*EM*	*AM*	*PM*	*#*	*Mean*	*Median*	
12.	Hassan	0.8	8.9	11.3	79.0	124	25.5	25.0	9.7
13.	Kodagu	0.0	8.5	17.0	74.5	141	26.9	25.0	8.5
14.	Kolar	0.6	15.1	14.5	69.8	159	24.3	24.0	15.7
15.	Mandya	0.0	6.0	7.8	86.2	116	25.5	25.0	6.0
16.	Mysore	0.9	2.6	12.1	84.5	116	26.3	26.0	3.4
17.	Raichur	7.3	23.0	18.8	50.9	165	22.9	23.0	30.3
18.	Shimoga	0.5	4.8	10.1	84.6	188	26.6	26.0	5.3
19.	Tumkur	0.9	5.1	23.1	70.9	117	25.2	24.0	6.0
20.	Uttara Kannada	0.0	3.3	9.3	87.3	150	27.9	28.0	3.3
7	**Kerala**								
1.	Alappuzha	0.0	1.7	1.7	96.6	174	28.1	28.0	1.7
2.	Ernakulam	0.0	0.6	5.1	94.2	156	28.5	28.0	0.6
3.	Idukki	0.0	4.3	10.7	85.0	140	25.9	26.0	4.3
4.	Kannur	0.0	0.0	7.5	92.5	146	28.4	28.0	0.0
5.	Kasaragod	0.0	1.7	5.8	92.5	120	27.7	27.5	1.7
6.	Kollam	0.0	3.0	3.6	93.5	169	28.3	28.0	3.0
7.	Kottayam	0.0	2.5	3.1	94.4	161	28.3	28.0	2.5
8.	Kozhikode	0.0	2.2	8.9	88.9	180	26.8	27.0	2.2
9.	Malappuram	0.0	9.2	19.6	71.2	184	24.8	24.0	9.2
10.	Palakkad	0.0	1.3	8.7	89.9	149	27.3	27.0	1.3
11.	Pathanamthitta	0.0	0.0	5.2	94.8	116	27.7	28.0	0.0
12.	Thiruvananthapuram	0.0	2.8	4.6	92.7	109	28.0	28.0	2.8
13.	Thrissur	0.0	1.9	1.9	96.1	155	29.1	29.0	1.9
14.	Wayanad	0.0	8.4	9.1	82.5	143	25.8	26.0	8.4
8	**Madhya Pradesh**								
1.	Balaghat	0.0	20.5	24.4	55.1	78	23.8	24.0	20.5
2.	Bastar	9.0	29.5	21.8	39.7	78	22.4	22.0	38.5
3.	Betul	0.0	13.9	23.6	62.5	72	24.1	25.0	13.9
4.	Bhind	9.4	42.9	21.2	26.5	170	21.1	20.0	52.4
5.	Bhopal	5.1	17.7	25.3	51.9	79	23.4	23.0	22.8
6.	Bilaspur(MP)	4.1	33.6	21.2	41.1	146	22.7	22.0	37.7
7.	Chattarpur	18.5	46.7	19.6	15.2	92	20.0	19.5	65.2
8.	Chhindwara	1.7	19.2	20.8	58.3	120	23.8	24.0	20.8
9.	Damoh	14.3	38.1	21.4	26.2	126	21.1	20.0	52.4
10.	Datia	6.3	50.6	14.6	28.5	158	20.9	20.0	57.0
11.	Dewas	13.3	40.6	17.8	28.3	180	21.1	20.0	53.9
12.	Dhar	12.4	39.6	20.7	27.2	169	21.0	20.0	52.1
13.	Durg	6.3	19.8	22.5	51.4	111	23.1	23.0	26.1
14.	East Nimar	3.7	27.3	17.4	51.6	161	22.8	23.0	31.1
15.	Guna	24.3	38.3	11.3	26.1	115	20.4	19.0	62.6
16.	Gwalior	2.8	25.5	25.5	46.2	106	22.8	22.0	28.3
17.	Hoshangabad	1.2	27.9	24.4	46.5	86	22.9	22.0	29.1
18.	Indore	8.4	20.3	14.7	56.6	143	23.2	23.0	28.7
19.	Jabalpur	8.6	11.8	17.2	62.4	93	23.7	24.0	20.4
20.	Jhabua	30.5	39.6	13.6	16.2	154	19.3	19.0	70.1
21.	Mandla	5.3	31.6	33.3	29.8	57	21.4	22.0	36.8
22.	Mandsaur	25.0	33.6	16.4	25.0	140	20.2	20.0	58.6
23.	Morena	26.6	42.2	20.3	10.9	128	19.1	18.0	68.8
24.	Narsimhapur	1.3	30.3	24.3	44.1	152	22.7	22.0	31.6
25.	Panna	25.6	44.9	16.7	12.8	78	19.6	20.0	70.5
26.	Raigarh(M P)	0.0	19.5	28.6	51.9	77	23.0	23.0	19.5

Appendix - VI (Continued)

Sr. No.	State/district	Category of marriage (percentages add to 100)				Total marri-ages	Average age at marraige		Percent of marri-ages < 21 years
		CM	EM	AM	PM	#	Mean	Median	
27.	Raipur	6.8	37.3	16.9	39.0	59	21.6	21.0	44.1
28.	Raisen	2.3	26.9	33.8	36.9	130	22.1	22.0	29.2
29.	Rajgarh	32.0	25.5	20.3	22.2	153	19.9	19.0	57.5
30.	Rajnandgaon	6.5	33.1	24.2	36.3	124	22.2	21.0	39.5
31.	Ratlam	17.9	24.3	20.0	37.9	140	21.7	21.0	42.1
32.	Rewa	19.6	37.1	19.6	23.7	97	20.3	20.0	56.7
33.	Sagar	6.8	35.6	22.0	35.6	118	22.0	22.0	42.4
34.	Satna	17.1	45.7	17.9	19.3	140	20.4	20.0	62.9
35.	Sehore	19.9	29.4	14.7	36.0	136	21.4	21.0	49.3
36.	Seoni	2.8	18.1	34.7	44.4	72	23.0	22.0	20.8
37.	Shahdol	16.7	36.7	13.3	33.3	30	21.4	20.0	53.3
38.	Shajapur	25.7	36.4	15.7	22.1	140	20.1	19.0	62.1
39.	Shivpuri	21.5	43.8	12.4	22.3	121	20.0	20.0	65.3
40.	Sidhi	27.6	41.0	18.1	13.3	105	19.4	19.0	68.6
41.	Surguja	21.3	36.1	17.2	25.4	122	20.3	20.0	57.4
42.	Tikamgarh	24.0	52.0	12.8	11.2	125	19.2	18.0	76.0
43.	Ujjain	12.3	23.9	23.2	40.6	155	22.1	22.0	36.1
44.	Vidisha	14.8	38.1	25.2	21.9	155	20.9	20.0	52.9
45.	West Nimar	12.3	28.5	26.9	32.3	130	21.4	21.0	40.8
9	**Maharashtra**								
1.	Ahmadnagar	0.0	14.0	23.4	62.6	171	24.0	23.0	14.0
2.	Akola	0.6	14.8	27.1	57.4	155	23.6	23.0	15.5
3.	Amravali	0.0	4.7	17.4	77.9	86	25.3	25.0	4.7
4.	Aurangabad(Mah)	2.0	23.5	24.2	50.3	153	23.0	23.0	25.5
5.	Bhandara	0.0	1.8	14.7	83.5	109	25.7	25.0	1.8
6.	Bid	4.4	25.4	34.2	36.0	114	21.9	22.0	29.8
7.	Buldana	0.0	7.5	29.6	62.9	159	24.1	24.0	7.5
8.	Chandrapur	4.1	10.2	17.3	68.4	98	24.3	25.0	14.3
9.	Dhule	2.7	18.5	26.0	52.7	146	23.0	23.0	21.2
10.	Gadchiroli	1.8	19.1	26.4	52.7	110	23.3	23.0	20.9
11.	Greater Bombay (Mum	0.7	5.0	12.9	81.4	140	26.2	26.0	5.7
12.	Jalgaon	0.7	20.7	25.0	53.6	140	23.3	23.0	21.4
13.	Jalna	5.5	27.4	26.0	41.1	146	22.5	22.0	32.9
14.	Kolhapur	1.1	8.9	12.8	77.1	179	25.0	25.0	10.1
15.	Latur	2.6	17.9	26.5	53.0	151	23.0	23.0	20.5
16.	Nagpur	0.0	2.6	12.2	85.3	156	25.8	25.0	2.6
17.	Nanded	4.4	27.4	28.1	40.0	135	22.5	22.0	31.9
18.	Nashik	2.9	18.5	25.4	53.2	173	23.2	23.0	21.4
19.	Osmanabad	3.6	14.4	22.3	59.7	139	23.8	24.0	18.0
20.	Parbhani	4.9	28.4	29.6	37.0	162	22.2	22.0	33.3
21.	Pune	0.6	9.0	24.7	65.7	166	24.4	24.0	9.6
22.	Raigarh (MAH)	0.0	5.8	29.8	64.4	104	24.3	24.0	5.8
23.	Ratnagiri	0.0	9.0	25.5	65.5	145	24.9	24.0	9.0
24.	Sangli	0.5	15.3	17.4	66.8	190	24.3	25.0	15.8
25.	Satara	0.9	6.8	17.9	74.4	117	24.6	24.0	7.7
26.	Sindhudurg	0.0	3.4	12.3	84.4	179	26.8	26.0	3.4
27.	Solapur	0.8	13.2	22.5	63.6	129	24.4	24.0	14.0
28.	Thane	1.8	8.2	20.0	70.0	110	24.7	25.0	10.0
29.	Wardha	0.0	2.8	5.6	91.7	108	26.3	26.0	2.8
30.	Yavatmal	0.0	11.3	19.4	69.4	160	24.5	25.0	11.3

Appendix - VI (Continued)

Sr. No.	*State/district*	*Category of marriage (percentages add to 100)*				*Total marri-ages*	*Average age at marraige*		*Percent of marri-ages < 21 years*
		CM	*EM*	*AM*	*PM*	*#*	*Mean*	*Median*	
10	**Orissa**								
1.	Anugul	0.9	20.0	25.5	53.6	110	23.7	23.0	20.9
2.	Balangir	4.0	25.0	21.0	50.0	124	23.2	22.5	29.0
3.	Balasore	0.0	6.9	14.5	78.6	145	25.9	25.0	6.9
4.	Bargarh	1.7	17.5	20.8	60.0	120	23.7	23.0	19.2
5.	Baudh	1.6	30.7	23.6	44.1	127	22.9	22.0	32.3
6.	Bhadrak	0.0	8.1	11.5	80.4	148	26.0	26.0	8.1
7.	Cuttack	1.2	7.6	10.0	81.2	170	25.8	26.0	8.8
8.	Debagarh	0.0	13.3	15.0	71.7	120	24.7	25.0	13.3
9.	Dhenkanal	0.7	11.4	12.8	75.2	149	25.4	25.0	12.1
10.	Gajapati	2.9	15.1	15.8	66.2	139	24.1	24.0	18.0
11.	Ganjam	0.7	13.8	11.2	74.3	152	24.7	25.0	14.5
12.	Jagatsinghapur	0.0	1.4	5.6	93.1	144	26.6	27.0	1.4
13.	Jajapur	0.0	1.8	11.8	86.4	110	26.1	26.0	1.8
14.	Jharsuguda	0.0	13.6	21.4	65.0	103	24.1	24.0	13.6
15.	Kalahandi	3.4	35.3	21.6	39.7	116	22.5	22.0	38.8
16.	Kendrapara	0.5	2.6	7.4	89.5	190	25.9	26.0	3.2
17.	Kendujhar	2.2	14.0	20.6	63.2	136	24.4	24.0	16.2
18.	Khordha	0.0	6.6	10.9	82.5	137	25.6	25.0	6.6
19.	Koraput	9.2	40.3	15.1	35.3	119	21.7	21.0	49.6
20.	Malkangiri	8.2	44.5	13.6	33.6	110	21.5	20.0	52.7
21.	Mayurbhanj	1.5	18.2	15.2	65.2	132	24.4	24.5	19.7
22.	Nabarangapur	8.4	35.5	20.6	35.5	107	22.5	21.0	43.9
23.	Nayagarh	1.9	12.3	17.9	67.9	162	24.3	24.0	14.2
24.	Nuapada	3.0	24.8	20.8	51.5	101	23.3	23.0	27.7
25.	Phulbani	2.6	30.4	10.4	56.5	115	23.5	23.0	33.0
26.	Puri	0.0	9.4	14.0	76.6	171	25.6	25.0	9.4
27.	Rayagada	1.5	27.6	17.9	53.0	134	23.2	23.0	29.1
28.	Sambalpur	0.8	5.9	20.3	72.9	118	25.7	25.0	6.8
29.	Sonapur	0.9	14.8	27.8	56.5	115	24.0	23.0	15.7
30.	Sundargarh	0.9	6.6	12.3	80.2	106	25.3	25.0	7.5
11	**Punjab**								
1.	Amritsar	1.8	16.1	22.6	59.5	168	23.7	23.0	17.9
2.	Bathinda	2.1	25.4	25.4	47.1	189	22.7	22.0	27.5
3.	Faridkot	2.7	28.0	25.3	44.1	186	22.7	22.0	30.6
4.	Fatehgarh Sahib	1.1	17.8	33.0	48.1	185	22.9	22.0	18.9
5.	Firozpur	3.6	32.6	21.3	42.5	221	22.4	22.0	36.2
6.	Gurdaspur	0.6	10.2	17.5	71.7	166	24.7	25.0	10.8
7.	Hoshiarpur	0.0	6.4	13.5	80.1	171	25.4	25.0	6.4
8.	Jalandhar	0.7	10.7	18.7	70.0	150	24.7	24.0	11.3
9.	Kapurthala	1.2	13.0	22.2	63.6	162	24.2	24.0	14.2
10.	Ludhiana	0.0	12.1	21.2	66.7	132	24.1	24.0	12.1
11.	Mansa	3.3	28.6	27.5	40.7	182	22.2	22.0	31.9
12.	Moga	1.8	23.5	24.7	50.0	166	23.6	22.5	25.3
13.	Muktsar	5.7	30.9	26.9	36.6	175	22.5	22.0	36.6
14.	Nawanshahr	0.0	11.5	20.0	68.5	165	24.3	24.0	11.5
15.	Patiala	2.1	21.8	25.4	50.8	193	22.8	23.0	23.8
16.	Rupnagar	1.8	10.9	21.2	66.1	165	24.2	24.0	12.7
17.	Sangrur	1.1	26.4	25.3	47.2	178	22.9	22.0	27.5
12	**Rajasthan**								
1.	Ajmer	19.8	20.8	17.8	41.6	101	21.7	22.0	40.6

Appendix - VI (Continued)

Sr. No.	State/district	Category of marriage (percentages add to 100)				Total marri-ages	Average age at marraige		Percent of marri-ages < 21 years
		CM	EM	AM	PM	#	Mean	Median	
2.	Alwar	20.5	36.1	16.9	26.5	166	20.5	20.0	56.6
3.	Banswara	24.5	43.4	11.9	20.3	143	19.6	19.0	67.8
4.	Barmer	16.3	40.4	19.9	23.5	166	20.4	20.0	56.6
5.	Bharatpur	16.0	37.7	20.4	25.9	162	20.8	20.0	53.7
6.	Bhilwara	28.0	30.0	11.0	31.0	100	20.4	20.0	58.0
7.	Bikaner	11.7	40.7	18.6	29.0	145	21.3	20.0	52.4
8.	Bundi	36.3	36.3	11.5	15.9	113	19.1	18.0	72.6
9.	Chittaurgarh	33.3	33.3	11.1	22.2	72	19.7	20.0	66.7
10.	Churu	12.0	51.6	20.3	16.1	192	20.1	20.0	63.5
11.	Dausa	20.9	46.2	17.1	15.8	158	19.7	20.0	67.1
12.	Dhaulpur	20.4	43.1	17.5	19.0	137	19.9	20.0	63.5
13.	Dungarpur	6.7	40.0	25.0	28.3	180	21.4	21.0	46.7
14.	Ganganagar	13.5	41.1	21.5	23.9	163	20.7	20.0	54.6
15.	Hanumangarh	19.2	43.5	16.6	20.7	193	20.3	20.0	62.7
16.	Jaipur	18.1	24.6	23.2	34.1	138	21.2	21.0	42.8
17.	Jaisalmer	8.8	28.4	22.5	40.2	102	22.0	22.0	37.3
18.	Jalor	13.6	44.4	22.2	19.7	198	20.4	20.0	58.1
19.	Jhalawar	29.8	31.3	16.0	22.9	131	20.1	20.0	61.1
20.	Jhunjhunun	7.2	28.3	27.1	37.3	166	21.7	22.0	35.5
21.	Jodhpur	8.2	34.4	19.7	37.7	122	21.8	21.0	42.6
22.	Kota	16.0	37.0	18.5	28.6	119	21.0	20.0	52.9
23.	Nagaur	16.4	39.0	19.9	24.7	146	20.6	20.0	55.5
24.	Pali	13.3	35.4	26.6	24.7	158	20.7	21.0	48.7
25.	Rajsamand	15.5	34.5	22.4	27.6	116	21.0	20.5	50.0
26.	Sawai Madhopur	26.4	31.9	18.7	23.1	91	19.8	20.0	58.2
27.	Sikar	11.6	30.1	25.3	32.9	146	21.3	21.0	41.8
28.	Sirohi	10.5	24.4	23.3	41.9	86	22.3	22.0	34.9
29.	Tonk	20.6	40.2	16.5	22.7	97	20.0	20.0	60.8
30.	Udaipur	16.2	43.8	16.2	23.8	130	20.8	20.0	60.0
13	**Tamil Nadu**								
1.	Chengalpattu	0.0	7.1	19.3	73.6	140	25.6	25.0	7.1
2.	Chennai	0.0	4.0	8.1	87.9	99	26.8	27.0	4.0
3.	Coimbatore	1.3	6.5	11.7	80.5	77	26.3	27.0	7.8
4.	Dharmapuri	0.6	13.4	17.1	68.9	164	24.5	25.0	14.0
5.	Dindigul	0.0	7.0	12.3	80.7	114	25.7	25.5	7.0
6.	Kanniyakumari	0.0	0.7	4.3	95.0	139	28.0	28.0	0.7
7.	Madurai	0.9	7.3	7.3	84.4	109	26.6	27.0	8.3
8.	Namakkal	0.0	9.5	9.5	81.1	95	26.1	25.0	9.5
9.	North Arcot	1.4	6.4	17.7	74.5	141	25.6	25.0	7.8
10.	Periyar	1.3	5.2	10.4	83.1	77	26.4	26.0	6.5
11.	Pudukkottai	0.0	9.8	6.6	83.6	122	25.7	25.0	9.8
12.	Ramanathapuram	0.0	7.0	19.8	73.3	86	25.2	25.0	7.0
13.	Salem	0.0	9.0	19.5	71.4	133	25.3	25.0	9.0
14.	Sivaganganagar	0.0	4.3	14.3	81.4	140	26.0	26.0	4.3
15.	South Arcot	0.9	10.6	17.7	70.8	113	25.3	25.0	11.5
16.	Thanjavur	0.0	6.4	11.0	82.6	109	26.9	27.0	6.4
17.	The Nilgiris	0.0	1.6	4.8	93.5	62	27.6	28.0	1.6
18.	Theni	1.4	11.0	12.3	75.3	73	25.5	25.0	12.3
19.	Tiruchirappalli	0.0	5.3	7.4	87.2	94	28.0	27.0	5.3
20.	Tirunelveli	0.0	0.0	10.2	89.8	98	26.1	25.0	0.0

Appendix - VI (Continued)

Sr. No.	*State/district*	*Category of marriage (percentages add to 100)*				*Total marri-ages*	*Average age at marraige*		*Percent of marri-ages < 21 years*
		CM	*EM*	*AM*	*PM*	*#*	*Mean*	*Median*	
21.	Tiruvanamalai	1.5	11.5	21.4	65.6	131	25.1	25.0	13.0
22.	Tutikorin	0.0	3.6	11.8	84.5	110	26.6	27.0	3.6
23.	Virudhunagar	0.8	9.2	17.7	72.3	130	25.4	25.0	10.0
14	**Uttar Pradesh**								
1.	Agra	5.3	38.2	25.7	30.9	152	21.6	21.0	43.4
2.	Aligarh	7.0	39.0	29.1	25.0	172	21.3	21.0	45.9
3.	Allahabad	12.5	47.8	16.2	23.5	136	20.7	20.0	60.3
4.	Almora	0.0	3.0	33.0	64.0	100	24.1	23.0	3.0
5.	Ambedkarnagar	30.2	36.8	12.3	20.8	106	19.5	18.5	67.0
6.	Azamgarh	16.7	47.8	13.8	21.7	138	20.1	20.0	64.5
7.	Bahraich	29.2	42.3	12.3	16.2	130	19.5	19.0	71.5
8.	Ballia	8.9	31.7	16.8	42.6	101	21.9	22.0	40.6
9.	Banda	20.0	45.2	10.4	24.4	135	20.3	20.0	65.2
10.	Barabanki	15.9	47.7	16.6	19.9	151	20.3	20.0	63.6
11.	Bareilly	6.5	42.4	26.1	25.0	92	21.3	21.0	48.9
12.	Basti	26.3	38.0	13.9	21.9	137	19.9	20.0	64.2
13.	Bhadohi	26.8	50.3	13.4	9.5	179	19.0	18.0	77.1
14.	Bijnor	1.4	24.5	30.2	43.9	139	22.5	22.0	25.9
15.	Budaun	14.8	41.9	25.8	17.4	155	20.4	20.0	56.8
16.	Bulandshahar	3.2	36.0	31.1	29.7	222	21.7	22.0	39.2
17.	Chamoli	0.0	11.4	27.3	61.4	88	24.0	24.0	11.4
18.	Dehradun	0.8	7.6	23.5	68.1	119	24.9	25.0	8.4
19.	Deoria	23.6	49.3	8.6	18.6	140	19.9	18.5	72.9
20.	Etah	3.2	42.7	35.5	18.5	124	21.2	21.0	46.0
21.	Etawah	1.9	37.9	28.6	31.7	161	21.8	21.0	39.8
22.	Faizabad	32.1	37.5	14.3	16.1	112	19.4	18.0	69.6
23.	Farrukhabad	8.0	37.4	25.2	29.4	163	21.4	21.0	45.4
24.	Fatehpur	4.5	42.7	25.3	27.5	178	21.4	21.0	47.2
25.	Firozabad	6.5	48.4	17.4	27.7	155	21.1	20.0	54.8
26.	Ghaziabad	4.9	26.8	26.8	41.5	142	22.2	22.0	31.7
27.	Ghazipur	20.8	36.9	17.7	24.6	130	20.7	20.0	57.7
28.	Gonda	28.3	42.8	14.5	14.5	152	19.4	19.0	71.1
29.	Gorakhpur	27.2	30.7	15.8	26.3	114	20.3	20.0	57.9
30.	Hamirpur (UP)	7.2	53.6	17.4	21.7	138	20.6	20.0	60.9
31.	Hardoi	6.7	45.7	23.8	23.8	105	21.0	20.0	52.4
32.	Hardwar	4.7	22.0	29.9	43.3	127	22.5	22.0	26.8
33.	Hathras	5.0	41.5	27.0	26.4	159	21.3	21.0	46.5
34.	Jalaun	9.3	44.9	20.3	25.4	118	21.0	20.0	54.2
35.	Jaunpur	21.5	41.5	17.5	19.5	200	19.8	19.0	63.0
36.	Jhansi	14.0	43.9	14.9	27.2	114	21.0	20.0	57.9
37.	Kanpur Dehat	5.3	34.5	25.7	34.5	113	21.8	21.0	39.8
38.	Kanpur Nagar	1.7	25.2	24.4	48.7	119	23.1	22.0	26.9
39.	Kheri	9.2	55.6	17.6	17.6	142	20.5	20.0	64.8
40.	Lalitpur	34.9	45.2	7.1	12.7	126	18.7	18.0	80.2
41.	Lucknow	6.7	36.2	17.1	40.0	105	22.2	22.0	42.9
42.	Maharajganj	44.3	35.7	5.7	14.3	70	18.4	18.0	80.0
43.	Mahoba	19.9	41.1	19.9	19.2	146	20.2	20.0	61.0
44.	Mainpuri	5.9	53.8	13.0	27.2	169	21.0	20.0	59.8
45.	Mathura	6.2	40.7	25.3	27.8	194	21.5	21.0	46.9
46.	Mau	8.9	47.9	17.1	26.0	146	20.7	20.0	56.8
47.	Meerut	2.9	29.7	39.9	27.5	138	21.6	22.0	32.6

Appendix - VI (Continued)

Sr. No.	State/district	Category of marriage (percentages add to 100) CM	EM	AM	PM	Total marriages #	Average age at marraige Mean	Median	Percent of marriages < 21 years
48.	Mirzapur	16.8	50.4	16.1	16.8	137	20.1	20.0	67.2
49.	Muradabad	3.5	40.6	24.5	31.5	143	21.5	21.0	44.1
50.	Muzaffarnagar	5.2	26.0	35.1	33.8	154	22.0	21.0	31.2
51.	Nainital	1.4	19.4	24.5	54.7	139	23.9	23.0	20.9
52.	Pauri Garhwal	0.0	7.5	15.1	77.4	106	24.7	25.0	7.5
53.	Pilibhit	12.7	46.5	17.8	22.9	157	20.5	20.0	59.2
54.	Pithoragarh	3.0	17.2	30.3	49.5	99	23.1	22.0	20.2
55.	Pratapgarh	21.3	52.9	9.0	16.8	155	19.8	19.0	74.2
56.	Rae Bareli	15.0	46.5	22.0	16.5	127	20.4	20.0	61.4
57.	Rampur	6.2	34.5	26.5	32.7	113	21.6	22.0	40.7
58.	Saharanpur	3.0	27.3	37.1	32.6	132	22.1	21.0	30.3
59.	Shajahanabad	15.0	46.3	16.3	22.4	147	20.3	20.0	61.2
60.	Siddharthnagar	38.1	41.3	9.5	11.1	63	18.6	18.0	79.4
61.	Sitapur	14.2	45.5	17.2	23.1	134	20.6	20.0	59.7
62.	Sonbhadra	20.7	39.1	13.8	26.4	87	20.3	20.0	59.8
63.	Sultanpur	20.8	46.4	19.2	13.6	125	19.4	19.0	67.2
64.	Tehri Garhwal	1.0	15.7	35.3	48.0	102	23.3	22.0	16.7
65.	Udhamsingh Nagar	5.3	29.3	28.6	36.8	133	22.0	22.0	34.6
66.	Unnao	9.0	47.0	15.0	29.0	100	21.1	20.0	56.0
67.	Uttarkashi	2.2	23.6	28.1	46.1	89	22.8	22.0	25.8
68.	Varanasi	16.7	41.7	14.2	27.5	120	21.0	20.0	58.3
15	**West Bengal**								
1.	Bankura	3.1	15.7	20.8	60.4	159	24.2	24.0	18.9
2.	Barddhaman	3.2	24.2	14.2	58.4	190	24.5	24.0	27.4
3.	Birbhum	4.4	25.0	28.7	41.9	136	23.2	22.0	29.4
4.	Dakshin Dinajpur	3.5	22.2	16.0	58.3	144	24.3	24.0	25.7
5.	Darjiling	5.2	17.6	13.1	64.1	153	24.8	24.0	22.9
6.	Haora	3.2	9.5	15.2	72.2	158	25.9	25.5	12.7
7.	Hugli	1.2	15.9	14.6	68.3	164	25.3	25.0	17.1
8.	Jalpaiguri	0.0	25.3	18.8	55.9	170	24.3	23.5	25.3
9.	Koch Bihar	5.2	19.4	19.4	56.0	134	23.8	24.0	24.6
10.	Kolkata	0.8	10.8	8.3	80.0	120	27.0	27.0	11.7
11.	Maldah	5.4	17.4	18.8	58.4	149	23.8	24.0	22.8
12.	Medinipur	1.7	17.8	20.7	59.8	174	23.9	24.0	19.5
13.	Murshidabad	9.2	34.2	19.6	37.0	184	21.9	21.0	43.5
14.	Nadia	0.7	16.8	18.9	63.6	143	24.8	24.0	17.5
15.	North 24 Parganas	0.0	14.1	16.3	69.6	135	26.3	26.0	14.1
16.	Puruliya	8.8	22.0	19.5	49.7	159	23.4	22.0	30.8
17.	South 24 Parganas	2.5	21.0	25.5	51.0	157	24.0	23.0	23.6
18.	Uttar Dinajpur	3.9	20.6	16.1	59.4	155	24.1	24.0	24.5
16	**Andaman & Nicobar**								
1.	Andaman	0.0	4.3	15.9	79.7	69	25.3	25.0	4.3
2.	Nicobar	0.0		18.7	81.3	75	27.4	26.0	0.0
17	**Arunachal Pradesh**								
1.	Changlang	4.5	31.3	20.9	43.3	67	23.0	22.0	35.8
2.	Dibang Valley	7.9	23.7	23.7	44.7	38	23.5	22.0	31.6
3.	East Kameng	0.0	51.1	17.0	31.9	47	22.0	20.0	51.1
4.	East Siang	4.3	52.2	15.2	28.3	46	21.5	20.0	56.5
5.	Lohit	2.6	26.3	13.2	57.9	38	23.4	23.0	28.9
6.	Lower Subansiri	8.8	29.4	17.6	44.1	34	23.0	21.5	38.2

Appendix - VI (Continued)

Sr. No.	State/district	Category of marriage (percentages add to 100)				Total marri-ages	Average age at marraige		Percent of marri-ages < 21 years
		CM	EM	AM	PM	#	Mean	Median	
7.	Papum Pare	0.0	40.0	20.0	40.0	25	23.2	22.0	40.0
8.	Tawang	0.0	7.7	15.4	76.9	26	25.1	24.0	7.7
9.	Tirap	5.9	11.8	17.6	64.7	17	24.2	25.0	17.6
10.	Upper Siang	0.0	21.7	13.0	65.2	23	22.9	23.0	21.7
11.	Upper Subansiri	1.4	23.2	20.3	55.1	69	23.6	23.0	24.6
12.	West Kameng	2.4	31.7	24.4	41.5	41	23.1	22.0	34.1
13.	West Siang	0.0	17.4	10.9	71.7	46	24.9	25.0	17.4
18	**Chandigarh**								
1.	Chandigarh	0.0	9.3	11.1	79.6	54	24.9	25.0	9.3
19	**Dadra & Nagar Haveli**								
1.	Dadra & Nagar Havel	9.5	37.1	20.7	32.8	116	21.4	21.0	46.6
20	**Daman & Diu**								
1.	Daman	0.6	11.3	22.5	65.6	160	24.4	25.0	11.9
2.	Diu	0.7	16.3	18.4	64.6	147	24.3	24.0	17.0
21	**Delhi**								
1.	Delhi	1.0	11.8	16.7	70.6	102	24.4	24.5	12.7
22	**Goa**								
1.	North Goa	0.0	1.7	3.4	94.8	116	29.1	29.5	1.7
2.	South Goa	0.0	1.5	6.8	91.7	132	28.6	28.0	1.5
23	**Himachal Pradesh**								
1.	Bilaspur(Pra.Him)	0.0	5.6	18.1	76.4	144	24.9	25.0	5.6
2.	Chamba	0.0	6.3	22.3	71.4	175	24.8	24.0	6.3
3.	Hamirpur(HP)	1.7	4.1	5.8	88.4	172	25.5	26.0	5.8
4.	Kangra	0.0	1.3	3.9	94.7	152	26.2	26.0	1.3
5.	Kinnaur	1.0	12.7	15.7	70.6	102	24.4	24.0	13.7
6.	Kullu	0.0	13.0	16.7	70.4	108	24.4	24.0	13.0
7.	Lahul & Spiti	0.0	11.0	24.7	64.4	73	25.0	24.0	11.0
8.	Mandi	0.6	4.2	19.6	75.6	168	24.7	24.0	4.8
9.	Shimla	0.9	6.9	12.1	80.2	116	26.1	26.0	7.8
10.	Sirmaur	0.0	13.3	23.3	63.3	150	24.0	24.0	13.3
11.	Solan	0.6	7.9	20.8	70.8	178	24.3	24.0	8.4
12.	Una	0.0	1.8	6.7	91.5	165	25.9	26.0	1.8
24	**Jammu & Kashmir**								
1.	Anantanag	0.0	7.7	15.4	76.9	26	25.1	25.0	7.7
2.	Badgam	2.3	31.8	20.5	45.5	44	22.3	22.0	34.1
3.	Baramula	0.0	15.2	12.1	72.7	66	25.9	25.0	15.2
4.	Doda	0.0	1.5	11.9	86.6	67	26.5	26.0	1.5
5.	Jammu	0.0		4.7	95.3	64	27.0	27.0	0.0
6.	Kargil	1.2	12.2	11.0	75.6	82	23.6	24.0	13.4
7.	Kathua	0.0	0.9	0.9	98.1	107	28.5	28.0	0.9
8.	Kupwara	0.0	18.2	13.6	68.2	44	24.6	25.0	18.2
9.	Leh	0.0	16.4	12.7	70.9	55	24.1	24.0	16.4
10.	Pulwama	6.7	16.7	20.0	56.7	30	23.0	23.0	23.3
11.	Punch	0.0	3.1	4.6	92.3	65	24.5	24.0	3.1
12.	Rajauri	0.0	0.9	5.6	93.5	107	23.6	24.0	0.9
13.	Srinagar	0.0	30.8	50.0	19.2	26	21.3	22.0	30.8
14.	Udhampur	0.0	3.4	23.9	72.7	88	23.9	23.5	3.4

Appendix - VI (Continued)

Sr. No.	State/district	Category of marriage (percentages add to 100)				Total marriages	Average age at marriage		Percent of marriages < 21 years
		CM	EM	AM	PM	#	Mean	Median	
25	**Lakshadweep**								
1.	Lakshadweep	0.0	9.2	13.3	77.6	98	25.7	26.0	9.2
26	**Manipur**								
1.	Bishnupur	1.5	16.4	15.7	66.4	134	26.1	25.0	17.9
2.	Chandel	8.0	13.3	9.3	69.3	75	24.8	25.0	21.3
3.	Churachandpur	0.0	15.0	12.1	72.9	107	25.4	25.0	15.0
4.	Imphal	2.2	8.7	12.0	77.2	92	28.0	27.0	10.9
5.	Senapati	3.6	16.1	7.1	73.2	56	25.3	25.0	19.6
6.	Tamenglong	1.9	22.1	13.5	62.5	104	24.6	24.0	24.0
7.	Thoubal	1.4	15.1	13.7	69.9	146	25.5	25.0	16.4
8.	Ukhrul	1.9	16.7	7.4	74.1	54	26.7	27.0	18.5
27	**Meghalaya**								
1.	East Garo Hills	6.1	33.3	6.1	54.5	33	22.5	23.0	39.4
2.	East Khasi Hills	0.0	52.6	21.1	26.3	19	21.3	20.0	52.6
3.	Jaintia Hills	0.0		6.7	93.3	15			
4.	Ri Bhoi	2.9	65.7	25.7	5.7	35	20.2	20.0	68.6
5.	West Garo Hills	0.0	33.3		66.7	6	24.3	24.0	33.3
6.	West Khasi Hills	0.0	51.3	23.1	25.6	39	21.3	20.0	51.3
28	**Mizoram**								
1.	Aizwal	1.5	22.4	18.7	57.5	134	24.5	24.0	23.9
2.	Chhimtuipui	6.0	20.0	18.0	56.0	50	23.9	24.0	26.0
3.	Lunglei	1.5	10.8	12.3	75.4	65	26.3	25.0	12.3
29	**Nagaland**								
1.	Kohima	4.1	65.3	24.5	6.1	49	20.0	20.0	69.4
2.	Mokokchung	0.0	9.4	12.5	78.1	32	25.2	24.0	9.4
3.	Mon	1.2	23.2	25.6	50.0	82	22.8	22.5	24.4
4.	Phek	10.5	21.1	21.1	47.4	19	22.1	22.0	31.6
5.	Tuensang	0.0	4.5	20.5	75.0	88	24.9	24.0	4.5
6.	Wokha	1.9	5.8	7.7	84.6	52	25.1	25.0	7.7
7.	Zunheboto	8.1	24.2	19.4	48.4	124	22.3	22.0	32.3
30	**Pondicherry**								
1.	Karaikal	0.0	4.2	15.6	80.2	96	26.4	26.0	4.2
2.	Mahe	0.0	1.1	2.2	96.8	186	29.7	29.0	1.1
3.	Pondicherry	0.0	0.8	8.5	90.8	130	27.5	27.0	0.8
4.	Yanam	0.0	13.4	20.9	65.7	67	24.7	24.0	13.4
31	**Sikkim**								
1.	East Sikkim	1.7	7.5	13.3	77.5	120	25.8	25.0	9.2
2.	North Sikkim	4.7	23.4	15.6	56.3	64	24.5	24.0	28.1
3.	South Sikkim	2.7	27.0	21.6	48.6	37	23.2	22.0	29.7
4.	West Sikkim	3.3	17.6	19.8	59.3	91	24.0	23.0	20.9
32	**Tripura**								
1.	North Tripura	1.5	6.9	10.7	80.9	131	27.5	27.0	8.4
2.	South Tripura	2.3	4.5	9.8	83.5	133	27.2	28.0	6.8
3.	West Tripura	0.7	5.5	8.9	84.9	146	28.6	28.0	6.2

APPENDIX - VII

Per cent of Marriages below legal Minimum Age of 21 years and Average Age at Marriage in each District by place of Residence - BOYS

Sr. No.	State/District	Age at Marriage: < 21 years (%) Rural	Urban	Mean Rural	Urban	Median Rural	Urban	Total Number of marriages Rural	Urban
1	**Andhra Pradesh**								
1.	Adilabad	33.7	22.7	22.3	23.1	22.0	24.0	86	22
2.	Anantapur	24.2	10.5	23.8	25.0	23.0	25.0	62	19
3.	Chittoor	23.1	5.3	24.0	27.3	24.0	26.0	39	19
4.	Cuddapah	17.2	38.5	23.3	23.7	22.0	23.0	64	13
5.	East Godavari	32.3	11.8	22.1	24.3	22.0	24.0	65	17
6.	Guntur	44.4	11.1	21.3	23.5	21.0	22.5	45	36
7.	Hyderabad	**	0.9	NA	26.5	NA	26.0	**	115
8.	Karimnagar	37.7	**	22.1	NA	22.0	NA	61	**
9.	Khammam	32.7	18.2	22.5	23.3	23.0	23.0	55	11
10.	Krishna	50.9	22.2	21.2	25.3	20.0	25.0	108	45
11.	Kurnool	24.7	14.8	23.2	24.9	24.0	25.0	73	27
12.	Mahbubnagar	46.9	22.2	21.6	24.7	22.0	25.0	64	9
13.	Medak	26.0	26.7	23.1	22.5	23.0	22.0	100	15
14.	Nalgonda	42.6	25.0	21.8	23.2	22.0	24.0	136	16
15.	Nellore	22.2	19.0	23.1	23.8	23.0	23.0	63	21
16.	Nizamabad	40.2	22.2	21.9	24.6	21.5	25.0	92	9
17.	Prakasam	25.5	28.6	23.0	23.5	22.0	23.0	55	14
18.	Rangareddi	24.7	5.5	22.8	25.7	22.0	26.0	85	55
19.	Srikakulam	23.0	22.2	23.3	24.6	23.0	25.0	113	9
20.	Vishkhapatanam	35.6	28.2	22.6	23.8	23.0	25.0	59	39
21.	Vizianagaram	35.6	6.3	22.5	22.9	22.0	23.0	73	16
22.	Warangal	39.0	42.1	21.3	22.6	22.0	22.0	77	19
23.	West Godavari	24.8	26.7	23.0	22.9	23.0	24.0	105	15
2	**Assam**								
1.	Barpeta	3.9	0.0	27.4	28.6	28.0	29.0	155	7
2.	Bongaigaon	15.3	0.0	25.7	27.8	26.0	26.5	98	8
3.	Cachar	4.5	0.0	28.5	32.6	30.0	34.5	88	10
4.	Darrang	4.5	25.0	28.0	26.0	28.0	27.0	88	8
5.	Dhemaji	1.6	0.0	27.7	27.8	28.0	29.0	311	11
6.	Dhubri	3.2	4.3	26.1	27.6	26.0	27.0	125	23
7.	Dibrugarh	38.7	11.1	24.4	27.0	25.0	27.0	31	9
8.	Goalpara	12.8	0.0	26.6	31.7	27.0	32.0	125	6
9.	Golaghat	13.7	0.0	25.7	29.5	25.0	30.0	131	13
10.	Hailakandi	5.3	0.0	29.1	30.4	29.0	30.0	75	11
11.	Jorhat	2.3	0.0	27.8	29.5	28.0	30.0	214	25
12.	Kamrup	4.9	5.9	27.4	29.8	28.0	30.0	122	51
13.	Karbi Anglong	16.0	0.0	22.3	24.8	21.0	23.0	106	4
14.	Karimganj	3.7	0.0	29.6	32.3	28.0	32.0	134	9
15.	Lakhimpur	39.1	0.0	19.3	22.5	18.0	22.5	23	2
16.	Marigaon	8.4	0.0	26.6	29.6	27.0	30.0	214	8

Appendix - VII (Continued)

Sr. No.	State/District	Age at Marriage < 21 years (%) Rural	Urban	Mean Rural	Mean Urban	Median Rural	Median Urban	Total Number of marriages Rural	Urban
17.	Nagaon	14.1	3.3	25.0	26.8	25.0	27.0	163	30
18.	Nalbari	2.5	0.0	28.9	30.0	30.0	30.0	122	2
19.	North Cachar Hills	15.7	9.5	24.2	25.2	25.0	25.0	51	21
20.	Sibsagar	9.6	12.5	27.8	27.4	28.0	27.5	52	8
21.	Sonitpur	12.7	0.0	25.9	28.2	25.0	28.0	110	13
22.	Tinsukia	24.3	5.6	24.1	30.0	24.0	29.5	111	18
3	**Bihar**								
1.	Araria	36.1	18.2	22.4	23.7	22.0	23.0	144	11
2.	Aurangabad(Bih)	64.4	50.0	20.3	21.5	20.0	21.0	216	8
3.	Begusarai	47.3	42.9	21.1	21.6	21.0	21.5	201	14
4.	Bhagalpur	36.7	11.8	23.2	23.4	22.0	23.0	150	17
5.	Bhojpur	62.1	55.6	20.3	22.0	20.0	20.0	190	9
6.	Buxar	50.3	43.8	21.0	22.1	20.0	21.5	185	16
7.	Darbhanga	42.0	21.4	21.7	24.2	21.0	24.5	200	14
8.	Deoghar	51.1	22.2	21.1	24.2	20.0	22.5	133	18
9.	Dhanbad	37.1	37.8	22.1	22.1	22.0	21.0	70	37
10.	Dumka	28.8	27.3	22.8	24.3	22.0	24.0	132	11
11.	Gaya	61.8	16.0	19.8	22.8	20.0	23.0	136	25
12.	Giridih	55.5	33.3	20.8	23.1	20.0	22.0	164	18
13.	Godda	25.9	25.0	23.1	22.8	22.0	21.0	116	4
14.	Gopalganj	58.9	23.1	20.6	22.2	20.0	23.0	202	13
15.	Gulma	20.9	0.0	23.7	25.4	24.0	25.5	115	8
16.	Hazaribagh	43.8	17.9	21.2	23.7	21.0	22.0	130	39
17.	Jehanabad	58.3	45.5	20.7	21.4	20.0	22.0	192	11
18.	Katihar	38.7	0.0	22.4	26.8	22.0	24.0	124	9
19.	Khagaria	44.4	33.3	21.7	22.9	21.0	21.0	153	9
20.	Kishanganj	20.9	27.8	23.8	25.3	24.0	25.0	134	18
21.	Lohardaga	22.4	0.0	22.8	26.7	22.0	26.0	107	12
22.	Madhepura	56.2	0.0	21.1	24.9	20.0	23.5	137	10
23.	Madhubani	57.1	15.4	20.7	24.9	20.0	25.0	170	13
24.	Munger	66.1	38.1	20.1	22.6	20.0	22.0	124	21
25.	Muzaffarpur	43.2	6.7	21.5	25.3	21.0	25.0	155	15
26.	Nalanda	54.7	41.2	20.8	23.6	20.0	22.0	150	17
27.	Nawada	64.6	100.0	19.9	18.4	20.0	19.0	189	8
28.	Palamu	62.7	16.7	20.3	27.2	20.0	29.0	150	6
29.	Pashchim Champaran	45.7	31.4	21.5	23.3	21.0	23.0	116	51
30.	Pashchmi Singhbhum	25.9	11.8	23.4	24.9	25.0	23.0	81	17
31.	Patna	57.2	17.6	21.0	24.5	20.0	25.0	152	17
32.	Purba Champaran	45.4	0.0	21.9	26.0	22.0	27.0	185	5
33.	Purbi Singhbhum	12.3	6.0	24.5	27.8	25.0	28.0	73	67
34.	Purnia	30.0	7.1	22.9	23.5	22.0	24.0	150	14
35.	Ranchi	18.8	30.4	23.6	24.1	24.0	25.0	85	23
36.	Rohtas	71.0	50.0	19.3	20.3	18.0	21.0	145	8
37.	Saharsa	52.4	16.7	21.3	25.7	20.0	25.0	170	12
38.	Sahibganj	50.0	0.0	21.5	21.0	20.5	21.0	150	1
39.	Samastipur	48.0	42.9	21.5	22.0	21.0	21.0	204	7
40.	Saran	39.0	21.4	22.3	24.5	22.0	24.0	205	14
41.	Sitamarhi	48.7	36.4	21.3	22.8	21.0	22.0	150	11
42.	Siwan	38.3	0.0	22.3	23.8	22.0	22.5	183	8
43.	Vaishali	47.1	27.3	21.1	22.8	21.0	24.0	206	11

Appendix - VII (Continued)

Sr. No.	State/District	Age at Marriage						Total Number of marriages	
		< 21 years (%)		Mean		Median			
		Rural	Urban	Rural	Urban	Rural	Urban	Rural	Urban
4	**Gujarat**								
1.	Ahmadabad	51.6	19.0	21.6	23.7	20.0	23.0	62	100
2.	Amreli	32.8	15.8	22.1	23.7	22.0	23.0	198	38
3.	Banas Kantha	58.7	33.3	19.8	22.2	20.0	22.0	143	15
4.	Bharuch	31.0	12.5	23.2	24.9	22.0	25.0	155	32
5.	Bhavnagar	48.3	16.7	20.9	22.8	21.0	23.0	116	54
6.	Gandhinagar	46.9	28.2	21.3	23.1	21.0	23.0	113	39
7.	Jamnagar	30.3	16.3	22.5	24.2	22.0	23.0	122	49
8.	Junagadh	24.0	15.2	22.6	23.7	22.0	23.0	167	79
9.	Kachchh	31.1	16.7	22.2	23.8	22.0	23.0	103	30
10.	Kheda	40.2	6.7	21.7	23.9	22.0	23.5	184	30
11.	Mahesana	42.9	30.3	21.1	22.2	21.0	22.0	91	33
12.	Panch Mahals	51.9	6.3	20.7	25.4	20.0	26.0	181	16
13.	Rajkot	27.6	4.7	22.2	25.1	22.0	25.0	105	64
14.	Sabar Kantha	47.2	35.7	21.0	22.3	21.0	22.0	199	14
15.	Surat	23.7	16.4	22.6	23.6	23.0	24.0	59	67
16.	Surendranagar	32.3	16.3	22.1	24.0	22.0	24.0	130	43
17.	The Dangs	63.3	33.3	20.2	22.8	20.0	22.5	120	12
18.	Vadodara	55.4	26.7	21.2	23.3	20.0	22.5	112	60
19.	Valsad	10.3	0.0	24.4	26.3	24.0	27.0	136	21
5	**Haryana**								
1.	Ambala	28.6	7.1	22.6	25.4	22.0	25.0	105	42
2.	Bhiwani	47.3	22.2	21.3	22.7	21.0	23.0	167	27
3.	Faridabad	44.3	17.3	21.5	23.7	21.0	24.0	106	98
4.	Gurgaon	51.1	19.4	20.9	24.2	20.0	24.0	141	31
5.	Hisar	52.8	15.4	21.0	24.6	20.0	24.0	108	26
6.	Jind	35.9	24.0	21.5	23.5	21.0	22.0	145	25
7.	Kaithal	30.5	9.5	22.0	24.3	22.0	24.0	141	21
8.	Karnal	20.8	7.7	22.4	23.8	22.0	24.0	125	39
9.	Kurukshetra	26.7	13.3	22.4	24.0	22.0	24.5	116	30
10.	Mahendragarh	46.5	17.4	20.9	22.9	21.0	23.0	159	23
11.	Panchkula	20.7	1.9	22.5	25.9	22.0	26.0	121	53
12.	Panipat	44.3	16.7	21.2	23.2	21.0	23.5	122	36
13.	Rewari	44.7	19.4	21.1	23.0	21.0	23.0	179	31
14.	Rohtak	20.7	18.2	22.9	23.7	23.0	24.5	135	22
15.	Sirsa	43.8	14.3	21.7	24.2	21.0	25.0	130	35
16.	Sonipat	37.0	14.3	21.9	23.9	22.0	24.0	146	35
17.	Yamunanagar	21.3	6.5	22.8	24.6	22.0	24.5	122	46
6	**Karnataka**								
1.	Bangalore	10.3	1.5	25.4	26.3	25.0	26.0	29	66
2.	Bangalore Rural	1.2	0.0	26.0	26.6	25.0	27.0	82	14
3.	Belgaum	25.0	3.8	23.6	25.9	23.0	25.0	112	26
4.	Bellary	13.9	13.9	24.3	26.0	24.0	25.0	122	36
5.	Bidar	31.1	25.0	22.6	22.7	22.0	22.0	151	24
6.	Bijapur	25.7	24.3	23.7	24.4	24.0	25.0	140	37
7.	Chikmagalur	10.9	0.0	26.0	29.0	26.0	29.0	156	29
8.	Chitradurga	14.0	11.4	24.6	27.3	24.0	28.0	143	44
9.	Dakshina Kannada	2.9	4.8	27.1	29.4	27.0	29.0	102	42
10.	Dharwad	12.2	12.2	24.5	25.7	24.0	25.0	90	49
11.	Gulbarga	35.5	6.9	22.3	25.8	22.0	25.0	107	29
12.	Hassan	9.3	11.8	25.1	27.9	25.0	28.0	107	17
13.	Kodagu	8.5	8.7	26.8	27.3	25.0	25.0	118	23

Appendix - VII (Continued)

Sr. No.	State/District	Age at Marriage						Total Number of marriages	
		< 21 years (%)		Mean		Median			
		Rural	Urban	Rural	Urban	Rural	Urban	Rural	Urban
14.	Kolar	15.5	16.7	24.0	25.7	24.0	25.0	129	30
15.	Mandya	7.4	0.0	25.5	25.5	25.0	25.0	95	21
16.	Mysore	3.4	3.7	25.9	27.6	25.0	28.0	89	27
17.	Raichur	34.1	16.7	22.5	24.4	22.0	24.5	129	36
18.	Shimoga	6.1	2.4	26.5	27.1	26.0	27.0	147	41
19.	Tumkur	6.7	0.0	24.7	29.4	24.0	30.5	105	12
20.	Uttara Kannada	3.4	2.9	27.7	28.8	27.5	28.0	116	34
7	**Kerala**								
1.	Alappuzha	0.8	4.0	28.0	28.3	28.0	28.0	124	50
2.	Ernakulam	1.2	0.0	27.6	29.6	28.0	29.0	86	70
3.	Idukki	4.5	0.0	25.9	24.5	26.0	25.0	134	6
4.	Kannur	0.0	0.0	28.4	28.5	28.0	28.0	66	80
5.	Kasaragod	1.9	0.0	27.9	26.6	28.0	26.0	104	16
6.	Kollam	3.3	0.0	28.4	27.8	28.0	27.5	151	18
7.	Kottayam	2.2	4.3	28.3	27.8	28.0	28.0	138	23
8.	Kozhikode	2.7	1.4	26.2	27.8	26.0	27.0	111	69
9.	Malappuram	7.6	28.6	24.8	24.2	24.0	24.5	170	14
10.	Palakkad	1.6	0.0	27.2	28.1	27.0	29.0	126	23
11.	Pathanamthitta	0.0	0.0	27.7	27.5	27.5	28.5	106	10
12.	Thiruvananthapuram	2.5	3.4	28.0	28.1	28.0	28.0	80	29
13.	Thrissur	2.6	0.0	28.7	30.4	28.0	29.0	116	39
14.	Wayanad	8.7	0.0	25.7	28.4	26.0	27.0	138	5
8	**Madhya Pradesh**								
1.	Balaghat	20.3	22.2	23.6	25.7	24.0	28.0	69	9
2.	Bastar	43.5	0.0	21.9	26.6	22.0	25.0	69	9
3.	Betul	13.0	33.3	24.0	25.0	25.0	27.0	69	3
4.	Bhind	56.2	36.4	20.9	22.2	20.0	22.0	137	33
5.	Bhopal	50.0	17.9	20.9	23.9	20.0	24.0	12	67
6.	Bilaspur(MP)	43.3	11.5	22.0	26.1	21.5	26.0	120	26
7.	Chattarpur	72.9	40.9	19.4	21.8	18.5	21.0	70	22
8.	Chhindwara	25.8	3.7	23.0	26.7	22.0	27.0	93	27
9.	Damoh	56.9	33.3	20.6	23.0	20.0	22.5	102	24
10.	Datia	64.6	21.4	20.4	23.6	20.0	24.0	130	28
11.	Dewas	59.7	37.0	20.5	22.9	20.0	22.0	134	46
12.	Dhar	54.8	21.4	20.7	24.8	20.0	26.0	155	14
13.	Durg	27.1	23.1	22.7	24.5	22.0	25.5	85	26
14.	East Nimar	38.9	15.1	22.0	24.5	22.0	24.0	108	53
15.	Guna	71.3	23.8	19.6	23.8	18.0	23.0	94	21
16.	Gwalior	40.8	17.5	21.5	24.0	21.0	24.0	49	57
17.	Hoshangabad	34.4	13.6	22.2	24.9	22.0	26.0	64	22
18.	Indore	59.6	13.5	20.8	24.4	20.0	24.0	47	96
19.	Jabalpur	35.3	2.4	21.4	26.5	22.0	26.0	51	42
20.	Jhabua	74.6	16.7	18.9	24.0	18.0	24.0	142	12
21.	Mandla	37.0	33.3	21.3	22.0	22.0	23.0	54	3
22.	Mandsaur	72.3	23.1	19.0	23.4	19.0	23.0	101	39
23.	Morena	72.8	52.0	18.9	19.9	18.0	20.0	103	25
24.	Narsimhapur	33.6	19.0	22.6	23.0	22.0	22.0	131	21
25.	Panna	76.1	36.4	19.0	23.0	19.0	22.0	67	11
26.	Raigarh(M P)	21.1	0.0	22.9	24.3	22.0	23.5	71	6
27.	Raipur	42.3	57.1	21.7	21.1	21.0	20.0	52	7
28.	Raisen	32.7	13.0	21.9	23.0	22.0	22.0	107	23

Appendix - VII (Continued)

Sr. No.	State/District	Age at Marriage						Total Number of marriages	
		< 21 years (%)		Mean		Median			
		Rural	Urban	Rural	Urban	Rural	Urban	Rural	Urban
29.	Rajgarh	59.5	48.1	19.9	20.2	19.0	21.0	126	27
30.	Rajnandgaon	41.8	21.4	21.9	24.3	21.0	24.5	110	14
31.	Ratlam	52.8	23.5	20.9	23.1	20.0	23.0	89	51
32.	Rewa	64.6	22.2	19.8	22.5	20.0	23.0	79	18
33.	Sagar	54.9	13.9	20.8	24.8	20.0	25.0	82	36
34.	Satna	71.0	42.5	19.9	21.7	20.0	21.0	100	40
35.	Sehore	56.5	21.4	20.8	23.6	20.0	24.0	108	28
36.	Seoni	23.8	0.0	22.7	25.1	22.0	25.0	63	9
37.	Shahdol	63.6	25.0	20.9	22.8	19.5	22.5	22	8
38.	Shajapur	70.3	31.0	19.5	22.2	19.0	22.0	111	29
39.	Shivpuri	71.6	31.6	19.6	22.3	19.0	22.0	102	19
40.	Sidhi	68.6	**	19.4	NA	19.0	NA	105	**
41.	Surguja	64.2	12.5	19.9	23.1	20.0	23.5	106	16
42.	Tikamgarh	78.1	65.0	18.9	21.0	18.0	20.0	105	20
43.	Ujjain	48.3	19.7	21.0	23.7	21.0	23.0	89	66
44.	Vidisha	56.8	30.4	20.2	24.5	20.0	24.0	132	23
45.	West Nimar	49.0	15.6	20.9	22.9	21.0	22.5	98	32
9	**Maharashtra**								
1.	Ahmadnagar	14.7	6.7	23.8	25.5	23.0	25.0	156	15
2.	Akola	17.8	11.1	23.5	23.9	23.0	23.0	101	54
3.	Amravali	4.7	4.5	25.5	24.6	25.0	24.5	64	22
4.	Aurangabad(Mah)	29.4	15.9	22.7	23.8	22.0	24.0	109	44
5.	Bhandara	2.2	0.0	25.4	27.3	25.0	26.5	91	18
6.	Bid	32.3	13.3	21.7	23.4	22.0	22.0	99	15
7.	Buldana	8.0	5.9	23.7	25.3	23.0	25.5	125	34
8.	Chandrapur	16.0	5.9	23.6	27.6	24.0	26.0	81	17
9.	Dhule	25.0	8.8	22.4	25.0	22.0	24.5	112	34
10.	Gadchiroli	24.1	11.1	22.8	24.9	22.0	25.0	83	27
11.	Greater Bombay (Mum	**	5.7	NA	26.2	NA	26.0	**	140
12.	Jalgaon	22.0	19.4	23.0	24.3	23.0	25.0	109	31
13.	Jalna	31.8	42.9	22.5	22.9	22.0	21.0	132	14
14.	Kolhapur	12.3	2.4	24.7	26.0	25.0	26.0	138	41
15.	Latur	25.6	0.0	22.4	25.6	22.0	25.5	121	30
16.	Nagpur	0.0	4.8	26.0	25.6	25.0	25.0	73	83
17.	Nanded	35.3	21.2	22.1	23.5	22.0	23.0	102	33
18.	Nashik	24.6	15.3	22.7	24.3	22.0	25.0	114	59
19.	Osmanabad	18.3	15.8	23.8	23.9	24.0	24.0	120	19
20.	Parbhani	40.5	12.2	21.7	23.6	21.0	24.0	121	41
21.	Pune	8.1	11.3	23.9	25.0	24.0	25.0	86	80
22.	Raigarh(MAH)	6.7	0.0	24.1	26.1	24.0	25.0	90	14
23.	Ratnagiri	9.7	0.0	24.6	28.1	24.0	27.0	134	11
24.	Sangli	16.1	14.6	24.2	24.3	25.0	24.0	149	41
25.	Satara	7.9	6.3	24.5	25.1	24.0	24.0	101	16
26.	Sindhudurg	3.6	0.0	26.7	28.5	26.0	28.0	168	11
27.	Solapur	12.4	17.5	24.3	24.5	24.0	25.0	89	40
28.	Thane	18.2	6.5	23.3	25.3	23.0	25.0	33	77
29.	Wardha	3.5	0.0	26.1	27.1	26.0	27.0	85	23
30.	Yavatmal	12.3	0.0	24.4	24.8	25.0	23.5	146	14
10	**Orissa**								
1.	Anugul	21.4	14.3	23.5	27.4	23.0	29.0	103	7
2.	Balangir	30.9	14.3	22.9	25.4	22.0	25.0	110	14
3.	Balasore	7.2	0.0	25.7	30.0	25.0	30.0	138	7

Appendix - VII (Continued)

Sr. No.	State/District	Age at Marriage						Total Number of marriages	
		< 21 years (%)		Mean		Median			
		Rural	Urban	Rural	Urban	Rural	Urban	Rural	Urban
4.	Bargarh	19.8	11.1	23.6	24.6	23.0	24.0	111	9
5.	Baudh	32.8	0.0	22.8	26.0	22.0	26.0	125	2
6.	Bhadrak	7.0	15.8	25.9	26.5	26.0	26.0	129	19
7.	Cuttack	8.6	10.0	25.8	25.8	26.0	25.5	140	30
8.	Debagarh	14.2	0.0	24.5	27.0	25.0	27.0	113	7
9.	Dhenkanal	12.8	0.0	25.2	27.8	25.0	27.0	141	8
10.	Gajapati	19.2	0.0	23.7	29.4	24.0	30.0	130	9
11.	Ganjam	13.9	20.0	24.7	25.1	25.0	25.0	137	15
12.	Jagatsinghapur	1.5	0.0	26.6	25.4	27.0	24.0	137	7
13.	Jajapur	2.0	0.0	26.0	26.5	26.0	26.0	102	8
14.	Jharsuguda	11.9	15.9	24.2	23.9	25.0	23.5	59	44
15.	Kalahandi	40.9	0.0	22.2	27.8	21.0	26.5	110	6
16.	Kendrapara	3.4	0.0	25.8	27.7	26.0	28.0	177	13
17.	Kendujhar	14.4	27.8	24.4	24.8	24.0	26.0	118	18
18.	Khordha	7.7	3.0	25.0	27.6	24.5	28.0	104	33
19.	Koraput	57.7	13.6	20.8	26.0	20.0	27.0	97	22
20.	Malkangiri	55.1	33.3	21.2	24.8	20.0	24.0	98	12
21.	Mayurbhanj	20.5	10.0	24.2	26.6	24.0	27.0	122	10
22.	Nabarangapur	46.1	0.0	22.2	28.0	21.0	28.0	102	5
23.	Nayagarh	14.3	0.0	24.3	28.0	24.0	28.0	161	1
24.	Nuapada	29.2	0.0	23.1	25.4	22.5	24.0	96	5
25.	Phulbani	32.7	37.5	23.4	24.5	23.0	24.5	107	8
26.	Puri	10.0	0.0	25.4	28.8	25.0	28.0	160	11
27.	Rayagada	30.2	26.3	22.9	23.7	22.5	24.0	96	38
28.	Sambalpur	7.6	3.8	25.2	27.6	25.0	27.5	92	26
29.	Sonapur	16.0	11.1	24.1	23.0	23.0	22.0	106	9
30.	Sundargarh	8.6	5.6	24.6	26.6	25.0	26.5	70	36
11	**Punjab**								
1.	Amritsar	23.0	7.3	22.9	25.4	23.0	25.0	113	55
2.	Bathinda	29.0	22.7	22.4	23.8	22.0	23.0	145	44
3.	Faridkot	31.0	29.5	22.7	22.7	22.0	23.0	142	44
4.	Fatehgarh Sahib	20.6	13.6	22.7	23.6	22.0	24.0	141	44
5.	Firozpur	40.4	18.6	21.9	24.4	22.0	24.0	178	43
6.	Gurdaspur	13.6	0.0	24.4	25.7	24.5	25.5	132	34
7.	Hoshiarpur	7.5	0.0	25.4	25.5	25.0	25.0	147	24
8.	Jalandhar	12.9	8.2	24.4	25.4	24.0	25.0	101	49
9.	Kapurthala	15.2	10.0	24.1	24.6	24.0	25.0	132	30
10.	Ludhiana	17.9	6.2	24.0	24.2	23.0	25.0	67	65
11.	Mansa	33.7	15.8	22.1	23.7	22.0	23.0	163	19
12.	Moga	30.8	5.6	23.0	25.9	22.0	25.0	130	36
13.	Muktsar	40.0	20.0	22.3	23.2	22.0	22.5	145	30
14.	Nawanshahr	11.0	18.2	24.2	25.7	24.0	25.0	154	11
15.	Patiala	27.5	13.7	22.6	23.5	22.0	24.0	142	51
16.	Rupnagar	14.6	7.1	23.8	25.4	23.0	25.0	123	42
17.	Sangrur	31.1	17.4	22.5	23.8	22.0	23.5	132	46
12	**Rajasthan**								
1.	Ajmer	71.2	8.2	19.2	24.3	19.0	24.0	52	49
2.	Alwar	63.7	5.0	19.8	25.0	20.0	25.0	146	20
3.	Banswara	71.0	33.3	19.4	22.4	18.0	24.0	131	12
4.	Barmer	58.8	38.9	20.3	21.4	20.0	21.5	148	18
5.	Bharatpur	56.2	43.8	20.5	21.8	20.0	22.0	130	32

Appendix - VII (Continued)

Sr. No.	State/District	Age at Marriage						Total Number of marriages	
		< 21 years (%)		Mean		Median			
		Rural	Urban	Rural	Urban	Rural	Urban	Rural	Urban
6.	Bhilwara	70.3	23.1	19.2	24.0	18.0	24.0	74	26
7.	Bikaner	75.9	21.0	19.8	23.2	20.0	22.5	83	62
8.	Bundi	84.3	29.2	18.1	22.8	18.0	23.0	89	24
9.	Chittaurgarh	71.4	33.3	19.1	23.8	19.0	25.0	63	9
10.	Churu	70.0	46.2	19.6	21.3	20.0	21.0	140	52
11.	Dausa	69.9	33.3	19.5	21.9	19.5	21.5	146	12
12.	Dhaulpur	64.4	57.9	19.8	20.4	20.0	19.0	118	19
13.	Dungarpur	50.0	0.0	21.1	26.2	20.5	25.5	168	12
14.	Ganganagar	61.1	28.1	20.2	22.8	20.0	23.0	131	32
15.	Hanumangarh	69.6	16.0	19.8	23.6	20.0	24.0	168	25
16.	Jaipur	56.5	20.8	19.5	23.8	20.0	24.0	85	53
17.	Jaisalmer	39.5	25.0	22.0	22.1	22.0	22.0	86	16
18.	Jalor	60.3	28.6	20.2	22.6	20.0	22.5	184	14
19.	Jhalawar	74.0	19.4	19.0	23.7	18.0	22.0	100	31
20.	Jhunjhunun	40.0	16.1	21.4	23.2	21.0	24.0	135	31
21.	Jodhpur	62.0	15.7	20.6	23.5	20.0	24.0	71	51
22.	Kota	71.6	22.2	19.7	23.2	20.0	23.0	74	45
23.	Nagaur	57.8	38.9	20.3	22.4	20.0	22.0	128	18
24.	Pali	50.0	44.1	20.6	20.9	20.5	21.0	124	34
25.	Rajsamand	52.5	33.3	20.9	21.7	20.0	21.0	101	15
26.	Sawai Madhopur	62.5	27.3	19.5	22.4	19.0	23.0	80	11
27.	Sikar	45.5	24.0	21.1	22.3	21.0	22.0	121	25
28.	Sirohi	39.1	17.6	21.9	24.1	22.0	24.0	69	17
29.	Tonk	62.0	57.7	19.8	20.4	20.0	20.0	71	26
30.	Udaipur	65.5	23.5	20.2	24.5	20.0	26.0	113	17
13	**Tamil Nadu**								
1.	Chengalpattu	9.3	4.6	24.4	26.9	25.0	27.0	75	65
2.	Chennai	**	4.0	NA	26.8	NA	27.0	**	99
3.	Coimbatore	11.9	2.9	25.8	26.9	25.0	27.0	42	35
4.	Dharmapuri	15.2	0.0	24.4	25.8	25.0	26.0	151	13
5.	Dindigul	9.1	0.0	25.0	27.9	25.0	27.0	88	26
6.	Kanniyakumari	0.8	0.0	28.0	28.2	28.0	28.0	126	13
7.	Madurai	15.4	1.8	25.1	28.0	25.0	27.0	52	57
8.	Namakkal	11.1	0.0	25.9	27.4	25.0	27.5	81	14
9.	North Arcot	9.2	4.7	25.8	25.0	25.0	25.0	98	43
10.	Periyar	5.6	8.7	26.4	26.5	26.0	26.0	54	23
11.	Pudukkottai	10.2	8.3	25.6	26.5	25.0	25.5	98	24
12.	Ramanathapuram	7.4	5.6	25.2	25.1	25.0	26.0	68	18
13.	Salem	8.8	9.5	25.2	25.5	25.0	25.0	91	42
14.	Sivaganganagar	5.8	0.0	25.7	26.8	26.0	26.0	103	37
15.	South Arcot	12.8	5.3	24.8	27.7	25.0	28.0	94	19
16.	Thanjavur	6.6	6.1	27.0	26.8	27.0	27.0	76	33
17.	The Nilgiris	0.0	3.7	27.7	27.6	28.0	27.0	35	27
18.	Theni	15.2	7.4	25.1	26.3	24.0	27.0	46	27
19.	Tiruchirappalli	6.0	3.7	28.2	27.3	27.0	27.0	67	27
20.	Tirunelveli	0.0	0.0	26.3	25.5	25.0	25.0	71	27
21.	Tiruvanamalai	14.5	0.0	25.0	26.2	25.0	26.0	117	14
22.	Tutikorin	6.3	0.0	26.1	27.3	26.0	27.0	63	47
23.	Virudhunagar	9.9	10.2	24.8	26.3	24.0	27.0	81	49
14	**Uttar Pradesh**								
1.	Agra	50.0	31.5	20.8	23.0	20.5	22.5	98	54
2.	Aligarh	47.8	38.2	21.1	22.2	21.0	22.0	138	34

Appendix - VII (Continued)

Sr. No.	*State/District*	*Age at Marriage*						*Total Number of marriages*	
		< 21 years (%)		*Mean*		*Median*			
		Rural	*Urban*	*Rural*	*Urban*	*Rural*	*Urban*	*Rural*	*Urban*
3.	Allahabad	68.4	18.2	20.1	24.2	20.0	23.0	114	22
4.	Almora	3.2	0.0	23.9	26.7	23.0	26.5	94	6
5.	Ambedkarnagar	68.0	33.3	19.4	22.7	18.0	25.0	103	3
6.	Azamgarh	63.1	87.5	20.2	19.3	20.0	19.5	130	8
7.	Bahraich	73.2	42.9	19.2	24.0	19.0	22.0	123	7
8.	Ballia	42.7	25.0	21.7	23.7	21.0	22.0	89	12
9.	Banda	65.0	66.7	20.2	20.8	20.0	20.0	123	12
10.	Barabanki	66.0	30.0	20.2	21.6	20.0	21.5	141	10
11.	Bareilly	63.2	25.7	20.1	23.1	20.0	22.0	57	35
12.	Basti	66.9	30.0	19.6	23.3	19.0	23.0	127	10
13.	Bhadohi	77.8	62.5	18.9	21.1	18.0	20.0	171	8
14.	Bijnor	27.8	16.7	22.2	24.0	22.0	23.0	115	24
15.	Budaun	59.3	40.0	20.1	22.1	20.0	22.0	135	20
16.	Bulandshahar	43.8	21.7	21.5	22.6	21.0	22.0	176	46
17.	Chamoli	11.1	14.3	23.8	25.9	24.0	25.0	81	7
18.	Dehradun	16.0	2.9	24.2	25.4	24.0	25.0	50	69
19.	Deoria	72.9	71.4	19.9	19.4	19.0	18.0	133	7
20.	Etah	49.5	28.6	21.0	22.4	21.0	22.0	103	21
21.	Etawah	39.6	40.9	21.8	22.1	21.0	22.0	139	22
22.	Faizabad	72.6	16.7	19.0	25.3	18.0	24.5	106	6
23.	Farrukhabad	47.9	30.4	21.1	23.4	21.0	23.0	140	23
24.	Fatehpur	49.1	31.6	21.4	21.9	21.0	22.0	159	19
25.	Firozabad	67.9	20.9	20.2	23.3	20.0	23.0	112	43
26.	Ghaziabad	36.7	23.1	21.7	23.0	21.0	23.0	90	52
27.	Ghazipur	59.7	16.7	20.5	24.3	20.0	22.0	124	6
28.	Gonda	71.6	50.0	19.3	22.0	19.0	21.0	148	4
29.	Gorakhpur	65.3	21.1	19.6	24.2	19.0	25.0	95	19
30.	Hamirpur(UP)	63.6	45.0	20.4	21.9	20.0	21.0	118	20
31.	Hardoi	54.3	36.4	20.7	23.1	20.0	22.0	94	11
32.	Hardwar	32.7	3.8	22.0	24.5	22.0	24.0	101	26
33.	Hathras	51.3	33.3	20.9	22.4	20.0	22.0	117	42
34.	Jalaun	57.1	44.4	20.9	21.1	20.0	21.0	91	27
35.	Jaunpur	64.8	14.3	19.8	21.4	19.0	22.0	193	7
36.	Jhansi	76.0	23.1	19.5	23.8	20.0	24.0	75	39
37.	Kanpur Dehat	39.4	50.0	21.8	20.8	21.0	21.0	109	4
38.	Kanpur Nagar	50.0	18.4	20.9	23.9	20.5	24.0	32	87
39.	Kheri	67.9	27.3	20.3	22.5	20.0	22.0	131	11
40.	Lalitpur	82.7	62.5	18.4	20.8	18.0	19.5	110	16
41.	Lucknow	67.3	16.0	20.5	24.0	20.0	25.0	55	50
42.	Maharajganj	79.4	100.0	18.5	16.5	18.0	16.5	68	2
43.	Mahoba	66.1	36.0	19.7	22.4	20.0	22.0	121	25
44.	Mainpuri	60.7	54.2	21.0	20.9	20.0	20.0	145	24
45.	Mathura	51.3	27.8	21.2	23.1	20.0	22.0	158	36
46.	Mau	63.1	25.0	20.2	23.6	20.0	24.0	122	24
47.	Meerut	30.3	35.5	21.9	21.2	22.0	21.0	76	62
48.	Mirzapur	70.9	20.0	19.7	24.7	20.0	25.5	127	10
49.	Muradabad	53.1	10.0	21.0	23.5	20.0	23.5	113	30
50.	Muzaffarnagar	34.1	13.6	21.5	25.2	21.0	24.0	132	22
51.	Nainital	27.6	4.9	23.2	25.7	22.0	25.0	98	41
52.	Pauri Garhwal	8.4	0.0	24.4	26.7	24.0	27.0	95	11
53.	Pilibhit	67.4	16.0	19.8	24.5	19.0	24.0	132	25

Appendix - VII (Continued)

Sr. No.	State/District	Age at Marriage						Total Number of marriages	
		< 21 years (%)		Mean		Median			
		Rural	Urban	Rural	Urban	Rural	Urban	Rural	Urban
54.	Pithoragarh	20.2	20.0	22.8	28.2	22.0	30.0	94	5
55.	Pratapgarh	76.5	16.7	19.7	22.7	19.0	23.0	149	6
56.	Rae Bareli	63.1	20.0	20.3	21.8	20.0	22.0	122	5
57.	Rampur	46.7	14.3	21.1	23.9	21.0	24.0	92	21
58.	Saharanpur	33.9	13.0	21.7	23.7	21.0	23.0	109	23
59.	Shajahanabad	66.1	41.4	19.8	22.2	19.0	22.0	118	29
60.	Siddharthnagar	82.0	0.0	18.5	23.5	18.0	23.5	61	2
61.	Sitapur	60.8	50.0	20.5	21.1	20.0	21.0	120	14
62.	Sonbhadra	65.4	11.1	19.8	24.6	19.0	25.0	78	9
63.	Sultanpur	68.6	25.0	19.4	21.0	19.0	21.5	121	4
64.	Tehri Garhwal	16.3	25.0	23.3	24.8	22.0	25.0	98	4
65.	Udhamsingh Nagar	40.0	14.3	21.6	23.6	22.0	23.5	105	28
66.	Unnao	59.3	35.7	20.7	23.1	20.0	22.0	86	14
67.	Uttarkashi	27.4	0.0	22.5	28.6	22.0	28.0	84	5
68.	Varanasi	73.0	16.1	19.4	25.4	19.0	25.0	89	31
15	**West Bengal**								
1.	Bankura	18.2	40.0	24.2	25.2	24.0	25.0	154	5
2.	Barddhaman	30.0	20.0	24.2	25.3	24.0	25.0	140	50
3.	Birbhum	31.3	0.0	23.0	26.9	22.0	28.0	128	8
4.	Dakshin Dinajpur	28.5	9.5	23.9	26.5	23.0	27.0	123	21
5.	Darjiling	28.0	10.9	24.1	26.4	23.0	27.0	107	46
6.	Haora	18.0	5.8	24.6	27.7	24.0	27.0	89	69
7.	Hugli	19.2	8.8	24.8	27.1	24.0	26.5	130	34
8.	Jalpaiguri	28.4	4.5	23.7	28.1	22.5	27.0	148	22
9.	Koch Bihar	26.0	0.0	23.7	26.6	24.0	27.0	127	7
10.	Kolkata	**	11.7	NA	27.0	NA	27.0	**	120
11.	Maldah	24.1	8.3	23.5	27.7	23.0	28.0	137	12
12.	Medinipur	19.8	16.7	24.0	23.3	24.0	22.0	162	12
13.	Murshidabad	41.8	64.3	22.0	20.9	21.0	20.0	170	14
14.	Nadia	17.9	15.4	24.3	27.0	24.0	27.5	117	26
15.	North 24 Parganas	16.9	11.4	24.5	28.0	24.0	28.0	65	70
16.	Puruliya	32.9	12.5	23.1	25.6	22.0	25.5	143	16
17.	South 24 Parganas	24.6	17.4	23.6	26.1	22.0	26.0	134	23
18.	Uttar Dinajpur	24.5	25.0	24.0	25.3	24.0	26.0	139	16
16	**Andaman & Nicobar**								
1.	Andaman	5.4	100.0	24.8	27.5	25.0	27.0	56	13
2.	Nicobar	0.0	**	27.4	NA	26.0	NA	75	**
17	**Arunachal Pradesh**								
1.	Changlang	36.9	0.0	23.0	23.0	22.0	23.0	65	2
2.	Dibang Valley	40.7	9.1	22.3	26.4	21.0	28.0	27	11
3.	East Kameng	63.2	0.0	21.2	25.3	20.0	25.0	38	9
4.	East Siang	59.0	42.9	21.3	22.6	20.0	22.0	39	7
5.	Lohit	30.6	0.0	23.2	27.0	23.0	27.0	36	2
6.	Lower Subansiri	41.7	30.0	22.9	23.1	22.0	21.0	24	10
7.	Papum Pare	35.7	45.5	24.5	21.5	23.5	21.0	14	11
8.	Tawang	7.7	**	25.1	NA	24.0	NA	26	**
9.	Tirap	20.0	0.0	24.1	25.0	24.0	25.0	15	2
10.	Upper Siang	25.0	0.0	22.7	24.3	23.0	24.0	20	3
11.	Upper Subansiri	25.0	23.5	23.5	23.9	23.0	24.0	52	17
12.	West Kameng	48.1	7.1	22.0	25.2	21.0	25.0	27	14
13.	West Siang	17.5	16.7	24.9	25.3	25.0	24.5	40	6

Appendix - VII (Continued)

Sr. No.	State/District	Age at Marriage						Total Number of marriages	
		< 21 years (%)		Mean		Median			
		Rural	Urban	Rural	Urban	Rural	Urban	Rural	Urban
18	**Chandigarh**								
1.	Chandigarh	**	9.3	NA	24.9	NA	25.0	**	54
19	**Dadra & Nagar Haveli**								
1.	Dadra & Nagar Havel	50.9	0.0	21.2	24.0	20.0	24.0	106	10
20	**Daman & Diu**								
1.	Daman	16.2	4.9	23.5	25.9	23.0	27.0	99	61
2.	Diu	29.7	4.1	22.3	26.3	22.0	26.0	74	73
21	**Delhi**								
1.	Delhi	14.8	12.0	23.1	24.9	22.0	25.0	27	75
22	**Goa**								
1.	North Goa	2.5	0.0	29.4	28.5	30.0	29.0	81	35
2.	South Goa	1.3	1.8	28.4	28.8	28.0	28.0	75	57
23	**Himachal Pradesh**								
1.	Bilaspur (Pra.Him)	5.9	0.0	24.9	25.4	25.0	25.5	136	8
2.	Chamba	6.8	0.0	24.6	27.1	24.0	27.0	162	13
3.	Hamirpur (HP)	5.4	25.0	25.4	26.8	26.0	27.0	168	4
4.	Kangra	1.4	0.0	26.2	25.8	26.0	26.0	148	4
5.	Kinnaur	13.7	**	24.4	NA	24.0	NA	102	**
6.	Kullu	13.0	**	24.4	NA	24.0	NA	108	**
7.	Lahul & Spiti	11.4	0.0	25.0	25.0	24.0	24.0	70	3
8.	Mandi	5.0	0.0	24.5	29.7	24.0	29.0	161	7
9.	Shimla	9.8	0.0	25.8	27.1	26.0	27.0	92	24
10.	Sirmaur	14.2	0.0	23.9	25.4	23.0	25.0	141	9
11.	Solan	9.8	0.0	24.0	26.0	24.0	26.0	153	25
12.	Una	1.9	0.0	25.8	27.2	26.0	26.5	155	10
24	**Jammu & Kashmir**								
1.	Anantanag	7.7	**	25.1	NA	25.0	NA	26	**
2.	Badgam	34.1	**	22.3	NA	22.0	NA	44	**
3.	Baramula	15.2	**	25.9	NA	25.0	NA	66	**
4.	Doda	1.5	**	26.5	NA	26.0	NA	67	**
5.	Jammu	0.0	**	27.0	NA	27.0	NA	64	**
6.	Kargil	13.4	**	23.6	NA	24.0	NA	82	**
7.	Kathua	0.9	**	28.5	NA	28.0	NA	107	**
8.	Kupwara	18.2	**	24.6	NA	25.0	NA	44	**
9.	Leh	16.4	**	24.1	NA	24.0	NA	55	**
10.	Pulwama	23.3	**	23.0	NA	23.0	NA	30	**
11.	Punch	3.1	**	24.5	NA	24.0	NA	65	**
12.	Rajauri	0.9	**	23.6	24.0	24.0	24.0	106	1
13.	Srinagar	30.8	**	21.3	NA	22.0	NA	26	**
14.	Udhampur	3.4	**	23.9	NA	23.5	NA	88	**
25	**Lakshadweep**								
1.	Lakshadweep	12.5	6.9	25.2	26.0	25.5	26.0	40	58
26	**Manipur**								
1.	Bishnupur	20.8	9.1	25.9	26.8	25.0	26.0	101	33
2.	Chandel	21.4	20.0	24.9	23.2	25.0	25.0	70	5
3.	Churachandpur	15.5	13.0	25.3	26.0	25.0	25.0	84	23

Appendix - VII (Continued)

Sr. No.	State/District	Age at Marriage						Total Number of marriages	
		< 21 years (%)		Mean		Median			
		Rural	Urban	Rural	Urban	Rural	Urban	Rural	Urban
4.	Imphal	10.3	11.8	27.2	29.4	27.0	29.5	58	34
5.	Senapati	20.4	0.0	25.3	24.5	25.0	24.5	54	2
6.	Tamenglong	28.1	0.0	24.4	25.5	24.0	25.0	89	15
7.	Thoubal	17.2	15.1	25.3	26.0	25.0	25.0	93	53
8.	Ukhrul	18.9	0.0	26.7	25.0	27.0	25.0	53	1
27	**Meghalaya**								
1.	East Garo Hills	37.5	100.0	22.6	20.0	23.5	20.0	32	1
2.	East Khasi Hills	60.0	25.0	20.5	24.3	20.0	24.5	15	4
3.	Jaintia Hills	0.0	0.0	25.1	25.6	25.0	26.0	7	8
4.	Ri Bhoi	68.6	**	20.2	NA	20.0	NA	35	**
5.	West Garo Hills	50.0	0.0	23.8	25.5	22.5	25.5	4	2
6.	West Khasi Hills	47.2	100.0	21.5	19.0	21.0	19.0	36	3
28	**Mizoram**								
1.	Aizwal	11.8	36.4	25.4	23.6	24.0	22.5	68	66
2.	Chhimtuipui	24.3	30.8	23.8	24.1	23.0	25.0	37	13
3.	Lunglei	5.0	24.0	26.8	25.6	25.0	25.0	40	25
29	**Nagaland**								
1.	Kohima	61.3	83.3	20.4	19.2	20.0	19.0	31	18
2.	Mokokchung	6.9	33.3	25.6	21.7	24.0	21.0	29	3
3.	Mon	25.0	0.0	22.8	25.5	22.0	25.5	80	2
4.	Phek	35.3	0.0	21.5	27.0	21.0	27.0	17	2
5.	Tuensang	5.2	0.0	25.1	23.5	24.0	23.0	77	11
6.	Wokha	8.0	0.0	25.0	26.5	25.0	26.5	50	2
7.	Zunheboto	30.3	37.1	22.4	22.3	23.0	22.0	89	35
30	**Pondicherry**								
1.	Karaikal	3.7	4.8	26.8	26.0	27.0	25.0	54	42
2.	Mahe	**	1.1	NA	29.7	NA	29.0	**	186
3.	Pondicherry	2.1	0.0	26.9	27.8	27.0	27.0	47	83
4.	Yanam	**	13.4	NA	24.7	NA	24.0	**	67
31	**Sikkim**								
1.	East Sikkim	8.7	11.8	25.7	26.2	25.0	26.0	103	17
2.	North Sikkim	30.0	0.0	24.3	26.8	24.0	24.5	60	4
3.	South Sikkim	29.7	**	23.2	NA	22.0	NA	37	**
4.	West Sikkim	21.3	0.0	24.0	24.5	23.0	24.5	89	2
32	**Tripura**								
1.	North Tripura	8.0	11.1	27.5	27.1	28.0	26.5	113	18
2.	South Tripura	5.6	28.6	27.3	26.7	28.0	26.0	126	7
3.	West Tripura	6.6	0.0	28.6	29.2	28.0	30.0	137	9

Note: In the column showing percent of marriages below legal minimum age, 0.0 indicates no marriage below 18 years.

** No marriage is reported in that category of characteristic/district.

NA Not applicable.

APPENDIX - VIII

Percent of Marriages below legal Minimum age of 21 years and Average Age at Marriage in each District by Caste-BOYS

Sr. No.	State/District	< 21 years (%)		Age at Marriage Mean		Median		Total Number of marriages	
		SC/ST/ OBC	OC	SC/ST OBC	OC	SC/ST OBC	OC	SC/ST OBC	OC
1	**Andhra Pradesh**								
1.	Adilabad	31.2	42.9	22.5	22.0	22.0	22.0	93	7
2.	Anantapur	27.8	5.0	23.9	24.7	23.0	25.0	54	20
3.	Chittoor	15.4	16.7	24.7	26.2	25.0	26.5	39	18
4.	Cuddapah	23.3	18.2	22.5	24.5	22.0	24.0	43	33
5.	East Godavari	29.2	26.7	22.4	22.9	22.0	23.0	65	15
6.	Guntur	36.7	10.5	21.7	24.5	21.5	26.0	60	19
7.	Hyderabad	0.0	0.0	26.2	26.5	25.0	26.0	33	61
8.	Karimnagar	44.9	0.0	21.5	24.9	21.0	25.0	49	11
9.	Khammam	30.4	27.8	22.5	22.9	22.5	23.5	46	18
10.	Krishna	45.4	35.6	21.9	23.4	21.0	24.0	108	45
11.	Kurnool	29.4	0.0	23.2	25.4	23.0	25.0	68	24
12.	Mahbubnagar	50.0	26.3	21.4	23.7	21.0	25.0	54	19
13.	Medak	29.9	15.6	22.7	24.0	22.0	25.0	77	32
14.	Nalgonda	46.4	14.8	21.5	23.9	21.0	24.0	125	27
15.	Nellore	25.4	6.7	22.7	25.5	22.0	26.0	67	15
16.	Nizamabad	46.8	25.0	22.1	22.4	21.0	22.5	62	36
17.	Prakasam	27.7	22.7	23.0	23.2	23.0	22.0	47	22
18.	Rangareddi	21.6	5.7	23.8	24.5	24.0	24.0	97	35
19.	Srikakulam	25.0	18.5	22.9	24.6	23.0	24.0	88	27
20.	Vishkhapatanam	45.3	8.8	22.0	25.1	21.5	25.0	64	34
21.	Vizianagaram	37.7	0.0	22.0	24.4	22.0	23.0	69	16
22.	Warangal	39.5	40.0	21.5	22.3	22.0	22.0	86	10
23.	West Godavari	35.1	8.1	22.1	24.8	22.0	25.0	77	37
2	**Assam**								
1.	Barpeta		4.4	29.2	27.2	30.5	28.0	26	136
2.	Bongaigaon	7.5	20.8	26.8	25.0	27.0	25.0	53	53
3.	Cachar	6.1	0.0	27.2	30.3	27.0	30.0	33	62
4.	Darrang	7.7	5.5	27.4	28.1	28.0	28.0	39	55
5.	Dhemaji	1.2	3.2	27.9	27.2	28.0	27.0	259	63
6.	Dhubri	3.4	3.4	27.1	26.1	27.0	26.0	29	119
7.	Dibrugarh	40.7	14.3	24.3	28.0	25.0	30.0	27	7
8.	Goalpara	12.8	11.3	26.6	27.1	27.0	27.0	78	53
9.	Golaghat	7.9	16.0	25.9	26.2	25.0	26.0	63	81
10.	Hailakandi	6.5	2.6	28.5	30.4	29.0	29.0	46	39
11.	Jorhat	2.9	0.0	27.6	28.9	28.0	30.0	170	65
12.	Kamrup	1.3	6.7	28.4	28.0	29.0	29.0	78	89
13.	Karbi Anglong	16.0	0.0	22.2	26.8	21.0	26.0	106	4
14.	Karimganj	0.0	4.4	30.9	29.3	31.0	28.0	50	90
15.	Lakhimpur	12.5	0.0	25.9	30.8	25.0	30.0	24	19

Appendix - VIII (Continued)

Sr. No.	State/District	Age at Marriage < 21 years (%)		Mean		Median		Total Number of marriages	
		SC/ST/ OBC	OC	SC/ST OBC	OC	SC/ST OBC	OC	SC/ST OBC	OC
16.	Marigaon	6.3	9.5	27.2	26.3	28.0	27.0	95	126
17.	Nagaon	2.3	16.2	27.1	24.6	26.5	25.0	44	142
18.	Nalbari	9.1	1.0	28.8	29.0	30.0	30.0	22	102
19.	North Cachar Hills	13.9	**	24.5	NA	25.0	NA	72	**
20.	Sibsagar	7.1	12.5	27.4	28.0	27.0	28.0	28	32
21.	Sonitpur	12.9	9.6	25.6	26.8	25.0	26.5	70	52
22.	Tinsukia	9.7	23.3	25.3	24.8	25.0	24.0	31	90
3	**Bihar**								
1.	Araria	37.4	20.8	22.3	23.7	22.0	23.0	131	24
2.	Aurangabad(Bih)	68.9	43.2	20.0	21.9	20.0	21.5	180	44
3.	Begusarai	51.0	39.4	20.7	22.1	20.0	21.5	147	66
4.	Bhagalpur	37.3	16.0	23.1	23.7	22.0	25.0	142	25
5.	Bhojpur	71.0	41.0	19.8	21.9	19.0	21.0	138	61
6.	Buxar	55.6	31.3	20.7	22.5	20.0	23.0	153	48
7.	Darbhanga	53.1	15.5	21.1	23.4	20.0	23.0	143	71
8.	Deoghar	53.1	17.4	20.9	25.0	20.0	25.0	128	23
9.	Dhanbad	41.8	25.0	21.7	23.4	21.0	24.0	79	28
10.	Dumka	29.9	11.1	22.8	23.6	22.0	22.0	134	9
11.	Gaya	61.4	29.4	19.8	22.3	20.0	22.0	127	34
12.	Giridih	52.8	57.1	21.1	20.7	20.0	20.0	161	21
13.	Godda	27.9	0.0	22.9	24.3	22.0	25.0	111	9
14.	Gopalganj	63.5	37.5	20.2	22.2	20.0	22.0	159	56
15.	Gulma	21.1	7.1	23.7	25.0	24.0	25.0	109	14
16.	Hazaribagh	39.6	22.2	21.5	24.0	21.0	22.5	149	18
17.	Jehanabad	65.0	32.6	20.2	22.4	20.0	22.0	157	46
18.	Katihar	40.4	24.2	22.2	24.2	22.0	23.0	99	33
19.	Khagaria	49.6	8.7	21.4	23.7	21.0	22.0	139	23
20.	Kishanganj	21.1	21.3	23.5	24.4	23.0	25.0	71	80
21.	Lohardaga	20.2	20.0	23.1	24.5	22.0	25.5	109	10
22.	Madhepura	56.3	26.3	21.1	23.0	20.0	23.0	128	19
23.	Madhubani	59.0	26.9	20.8	22.5	20.0	22.0	156	26
24.	Munger	68.1	38.7	20.1	21.8	20.0	21.0	113	31
25.	Muzaffarpur	42.8	28.1	21.3	24.1	21.0	24.0	138	32
26.	Nalanda	55.3	42.4	21.0	21.6	20.0	21.0	132	33
27.	Nawada	71.5	50.9	19.6	20.6	19.0	20.0	144	53
28.	Palamu	64.7	36.8	20.2	22.8	20.0	21.0	136	19
29.	Pashchim hamparan	42.0	37.5	21.9	23.1	22.0	22.0	143	24
30.	Pashchmi inghbhum	24.2	14.3	23.6	24.4	25.0	25.0	91	7
31.	Patna	57.8	39.0	20.8	22.9	20.0	22.0	128	41
32.	Purba Champaran	45.6	37.5	21.9	22.4	22.0	22.0	158	32
33.	Purbi Singhbhum	10.0	7.5	25.7	27.0	25.0	28.0	100	40
34.	Purnia	29.9	17.2	22.9	23.4	22.0	23.0	134	29
35.	Ranchi	22.0	17.6	23.6	24.4	24.0	25.0	91	17
36.	Rohtas	74.2	48.1	19.0	20.9	18.0	21.0	124	27
37.	Saharsa	59.2	11.8	20.9	24.7	20.0	25.0	147	34
38.	Sahibganj	49.6	50.0	21.6	21.2	21.0	20.5	125	26
39.	Samastipur	52.3	25.7	21.3	22.6	20.0	22.0	176	35
40.	Saran	42.8	25.0	22.0	23.5	21.0	24.0	159	60
41.	Sitamarhi	54.9	25.6	20.9	23.0	20.0	23.0	122	39
42.	Siwan	43.1	27.2	21.8	23.3	22.0	23.0	109	81
43	Vaishali	52.4	24.5	20.8	22.7	20.0	23.0	168	49

Appendix - VIII (Continued)

Sr. No.	State/District	Age at Marriage < 21 years (%) SC/ST/OBC	OC	Mean SC/ST OBC	OC	Median SC/ST OBC	OC	Total Number of marriages SC/ST OBC	OC
4	**Gujarat**								
1.	Ahmadabad	42.4	17.1	21.9	24.3	21.5	24.0	92	70
2.	Amreli	40.0	18.5	21.5	23.1	21.0	23.0	95	108
3.	Banas Kantha	59.8	54.2	19.7	20.5	20.0	20.0	92	59
4.	Bharuch	34.9	18.2	22.9	24.4	22.0	24.0	109	77
5.	Bhavnagar	44.0	30.0	21.2	21.9	21.0	22.0	100	70
6.	Gandhinagar	60.2	10.3	20.3	24.3	20.0	24.0	88	58
7.	Jamnagar	39.1	11.5	22.0	24.2	22.0	24.0	92	78
8.	Junagadh	19.6	25.6	23.2	22.6	23.0	22.0	158	78
9.	Kachchh	31.3	22.6	22.3	22.9	22.0	23.0	80	53
10.	Kheda	43.2	20.7	21.4	23.3	21.0	23.5	81	58
11.	Mahesana	44.0	32.7	20.8	22.2	21.0	22.0	75	49
12.	Panch Mahals	55.5	19.4	20.4	24.2	20.0	24.0	155	36
13.	Rajkot	25.7	13.7	22.6	23.8	22.0	23.0	74	95
14.	Sabar Kantha	52.6	33.3	20.7	22.0	20.0	22.0	135	72
15.	Surat	27.5	10.5	22.7	23.7	23.0	24.0	69	57
16.	Surendranagar	27.8	22.4	22.5	23.2	22.0	23.0	72	67
17.	The Dangs	62.2	20.0	20.3	24.0	20.0	25.0	127	5
18.	Vadodara	58.4	12.0	20.8	24.6	20.0	24.0	113	50
19.	Valsad	5.7	10.0	24.7	26.2	24.0	25.0	106	20
5	**Haryana**								
1.	Ambala	23.3	22.4	22.8	23.8	22.0	24.0	60	85
2.	Bhiwani	48.4	39.4	21.5	21.5	21.0	22.0	95	99
3.	Faridabad	42.4	22.3	21.5	23.4	21.0	24.0	92	112
4.	Gurgaon	37.3	52.0	21.6	21.2	21.0	20.0	67	102
5.	Hisar	47.0	44.1	21.2	22.1	21.0	22.0	66	68
6.	Jind	32.5	35.6	21.7	21.9	22.0	21.0	80	90
7.	Kaithal	35.8	22.3	21.4	23.0	21.0	23.0	67	94
8.	Karnal	20.6	15.6	22.1	23.1	22.0	23.0	68	96
9.	Kurukshetra	31.9	20.2	22.0	23.1	22.0	23.0	47	99
10.	Mahendragarh	48.9	27.5	20.8	22.0	21.0	22.0	131	51
11.	Panchkula	20.2	9.4	23.1	24.0	23.0	24.0	89	85
12.	Panipat	49.2	30.5	20.7	22.3	21.0	22.0	61	95
13.	Rewari	37.8	48.4	21.6	20.8	21.0	21.0	148	62
14.	Rohtak	19.2	21.0	22.8	23.1	22.5	23.0	52	105
15.	Sirsa	41.0	34.5	21.7	22.6	22.0	22.0	78	87
16.	Sonipat	48.3	25.2	21.4	22.8	21.0	22.0	58	123
17.	Yamunanagar	24.4	9.0	22.6	24.1	22.0	24.0	90	78
6	**Karnataka**								
1.	Bangalore	3.3	4.3	26.4	26.7	26.0	27.0	30	47
2.	Bangalore Rural	1.2	0.0	26.1	26.0	25.0	26.5	85	8
3.	Belgaum	28.4	13.0	22.9	25.2	22.0	25.0	67	54
4.	Bellary	17.1	3.6	23.8	27.6	23.0	26.5	105	28
5.	Bidar	36.5	28.9	22.0	22.9	21.5	22.0	52	97
6.	Bijapur	28.0	17.5	23.5	24.7	23.0	25.0	93	63
7.	Chikmagalur	26.8	2.6	24.7	27.4	25.0	27.0	41	116
8.	Chitradurga	14.2	5.0	24.9	27.4	24.5	28.0	134	40
9.	Dakshina Kannada	2.1	4.8	28.3	28.6	28.0	28.5	47	62
10.	Dharwad	16.1	5.8	24.2	26.1	24.0	26.0	62	52
11.	Gulbarga	43.1	20.9	21.8	23.8	21.5	24.0	58	67

Appendix - VIII (Continued)

Sr. No.	State/District	Age at Marriage < 21 years (%) SC/ST/ OBC	OC	Mean SC/ST OBC	OC	Median SC/ST OBC	OC	Total Number of marriages SC/ST OBC	OC
12.	Hassan	11.0	4.2	25.3	26.7	25.0	27.0	100	24
13.	Kodagu	6.1	6.8	25.2	28.8	25.0	28.0	33	73
14.	Kolar	15.9	0.0	24.0	27.7	24.0	27.0	126	15
15.	Mandya	5.9	6.6	25.2	25.8	25.0	25.0	51	61
16.	Mysore	4.1	2.6	25.5	27.5	25.0	27.0	73	39
17.	Raichur	33.3	29.9	22.2	23.3	22.0	23.0	60	97
18.	Shimoga	8.9	0.0	26.1	28.0	25.0	28.0	101	68
19.	Tumkur	9.4	2.2	24.9	25.6	24.0	25.0	64	46
20.	Uttara Kannada	3.8	2.0	26.8	30.1	26.0	30.0	80	50
7	**Kerala**								
1.	Alappuzha	2.9	0.0	28.2	28.8	28.0	28.0	105	49
2.	Ernakulam	0.0	0.0	28.4	30.1	28.0	30.0	38	30
3.	Idukki	3.9	5.1	25.3	27.2	25.0	28.0	76	39
4.	Kannur	0.0	0.0	30.1	31.3	30.0	31.0	78	6
5.	Kasaragod	2.4	0.0	27.3	29.2	27.0	30.0	85	24
6.	Kollam	1.3	2.4	28.8	29.0	28.0	28.0	79	42
7.	Kottayam	4.8	0.0	27.7	28.8	28.0	28.5	63	22
8.	Kozhikode	2.9	0.0	26.7	29.3	27.0	28.0	139	16
9.	Malappuram	4.8	0.0	26.9	28.0	26.0	28.0	42	5
10.	Palakkad	2.0	0.0	26.7	29.2	26.0	29.0	102	38
11.	Pathanamthitta	0.0	0.0	27.2	27.8	27.0	28.0	57	43
12.	Thiruvananthapuram	1.8	0.0	28.1	28.7	28.0	28.0	55	24
13.	Thrissur	1.2	0.0	29.0	30.2	28.0	29.0	84	48
14.	Wayanad	11.1	11.8	25.3	25.9	25.0	26.0	54	17
8	**Madhya Pradesh**								
1.	Balaghat	22.2	14.3	23.6	25.0	24.0	24.5	63	14
2.	Bastar	45.9	7.1	21.9	24.6	21.0	25.0	61	14
3.	Betul	13.8	14.3	24.0	24.3	25.0	24.5	58	14
4.	Bhind	64.6	40.9	20.4	21.8	20.0	21.0	82	88
5.	Bhopal	32.4	14.3	22.1	24.6	22.0	24.0	37	42
6.	Bilaspur(MP)	40.5	20.0	22.3	26.5	22.0	26.0	126	15
7.	Chattarpur	79.4	32.1	19.1	22.1	18.0	21.5	63	28
8.	Chhindwara	24.0	0.0	23.4	26.6	23.0	27.0	104	16
9.	Damoh	60.0	29.0	20.4	23.2	20.0	23.0	95	31
10.	Datia	63.7	32.4	20.4	23.0	20.0	23.5	124	34
11.	Dewas	61.1	37.0	20.4	22.9	20.0	22.0	126	54
12.	Dhar	54.8	34.8	20.7	23.0	20.0	22.0	146	23
13.	Durg	29.8	6.7	22.5	26.3	22.0	27.0	94	15
14.	East Nimar	40.2	13.5	21.8	24.7	21.0	24.5	107	52
15.	Guna	74.1	27.6	19.5	23.0	18.0	23.0	85	29
16.	Gwalior	39.3	13.3	21.9	24.1	21.0	24.0	61	45
17.	Hoshangabad	31.6	24.1	22.3	23.9	22.0	25.0	57	29
18.	Indore	34.8	17.6	22.7	24.0	22.0	24.0	92	51
19.	Jabalpur	27.4	6.5	22.6	26.0	23.0	26.0	62	31
20.	Jhabua	73.0	0.0	19.0	25.0	19.0	24.0	148	3
21.	Mandla	37.0	100.0	21.4	20.0	22.0	20.0	54	1
22.	Mandsaur	70.8	37.3	19.2	22.0	19.0	21.0	89	51
23.	Morena	72.7	61.1	19.0	19.4	18.0	19.0	66	54
24.	Narsimhapur	35.7	20.0	22.3	23.9	22.0	24.0	115	35
25.	Panna	83.7	37.5	18.9	21.6	20.0	22.0	49	16
26.	Raigarh(M P)	20.0	0.0	23.0	23.7	22.0	23.5	70	6

Appendix - VIII (Continued)

Sr. No.	State/District	< 21 years (%)		Age at Marriage Mean		Median		Total Number of marriages	
		SC/ST/ OBC	OC	SC/ST OBC	OC	SC/ST OBC	OC	SC/ST OBC	OC
27.	Raipur	45.1	37.5	21.3	23.6	21.0	23.5	51	8
28.	Raisen	33.0	17.2	21.8	22.8	22.0	22.0	97	29
29.	Rajgarh	63.7	39.1	19.1	22.1	19.0	22.0	102	46
30.	Rajnandgaon	41.0	0.0	22.1	24.8	21.0	25.0	117	5
31.	Ratlam	55.7	23.2	20.3	23.6	20.0	25.0	79	56
32.	Rewa	72.3	40.8	19.2	21.6	18.0	21.0	47	49
33.	Sagar	54.1	25.6	21.2	23.0	20.0	22.0	74	39
34.	Satna	72.0	45.7	19.9	21.4	20.0	21.0	93	46
35.	Sehore	49.4	42.1	21.2	22.3	21.0	21.0	87	38
36.	Seoni	23.8	0.0	22.7	25.1	22.0	24.0	63	9
37.	Shahdol	53.3	40.0	21.5	22.6	20.0	22.0	15	5
38.	Shajapur	65.6	55.3	19.7	20.7	19.0	20.0	93	47
39.	Shivpuri	72.3	38.5	19.6	21.8	19.0	21.0	94	26
40.	Sidhi	74.7	51.7	18.8	20.9	18.0	20.0	75	29
41.	Surguja	62.6	33.3	19.9	22.1	20.0	22.0	99	21
42.	Tikamgarh	82.0	28.6	18.6	24.1	18.0	25.0	111	14
43.	Ujjain	45.6	17.3	21.3	23.8	21.0	23.0	103	52
44.	Vidisha	61.3	30.2	20.1	22.9	20.0	22.0	111	43
45.	West Nimar	46.0	19.2	21.1	23.0	21.0	23.0	100	26
9	**Maharashtra**								
1.	Ahmadnagar	19.7	9.5	23.7	24.2	23.0	24.0	76	95
2.	Akola	15.3	14.5	23.6	23.8	24.0	23.0	98	55
3.	Amravali	2.9	14.3	25.3	25.4	25.0	25.5	69	14
4.	Aurangabad(Mah)	30.9	16.9	23.0	23.4	22.0	23.0	55	77
5.	Bhandara	2.0	0.0	25.7	25.9	25.0	25.0	98	11
6.	Bid	47.4	19.7	21.0	22.6	21.0	22.0	38	66
7.	Buldana	8.4	5.0	24.2	23.8	24.0	23.5	119	40
8.	Chandrapur	15.3	8.3	24.2	25.3	24.0	25.5	85	12
9.	Dhule	25.0	9.8	23.0	23.2	22.5	23.0	100	41
10.	Gadchiroli	21.4	0.0	23.3	24.7	23.0	24.5	103	6
11.	Greater Bombay (Mumbai)	7.9	4.0	26.5	26.2	25.0	26.0	38	101
12.	Jalgaon	27.6	15.8	22.9	23.9	22.0	24.0	76	57
13.	Jalna	37.7	29.4	22.2	22.7	22.0	22.0	61	85
14.	Kolhapur	11.5	9.3	24.7	25.0	25.0	25.0	52	118
15.	Latur	21.9	18.8	22.8	23.2	22.0	23.0	64	85
16.	Nagpur	2.4	3.1	25.9	25.5	25.0	25.0	124	32
17.	Nanded	35.5	27.6	22.0	23.1	22.0	22.0	76	58
18.	Nashik	25.4	21.3	22.4	23.5	22.0	23.0	63	94
19.	Osmanabad	27.1	11.5	23.6	24.0	24.0	23.0	59	78
20.	Parbhani	28.2	39.0	22.2	22.2	22.0	21.0	78	77
21.	Pune	11.3	8.4	23.7	25.0	24.0	25.0	71	95
22.	Raigarh (MAH)	4.2	9.4	24.6	23.7	25.0	23.0	72	32
23.	Ratnagiri	7.0	11.9	24.8	25.0	24.0	25.0	86	59
24.	Sangli	23.0	10.9	23.4	24.8	24.0	25.0	61	119
25.	Satara	11.9	5.3	23.9	24.9	24.0	24.0	42	75
26.	Sindhudurg	2.8	3.8	27.2	26.5	27.0	26.0	71	106
27.	Solapur	16.1	12.3	23.9	24.8	23.0	24.0	62	65
28.	Thane	13.0	7.5	24.3	25.0	24.5	25.0	54	53
29.	Wardha	3.1	0.0	26.3	26.6	26.0	26.0	96	12
30.	Yavatmal	13.1	3.6	24.3	24.8	24.5	25.0	130	28

Appendix - VIII (Continued)

Sr. No.	State/District	Age at Marriage < 21 years (%) SC/ST/OBC	OC	Mean SC/ST OBC	OC	Median SC/ST OBC	OC	Total Number of marriages SC/ST OBC	OC
10	**Orissa**								
1.	Anugul	21.0	20.7	23.4	24.7	22.0	25.0	81	29
2.	Balangir	34.3	5.0	22.5	26.6	22.0	27.5	102	20
3.	Balasore	9.6	2.0	25.3	27.1	25.0	27.0	94	51
4.	Bargarh	20.9	0.0	23.4	26.8	23.0	27.0	110	10
5.	Baudh	34.7	0.0	22.5	27.1	22.0	28.0	118	9
6.	Bhadrak	13.6	1.5	25.7	26.4	26.0	26.0	81	67
7.	Cuttack	10.7	6.0	25.2	26.8	25.0	27.0	103	67
8.	Debagarh	15.1	0.0	24.4	26.6	24.5	25.5	106	14
9.	Dhenkanal	17.6	4.7	24.9	25.9	25.0	25.5	85	64
10.	Gajapati	20.2	0.0	23.6	28.3	23.5	28.0	124	15
11.	Ganjam	15.7	11.4	24.6	25.1	25.0	25.0	108	44
12.	Jagatsinghapur	1.5	1.3	26.5	26.6	26.5	27.0	66	78
13.	Jajapur	1.4	2.8	25.6	27.1	25.0	27.0	73	36
14.	Jharsuguda	14.1	9.1	24.1	24.1	24.0	24.0	92	11
15.	Kalahandi	43.4	11.8	21.9	26.3	21.0	26.0	99	17
16.	Kendrapara	3.1	3.2	25.8	26.1	26.0	26.0	128	62
17.	Kendujhar	15.4	0.0	24.3	27.4	24.0	26.0	123	7
18.	Khordha	8.4	3.8	25.0	26.5	24.0	26.0	83	52
19.	Koraput	57.6	10.0	20.9	25.7	20.0	26.0	99	20
20.	Malkangiri	53.8	25.0	21.4	25.0	20.0	25.5	106	4
21.	Mayurbhanj	22.6	7.7	23.9	26.4	23.0	26.0	106	26
22.	Nabarangapur	47.2	27.8	22.4	22.7	21.0	22.0	89	18
23.	Nayagarh	15.7	7.9	24.2	24.6	24.0	25.0	121	38
24.	Nuapada	32.1	10.0	22.6	25.8	22.0	25.0	81	20
25.	Phulbani	32.4	38.5	23.6	22.5	24.0	21.0	102	13
26.	Puri	17.9	5.3	23.8	26.5	23.0	26.0	56	114
27.	Rayagada	31.4	8.3	22.8	26.5	22.0	26.5	121	12
28.	Sambalpur	8.3	0.0	25.0	28.7	24.0	27.5	96	20
29.	Sonapur	18.2	0.0	23.7	25.4	23.0	25.0	99	16
30.	Sundargarh	9.4	0.0	24.6	27.9	25.0	28.0	85	21
11	**Punjab**								
1.	Amritsar	21.3	15.9	23.5	23.9	23.0	24.0	61	107
2.	Bathinda	39.7	20.7	22.1	23.0	22.0	22.0	68	121
3.	Faridkot	36.5	25.7	22.2	23.1	22.0	22.0	85	101
4.	Fatehgarh Sahib	19.3	18.6	23.0	22.8	22.0	22.0	88	97
5.	Firozpur	48.5	26.6	21.7	22.9	21.0	22.5	97	124
6.	Gurdaspur	11.3	10.8	24.7	24.7	25.0	25.0	62	102
7.	Hoshiarpur	7.7	4.5	24.9	26.2	25.0	26.0	104	67
8.	Jalandhar	16.5	5.6	23.9	25.6	24.0	25.0	79	71
9.	Kapurthala	16.4	12.4	23.7	24.7	23.0	25.0	73	89
10.	Ludhiana	18.2	7.8	23.5	24.5	23.0	25.0	55	77
11.	Mansa	29.7	33.3	22.4	22.1	22.0	22.0	74	108
12.	Moga	39.2	14.1	22.4	24.6	22.0	25.0	74	92
13.	Muktsar	50.0	19.5	21.3	23.9	20.5	23.0	98	77
14.	Nawanshahr	13.0	7.1	24.3	24.4	25.0	24.0	123	42
15.	Patiala	28.9	20.5	22.3	23.1	22.0	23.0	76	117
16.	Rupnagar	21.0	4.8	23.7	24.7	24.0	25.0	81	84
17.	Sangrur	25.0	29.2	22.7	23.0	22.0	22.0	72	106
12	**Rajasthan**								
1.	Ajmer	51.7	25.6	20.5	23.3	20.0	23.0	58	43

Appendix - VIII (Continued)

Sr. No.	State/District	< 21 years (%)		Age at Marriage Mean		Median		Total Number of marriages	
		SC/ST/ OBC	OC	SC/ST OBC	OC	SC/ST OBC	OC	SC/ST OBC	OC
2.	Alwar	75.0	37.8	19.0	22.0	19.0	22.0	84	82
3.	Banswara	77.6	38.9	18.9	21.8	18.0	22.0	107	36
4.	Barmer	61.6	52.7	20.2	20.7	20.0	20.0	73	93
5.	Bharatpur	61.3	48.5	19.9	21.3	20.0	21.0	62	99
6.	Bhilwara	72.4	38.1	19.1	22.2	18.0	22.5	58	42
7.	Bikaner	48.9	55.2	21.2	21.2	21.0	20.0	47	96
8.	Bundi	83.5	47.1	18.3	21.0	18.0	21.0	79	34
9.	Chittaurgarh	81.4	44.8	18.5	21.4	18.0	21.0	43	29
10.	Churu	69.4	58.9	19.6	20.4	20.0	20.0	85	107
11.	Dausa	75.2	31.0	19.1	22.1	19.0	22.0	129	29
12.	Dhaulpur	70.4	53.6	19.4	20.6	19.0	20.0	81	56
13.	Dungarpur	62.4	29.9	20.5	22.4	20.0	22.0	93	87
14.	Ganganagar	67.9	48.2	20.0	21.0	20.0	21.0	53	110
15.	Hanumangarh	69.0	57.8	19.9	20.5	20.0	20.0	84	109
16.	Jaipur	64.2	29.8	19.7	22.1	19.0	22.0	53	84
17.	Jaisalmer	39.0	36.1	21.9	22.1	21.0	22.0	41	61
18.	Jalor	63.7	52.1	19.8	20.9	20.0	20.0	102	96
19.	Jhalawar	70.6	50.8	19.2	21.2	18.0	20.0	68	63
20.	Jhunjhunun	44.2	26.3	21.2	22.3	21.0	22.0	86	80
21.	Jodhpur	54.2	35.1	21.2	22.2	20.0	22.0	48	74
22.	Kota	66.3	25.6	19.8	23.4	20.0	23.0	80	39
23.	Nagaur	60.0	51.3	20.4	20.7	20.0	20.0	70	76
24.	Pali	52.4	44.6	20.4	21.0	20.0	21.0	84	74
25.	Rajsamand	68.2	38.9	20.3	21.4	20.0	21.0	44	72
26.	Sawai Madhopur	65.6	43.3	19.1	21.2	19.0	22.0	61	30
27.	Sikar	44.6	38.9	20.8	21.9	21.0	21.5	74	72
28.	Sirohi	42.9	20.0	21.5	23.8	21.0	24.0	56	30
29.	Tonk	72.0	48.9	19.4	20.6	20.0	21.0	50	47
30.	Udaipur	76.6	43.9	19.4	22.1	19.0	21.0	64	66
13	**Tamil Nadu**								
1.	Chengalpattu	7.4	0.0	25.3	31.8	25.0	30.0	135	5
2.	Chennai	4.4	0.0	26.5	29.1	26.0	29.5	91	8
3.	Coimbatore	8.7	0.0	26.3	26.1	27.0	26.0	69	8
4.	Dharmapuri	14.2	0.0	24.5	28.5	25.0	28.5	162	2
5.	Dindigul	7.1	0.0	25.7	23.0	26.0	23.0	113	1
6.	Kanniyakumari	0.9	0.0	27.8	28.8	28.0	29.0	109	30
7.	Madurai	8.3	0.0	26.5	32.0	27.0	32.0	108	1
8.	Namakkal	9.5	**	26.1	NA	25.0	NA	95	**
9.	North Arcot	8.1	0.0	25.6	24.3	25.0	25.0	135	6
10.	Periyar	5.6	20.0	26.6	24.0	26.0	25.0	72	5
11.	Pudukkottai	9.9	0.0	25.7	26.0	25.0	26.0	121	1
12.	Ramanathapuram	6.0	50.0	25.1	26.0	25.0	26.0	84	2
13.	Salem	9.1	0.0	25.3	21.0	25.0	21.0	132	1
14.	Sivaganganagar	4.4	0.0	25.8	32.0	26.0	31.0	136	4
15.	South Arcot	11.9	0.0	25.2	28.7	25.0	27.0	109	3
16.	Thanjavur	6.9	0.0	26.7	30.3	26.0	30.0	101	8
17.	The Nilgiris	1.7	0.0	27.6	27.5	28.0	27.5	60	2
18.	Theni	12.3	**	25.5	NA	25.0	NA	73	**
19.	Tiruchirappalli	5.7	0.0	27.8	30.0	27.0	29.0	87	7
20.	Tirunelveli	0.0	0.0	26.1	30.0	25.0	30.0	97	1

Appendix - VIII (Continued)

Sr. No.	State/District	< 21 years (%) SC/ST/ OBC	< 21 years (%) OC	Age at Marriage Mean SC/ST OBC	Mean OC	Median SC/ST OBC	Median OC	Total Number of marriages SC/ST OBC	Total Number of marriages OC
21.	Tiruvanamalai	13.5	0.0	25.0	27.4	25.0	26.0	126	5
22.	Tutikorin	3.7	0.0	26.6	29.0	27.0	29.0	109	1
23.	Virudhunagar	10.1	0.0	25.3	31.0	25.0	31.0	129	1
14	**Uttar Pradesh**								
1.	Agra	55.6	25.8	20.6	23.1	20.0	23.0	90	62
2.	Aligarh	49.5	41.3	21.0	21.6	21.0	21.0	97	75
3.	Allahabad	62.1	56.1	20.5	21.2	20.0	20.0	95	41
4.	Almora	6.3	2.4	23.1	24.2	22.0	24.0	16	83
5.	Ambedkarnagar	71.3	47.4	18.9	22.4	18.0	21.0	87	19
6.	Azamgarh	74.2	42.5	19.5	21.5	19.0	22.0	97	40
7.	Bahraich	75.3	64.1	18.9	20.7	19.0	20.0	89	39
8.	Ballia	63.8	9.3	20.0	24.5	20.0	24.0	58	43
9.	Banda	75.7	51.7	19.5	21.3	19.0	20.0	74	60
10.	Barabanki	72.8	43.8	19.6	21.8	20.0	21.0	103	48
11.	Bareilly	43.3	51.6	20.9	21.5	21.0	20.0	30	62
12.	Basti	71.8	54.2	19.2	20.8	18.0	20.0	78	59
13.	Bhadohi	81.5	63.6	18.8	19.9	18.0	20.0	135	44
14.	Bijnor	24.6	25.4	22.2	22.9	22.0	22.0	65	71
15.	Budaun	62.1	47.1	20.0	21.0	20.0	21.0	103	51
16.	Bulandshahar	56.0	20.8	21.0	22.5	20.0	22.0	116	106
17.	Chamoli	12.5	11.4	22.6	24.1	21.0	24.0	8	79
18.	Dehradun	14.3	6.0	24.1	25.2	24.0	25.0	35	83
19.	Deoria	86.0	48.9	18.8	22.0	18.0	21.0	93	45
20.	Etah	57.4	37.1	20.8	21.5	20.0	22.0	54	70
21.	Etawah	45.8	27.8	21.2	23.1	21.0	23.0	107	54
22.	Faizabad	77.3	58.7	18.4	20.7	18.0	20.0	66	46
23.	Farrukhabad	48.5	40.6	21.1	21.9	21.0	21.0	99	64
24.	Fatehpur	52.1	37.3	21.1	22.1	20.0	22.0	119	59
25.	Firozabad	63.2	36.7	20.5	22.4	20.0	22.0	106	49
26.	Ghaziabad	44.0	17.9	21.2	23.3	21.0	24.0	75	67
27.	Ghazipur	69.4	21.9	19.7	23.7	19.0	23.5	98	32
28.	Gonda	77.3	66.3	19.0	19.6	18.0	19.5	66	86
29.	Gorakhpur	72.5	23.5	19.1	23.3	18.0	24.5	80	34
30.	Hamirpur (UP)	69.7	27.6	20.1	22.3	20.0	22.0	109	29
31.	Hardoi	63.5	42.3	20.5	21.5	20.0	21.0	52	52
32.	Hardwar	31.6	12.5	22.2	23.4	22.0	23.0	95	32
33.	Hathras	50.9	37.3	20.9	22.1	20.0	22.0	108	51
34.	Jalaun	63.9	39.1	20.3	21.9	20.0	22.0	72	46
35.	Jaunpur	66.4	55.4	19.4	20.6	19.0	20.0	122	74
36.	Jhansi	70.3	35.0	19.8	23.1	20.0	23.0	74	40
37.	Kanpur Dehat	50.6	12.1	21.4	22.8	20.0	23.0	79	33
38.	Kanpur Nagar	39.6	15.6	22.1	23.9	22.0	24.0	53	64
39.	Kheri	71.4	50.0	20.1	21.4	20.0	20.5	98	44
40.	Lalitpur	84.6	60.0	18.2	21.6	18.0	20.0	104	20
41.	Lucknow	57.4	16.2	20.7	24.9	20.0	25.0	68	37
42.	Maharajganj	87.7	46.2	17.8	21.5	17.0	21.0	57	13
43.	Mahoba	69.5	39.0	19.5	21.8	19.0	21.0	105	41
44.	Mainpuri	63.4	45.7	20.7	22.1	20.0	22.0	134	35
45.	Mathura	53.6	42.2	20.8	22.0	20.0	22.0	84	109
46.	Mau	64.4	38.1	20.2	22.0	20.0	22.0	104	42
47.	Meerut	25.5	36.0	21.7	21.6	22.0	21.0	55	75

Appendix - VIII (Continued)

Sr. No.	State/District	< 21 years (%)		Age at Marriage Mean		Median		Total Number of marriages	
		SC/ST/ OBC	OC	SC/ST OBC	OC	SC/ST OBC	OC	SC/ST OBC	OC
48.	Mirzapur	70.4	59.0	19.9	20.5	20.0	20.0	98	39
49.	Muradabad	52.8	29.6	20.9	22.5	20.0	22.0	89	54
50.	Muzaffarnagar	40.2	21.1	21.0	23.2	21.0	22.0	82	71
51.	Nainital	28.6	18.4	22.5	24.4	22.0	24.0	35	103
52.	Pauri Garhwal	0.0	9.0	24.6	24.7	24.0	25.0	17	89
53.	Pilibhit	71.3	26.8	19.7	22.8	19.0	22.0	115	41
54.	Pithoragarh	27.8	18.5	22.6	23.2	22.0	23.0	18	81
55.	Pratapgarh	81.6	59.6	19.2	21.1	18.0	20.0	103	52
56.	Rae Bareli	75.3	42.6	19.6	21.4	20.0	21.0	73	54
57.	Rampur	46.3	27.3	21.2	22.5	21.0	22.0	80	33
58.	Saharanpur	31.1	30.9	21.8	22.5	21.5	21.0	74	55
59.	Shajahanabad	65.9	53.6	19.9	20.9	20.0	20.0	91	56
60.	Siddharthnagar	93.5	65.6	17.0	20.2	16.0	20.0	31	32
61.	Sitapur	64.4	45.5	20.2	21.8	20.0	21.0	101	33
62.	Sonbhadra	64.4	48.1	19.9	21.1	19.0	21.0	59	27
63.	Sultanpur	74.0	56.3	19.0	20.1	19.0	20.0	77	48
64.	Tehri Garhwal	9.1	17.6	24.0	23.2	24.0	22.0	11	91
65.	Udhamsingh Nagar	41.6	25.0	21.6	22.7	21.0	22.0	77	56
66.	Unnao	59.2	48.3	20.8	21.6	20.0	21.0	71	29
67.	Uttarkashi	36.4	23.7	21.6	23.1	22.0	22.0	11	76
68.	Varanasi	66.3	42.5	20.0	22.8	20.0	22.0	80	40
15	**West Bengal**								
1.	Bankura	21.1	15.2	24.1	24.6	24.0	24.0	71	79
2.	Barddhaman	43.7	14.3	22.4	26.3	22.0	25.0	87	98
3.	Birbhum	33.9	21.7	21.6	24.8	21.5	25.0	62	69
4.	Dakshin Dinajpur	26.9	19.6	24.0	25.2	24.0	25.0	67	56
5.	Darjiling	25.7	20.3	24.5	25.1	24.0	25.0	74	79
6.	Haora	5.7	12.8	25.9	26.1	26.0	25.0	35	109
7.	Hugli	31.7	8.1	23.3	26.6	23.0	26.0	63	99
8.	Jalpaiguri	26.2	22.4	23.7	25.0	23.0	25.0	103	49
9.	Koch Bihar	21.9	29.8	23.7	23.7	24.0	24.0	73	57
10.	Kolkata	18.2	10.0	25.4	27.4	24.0	27.5	22	90
11.	Maldah	20.3	27.1	23.9	23.7	24.0	22.0	74	59
12.	Medinipur	28.8	14.5	23.9	24.0	24.0	24.0	52	110
13.	Murshidabad	39.0	45.4	21.6	22.0	21.0	21.0	41	141
14.	Nadia	23.4	14.6	24.2	25.1	23.0	25.0	47	96
15.	North 24 Parganas	16.7	13.9	25.5	26.4	24.5	26.0	24	108
16.	Puruliya	27.2	32.2	23.6	23.3	22.5	23.0	92	59
17.	South 24 Parganas	19.7	25.8	24.8	23.4	25.0	22.0	61	89
18.	Uttar Dinajpur	22.0	24.7	24.6	23.9	24.0	24.0	59	73
16	**Andaman & Nicobar**								
1.	Andaman	0.0	3.8	25.4	25.9	25.0	26.0	17	26
2.	Nicobar	0.0	0.0	27.5	28.2	26.5	26.5	66	6
17	**Arunachal Pradesh**								
1.	Changlang	31.3	22.2	23.6	22.8	22.5	22.0	48	9
2.	Dibang Valley	34.5	12.5	22.6	27.1	22.0	28.0	29	8
3.	East Kameng	58.5	0.0	21.2	27.6	20.0	28.0	41	5
4.	East Siang	58.1	33.3	21.4	23.3	20.0	22.0	43	3
5.	Lohit	32.4	0.0	23.3	24.3	23.0	23.5	34	4
6.	Lower Subansiri	40.6	0.0	22.8	25.5	21.5	25.5	32	2

Appendix - VIII (Continued)

Sr. No.	State/District	Age at Marriage < 21 years (%) SC/ST/OBC	< 21 years (%) OC	Mean SC/ST OBC	Mean OC	Median SC/ST OBC	Median OC	Total Number of marriages SC/ST OBC	Total Number of marriages OC
7.	Papum Pare	41.7	0.0	23.1	24.0	21.5	24.0	24	1
8.	Tawang	10.0	0.0	24.0	29.0	24.0	28.0	20	6
9.	Tirap	18.8	0.0	24.1	25.0	24.5	25.0	16	1
10.	Upper Siang	21.7	**	22.9	NA	23.0	NA	23	**
11.	Upper Subansiri	25.4	20.0	23.2	28.8	23.0	30.0	63	5
12.	West Kameng	36.4	25.0	22.8	24.4	21.0	24.5	33	8
13.	West Siang	18.2	0.0	25.0	24.0	25.0	24.0	44	1
18	**Chandigarh**								
1.	Chandigarh	28.6	4.3	21.9	25.5	22.0	26.0	7	46
19	**Dadra & Nagar Haveli**								
1.	Dadra & Nagar Havel	53.8	18.2	20.9	23.0	20.0	23.5	93	22
20	**Daman & Diu**								
1.	Daman	14.3	10.3	24.1	25.1	24.0	25.0	98	39
2.	Diu	22.0	6.4	23.9	25.0	23.0	24.0	100	47
21	**Delhi**								
1.	Delhi	31.8	6.4	22.6	24.9	22.0	25.0	22	78
22	**Goa**								
1.	North Goa	0.0	1.5	29.1	29.5	29.0	30.0	26	67
2.	South Goa	7.7	1.4	27.6	28.4	25.0	28.0	13	72
23	**Himachal Pradesh**								
1.	Bilaspur (Pra. Him.)	7.1	5.2	25.0	24.9	24.0	25.0	28	116
2.	Chamba	7.2	5.7	23.8	25.4	23.0	25.0	69	106
3.	Hamirpur (HP)	15.2	3.6	24.2	25.7	24.0	26.0	33	139
4.	Kangra	1.7	1.1	26.1	26.3	26.0	26.0	59	93
5.	Kinnaur	17.5	7.7	23.8	25.2	23.0	25.0	63	39
6.	Kullu	22.7	10.5	23.4	24.6	23.0	24.5	22	86
7.	Lahul & Spiti	14.0	0.0	25.2	24.6	24.0	24.5	57	16
8.	Mandi	7.4	3.5	24.1	25.0	24.0	25.0	54	114
9.	Shimla	18.2	5.3	24.8	26.4	25.5	26.5	22	94
10.	Sirmaur	15.8	11.8	23.6	24.2	24.0	24.0	57	93
11.	Solan	8.3	8.5	23.1	24.6	23.0	25.0	36	142
12.	Una	3.1	1.0	25.3	26.3	25.0	26.0	65	100
24	**Jammu & Kashmir**								
1.	Anantanag	8.7	0.0	25.2	24.0	25.0	23.0	23	3
2.	Badgam	33.3	15.4	22.4	23.5	22.0	23.0	15	13
3.	Baramula	10.8	20.7	26.6	24.9	25.0	25.0	37	29
4.	Doda	0.0	2.0	27.1	26.3	26.0	26.0	17	50
5.	Jammu	0.0	0.0	27.2	26.9	26.0	27.0	17	47
6.	Kargil	13.4	**	23.6	NA	24.0	NA	82	**
7.	Kathua	0.0	1.2	27.0	28.9	27.0	29.0	23	84
8.	Kupwara	33.3	4.3	22.8	26.3	22.0	26.0	21	23
9.	Leh	16.4	**	24.1	NA	24.0	NA	55	**
10.	Pulwama	42.9	17.4	22.6	23.2	24.0	23.0	7	23
11.	Punch	4.3	2.4	24.1	24.7	24.0	24.0	23	42
12.	Rajauri	1.4	0.0	23.8	23.3	24.0	23.0	71	36
13.	Srinagar	25.0	31.8	21.5	21.2	22.5	22.0	4	22
14.	Udhampur	5.3		23.2	25.1	23.0	25.0	57	31

Appendix - VIII (Continued)

Sr. No.	State/District	< 21 years (%)		Age at Marriage Mean		Median		Total Number of marriages	
		SC/ST/ OBC	OC	SC/ST OBC	OC	SC/ST OBC	OC	SC/ST OBC	OC
25	**Lakshadweep**								
1.	Lakshadweep	9.2	**	25.7	NA	26.0	NA	98	**
26	**Manipur**								
1.	Bishnupur	17.0	18.5	26.0	25.9	25.0	25.0	47	81
2.	Chandel	21.6	0.0	24.8	26.0	25.0	26.0	74	1
3.	Churachandpur	14.3	22.2	25.6	24.3	25.0	23.0	98	9
4.	Imphal	0.0	13.0	29.2	27.9	28.0	27.0	13	77
5.	Senapati	21.2	0.0	25.3	25.8	25.0	26.0	52	4
6.	Tamenglong	24.0	**	24.6	NA	24.0	NA	104	**
7.	Thoubal	22.2	14.7	24.7	25.8	23.0	25.0	36	109
8.	Ukhrul	17.0	100.0	26.8	18.0	27.0	18.0	53	1
27	**Meghalaya**								
1.	East Garo Hills	39.4	50.0	22.5	25.0	23.0	25.0	33	2
2.	East Khasi Hills	52.9	**	20.9	NA	20.0	NA	17	**
3.	Jaintia Hills	0.0	**	25.4	NA	26.0	NA	15	**
4.	Ri Bhoi	68.6	**	20.2	NA	20.0	NA	35	**
5.	West Garo Hills	50.0	**	22.0	NA	21.5	NA	4	**
6.	West Khasi Hills	51.3	**	21.3	NA	20.0	NA	39	**
28	**Mizoram**								
1.	Aizwal	23.9	**	24.5	NA	24.0	NA	134	**
2.	Chhimtuipui	26.5	0.0	23.9	25.0	24.0	25.0	49	1
3.	Lunglei	12.3	**	26.3	NA	25.0	NA	65	**
29	**Nagaland**								
1.	Kohima	69.4	**	20.0	NA	20.0	NA	49	**
2.	Mokokchung	9.4	**	25.2	NA	24.0	NA	32	**
3.	Mon	25.0		22.7	27.5	22.0	27.5	80	2
4.	Phek	31.6	**	22.1	NA	22.0	NA	19	**
5.	Tuensang	4.7	**	24.9	NA	24.0	NA	85	**
6.	Wokha	7.8	0.0	25.1	22.0	25.0	22.0	51	1
7.	Zunheboto	32.3	**	22.3	NA	22.0	NA	124	**
30	**Pondicherry**								
1.	Karaikal	4.3	0.0	26.5	25.0	26.0	25.0	94	1
2.	Mahe	1.1	0.0	29.6	31.9	29.0	30.0	179	7
3.	Pondicherry	0.8	0.0	27.5	28.8	27.0	29.0	126	4
4.	Yanam	17.0	0.0	24.5	25.5	24.0	24.5	53	14
31	**Sikkim**								
1.	East Sikkim	13.3	5.0	25.8	25.8	25.0	26.0	60	60
2.	North Sikkim	30.2	18.2	24.4	24.9	24.0	25.0	53	11
3.	South Sikkim	26.7	27.8	24.2	22.9	25.0	22.0	15	18
4.	West Sikkim	20.6	21.4	23.9	24.3	23.0	24.0	63	28
32	**Tripura**								
1.	North Tripura	8.8	7.9	27.5	27.4	28.0	27.0	68	63
2.	South Tripura	12.3	2.6	25.4	28.7	25.0	29.0	57	76
3.	West Tripura	4.3	8.0	27.9	29.1	27.5	30.0	70	75

Note: In the column showing percent of marriages below legal minimum age, 0.0 indicates no marriage below 21 years.

** No marriage is reported in that category of characteristic/district.

NA Not applicable.

APPENDIX - IX

Percent of Marriages below legal Minimum Age of 21 years and Average Age at Marriage in each District by Economic status-BOYS

Sr. No.	State/District	Age at marriage: < 21 years (%) Economic status			Mean Economic status			Median Economic status			Total number of marriages Economic status		
		Low	Medium	High	Low	Medium	High	Low	Medium	High	Low	Medium	High
1	**Andhra Pradesh**												
1.	Adilabad	31.6	36.4	13.3	22.4	22.1	24.1	22.0	22.0	24.0	38	55	15
2.	Anantapur	33.3	21.9	8.0	22.9	23.7	25.8	23.0	24.0	25.0	24	32	25
3.	Chittoor	26.3	11.8	13.6	23.3	27.0	25.2	24.0	25.0	26.0	19	17	22
4.	Cuddapah	21.4	26.7	17.6	23.4	22.0	23.9	24.0	22.0	23.0	28	15	34
5.	East Godavari	36.4	28.6	20.0	21.7	22.7	23.0	21.5	22.0	22.0	22	35	25
6.	Guntur	53.6	18.5	15.4	20.9	22.4	23.7	20.0	22.0	23.0	28	27	26
7.	Hyderabad	0.0	6.7	0.0	27.0	25.0	26.7	26.0	25.0	26.0	3	15	97
8.	Karimnagar	52.9	39.4	9.1	21.2	21.7	24.6	20.0	22.0	25.0	17	33	11
9.	Khammam	29.6	37.5	20.0	22.1	22.7	23.3	22.0	23.0	24.0	27	24	15
10.	Krishna	51.4	35.9	33.3	21.7	22.4	23.5	20.0	22.0	23.0	72	39	42
11.	Kurnool	23.8	39.1	14.3	22.4	22.8	24.5	23.0	22.0	25.0	21	23	56
12.	Mahbubnagar	46.2	50.0	34.6	21.5	21.2	23.1	22.0	20.5	23.5	13	34	26
13.	Medak	50.0	35.7	21.0	21.0	22.0	23.6	21.0	21.0	23.0	6	28	81
14.	Nalgonda	51.4	40.3	32.6	21.6	21.8	22.6	20.0	22.0	23.0	37	72	43
15.	Nellore	27.6	37.5	10.3	22.8	22.8	23.8	22.0	22.0	23.0	29	16	39
16.	Nizamabad	42.9	48.0	33.9	21.6	21.8	22.5	21.5	21.0	22.0	14	25	62
17.	Prakasam	26.9	31.8	19.0	22.7	22.9	23.8	22.5	22.0	25.0	26	22	21
18.	Rangareddi	57.1	17.7	7.8	20.5	23.6	25.0	20.0	24.0	25.0	14	62	64
19.	Srikakulam	30.9	18.2	13.0	22.3	24.3	24.2	22.0	24.0	24.0	55	44	23
20.	Vishkhapatanam	50.0	39.3	22.0	21.1	22.3	24.4	21.0	23.0	25.0	20	28	50
21.	Vizianagaram	40.5	23.1	19.0	22.3	22.8	23.0	22.0	23.0	23.0	42	26	21
22.	Warangal	46.4	41.7	25.0	21.0	21.1	23.5	21.5	21.5	24.0	28	48	20
23.	West Godavari	48.7	14.5	11.5	21.6	23.3	24.7	21.0	23.0	25.0	39	55	26
2	**Assam**												
1.	Barpeta	6.5	0.0	0.0	26.7	28.5	28.5	27.0	29.0	28.5	92	66	4

Appendix - IX (Continued)

Sr. No.	State/District	Age at marriage: < 21 years (%) Economic status: Low	Medium	High	Mean Economic status: Low	Medium	High	Median Economic status: Low	Medium	High	Total number of marriages Economic status: Low	Medium	High
2.	Bongaigaon	20.0	4.0	0.0	25.1	27.1	28.2	26.0	28.0	28.0	70	25	11
3.	Cachar	7.0	0.0	0.0	27.5	31.2	30.6	27.0	31.0	30.5	57	27	14
4.	Darrang	4.3	11.8	10.0	27.8	28.6	26.1	28.0	29.0	26.5	69	17	10
5.	Dhemaji	1.2	3.0	0.0	27.6	28.0	28.8	28.0	29.0	30.0	241	66	15
6.	Dhubri	4.5	0.0	0.0	25.9	27.8	27.8	26.0	28.0	27.5	112	24	12
7.	Dibrugarh	58.8	27.3	0.0	22.5	25.0	28.5	20.0	25.0	28.5	17	11	12
8.	Goalpara	16.5	6.1	0.0	26.1	27.1	30.6	26.0	28.0	30.0	85	33	13
9.	Golaghat	15.7	0.0	4.0	24.9	28.5	30.0	25.0	28.0	31.0	108	11	25
10.	Hailakandi	6.8	0.0	0.0	28.6	30.7	31.0	28.0	31.0	29.0	59	20	7
11.	Jorhat	5.2	0.0	0.0	27.0	28.3	30.0	27.0	28.0	30.0	97	119	23
12.	Kamrup	10.3	2.1	1.7	25.9	28.5	30.3	26.0	29.0	30.0	68	47	58
13.	Karbi Anglong	17.0	10.5	0.0	22.3	22.3	25.3	21.0	21.0	23.0	88	19	3
14.	Karimganj	3.2	6.7	0.0	28.6	31.7	32.6	27.0	30.5	32.0	94	30	19
15.	Lakhimpur	7.4	14.3	0.0	27.0	27.4	31.9	26.0	26.0	32.0	27	7	9
16.	Marigaon	10.5	3.2	7.4	26.0	28.0	27.3	26.0	29.0	28.0	133	62	27
17.	Nagaon	15.4	4.2	3.8	24.8	26.8	26.8	25.0	26.5	26.0	143	24	26
18.	Nalbari	6.3	0.0	6.3	27.7	29.6	28.3	28.0	30.0	29.5	32	76	16
19.	North Cachar Hills	25.9	6.7	6.7	23.6	24.7	25.6	25.0	25.0	25.0	27	30	15
20.	Sibsagar	16.0	20.0	0.0	26.4	27.1	29.2	27.0	27.5	30.0	25	10	25
21.	Sonitpur	13.2	7.7	5.3	25.4	26.3	29.3	25.0	26.0	30.0	91	13	19
22.	Tinsukia	20.3	33.3	9.1	24.5	23.6	28.4	24.5	22.0	28.0	74	33	22
3	**Bihar**												
1.	Araria	36.7	33.3	0.0	22.3	22.9	25.0	22.0	22.0	25.0	139	9	7
2.	Aurangabad(Bih)	70.6	56.1	41.7	19.9	20.9	22.1	19.0	20.0	22.0	143	57	24
3.	Begusarai	58.9	43.2	36.2	20.3	21.6	21.6	20.0	21.0	22.0	73	95	47
4.	Bhagalpur	44.2	32.1	7.1	22.6	23.2	25.0	21.0	23.0	25.0	86	53	28
5.	Bhojpur	72.4	51.3	51.6	19.7	21.4	20.9	19.0	20.0	20.0	98	39	62
6.	Buxar	60.4	43.9	33.3	20.4	21.6	22.2	20.0	21.0	23.0	96	66	39

Appendix - IX (Continued)

Sr. No.	State/District	Age at marriage: < 21 years (%) Economic status			Mean Economic status			Median Economic status			Total number of marriages Economic status		
		Low	Medium	High	Low	Medium	High	Low	Medium	High	Low	Medium	High
7.	Darbhanga	53.8	32.9	17.6	21.1	22.2	23.2	20.0	22.0	22.5	104	76	34
8.	Deoghar	53.8	57.1	12.5	20.8	20.5	25.3	20.0	20.0	25.0	106	21	24
9.	Dhanbad	47.4	21.4	27.8	21.2	23.5	22.9	21.0	24.5	22.5	57	14	36
10.	Dumka	30.5	25.0	0.0	22.7	22.3	26.5	22.0	22.5	26.0	131	4	8
11.	Gaya	68.3	60.0	25.0	19.4	20.3	22.0	19.0	20.0	22.0	82	35	44
12.	Giridih	56.7	44.8	42.1	20.8	21.7	22.1	20.0	22.0	21.0	134	29	19
13.	Godda	28.9	12.5	23.8	22.9	24.6	22.5	22.0	24.5	22.0	83	16	21
14.	Gopalganj	75.0	60.7	35.9	19.6	20.4	21.9	19.5	20.0	22.0	76	61	78
15.	Gulma	21.1	11.1	0.0	23.6	25.4	24.8	24.0	25.0	26.0	109	9	5
16.	Hazaribagh	39.1	44.1	24.0	21.5	21.1	24.0	21.5	21.0	23.0	110	34	25
17.	Jehanabad	71.6	57.6	37.5	19.6	20.5	22.5	19.0	20.0	22.0	81	66	56
18.	Katihar	41.2	14.3	0.0	22.0	26.4	27.2	22.0	24.0	25.5	114	7	12
19.	Khagaria	56.2	35.2	31.4	21.3	21.8	22.7	20.0	22.0	22.0	73	54	35
20.	Kishanganj	20.4	20.0	40.0	23.8	27.4	24.7	24.0	26.0	25.0	137	5	10
21.	Lohardaga	23.8	0.0	0.0	22.8	25.3	26.5	22.0	25.0	26.0	101	12	6
22.	Madhepura	63.4	17.4	16.7	20.7	23.0	24.0	20.0	22.0	24.5	112	23	12
23.	Madhubani	61.2	44.4	22.2	20.4	21.7	23.9	20.0	21.0	24.0	129	36	18
24.	Munger	76.9	53.8	32.1	19.4	21.3	22.1	19.0	20.0	21.0	78	39	28
25.	Muzaffarpur	44.9	36.4	28.6	21.5	22.0	22.8	21.0	22.0	23.5	98	44	28
26.	Nalanda	63.3	50.0	34.4	20.1	21.5	23.1	20.0	20.5	22.5	79	56	32
27.	Nawada	72.2	75.0	49.2	19.2	19.5	21.1	18.0	19.5	21.0	90	48	59
28.	Palamu	66.9	27.8	20.0	20.1	22.7	26.2	20.0	22.5	29.0	133	18	5
29.	Pashchim Champaran	61.5	44.2	30.6	21.2	21.2	22.9	20.0	21.0	22.0	39	43	85
30.	Pashchmi Singhbhum	28.2	11.1	0.0	23.1	24.7	27.3	25.0	25.0	26.0	78	9	11
31.	Patna	64.2	37.8	30.8	20.3	22.5	23.7	20.0	22.0	23.0	106	37	26
32.	Purba Champaran	47.1	43.1	27.8	21.7	22.1	23.4	21.0	22.0	24.5	121	51	18
33.	Purbi Singhbhum	13.6	7.7	5.5	24.3	25.8	28.0	25.0	25.0	28.0	59	26	55
34.	Purnia	29.3	42.9	0.0	22.9	22.0	24.1	22.0	22.0	25.0	147	7	10
35	Ranchi	23.7	25.0	6.3	23.3	24.2	25.4	24.0	23.0	26.0	76	16	16

Appendix - IX (Continued)

Sr. No.	State/District	Age at marriage									Total number of marriages		
		< 21 years (%) Economic status			Mean Economic status			Median Economic status			Economic status		
		Low	Medium	High	Low	Medium	High	Low	Medium	High	Low	Medium	High
36.	Rohtas	79.7	79.5	37.1	18.5	18.8	21.7	18.0	18.0	21.0	79	39	35
37.	Saharsa	57.8	39.4	19.0	20.9	22.1	25.0	20.0	22.0	25.0	128	33	21
38.	Sahibganj	51.8	28.6	0.0	21.4	22.9	25.0	20.0	25.0	25.0	141	7	3
39.	Samastipur	56.9	40.5	30.4	20.9	22.0	22.7	20.0	22.0	23.0	109	79	23
40.	Saran	46.7	40.5	23.3	21.7	22.3	23.5	21.0	22.0	24.0	75	84	60
41.	Sitamarhi	58.8	33.3	45.8	20.8	22.1	22.0	20.0	22.0	21.0	80	57	24
42.	Siwan	63.2	42.3	26.6	20.8	22.2	22.9	20.0	22.0	22.0	19	78	94
43.	Vaishali	70.1	33.0	20.0	19.9	21.8	23.2	20.0	22.0	24.0	87	100	30
4	**Gujarat**												
1.	Ahmadabad	80.0	40.0	24.8	19.9	22.1	23.5	18.5	21.0	23.0	10	35	117
2.	Amreli	33.8	27.7	29.2	21.6	22.3	23.2	22.0	22.0	23.0	77	94	65
3.	Banas Kantha	65.0	52.0	54.4	19.8	19.9	20.3	19.0	20.0	20.0	40	50	68
4.	Bharuch	43.9	23.9	12.0	22.0	23.9	25.0	21.0	24.0	24.0	66	71	50
5.	Bhavnagar	75.0	50.6	25.8	19.5	20.9	22.1	19.0	20.0	22.0	4	77	89
6.	Gandhinagar	70.0	51.0	30.1	18.5	21.0	23.0	18.0	20.0	23.0	20	49	83
7.	Jamnagar	6.7	36.2	24.8	25.5	22.0	23.1	25.0	22.0	23.0	15	47	109
8.	Junagadh	45.5	18.8	11.8	21.3	23.1	23.8	21.0	23.0	23.0	44	117	85
9.	Kachchh	43.8	29.3	23.7	21.8	22.3	22.9	22.0	22.0	22.0	16	41	76
10.	Kheda	47.1	37.1	23.0	21.1	21.9	23.0	21.0	22.0	23.0	70	70	74
11.	Mahesana	50.0	44.4	37.6	19.8	20.6	21.7	19.5	21.0	22.0	4	27	93
12.	Panch Mahals	55.6	49.2	17.9	20.4	20.8	24.7	20.0	21.0	24.5	108	61	28
13.	Rajkot	28.6	33.3	16.3	21.6	21.2	23.7	21.0	21.0	23.0	7	21	141
14.	Sabar Kantha	46.1	53.4	39.6	21.0	20.7	21.8	21.0	20.0	21.0	102	58	53
15.	Surat	54.5	25.0	13.8	20.5	22.1	23.9	20.0	22.0	24.0	11	28	87
16.	Surendranagar	43.2	26.7	19.6	21.7	22.7	23.0	22.0	22.0	23.0	37	90	46
17.	The Dangs	62.5	61.7	0.0	20.3	20.3	27.7	20.0	20.0	28.0	48	81	3
18.	Vadodara	66.0	52.9	25.4	20.0	21.6	23.5	19.5	20.0	23.0	50	51	71
19.	Valsad	15.5	6.8	0.0	23.6	24.9	26.0	22.0	24.5	25.5	71	44	42

Appendix - IX (Continued)

Sr. No.	State/District	Age at marriage									Total number of marriages		
		< 21 years (%) Economic status			Mean Economic status			Median Economic status			Economic status		
		Low	Medium	High	Low	Medium	High	Low	Medium	High	Low	Medium	High
5	**Haryana**												
1.	Ambala	42.9	24.3	18.6	22.6	22.6	24.2	22.0	22.0	24.0	7	70	70
2.	Bhiwani	82.4	46.9	32.1	18.8	21.2	22.4	18.0	21.0	22.0	17	96	81
3.	Faridabad	41.7	39.7	26.4	21.1	21.6	23.2	21.0	22.0	24.0	12	63	129
4.	Gurgaon	100.0	53.3	23.5	17.4	20.7	23.4	17.5	20.0	23.0	14	90	68
5.	Hisar	100.0	57.8	20.8	19.3	20.9	23.1	20.0	20.0	23.0	3	83	48
6.	Jind	14.3	41.6	20.0	21.3	21.1	23.4	22.0	21.0	23.0	7	113	50
7.	Kaithal	66.7	31.0	22.2	22.3	21.8	23.0	20.0	22.0	22.5	3	87	72
8.	Karnal	33.3	25.6	7.9	21.0	22.2	23.4	21.5	22.0	23.0	6	82	76
9.	Kurukshetra	40.0	33.8	12.9	22.2	22.0	23.6	22.0	22.0	24.0	5	71	70
10.	Mahendragarh	83.3	40.5	42.3	18.2	21.2	21.3	18.5	21.0	21.0	6	79	97
11.	Panchkula	0.0	26.3	6.3	25.3	22.0	24.7	26.0	22.0	25.0	3	76	95
12.	Panipat	0.0	43.7	31.4	23.0	21.1	22.3	23.0	21.0	22.5	1	87	70
13.	Rewari	0.0	35.9	45.0	25.7	21.7	21.1	25.0	22.0	21.0	3	78	129
14.	Rohtak	100.0	23.5	17.0	20.0	22.6	23.3	20.0	22.0	23.5	1	68	88
15.	Sirsa	75.0	41.9	25.3	20.0	21.7	23.2	20.0	21.0	23.0	16	74	75
16.	Sonipat	**	42.1	22.1	NA	21.8	22.9	NA	21.0	23.0	**	95	86
17.	Yamunanagar	23.1	20.0	13.3	22.9	22.8	23.9	22.0	23.0	23.0	13	80	75
6	**Karnataka**												
1.	Bangalore	0.0	11.4	0.0	25.0	24.6	27.0	25.0	24.0	26.0	3	35	57
2.	Bangalore Rural	0.0	0.0	6.7	24.3	26.5	26.6	24.5	27.0	28.0	18	63	15
3.	Belgaum	29.6	20.3	15.6	22.5	24.1	25.3	22.0	24.0	25.0	27	79	32
4.	Bellary	16.3	15.0	0.0	23.8	24.5	27.9	23.0	24.0	27.0	43	100	15
5.	Bidar	37.5	29.2	20.0	22.1	22.5	24.5	21.0	22.0	25.0	40	120	15
6.	Bijapur	35.0	26.1	7.7	23.7	23.3	26.3	24.0	23.0	26.0	40	111	26
7.	Chikmagalur	80.0	7.8	0.0	20.4	26.5	28.8	20.0	27.0	30.0	5	167	13
8.	Chitradurga	22.2	15.1	0.0	23.9	24.7	28.7	22.5	24.0	29.0	18	139	30
9.	Dakshina Kannada	10.0	2.1	0.0	27.8	27.6	28.5	27.0	27.0	29.0	30	94	20

Appendix - IX (Continued)

Sr. No.	State/District	Age at marriage: < 21 years (%) Economic status			Mean Economic status			Median Economic status			Total number of marriages Economic status		
		Low	Medium	High	Low	Medium	High	Low	Medium	High	Low	Medium	High
10.	Dharwad	16.7	14.4	0.0	22.3	24.6	27.0	22.5	24.0	26.0	6	111	22
11.	Gulbarga	40.5	18.2	11.1	21.9	24.4	24.4	22.0	25.0	25.0	74	44	18
12.	Hassan	12.5	10.8	0.0	22.3	25.4	28.1	22.5	25.0	28.0	8	102	14
13.	Kodagu	0.0	13.4	4.4	26.7	24.6	29.1	25.0	24.0	29.0	6	67	68
14.	Kolar	10.0	19.4	8.3	23.7	23.8	26.2	23.0	24.0	26.0	20	103	36
15.	Mandya	10.0	6.6	0.0	24.2	25.3	27.7	24.0	25.0	27.0	30	61	25
16.	Mysore	18.2	2.5	0.0	24.9	25.7	28.5	24.0	25.0	28.0	11	79	26
17.	Raichur	45.2	30.8	9.4	21.5	22.6	25.6	21.0	22.0	26.5	42	91	32
18.	Shimoga	14.3	7.1	0.0	26.7	25.5	28.2	25.0	25.0	28.0	21	99	68
19.	Tumkur	0.0	6.9	0.0	24.0	24.8	29.5	24.0	24.0	31.0	4	102	11
20.	Uttara Kannada	0.0	4.2	0.0	27.0	27.8	28.6	24.5	27.5	28.0	6	118	26
7	**Kerala**												
1.	Alappuzha	7.7	5.7	0.0	30.5	27.1	28.1	30.0	27.0	28.0	13	35	126
2.	Ernakulam	0.0	3.7	0.0	36.0	27.5	28.7	36.0	27.0	29.0	1	27	128
3.	Idukki	0.0	5.7	3.9	25.0	24.3	26.4	24.0	24.0	27.0	3	35	102
4.	Kannur	0.0	0.0	0.0	24.1	28.4	29.0	22.5	28.0	28.0	8	77	61
5.	Kasaragod	0.0	1.8	1.7	26.8	27.6	27.9	28.0	27.0	28.0	5	57	58
6.	Kollam	13.3	1.1	0.0	25.1	29.0	29.0	26.0	28.0	28.0	30	87	52
7.	Kottayam	0.0	3.3	2.3	27.5	26.9	29.4	28.0	27.0	29.0	13	61	87
8.	Kozhikode	0.0	8.7	1.3	22.0	25.6	27.1	21.0	25.0	27.0	3	23	154
9.	Malappuram	16.0	7.9	8.4	23.5	24.6	25.4	22.0	24.0	25.0	25	76	83
10.	Palakkad	0.0	7.7	0.0	27.7	25.8	27.6	25.5	25.0	27.0	6	26	117
11.	Pathanamthitta	0.0	0.0	0.0	27.5	27.5	28.1	27.5	27.0	28.0	2	74	40
12.	Thiruvananthapuram	0.0	4.8	1.5	26.0	27.7	28.3	26.0	27.5	28.0	1	42	66
13.	Thrissur	0.0	3.1	1.7	27.2	28.3	29.4	28.0	27.5	29.0	6	32	117
14.	Wayanad	18.5	12.8	2.6	24.4	25.0	26.6	24.0	25.0	27.0	27	39	77
8	**Madhya Pradesh**												
1.	Balaghat	23.6	16.7	0.0	23.1	24.7	28.0	23.0	24.5	28.0	55	18	5

Appendix - IX (Continued)

Sr. No.	State/District	Age at marriage < 21 years (%) Economic status			Mean Economic status			Median Economic status			Total number of marriages Economic status		
		Low	Medium	High	Low	Medium	High	Low	Medium	High	Low	Medium	High
2.	Bastar	44.3	18.2	16.7	21.5	25.8	25.2	21.0	25.0	26.0	61	11	6
3.	Betul	15.8	11.1	0.0	23.9	24.2	25.3	24.0	25.0	25.5	57	9	6
4.	Bhind	62.5	57.1	43.2	20.5	20.4	22.1	20.0	20.0	21.0	40	56	74
5.	Bhopal	42.3	28.6	7.7	21.3	23.4	24.8	21.5	22.5	25.0	26	14	39
6.	Bilaspur(MP)	50.5	8.3	9.5	21.8	24.7	25.0	20.0	23.0	25.0	101	24	21
7.	Chattarpur	71.2	66.7	35.7	19.5	19.9	22.4	19.0	20.0	22.0	66	12	14
8.	Chhindwara	25.3	13.6	6.7	22.9	25.2	27.1	22.0	25.5	27.0	83	22	15
9.	Damoh	62.0	35.7	20.0	20.1	22.4	24.5	20.0	23.5	23.5	92	14	20
10.	Datia	66.7	54.8	48.9	20.5	20.9	21.5	20.0	20.0	21.0	51	62	45
11.	Dewas	63.5	42.6	43.5	20.6	21.6	22.2	19.0	21.0	22.0	96	61	23
12.	Dhar	59.8	36.4	41.4	20.3	22.9	21.8	20.0	22.0	21.0	107	33	29
13.	Durg	33.8	19.0	12.0	22.3	23.1	25.1	22.0	23.0	26.0	65	21	25
14.	East Nimar	40.9	32.3	9.5	21.5	23.0	25.3	21.5	23.0	25.0	88	31	42
15.	Guna	75.7	31.6	45.5	19.0	22.7	22.9	18.0	22.0	21.5	74	19	22
16.	Gwalior	41.7	35.3	24.7	21.1	21.9	23.3	21.0	22.0	23.0	12	17	77
17.	Hoshangabad	38.1	24.0	15.8	22.0	23.3	24.1	22.0	24.0	25.0	42	25	19
18.	Indore	44.4	28.6	17.5	22.0	23.4	23.9	22.0	24.0	24.0	45	35	63
19.	Jabalpur	30.2	23.1	0.0	22.2	23.8	26.7	22.0	23.0	27.0	53	13	27
20.	Jhabua	77.7	40.0	11.1	18.7	21.1	24.7	18.0	23.0	26.0	130	15	9
21.	Mandla	40.5	40.0	20.0	21.2	21.0	22.1	22.0	21.0	21.5	42	5	10
22.	Mandsaur	77.8	53.6	36.7	18.6	20.2	22.3	19.0	20.0	22.0	63	28	49
23.	Morena	71.4	73.9	64.3	19.0	18.3	19.4	18.0	18.0	19.0	49	23	56
24.	Narsimhapur	35.5	28.0	11.8	22.4	23.0	24.4	22.0	23.0	25.0	110	25	17
25.	Panna	78.1	0.0	50.0	18.9	24.8	22.1	19.5	24.5	21.0	64	4	10
26.	Raigarh(M P)	24.1	0.0	12.5	22.8	23.9	23.1	22.0	24.0	23.5	58	11	8
27.	Raipur	50.0	46.7	12.5	21.1	21.7	24.0	20.5	21.0	24.5	36	15	8
28.	Raisen	35.3	19.4	11.1	21.7	22.8	23.0	22.0	22.0	23.0	85	36	9
29.	Rajgarh	57.6	62.9	47.4	19.8	19.9	20.6	19.0	19.0	21.0	99	35	19
30.	Rajnandgaon	44.2	20.8	40.0	21.7	24.1	22.0	21.0	23.0	21.0	95	24	5

Appendix - IX (Continued)

Sr. No.	State/District	Age at marriage: < 21 years (%) Economic status			Mean Economic status			Median Economic status			Total number of marriages Economic status		
		Low	Medium	High	Low	Medium	High	Low	Medium	High	Low	Medium	High
31.	Ratlam	56.9	55.6	14.6	20.3	21.0	23.9	20.0	20.0	24.0	65	27	48
32.	Rewa	68.8	43.8	23.5	19.5	21.3	22.6	18.5	21.0	22.0	64	16	17
33.	Sagar	55.1	33.3	4.5	20.7	23.3	25.7	20.0	22.0	26.0	78	18	22
34.	Satna	74.2	55.6	20.0	19.4	21.8	23.3	19.0	20.0	24.0	93	27	20
35.	Sehore	65.8	35.7	21.9	20.2	22.1	23.6	19.0	22.5	23.5	76	28	32
36.	Seoni	20.5	31.3	8.3	22.4	23.2	24.8	22.0	22.0	25.0	44	16	12
37.	Shahdol	63.6	50.0	16.7	20.8	20.5	24.0	19.0	20.5	24.0	22	2	6
38.	Shajapur	68.1	61.5	39.1	19.8	20.1	21.1	19.0	19.5	22.0	91	26	23
39.	Shivpuri	71.4	62.5	60.0	19.5	20.3	20.5	19.0	20.0	20.0	49	32	40
40.	Sidhi	73.1	42.9	20.0	19.0	21.7	22.2	18.0	22.0	21.0	93	7	5
41.	Surguja	62.5	0.0	0.0	20.0	25.2	23.4	20.0	25.0	23.0	112	5	5
42.	Tikamgarh	82.8	71.7	66.7	18.7	19.4	20.5	18.0	18.5	20.0	58	46	21
43.	Ujjain	47.4	38.1	19.6	21.2	22.2	23.4	21.0	21.0	23.0	78	21	56
44.	Vidisha	60.5	45.0	19.0	19.9	22.7	24.2	20.0	21.5	24.0	114	20	21
45.	West Nimar	47.3	34.2	27.8	20.8	22.0	22.4	21.0	22.0	22.0	74	38	18
9	**Maharashtra**												
1.	Ahmadnagar	23.7	16.4	6.9	22.8	24.3	24.4	22.0	24.0	23.0	38	61	72
2.	Akola	21.1	11.9	12.9	22.9	24.0	24.1	22.0	24.0	24.0	57	67	31
3.	Amravali	7.3	3.7	0.0	24.3	25.6	26.9	24.0	25.0	26.5	41	27	18
4.	Aurangabad(Mah)	29.7	27.9	18.8	22.1	22.8	24.0	22.0	22.5	24.0	37	68	48
5.	Bhandara	2.4	2.1	0.0	24.6	26.1	27.1	25.0	25.0	26.5	41	48	20
6.	Bid	40.7	19.4	16.7	21.1	22.5	23.3	21.0	22.0	24.0	59	31	24
7.	Buldana	12.0	2.1	3.4	23.4	24.7	25.1	23.0	24.0	25.0	83	47	29
8.	Chandrapur	11.4	20.0	5.6	24.4	23.8	25.6	25.0	23.0	25.0	35	45	18
9.	Dhule	31.7	23.8	7.1	21.8	22.6	24.9	22.0	22.0	24.0	41	63	42
10.	Gadchiroli	23.4	17.9	28.6	22.6	23.6	25.4	22.0	23.0	27.0	47	56	7
11.	Greater Bombay (Mumbai)	0.0	7.8	2.1	25.7	25.7	27.3	25.0	25.0	27.0	3	90	47
12.	Jalgaon	32.5	20.8	13.5	22.3	23.3	24.1	22.0	23.0	24.0	40	48	52

Appendix - IX (Continued)

Sr. No.	State/District	Age at marriage									Total number of marriages		
		< 21 years (%) Economic status			Mean Economic status			Median Economic status			Economic status		
		Low	Medium	High	Low	Medium	High	Low	Medium	High	Low	Medium	High
13.	Jalna	35.7	32.2	23.5	22.2	22.5	23.6	22.0	22.0	25.0	70	59	17
14.	Kolhapur	24.1	13.3	1.3	23.1	24.5	26.3	22.0	25.0	26.0	29	75	75
15.	Latur	17.9	26.2	15.5	22.4	22.4	24.0	23.0	22.0	24.0	28	65	58
16.	Nagpur	8.7	0.0	2.7	25.9	25.5	26.0	26.0	25.0	26.0	23	58	75
17.	Nanded	47.3	22.2	19.2	21.3	23.1	23.6	21.0	22.0	23.0	55	54	26
18.	Nashik	33.3	20.5	13.2	21.7	23.3	24.4	21.0	23.0	24.0	42	78	53
19.	Osmanabad	33.3	19.4	0.0	22.5	23.4	26.2	22.0	23.0	26.5	33	72	34
20.	Parbhani	38.5	37.3	11.1	22.0	21.9	23.6	22.0	22.0	24.0	52	83	27
21.	Pune	13.8	7.6	9.9	24.5	24.1	24.7	24.0	24.0	24.0	29	66	71
22.	Raigarh(MAH)	6.7	4.8	7.7	23.1	24.3	25.0	23.0	24.0	24.5	15	63	26
23.	Ratnagiri	0.0	11.5	7.3	25.5	24.8	24.9	25.5	23.0	25.0	2	61	82
24.	Sangli	27.9	15.0	9.0	23.0	24.2	25.1	22.0	25.0	25.0	43	80	67
25.	Satara	20.0	6.5	0.0	23.4	24.4	25.8	23.0	24.0	25.0	25	62	30
26.	Sindhudurg	8.3	2.6	2.5	25.6	26.7	27.7	25.0	26.0	28.0	24	115	40
27.	Solapur	15.8	9.3	16.7	24.1	24.3	24.6	22.5	24.0	24.0	38	43	48
28.	Thane	10.0	10.8	9.5	24.1	24.3	25.0	24.0	24.0	25.0	10	37	63
29.	Wardha	5.6	2.5	0.0	24.8	26.9	27.2	25.0	27.0	27.0	36	40	32
30.	Yavatmal	16.7	6.9	4.2	24.1	24.5	25.7	24.5	24.0	25.0	78	58	24
10	**Orissa**												
1.	Anugul	22.8	13.3	18.8	23.2	25.0	25.2	22.0	25.0	25.0	79	15	16
2.	Balangir	37.0	11.1	0.0	22.2	24.7	27.9	21.5	24.0	29.0	92	18	14
3.	Balasore	7.3	8.3	0.0	25.5	26.5	27.6	25.0	26.0	28.0	96	36	13
4.	Bargarh	26.6	8.7	0.0	22.8	25.0	25.9	22.0	25.0	25.5	79	23	18
5.	Baudh	34.2	0.0	0.0	22.8	25.0	21.5	22.0	25.0	21.5	120	5	2
6.	Bhadrak	8.8	10.0	0.0	25.8	26.8	27.1	26.0	27.0	26.0	125	10	13
7.	Cuttack	8.6	11.1	7.3	25.5	25.6	26.7	25.0	26.0	27.0	93	36	41
8.	Debagarh	15.9	8.3	0.0	23.9	26.8	27.1	24.0	27.0	27.5	88	24	8
9.	Dhenkanal	15.2	0.0	6.3	24.8	25.7	27.1	25.0	26.0	27.0	105	12	32

Appendix - IX (Continued)

Sr. No.	State/District	Age at marriage < 21 years (%) Economic status			Mean Economic status			Median Economic status			Total number of marriages Economic status		
		Low	Medium	High	Low	Medium	High	Low	Medium	High	Low	Medium	High
10.	Gajapati	24.5	10.0	0.0	23.2	24.0	27.4	23.0	23.0	27.0	94	20	25
11.	Ganjam	19.4	9.1	11.1	24.0	24.8	25.5	24.0	25.0	25.0	67	22	63
12.	Jagatsinghapur	2.0	0.0	0.0	26.2	27.4	27.6	26.0	27.0	28.0	100	16	28
13.	Jajapur	2.7	0.0	0.0	25.7	26.4	27.1	26.0	25.0	27.0	74	12	24
14.	Jharsuguda	17.5	10.0	15.4	23.3	24.5	24.7	23.0	25.0	25.0	40	50	13
15.	Kalahandi	40.2	44.4	0.0	22.0	22.5	29.1	22.0	21.0	29.0	82	27	7
16.	Kendrapara	4.1	0.0	0.0	25.4	28.0	27.3	25.0	28.0	27.0	147	10	33
17.	Kendujhar	16.4	0.0	30.8	24.1	26.5	25.3	24.0	27.0	27.0	110	13	13
18.	Khordha	12.3	3.7	1.9	23.9	26.2	27.0	24.0	26.0	27.0	57	27	53
19.	Koraput	59.5	50.0	0.0	20.8	21.4	27.1	20.0	21.0	28.0	74	30	15
20.	Malkangiri	54.0	37.5	50.0	21.4	23.1	24.0	20.0	23.5	24.0	100	8	2
21.	Mayurbhanj	20.6	21.7	0.0	23.9	25.0	29.1	23.0	25.0	30.0	102	23	7
22.	Nabarangapur	48.4	16.7	0.0	22.1	24.8	26.5	21.0	24.0	27.5	95	6	6
23.	Nayagarh	18.0	9.7	6.5	23.8	24.7	25.5	23.5	25.0	26.0	100	31	31
24.	Nuapada	32.5	6.7	16.7	23.1	23.2	25.7	22.0	24.0	25.5	80	15	6
25.	Phulbani	30.7	41.7	33.3	23.3	23.5	26.3	24.0	22.5	27.0	88	24	3
26.	Puri	16.1	1.7	0.0	24.5	26.6	27.8	24.0	26.0	28.0	93	58	20
27.	Rayagada	34.8	22.2	11.1	22.3	24.0	25.8	22.0	24.0	26.5	89	27	18
28.	Sambalpur	10.0	0.0	0.0	25.1	26.7	27.7	24.0	27.0	26.0	80	23	15
29.	Sonapur	20.2	0.0	5.9	23.3	25.1	26.2	23.0	25.5	23.0	84	14	17
30.	Sundargarh	12.1	0.0		24.5	24.8	27.0	25.0	24.5	26.5	66	8	32
11	**Punjab**												
1.	Amritsar	33.3	25.3	8.0	21.2	22.8	25.0	21.5	22.0	25.0	6	87	75
2.	Bathinda	62.5	31.4	15.0	20.4	22.4	23.6	20.0	22.0	22.5	8	121	60
3.	Faridkot	57.1	35.3	18.6	21.0	22.3	23.6	20.0	22.0	24.0	14	102	70
4.	Fatehgarh Sahib	33.3	25.8	15.0	21.3	22.4	23.2	21.0	22.0	23.0	3	62	120
5.	Firozpur	55.2	36.0	28.4	20.8	22.4	23.1	20.0	22.0	23.0	29	125	67
6.	Gurdaspur	20.0	15.5	1.7	28.8	24.0	25.7	25.0	24.0	25.0	5	103	58

Appendix - IX (Continued)

Sr. No.	State/District	Age at marriage									Total number of marriages		
		< 21 years (%) Economic status			Mean Economic status			Median Economic status			Economic status		
		Low	Medium	High	Low	Medium	High	Low	Medium	High	Low	Medium	High
7.	Hoshiarpur	0.0	11.4	3.1	23.3	25.0	25.8	24.0	25.0	25.0	3	70	98
8.	Jalandhar	100.0	15.0	7.9	19.0	24.7	24.8	19.0	24.0	25.0	1	60	89
9.	Kapurthala	0.0	18.8	10.1	24.3	23.4	25.0	24.0	22.5	25.0	3	80	79
10.	Ludhiana	33.3	14.9	9.8	24.0	24.1	24.0	22.0	25.0	24.0	3	47	82
11.	Mansa	100.0	36.3	20.0	19.5	22.0	22.8	19.5	22.0	22.0	4	113	65
12.	Moga	42.9	34.5	13.3	22.3	22.3	25.2	22.0	22.0	25.0	7	84	75
13.	Muktsar	63.6	43.0	19.3	20.7	22.2	23.2	20.0	22.0	23.0	11	107	57
14.	Nawanshahr	0.0	13.5	10.1	22.0	24.3	24.3	22.0	24.0	25.0	2	74	89
15.	Patiala	16.7	31.5	16.8	22.2	22.2	23.5	22.0	22.0	23.0	6	92	95
16.	Rupnagar	25.0	17.6	10.0	21.8	24.2	24.3	22.5	24.0	24.0	4	51	110
17.	Sangrur	44.4	33.3	17.1	21.3	22.6	23.4	21.0	22.0	23.0	9	99	70
12	**Rajasthan**												
1.	Ajmer	70.6	50.0	31.4	18.8	21.1	22.5	19.0	21.0	22.0	17	14	70
2.	Alwar	85.0	76.0	47.9	18.1	19.2	21.1	17.5	19.0	21.0	20	25	121
3.	Banswara	75.2	83.3	25.0	19.0	19.1	22.9	18.0	18.0	24.0	101	18	24
4.	Barmer	63.0	46.2	43.8	20.2	21.4	20.5	20.0	21.0	21.0	108	26	32
5.	Bharatpur	81.8	69.0	45.0	18.2	19.7	21.4	18.0	20.0	21.0	11	42	109
6.	Bhilwara	79.2	80.0	41.1	18.4	18.8	21.9	18.0	16.0	22.0	24	20	56
7.	Bikaner	71.4	80.0	40.9	20.1	19.2	22.0	20.0	20.0	22.0	42	10	93
8.	Bundi	88.6	65.2	60.9	17.6	19.4	20.4	17.0	20.0	20.0	44	23	46
9.	Chittaurgarh	80.5	70.0	38.1	18.5	18.7	22.4	18.0	18.5	23.0	41	10	21
10.	Churu	87.5	73.0	58.3	18.9	19.7	20.3	18.5	19.0	20.0	16	37	139
11.	Dausa	75.0	86.7	59.0	18.8	18.3	20.3	18.0	18.0	20.0	28	30	100
12.	Dhaulpur	56.3	70.7	58.7	20.3	19.1	20.4	20.0	19.0	20.0	16	58	63
13.	Dungarpur	60.6	37.5	24.5	20.4	21.3	23.5	20.0	21.0	23.0	99	32	49
14.	Ganganagar	72.7	68.6	27.4	19.7	19.8	22.2	20.0	20.0	22.0	66	35	62
15.	Hanumangarh	57.4	74.6	56.6	20.1	19.5	21.0	20.0	20.0	20.0	54	63	76
16.	Jaipur	61.9	60.0	35.1	18.7	20.1	21.9	18.0	20.0	22.0	21	20	97

Appendix - IX (Continued)

Sr. No.	State/District	Age at marriage									Total number of marriages		
		< 21 years (%) Economic status			Mean Economic status			Median Economic status			Economic status		
		Low	*Medium*	*High*	*Low*	*Medium*	*High*	*Low*	*Medium*	*High*	*Low*	*Medium*	*High*
17.	Jaisalmer	39.0	46.4	27.3	22.0	21.7	22.2	22.0	21.0	22.0	41	28	33
18.	Jalor	67.9	48.8	45.1	19.7	20.5	21.7	20.0	21.0	21.0	106	41	51
19.	Jhalawar	73.0	64.0	31.3	19.3	19.8	22.4	19.0	19.0	22.0	74	25	32
20.	Jhunjhunun	50.0	37.9	34.6	20.5	21.3	21.8	20.5	22.0	22.0	4	29	133
21.	Jodhpur	50.0	54.5	35.7	21.7	20.9	22.1	20.5	20.0	22.0	30	22	70
22.	Kota	76.0	66.7	31.7	19.7	19.6	22.3	19.0	19.0	22.0	50	9	60
23.	Nagaur	75.0	54.2	52.0	19.7	20.6	20.7	19.5	20.0	20.0	20	24	102
24.	Pali	69.7	50.0	41.4	19.3	20.2	21.2	20.0	20.5	21.0	33	26	99
25.	Rajsamand	71.4	48.0	41.3	20.1	20.3	21.6	20.0	21.0	21.0	28	25	63
26.	Sawai Madhopur	69.6	65.4	47.6	18.9	18.9	20.9	18.0	18.0	21.0	23	26	42
27.	Sikar	58.3	70.0	35.1	20.5	19.7	21.7	20.0	19.0	22.0	12	20	114
28.	Sirohi	33.3	42.1	32.4	22.5	21.0	22.9	22.5	21.0	22.0	30	19	37
29.	Tonk	80.0	63.2	47.9	18.2	19.7	21.2	18.0	20.0	21.0	30	19	48
30.	Udaipur	76.0	64.0	43.6	19.6	20.2	22.1	19.0	20.0	21.0	50	25	55
13	**Tamil Nadu**												
1.	Chengalpattu	17.6	7.3	1.5	23.6	25.1	26.9	23.5	25.0	27.0	34	41	65
2.	Chennai	0.0	15.0	1.3	29.0	25.2	27.1	28.0	25.0	27.0	4	20	75
3.	Coimbatore	0.0	10.0	0.0	25.3	26.4	26.1	24.0	27.0	25.0	4	60	13
4.	Dharmapuri	24.0	12.1	12.5	23.9	24.2	25.4	25.0	24.0	25.0	25	91	48
5.	Dindigul	27.3	6.1	0.0	21.7	25.8	27.2	22.0	25.5	27.0	11	82	21
6.	Kanniyakumari	0.0	1.5	0.0	26.5	27.8	29.2	26.0	27.5	29.0	26	68	45
7.	Madurai	16.7	12.2	2.1	24.4	25.7	28.1	24.0	26.0	28.0	12	49	48
8.	Namakkal	18.8	7.0	9.1	25.0	26.3	26.4	24.5	26.0	26.5	16	57	22
9.	North Arcot	17.9	5.9	2.9	24.9	25.4	26.0	23.0	25.0	26.0	39	34	68
10.	Periyar	10.0	5.6	7.7	26.0	26.4	26.8	24.0	26.0	27.0	10	54	13
11.	Pudukkottai	6.3	11.8	7.1	25.5	25.8	25.9	25.0	25.0	25.0	32	76	14
12.	Ramanathapuram	14.3	6.1	4.3	24.1	25.4	25.3	23.5	25.0	26.0	14	49	23
13.	Salem	4.3	10.3	9.4	26.3	24.5	26.5	25.0	24.5	26.0	23	78	32

Appendix - IX (Continued)

Sr. No.	State/District	Age at marriage: < 21 years (%) Economic status			Mean Economic status			Median Economic status			Total number of marriages Economic status		
		Low	Medium	High	Low	Medium	High	Low	Medium	High	Low	Medium	High
14.	Sivaganganagar	5.9	4.3	3.2	24.6	26.1	26.3	25.0	26.0	27.0	17	92	31
15.	South Arcot	16.4	6.9	4.3	24.4	26.5	26.2	24.0	27.0	26.0	61	29	23
16.	Thanjavur	10.8	6.8	0.0	25.1	27.5	28.4	25.0	27.0	29.0	37	44	28
17.	The Nilgiris	0.0	2.0	0.0	25.0	27.9	26.7	25.0	28.0	27.0	1	51	10
18.	Theni	33.3	11.9	4.5	22.6	25.9	26.0	23.0	25.0	27.0	9	42	22
19.	Tiruchirappalli	12.0	4.0	0.0	26.5	28.1	29.6	27.0	28.0	29.0	25	50	19
20.	Tirunelveli	0.0	0.0	0.0	26.5	25.7	26.6	27.0	25.0	25.5	8	52	38
21.	Tiruvanamalai	17.4	9.1	12.2	23.9	24.9	26.8	22.5	25.0	26.0	46	44	41
22.	Tutikorin	0.0	5.1	2.2	27.2	25.9	27.5	26.0	25.0	27.0	6	59	45
23.	Virudhunagar	33.3	9.8	3.7	22.9	24.7	26.8	22.0	24.0	27.0	15	61	54
14	**Uttar Pradesh**												
1.	Agra	46.2	58.3	26.9	20.8	20.6	22.9	21.0	20.0	22.0	13	72	67
2.	Aligarh	61.9	48.9	41.3	20.0	20.9	21.7	20.0	21.0	22.0	21	47	104
3.	Allahabad	74.2	55.6	44.2	19.5	20.8	22.3	20.0	20.0	22.0	66	18	52
4.	Almora	0.0	6.8	0.0	24.0	23.4	24.7	23.0	23.0	24.0	7	44	49
5.	Ambedkarnagar	75.5	66.7	40.0	19.1	19.2	21.7	18.0	19.0	23.0	49	42	15
6.	Azamgarh	82.5	50.0	61.5	19.0	21.0	20.6	18.0	20.5	20.0	57	68	13
7.	Bahraich	75.3	60.6	75.0	19.0	20.0	20.7	19.0	20.0	19.0	81	33	16
8.	Ballia	65.0	37.9	26.1	19.6	22.2	23.2	19.5	22.0	24.0	20	58	23
9.	Banda	69.1	60.7	57.7	19.9	20.3	21.5	19.0	20.0	20.0	81	28	26
10.	Barabanki	74.1	57.3	55.6	19.9	20.5	20.9	20.0	20.0	20.0	58	75	18
11.	Bareilly	69.6	54.8	31.6	19.6	20.5	23.0	20.0	20.0	22.0	23	31	38
12.	Basti	83.9	64.3	36.4	18.5	19.9	21.7	18.0	19.0	22.0	31	84	22
13.	Bhadohi	86.3	78.4	64.5	18.5	19.0	19.7	18.0	19.0	19.0	80	37	62
14.	Bijnor	48.3	21.4	18.5	21.1	22.2	23.5	21.0	22.0	23.0	29	56	54
15.	Budaun	62.8	62.2	33.3	19.9	20.0	22.0	20.0	20.0	22.0	43	82	30
16.	Bulandshahar	52.9	42.5	35.2	20.8	21.3	22.1	20.0	21.0	22.0	17	80	125
17.	Chamoli	5.6	8.8	16.7	23.2	24.1	24.2	23.0	25.0	23.5	18	34	36

Appendix - IX (Continued)

Sr. No.	State/District	Age at marriage: < 21 years (%) Economic status Low	Medium	High	Mean Economic status Low	Medium	High	Median Economic status Low	Medium	High	Total number of marriages Economic status Low	Medium	High
18.	Dehradun	46.7	0.0	3.4	21.2	25.8	25.4	21.0	24.0	25.0	15	17	87
19.	Deoria	81.4	74.1	62.8	19.0	20.1	20.4	18.0	20.0	19.0	43	54	43
20.	Etah	52.8	44.7	42.0	20.1	21.5	21.7	20.0	21.0	22.0	36	38	50
21.	Etawah	51.4	35.5	39.4	21.1	22.0	21.9	20.0	22.0	21.0	35	93	33
22.	Faizabad	77.4	66.7	52.9	18.5	19.8	20.9	18.0	19.0	20.0	53	42	17
23.	Farrukhabad	56.1	48.1	30.2	20.8	21.0	22.8	20.0	21.0	22.0	41	79	43
24.	Fatehpur	55.8	51.1	32.1	20.9	21.6	22.0	20.0	20.0	22.0	77	45	56
25.	Firozabad	82.4	72.6	34.2	19.6	19.9	22.4	20.0	20.0	22.0	17	62	76
26.	Ghaziabad	60.0	50.0	20.2	19.8	21.6	22.7	20.0	20.5	23.0	5	48	89
27.	Ghazipur	61.1	63.6	48.8	20.1	21.1	21.1	19.0	20.0	21.0	54	33	43
28.	Gonda	71.7	73.5	56.3	19.3	19.3	20.1	19.0	18.0	20.0	53	83	16
29.	Gorakhpur	65.8	82.4	31.0	19.1	18.8	22.7	18.0	18.0	22.0	38	34	42
30.	Hamirpur (UP)	77.1	43.9	44.4	19.7	21.4	21.7	20.0	21.0	22.0	70	41	27
31.	Hardoi	58.2	42.4	52.9	20.7	21.6	20.7	20.0	21.0	20.0	55	33	17
32.	Hardwar	38.5	31.8	16.7	21.8	21.9	23.5	22.0	22.0	23.0	13	66	48
33.	Hathras	76.2	44.9	36.7	19.4	21.3	22.0	18.0	21.0	22.0	21	89	49
34.	Jalaun	76.1	51.6	31.7	19.8	21.4	22.0	19.5	20.0	22.0	46	31	41
35.	Jaunpur	70.8	65.6	41.9	19.0	19.8	21.8	18.0	20.0	21.0	96	61	43
36.	Jhansi	77.8	61.0	49.1	19.0	20.3	22.1	19.0	20.0	21.0	18	41	55
37.	Kanpur Dehat	47.6	40.0	32.6	21.6	21.7	22.0	21.5	21.0	21.5	42	25	46
38.	Kanpur Nagar	58.3	30.8	17.1	20.8	22.5	23.8	20.0	22.0	24.0	24	13	82
39.	Kheri	72.2	71.2	16.7	20.3	19.9	23.1	20.0	20.0	22.5	72	52	18
40.	Lalitpur	83.3	85.4	55.6	18.2	18.4	21.3	18.0	18.0	19.0	60	48	18
41.	Lucknow	75.0	55.9	17.0	20.7	20.7	24.0	20.0	20.0	25.0	24	34	47
42.	Maharajganj	83.3	70.0	85.0	18.5	19.0	17.8	17.0	18.0	18.0	30	20	20
43.	Mahoba	68.8	59.1	40.0	19.5	20.2	22.2	20.0	20.0	22.0	77	44	25
44.	Mainpuri	60.4	63.2	46.2	20.7	20.8	22.1	20.0	20.0	22.0	48	95	26
45.	Mathura	50.0	58.3	39.6	21.0	20.6	22.2	20.5	20.0	22.0	28	60	106
46.	Mau	69.2	59.1	28.6	19.9	20.4	23.1	20.0	20.0	24.0	52	66	28

Appendix - IX (Continued)

Sr. No.	State/District	Age at marriage: < 21 years (%) Economic status			Mean Economic status			Median Economic status			Total number of marriages Economic status		
		Low	Medium	High	Low	Medium	High	Low	Medium	High	Low	Medium	High
47.	Meerut	31.6	40.0	27.5	22.4	21.2	21.7	22.0	21.0	22.0	19	50	69
48.	Mirzapur	75.7	65.0	48.1	19.2	20.6	21.7	19.0	20.0	21.0	70	40	27
49.	Muradabad	57.9	54.0	13.5	19.9	20.9	23.8	20.0	20.0	24.0	19	87	37
50.	Muzaffarnagar	36.8	46.8	8.6	21.4	20.8	23.8	21.0	21.0	23.0	19	77	58
51.	Nainital	36.7	25.6	11.4	22.4	22.6	25.4	21.5	22.0	25.0	30	39	70
52.	Pauri Garhwal	0.0	15.2	5.8	24.8	24.0	25.0	25.0	23.0	25.0	21	33	52
53.	Pilibhit	72.4	64.5	29.7	19.8	19.7	23.1	19.0	19.5	23.0	58	62	37
54.	Pithoragarh	46.2	28.2	6.4	21.3	22.3	24.3	21.0	22.0	24.0	13	39	47
55.	Pratapgarh	76.7	80.0	52.6	19.6	20.0	21.2	18.5	19.5	20.0	116	20	19
56.	Rae Bareli	67.6	53.7	50.0	20.1	20.8	20.7	20.0	20.0	20.5	74	41	12
57.	Rampur	50.0	43.3	27.6	21.2	21.0	23.2	21.0	21.0	24.0	24	60	29
58.	Saharanpur	32.4	42.4	22.6	21.5	21.4	22.8	21.0	21.0	22.0	37	33	62
59.	Shajahanabad	72.5	60.4	32.0	19.5	20.5	22.0	19.0	20.0	22.0	69	53	25
60.	Siddharthnagar	94.4	74.2	71.4	17.1	19.2	19.4	17.0	20.0	18.5	18	31	14
61.	Sitapur	63.0	56.4	50.0	20.4	20.9	20.7	20.0	20.0	20.5	81	39	14
62.	Sonbhadra	67.1	66.7	21.4	19.7	21.7	23.1	19.0	20.0	23.5	70	3	14
63.	Sultanpur	71.2	68.6	46.7	19.3	19.4	20.3	18.0	20.0	21.0	59	51	15
64.	Tehri Garhwal	20.0	16.7	13.6	23.0	23.0	24.5	22.0	22.0	24.0	20	60	22
65.	Udhamsingh Nagar	41.5	42.2	21.3	21.2	21.4	23.4	21.0	21.0	23.0	41	45	47
66.	Unnao	62.3	50.0	44.0	20.7	20.6	22.2	20.0	20.5	21.0	61	14	25
67.	Uttarkashi	46.7	25.0	18.4	20.7	22.8	23.6	21.0	22.0	23.0	15	36	38
68.	Varanasi	71.4	74.2	40.7	19.7	18.8	23.0	20.0	18.0	22.0	35	31	54
15	**West Bengal**												
1.	Bankura	22.0	0.0	10.0	23.7	25.7	26.6	23.0	25.5	26.0	127	12	20
2.	Barddhaman	41.2	24.1	7.8	22.8	25.0	26.7	22.0	25.0	26.5	97	29	64
3.	Birbhum	37.1	26.1	4.2	21.6	24.0	28.5	21.0	24.0	29.5	89	23	24
4.	Dakshin Dinajpur	28.2	7.7	14.3	24.0	25.5	26.4	23.0	25.0	27.0	124	13	7
5.	Darjiling	26.9	27.3	6.5	24.1	24.6	26.9	23.0	24.0	27.0	78	44	31
6.	Haora	31.0	8.2	4.5	22.7	26.0	27.9	23.0	26.0	28.0	42	49	67

Appendix - IX (Continued)

Sr. No.	State/District	Age at marriage: < 21 years (%) Economic status: Low	Medium	High	Mean Economic status: Low	Medium	High	Median Economic status: Low	Medium	High	Total number of marriages Economic status: Low	Medium	High
7.	Hugli	27.8	21.9	1.7	23.9	24.8	27.3	23.0	24.0	27.0	72	32	60
8.	Jalpaiguri	29.1	20.5	0.0	23.8	24.6	29.8	23.0	24.0	30.0	117	44	9
9.	Koch Bihar	25.0	14.3	33.3	23.6	27.0	25.3	24.0	28.0	28.0	124	7	3
10.	Kolkata	28.6	15.0	5.7	24.3	25.6	28.8	25.0	25.0	28.0	7	60	53
11.	Maldah	25.0	25.0	9.5	23.4	23.6	26.2	23.0	23.5	27.0	100	28	21
12.	Medinipur	22.5	5.9	6.7	23.6	24.7	26.2	23.0	24.0	25.0	142	17	15
13.	Murshidabad	54.5	29.2	17.9	21.2	22.3	23.9	20.0	21.0	24.0	121	24	39
14.	Nadia	26.8	10.3	0.0	23.1	25.2	28.8	22.0	25.0	29.5	82	29	32
15.	North 24 Parganas	22.2	14.6	2.5	23.6	26.2	29.9	22.0	26.0	30.0	54	41	40
16.	Puruliya	34.4	41.7	8.0	22.5	22.6	27.9	22.0	21.5	28.0	122	12	25
17.	South 24 Parganas	30.7	17.1	10.7	23.1	24.7	25.9	22.0	24.0	26.5	88	41	28
18.	Uttar Dinajpur	26.1	0.0	21.4	23.8	27.3	26.0	24.0	25.0	26.0	134	7	14
16	**Andaman & Nicobar**												
1.	Andaman	7.4	0.0	5.9	23.9	26.8	25.4	24.0	27.0	26.0	27	25	17
2.	Nicobar	0.0	0.0	0.0	26.7	28.5	26.8	26.0	28.0	25.0	33	27	15
17	**Arunachal Pradesh**												
1.	Changlang	42.3	15.4	0.0	22.4	25.2	23.5	21.5	25.0	23.5	52	13	2
2.	Dibang Valley	37.0	18.2	**	22.7	25.3	NA	22.0	26.0	NA	27	11	**
3.	East Kameng	62.9	18.2	0.0	21.3	24.1	25	20.0	21.0	25	35	11	1
4.	East Siang	54.5	77.8	25.0	21.6	19.9	24.5	20.0	19.0	25	33	9	4
5.	Lohit	35.5	0.0	**	22.9	25.6	NA	23.0	26.0	NA	31	7	**
6.	Lower Subansiri	36.0	66.7	0.0	23.0	20.7	27	22.0	19.5	26	25	6	3
7.	Papum Pare	40.0	50.0	33.3	23.2	23.5	23.0	21.5	23.5	22	20	2	3
8.	Tawang	8.3	9.1	0.0	23.9	26.1	26.3	24.0	25.0	25	12	11	3
9.	Tirap	18.8	0.0	**	24.1	25.0	NA	24.5	25.0	NA	16	1	**
10.	Upper Siang	22.7	0.0	**	22.8	24.0	NA	23.0	24.0	NA	22	1	**
11.	Upper Subansiri	26.2	**	12.5	23.3	NA	25.9	23.0	NA	26.5	61	**	8
12.	West Kameng	44.4	10.0	25.0	22.1	25.5	24	21.0	25.0	23.5	27	10	4
13.	West Siang	20.0	0.0	0.0	24.7	22.0	28.5	25.0	22.0	27.5	40	2	4

Appendix - IX (Continued)

Sr. No.	State/District	Age at marriage: < 21 years (%) Economic status			Mean Economic status			Median Economic status			Total number of marriages Economic status		
		Low	Medium	High	Low	Medium	High	Low	Medium	High	Low	Medium	High
18	**Chandigarh**												
1.	Chandigarh	0.0	60.0	4.2	21.0	20.8	25.4	21.0	20.0	26.0	1	5	48
19	**Dadra & Nagar Haveli**												
1.	Dadra & Nagar Havel	61.0	51.3	25.0	20.0	21.0	23.4	20.0	20.0	23.5	41	39	36
20	**Daman & Diu**												
1	Daman	25.9	10.0	8.2	22.9	24.6	24.9	22.0	25.0	25.0	27	60	73
2	Diu	33.3	38.5	14.5	25.3	24.2	24.2	27.0	23.0	24.0	3	13	131
21	**Delhi**												
1.	Delhi	**	18.2	12.1	NA	22.7	24.6	NA	22.0	25.0	**	11	91
22	**Goa**												
1.	North Goa	33.3	1.1	0.0	25.7	29.2	29.3	25.0	29.0	30.0	3	89	24
2.	South Goa	0.0	1.9	0.0	23.0	28.4	29.8	23.0	28.0	29.0	2	107	23
23	**Himachal Pradesh**	.											
1.	Bilaspur(Pra.Him)	9.5	7.3	2.9	25.8	24.2	25.3	25.0	24.0	25.0	21	55	68
2.	Chamba	14.6	5.5	0.0	23.0	24.6	26.7	23.0	24.0	27.0	48	73	54
3.	Hamirpur(HP)	9.8	4.2	4.8	24.8	25.7	25.7	25.0	26.0	26.0	41	48	83
4.	Kangra	0.0	1.3	2.3	26.2	26.3	26.1	25.5	26.0	26.0	30	79	43
5.	Kinnaur	16.1	13.2	11.1	24.6	24.7	22.8	25.0	25.0	23.0	31	53	18
6.	Kullu	26.7	8.5	5.3	22.5	25.0	25.4	22.0	25.0	25.0	30	59	19
7.	Lahul & Spiti	12.0	10.8	9.1	25.5	24.5	25.9	24.0	23.0	25.0	25	37	11
8.	Mandi	7.5	7.9	0.0	24.0	24.1	25.7	23.5	24.0	25.0	40	63	65
9.	Shimla	14.7	8.2	0.0	25.0	26.2	26.9	24.0	26.0	27.0	34	49	33
10.	Sirmaur	27.1	7.1	6.8	22.6	24.8	24.6	22.0	25.0	24.0	48	28	74
11.	Solan	5.9	12.8	7.4	23.0	23.3	24.8	23.0	23.0	25.0	17	39	122
12.	Una	6.9	0.0	1.0	25.5	25.9	26.0	26.0	25.0	26.0	29	37	99
24	**Jammu & Kashmir**												
1.	Anantanag	0.0	8.3	8.3	23.0	24.2	26.3	23.0	24.0	26.0	2	12	12
2.	Badgam	0.0	36.4	35.5	24.0	22.8	22.0	24.0	23.0	22.0	2	11	31
3.	Baramula	25.0	12.5	0.0	24.6	26.1	28.1	25.0	26.5	29.0	28	24	14

Appendix - IX (Continued)

Sr. No.	State/District	Age at marriage: < 21 years (%) Economic status			Mean Economic status			Median Economic status			Total number of marriages Economic status		
		Low	Medium	High	Low	Medium	High	Low	Medium	High	Low	Medium	High
4.	Doda	2.9	0.0	0.0	25.8	26.8	28.1	26.0	27.0	28.0	34	25	8
5.	Jammu	0.0	0.0	0.0	26.3	26.2	27.7	25.0	26.5	28.0	18	16	30
6.	Kargil	14.3	10.0	0.0	23.6	23.4	24.5	24.0	24.0	24.5	70	10	2
7.	Kathua	0.0	3.4	0.0	27.8	27.5	29.4	27.0	28.0	29.0	26	29	52
8.	Kupwara	**	0.0	20.5	NA	23.6	24.7	NA	24.0	25.0	**	5	39
9.	Leh	16.7	16.7	0.0	24.2	24.5	21.0	24.0	24.0	21.0	48	6	1
10.	Pulwama	50.0	16.7	16.7	20.3	23.1	25.7	20.5	23.0	25.0	6	18	6
11.	Punch	7.7	0.0	0.0	23.8	24.8	25.3	24.0	24.5	25.0	26	30	9
12.	Rajauri	1.1	0.0	**	23.7	23.5	NA	24.0	24.0	NA	92	15	**
13.	Srinagar	0.0	57.1	23.5	21.5	20.6	21.5	21.5	20.0	22.0	2	7	17
14.	Udhampur	5.2	0.0	0.0	22.9	25.4	26.3	23.0	25.0	26.5	58	22	8
25	**Lakshadweep**												
1.	Lakshadweep	50.0	0.0	9.0	21.5	25.3	25.8	21.5	25.0	26.0	2	7	89
26	**Manipur**												
1.	Bishnupur	32.1	9.2	0.0	24.0	27.4	28.6	22.0	26.0	29.0	53	76	5
2.	Chandel	26.1	14.8	0.0	24.3	25.4	27.0	23.0	25.0	27.0	46	27	2
3.	Churachandpur	15.2	11.1	42.9	25.3	25.9	23.1	25.0	25.0	22.0	46	54	7
4.	Imphal	11.3	16.0	0.0	26.6	28.8	31.8	26.0	29.0	32.0	53	25	14
5.	Senapati	24.4	7.7	0.0	24.8	26.9	24.5	25.0	25.0	24.5	41	13	2
6.	Tamenglong	27.9	19.4	0.0	23.8	25.5	28.6	23.0	26.0	26.0	68	31	5
7.	Thoubal	18.6	15.2	25.0	25.0	25.8	24.5	25.0	25.0	25.0	43	99	4
8.	Ukhrul	19.0	16.7	**	26.2	28.3	NA	25.0	29.0	NA	42	12	**
27	**Meghalaya**												
1.	East Garo Hills	40.7	50.0	0.0	22.3	22.0	26.0	23.0	22.0	26.0	27	4	2
2.	East Khasi Hills	20.0	69.2	0.0	21.8	20.8	26.0	23.0	20.0	26.0	5	13	1
3.	Jaintia Hills	**	0.0	0.0	NA	25.6	25.3	NA	26.0	25.5	**	7	8
4.	Ri Bhoi	70.4	62.5	**	20.1	20.3	NA	20.0	19.5	NA	27	8	**
5.	West Garo Hills	66.7	0.0	**	21.0	27.7	NA	20.0	28.0	NA	3	3	**
6.	West Khasi Hills	50.0	53.3	33.3	20.7	21.3	22.3	19.5	20.0	22.0	6	30	3

Appendix - IX (Continued)

Sr. No.	State/District	Age at marriage < 21 years (%) Economic status			Mean Economic status			Median Economic status			Total number of marriages Economic status		
		Low	Medium	High	Low	Medium	High	Low	Medium	High	Low	Medium	High
28	**Mizoram**												
1	Aizwal	28.1	23.0	20.0	24.5	24.4	25.1	22.0	24.0	25.0	32	87	15
2.	Chhimtuipui	31.0	19.0	**	24.0	23.8	NA	22.0	24.0	NA	29	21	**
3.	Lunglei	14.3	13.2	0.0	22.6	26.5	29.0	23.0	25.0	28.0	7	53	5
29	**Nagaland**												
1	Kohima	71.4	59.3	86.7	20.0	20.5	19.0	20.0	20.0	19.0	7	27	15
2.	Mokokchung	7.1	11.1	**	25.4	25.0	NA	24.5	24.0	NA	14	18	**
3.	Mon	24.4	24.2	25.0	22.8	22.7	24.0	23.0	22.0	23.5	45	33	4
4.	Phek	31.3	33.3	**	21.7	24.0	NA	21.5	26.0	NA	16	3	**
5.	Tuensang	6.8	2.6	0.0	24.8	25.0	25.2	24.0	24.0	22.0	44	39	5
6.	Wokha	10.3	4.3	**	25.1	25.1	NA	25.0	25.0	NA	29	23	**
7.	Zunheboto	31.2	42.9	0.0	22.3	22.5	25.0	22.0	21.0	25.0	109	14	1
30	**Pondicherry**												
1.	Karaikal	7.5	0.0	0.0	25.4	26.9	28.2	25.0	27.0	27.0	53	18	25
2.	Mahe	**	0.0	1.1	NA	27.0	29.8	NA	27.0	29.0	**	7	179
3.	Pondicherry	4.8	0.0	0.0	25.0	28.0	28.0	25.0	28.0	28.0	21	44	65
4.	Yanam	0.0	7.1	18.6	23.3	24.1	25.3	22.5	23.5	25.0	10	14	43
31	**Sikkim**												
1.	East Sikkim	12.2	11.9	0.0	25.3	25.7	26.7	24.0	25.5	28.0	49	42	29
2.	North Sikkim	35.0	28.6	18.8	23.5	24.9	24.9	22.5	24.0	25.0	20	28	16
3.	South Sikkim	33.3	22.2	0.0	23.0	23.8	25.0	22.0	24.0	25.0	27	9	1
4.	West Sikkim	28.6	19.6	8.3	23.0	24.7	23.7	22.0	24.0	23.0	28	51	12
32	**Tripura**												
1.	North Tripura	9.7	9.1	0.0	27.2	27.5	28.9	28.0	27.0	27.0	103	11	17
2.	South Tripura	7.1	0.0	11.1	26.9	29.3	29.2	27.0	28.0	30.0	112	12	9
3.	West Tripura	8.0	0.0	0.0	27.9	28.8	32.6	28.0	28.5	34.0	112	16	18

Note: In the column showing percent of marriages below legal minimum age, 0.0 indicates no marriage below 18 years.

** No marriage is reported in that category of characteristic/district.

NA Not applicable.

APPENDIX - X

Percent of Marriages below legal Minimum Age of 21 years and Average Age at Marriage in each District by level of Female Literacy Rate -BOYS

Sr. No.	*State/district*	*Level of FLR*	*Age at marriage*			*Total Marriages (#)*
			< 21 years (%)	*Mean*	*Median*	
1	**Andhra Pradesh**					
1.	Mahbubnagar	Low	43.8	22.0	22.0	73
2.	Adilabad	Medium	31.5	22.5	22.0	108
3.	Anantapur	"	21.0	24.1	24.0	81
4.	Chittoor	"	17.2	25.1	25.0	58
5.	Cuddapah	"	20.8	23.4	22.0	77
6.	East Godavari	"	28.0	22.5	22.0	82
7.	Guntur	"	29.6	22.3	22.0	81
8.	Karimnagar	"	37.7	22.1	22.0	61
9.	Khammam	"	30.3	22.6	23.0	66
10.	Krishna	"	42.5	22.4	22.0	153
11.	Kurnool	"	22.0	23.7	24.5	100
12.	Medak	"	26.1	23.1	23.0	115
13.	Nalgonda	"	40.8	22.0	22.0	152
14.	Nellore	"	21.4	23.3	23.0	84
15.	Nizamabad	"	38.6	22.2	22.0	101
16.	Prakasam	"	26.1	23.1	23.0	69
17.	Rangareddi	"	17.1	23.9	24.0	140
18.	Srikakulam	"	23.0	23.4	23.0	122
19.	Vishkhapatanam	"	32.7	23.1	23.0	98
20.	Vizianagaram	"	30.3	22.6	22.0	89
21.	Warangal	"	39.6	21.6	22.0	96
22.	Hyderabad	high	0.9	26.5	26.0	115
23.	West Godavari	"	25.0	23.0	23.0	120
2	**Assam**					
1.	Barpeta	Medium	3.7	27.5	28.0	162
2.	Bongaigaon	"	14.2	25.9	26.0	106
3.	Cachar	"	4.1	28.9	30.0	98
4.	Darrang	"	6.3	27.8	28.0	96
5.	Dhemaji	"	1.6	27.7	28.0	322
6.	Dhubri	"	3.4	26.3	26.0	148
7.	Dibrugarh	"	32.5	25.0	26.0	40
8.	Goalpara	"	12.2	26.8	27.0	131
9.	Golaghat	"	12.5	26.1	25.5	144
10.	Hailakandi	"	4.7	29.3	29.0	86
11.	Karbi Anglong	"	15.5	22.4	21.0	110
12.	Karimganj	"	3.5	29.8	29.0	143
13.	Lakhimpur	"	7.0	28.1	28.0	43
14.	Marigaon	"	8.1	26.7	27.0	222
15.	Nagaon	"	12.4	25.3	25.0	193
16.	Nalbari	Medium	2.4	28.9	30.0	124

Appendix - X (Continued)

Sr. No.	State/district	Level of FLR	Age at marriage < 21 years (%)	Mean	Median	Total Marriages (#)
17.	North Cachar Hills	"	13.9	24.5	25.0	72
18.	Sonitpur	"	11.4	26.1	26.0	123
19.	Tinsukia	"	21.7	25.0	25.0	129
20.	Jorhat	High	2.1	28.0	28.0	239
21.	Kamrup	"	5.2	28.1	29.0	173
22.	Sibsagar	"	10.0	27.7	28.0	60
3	**Bihar**					
1.	Araria	Low	34.8	22.5	22.0	155
2.	Darbhanga	"	40.7	21.8	21.0	214
3.	Deoghar	"	47.7	21.5	21.0	151
4.	Dumka	"	28.7	22.9	22.0	143
5.	Giridih	"	53.3	21.1	20.0	182
6.	Godda	"	25.8	23.1	22.0	120
7.	Gopalganj	"	56.7	20.7	20.0	215
8.	Katihar	"	36.1	22.7	22.0	133
9.	Khagaria	"	43.8	21.8	21.0	162
10.	Kishanganj	"	21.7	24.0	24.0	152
11.	Madhepura	"	52.4	21.3	20.0	147
12.	Madhubani	"	54.1	21.0	20.0	183
13.	Nawada	"	66.0	19.8	20.0	197
14.	Palamu	"	60.9	20.6	20.0	156
15.	Pashchmi Singhbhum	"	23.5	23.7	25.0	98
16.	Purba Champaran	"	44.2	22.0	22.0	190
17.	Purnia	"	28.0	22.9	22.0	164
18.	Saharsa	"	50.0	21.6	20.5	182
19.	Sahibganj	"	49.7	21.5	21.0	151
20.	Samastipur	"	47.9	21.5	21.0	211
21.	Sitamarhi	"	47.8	21.4	21.0	161
22.	Aurangabad(Bih)	Medium	63.8	20.4	20.0	224
23.	Begusarai	"	47.0	21.1	21.0	215
24.	Bhagalpur	"	34.1	23.2	22.0	167
25.	Bhojpur	"	61.8	20.4	20.0	199
26.	Buxar	"	49.8	21.1	21.0	201
27.	Dhanbad	"	37.4	22.1	21.0	107
28.	Gaya	"	54.7	20.3	20.0	161
29.	Gulma	"	19.5	23.8	24.0	123
30.	Hazaribagh	"	37.9	21.8	22.0	169
31.	Jehanabad	"	57.6	20.7	20.0	203
32.	Lohardaga	"	20.2	23.2	23.0	119
33.	Munger	Medium	62.1	20.4	20.0	145
34.	Muzaffarpur	"	40.0	21.9	21.5	170
35.	Nalanda	"	53.3	21.1	20.0	167
36.	Pashchim Champaran	"	41.3	22.1	22.0	167
37.	Patna	"	53.3	21.3	20.0	169
38.	Purbi Singhbhum	"	9.3	26.1	26.0	140
39.	Ranchi	"	21.3	23.7	24.0	108
40.	Rohtas	"	69.9	19.3	18.0	153
41.	Saran	"	37.9	22.4	22.0	219
42.	Siwan	"	36.6	22.4	22.0	191
43.	Vaishali	"	46.1	21.2	21.0	217

Appendix - X (Continued)

Sr. No.	State/district	Level of FLR	Age at marriage < 21 years (%)	Mean	Median	Total Marriages (#)
4	**Gujarat**					
1.	Amreli	Medium	30.1	22.3	22.0	236
2.	Banas Kantha	"	56.3	20.0	20.0	158
3.	Bharuch	"	27.8	23.5	23.0	187
4.	Bhavnagar	"	38.2	21.5	21.0	170
5.	Gandhinagar	"	42.1	21.7	21.0	152
6.	Jamnagar	"	26.3	23.0	23.0	171
7.	Junagadh	"	21.1	23.0	23.0	246
8.	Kachchh	"	27.8	22.6	22.0	133
9.	Kheda	"	35.5	22.0	22.0	214
10.	Mahesana	"	39.5	21.4	21.0	124
11.	Panch Mahals	"	48.2	21.1	21.0	197
12.	Sabar Kantha	"	46.5	21.1	21.0	213
13.	Surendranagar	"	28.3	22.6	22.0	173
14.	The Dangs	"	60.6	20.5	20.0	132
15.	Vadodara	"	45.3	21.9	21.0	172
16.	Valsad	"	8.9	24.6	24.0	157
17.	Ahmadabad	High	31.5	22.9	22.0	162
18.	Rajkot	"	18.9	23.3	23.0	169
19.	Surat	"	19.8	23.2	23.0	126
5	**Haryana**					
1.	Bhiwani	Medium	43.8	21.5	21.0	194
2.	Faridabad	"	31.4	22.6	23.0	204
3.	Gurgaon	"	45.3	21.5	21.0	172
4.	Hisar	"	45.5	21.7	21.0	134
5.	Jind	"	34.1	21.8	21.0	170
6.	Kaithal	"	27.8	22.3	22.0	162
7.	Karnal	"	17.7	22.7	22.0	164
8.	Kurukshetra	"	24.0	22.8	22.0	146
9.	Mahendragarh	Medium	42.9	21.1	21.0	182
10.	Panchkula	"	38.0	21.7	22.0	158
11.	Panipat	"	41.0	21.4	21.0	210
12.	Rewari	"	20.4	23.0	23.0	157
13.	Rohtak	"	37.6	22.2	22.0	165
14.	Sirsa	"	32.6	22.3	22.0	181
15.	Sonipat	"	17.3	23.3	23.0	168
16.	Ambala	High	22.4	23.4	23.0	147
17.	Yamunanagar	"	14.9	23.5	23.0	174
6	**Karnataka**					
1.	Bangalore Rural	Medium	1.0	26.1	25.5	96
2.	Belgaum	"	21.0	24.1	23.0	138
3.	Bellary	"	13.9	24.7	24.0	158
4.	Bidar	"	30.3	22.6	22.0	175
5.	Bijapur	"	25.4	23.8	24.0	177
6.	Chikmagalur	"	9.2	26.5	27.0	185
7.	Chitradurga	"	13.4	25.3	25.0	187
8.	Dharwad	"	12.2	24.9	25.0	139
9.	Gulbarga	"	29.4	23.0	23.0	136
10.	Hassan	"	9.7	25.5	25.0	124
11.	Kolar	"	15.7	24.3	24.0	159
12.	Mandya	"	6.0	25.5	25.0	116

Appendix - X (Continued)

Sr. No.	State/district	Level of FLR	Age at marriage < 21 years (%)	Mean	Median	Total Marriages (#)
13.	Mysore	"	3.4	26.3	26.0	116
14.	Raichur	"	30.3	22.9	23.0	165
15.	Tumkur	"	6.0	25.2	24.0	117
16.	Bangalore	High	4.2	26.0	25.0	95
17.	Dakshina Kannada	"	3.5	27.8	27.0	144
18.	Kodagu	"	8.5	26.9	25.0	141
19.	Shimoga	"	5.3	26.6	26.0	188
20.	Uttara Kannada	"	3.3	27.9	28.0	150
7	**Kerala**					
1.	Alappuzha	High	1.7	28.1	28.0	174
2.	Ernakulam	"	0.6	28.5	28.0	156
3.	Idukki	"	4.3	25.9	26.0	140
4.	Kannur	"	0.0	28.4	28.0	146
5.	Kasaragod	"	1.7	27.7	27.5	120
6.	Kollam	"	3.0	28.3	28.0	169
7.	Kottayam	"	2.5	28.3	28.0	161
8.	Kozhikode	"	2.2	26.8	27.0	180
9.	Malappuram	"	9.2	24.8	24.0	184
10.	Palakkad	High	1.3	27.3	27.0	149
11.	Pathanamthitta	"	0.0	27.7	28.0	116
12.	Thiruvananthapuram	"	2.8	28.0	28.0	109
13.	Thrissur	"	1.9	29.1	29.0	155
14.	Wayanad	"	8.4	25.8	26.0	143
8	**Madhya Pradesh**					
1.	Jhabua	Low	70.1	19.3	19.0	154
2.	Balaghat	Medium	20.5	23.8	24.0	78
3.	Bastar	"	38.5	22.4	22.0	78
4.	Betul	"	13.9	24.1	25.0	72
5.	Bhind	"	52.4	21.1	20.0	170
6.	Bilaspur(MP)	"	37.7	22.7	22.0	146
7.	Chattarpur	"	65.2	20.0	19.5	92
8.	Chhindwara	"	20.8	23.8	24.0	120
9.	Damoh	"	52.4	21.1	20.0	126
10.	Datia	"	57.0	20.9	20.0	158
11.	Dewas	"	53.9	21.1	20.0	180
12.	Dhar	"	52.1	21.0	20.0	169
13.	Durg	"	26.1	23.1	23.0	111
14.	East Nimar	"	31.1	22.8	23.0	161
15.	Guna	"	62.6	20.4	19.0	115
16.	Gwalior	"	28.3	22.8	22.0	106
17.	Hoshangabad	"	29.1	22.9	22.0	86
18.	Indore	"	28.7	23.2	23.0	143
19.	Jabalpur	"	20.4	23.7	24.0	93
20.	Mandla	"	36.8	21.4	22.0	57
21.	Mandsaur	"	58.6	20.2	20.0	140
22.	Morena	"	68.8	19.1	18.0	128
23.	Panna	"	70.5	19.6	20.0	78
24.	Raigarh(M P)	"	19.5	23.0	23.0	77
25.	Raipur	"	44.1	21.6	21.0	59
26.	Raisen	"	29.2	22.1	22.0	130
27.	Rajgarh	"	57.5	19.9	19.0	153
28.	Ratlam	"	42.1	21.7	21.0	140

Appendix - X (Continued)

Sr. No.	State/district	Level of FLR	Age at marriage <21 years (%)	Mean	Median	Total Marriages (#)
29.	Rewa	"	56.7	20.3	20.0	97
30.	Sagar	"	42.4	22.0	22.0	118
31.	Satna	"	62.9	20.4	20.0	140
32.	Sehore	"	49.3	21.4	21.0	136
33.	Seoni	"	20.8	23.0	22.0	72
34.	Shahdol	"	53.3	21.4	20.0	30
35.	Shajapur	Medium	62.1	20.1	19.0	140
36.	Shivpuri	"	65.3	20.0	20.0	121
37.	Sidhi	"	68.6	19.4	19.0	105
38.	Surguja	"	57.4	20.3	20.0	122
39.	Tikamgarh	"	76.0	19.2	18.0	125
40.	Ujjain	"	36.1	22.1	22.0	155
41.	Vidisha	"	52.9	20.9	20.0	155
42.	West Nimar	"	40.8	21.4	21.0	130
43.	Bhopal	High	22.8	23.4	23.0	79
44.	Narsimhapur	"	31.6	22.7	22.0	152
45.	Rajnandgaon	"	39.5	22.2	21.0	124
9	**Maharashtra**					
1.	Ahmadnagar	Medium	14.0	24.0	23.0	171
2.	Aurangabad(Mah)	"	25.5	23.0	23.0	153
3.	Bid	"	29.8	21.9	22.0	114
4.	Buldana	"	7.5	24.1	24.0	159
5.	Chandrapur	"	14.3	24.3	25.0	98
6.	Dhule	"	21.2	23.0	23.0	146
7.	Gadchiroli	"	20.9	23.3	23.0	110
8.	Jalgaon	"	21.4	23.3	23.0	140
9.	Jalna	"	32.9	22.5	22.0	146
10.	Kolhapur	"	10.1	25.0	25.0	179
11.	Latur	"	20.5	23.0	23.0	151
12.	Nanded	"	31.9	22.5	22.0	135
13.	Nashik	"	21.4	23.2	23.0	173
14.	Osmanabad	"	18.0	23.8	24.0	139
15.	Parbhani	"	33.3	22.2	22.0	162
16.	Ratnagiri	"	9.0	24.9	24.0	145
17.	Solapur	"	14.0	24.4	24.0	129
18.	Yavatmal	"	11.3	24.5	25.0	160
19.	Akola	High	15.5	23.6	23.0	155
20.	Amravali	"	4.7	25.3	25.0	86
21.	Bhandara	"	1.8	25.7	25.0	109
22.	Greater Bombay (Mumbai)	"	5.7	26.2	26.0	140
23.	Nagpur	"	2.6	25.8	25.0	156
24.	Pune	"	9.6	24.4	24.0	166
25.	Raigarh (MAH)	"	5.8	24.3	24.0	104
26.	Sangli	"	15.8	24.3	25.0	190
27.	Satara	"	7.7	24.6	24.0	117
28.	Sindhudurg	"	3.4	26.8	26.0	179
29.	Thane	Medium	10.0	24.7	25.0	110
30.	Wardha	"	2.8	26.3	26.0	108
10	**Orissa**					
1.	Gajapati	Low	18.0	24.1	24.0	139
2.	Kalahandi	"	38.8	22.5	22.0	116

Appendix - X (Continued)

Sr. No.	*State/district*	*Level of FLR*	*Age at marriage* < 21 years (%)	*Mean*	*Median*	*Total Marriages (#)*
3.	Koraput	"	49.6	21.7	21.0	119
4.	Malkangiri	"	52.7	21.5	20.0	110
5.	Nabarangapur	"	43.9	22.5	21.0	107
6.	Nuapada	"	27.7	23.3	23.0	101
7.	Rayagada	"	29.1	23.2	23.0	134
8.	Anugul	Medium	20.9	23.7	23.0	110
9.	Balangir	"	29.0	23.2	22.5	124
10.	Balasore	"	6.9	25.9	25.0	145
11.	Bargarh	"	19.2	23.7	23.0	120
12.	Baudh	"	32.3	22.9	22.0	127
13.	Bhadrak	"	8.1	26.0	26.0	148
14.	Cuttack	"	8.8	25.8	26.0	170
15.	Debagarh	"	13.3	24.7	25.0	120
16.	Dhenkanal	"	12.1	25.4	25.0	149
17.	Ganjam	"	14.5	24.7	25.0	152
18.	Jajapur	"	1.8	26.1	26.0	110
19.	Jharsuguda	"	13.6	24.1	24.0	103
20.	Kendujhar	"	16.2	24.4	24.0	136
21.	Mayurbhanj	"	19.7	24.4	24.5	132
22.	Nayagarh	"	14.2	24.3	24.0	162
23.	Phulbani	"	33.0	23.5	23.0	115
24.	Sambalpur	"	6.8	25.7	25.0	118
25.	Sonapur	"	15.7	24.0	23.0	115
26.	Sundargarh	"	7.5	25.3	25.0	106
27.	Jagatsinghapur	High	1.4	26.6	27.0	144
28.	Kendrapara	"	3.2	25.9	26.0	190
29.	Khordha	"	6.6	25.6	25.0	137
30.	Puri	"	9.4	25.6	25.0	171
11	**Punjab**					
1.	Amritsar	Medium	17.9	23.7	23.0	168
2.	Bathinda	"	27.5	22.7	22.0	189
3.	Faridkot	"	30.6	22.7	22.0	186
4.	Firozpur	"	36.2	22.4	22.0	221
5.	Mansa	"	31.9	22.2	22.0	182
6.	Moga	"	25.3	23.6	22.5	166
7.	Muktsar	Medium	36.6	22.5	22.0	175
8.	Patiala	"	23.8	22.8	23.0	193
9.	Sangrur	"	27.5	22.9	22.0	178
10.	Fatehgarh Sahib	High	18.9	22.9	22.0	185
11.	Gurdaspur	"	10.8	24.7	25.0	166
12.	Hoshiarpur	"	6.4	25.4	25.0	171
13.	Jalandhar	"	11.3	24.7	24.0	150
14.	Kapurthala	"	14.2	24.2	24.0	162
15.	Ludhiana	"	12.1	24.1	24.0	132
16.	Nawanshahr	"	11.5	24.3	24.0	165
17.	Rupnagar	"	12.7	24.2	24.0	165
12	**Rajasthan**					
1.	Banswara	Low	67.8	19.6	19.0	143
2.	Dungarpur	"	46.7	21.4	21.0	180
3.	Jaisalmer	"	37.3	22.0	22.0	102
4.	Jalor	"	58.1	20.4	20.0	198

Appendix - X (Continued)

Sr. No.	State/district	Level of FLR	Age at marriage < 21 years (%)	Mean	Median	Total Marriages (#)
5.	Tonk	"	60.8	20.0	20.0	97
6.	Ajmer	Medium	40.6	21.7	22.0	101
7.	Alwar	"	56.6	20.5	20.0	166
8.	Barmer	"	56.6	20.4	20.0	166
9.	Bharatpur	"	53.7	20.8	20.0	162
10.	Bhilwara	"	58.0	20.4	20.0	100
11.	Bikaner	"	52.4	21.3	20.0	145
12.	Bundi	"	72.6	19.1	18.0	113
13.	Chittaurgarh	"	66.7	19.7	20.0	72
14.	Churu	"	63.5	20.1	20.0	192
15.	Dausa	"	67.1	19.7	20.0	158
16.	Dhaulpur	"	63.5	19.9	20.0	137
17.	Ganganagar	"	54.6	20.7	20.0	163
18.	Hanumangarh	"	62.7	20.3	20.0	193
19.	Jaipur	"	42.8	21.2	21.0	138
20.	Jhalawar	"	61.1	20.1	20.0	131
21.	Jhunjhunun	"	35.5	21.7	22.0	166
22.	Jodhpur	"	42.6	21.8	21.0	122
23.	Kota	"	52.9	21.0	20.0	119
24.	Nagaur	"	55.5	20.6	20.0	146
25.	Pali	"	48.7	20.7	21.0	158
26.	Rajsamand	"	50.0	21.0	20.5	116
27.	Sawai Madhopur	"	58.2	19.8	20.0	91
28.	Sikar	"	41.8	21.3	21.0	146
29.	Sirohi	Medium	34.9	22.3	22.0	86
30.	Udaipur	"	60.0	20.8	20.0	130
13	**Tamil Nadu**					
1.	Dharmapuri	Medium	14.0	24.5	25.0	164
2.	Dindigul	"	7.0	25.7	25.5	114
3.	Namakkal	"	9.5	26.1	25.0	95
4.	North Arcot	"	7.8	25.6	25.0	141
5.	Periyar	"	6.5	26.4	26.0	77
6.	Pudukkottai	"	9.8	25.7	25.0	122
7.	Ramanathapuram	"	7.0	25.2	25.0	86
8.	Salem	"	9.0	25.3	25.0	133
9.	Sivaganganagar	"	4.3	26.0	26.0	140
10.	South Arcot	"	11.5	25.3	25.0	113
11.	Theni	"	12.3	25.5	25.0	73
12.	Tirunelveli	"	0.0	26.1	25.0	98
13.	Virudhunagar	"	10.0	25.4	25.0	130
14.	Chengalpattu	High	7.1	25.6	25.0	140
15.	Chennai	"	4.0	26.8	27.0	99
16.	Coimbatore	"	7.8	26.3	27.0	77
17.	Kanniyakumari	"	0.7	28.0	28.0	139
18.	Madurai	"	8.3	26.6	27.0	109
19.	Thanjavur	"	6.4	26.9	27.0	109
20.	The Nilgiris	"	1.6	27.6	28.0	62
21.	Tiruchirappalli	"	5.3	28.0	27.0	94
22.	Tiruvanamalai		13.0	25.1	25.0	131
23.	Tutikorin	"	3.6	26.6	27.0	110
14	**Uttar Pradesh**					
1.	Bahraich	Low	71.5	19.5	19.0	130

Appendix - X (Continued)

Sr. No.	State/district	Level of FLR	Age at marriage < 21 years (%)	Mean	Median	Total Marriages (#)
2.	Budaun	"	56.8	20.4	20.0	155
3.	Gonda	"	71.1	19.4	19.0	152
4.	Lalitpur	"	80.2	18.7	18.0	126
5.	Maharajganj	"	80.0	18.4	18.0	70
6.	Muradabad	"	44.1	21.5	21.0	143
7.	Rampur	"	40.7	21.6	22.0	113
8.	Siddharthnagar	"	79.4	18.6	18.0	63
9.	Agra	Medium	43.4	21.6	21.0	152
10.	Aligarh	"	45.9	21.3	21.0	172
11.	Allahabad	"	60.3	20.7	20.0	136
12.	Almora	"	3.0	24.1	23.0	100
13.	Ambedkarnagar	"	67.0	19.5	18.5	106
14.	Azamgarh	Medium	64.5	20.1	20.0	138
15.	Ballia	"	40.6	21.9	22.0	101
16.	Banda	"	65.2	20.3	20.0	135
17.	Barabanki	"	63.6	20.3	20.0	151
18.	Bareilly	"	48.9	21.3	21.0	92
19.	Basti	"	64.2	19.9	20.0	137
20.	Bhadohi	"	77.1	19.0	18.0	179
21.	Bijnor	"	25.9	22.5	22.0	139
22.	Bulandshahar	"	39.2	21.7	22.0	222
23.	Chamoli	"	11.4	24.0	24.0	88
24.	Deoria	"	72.9	19.9	18.5	140
25.	Etah	"	46.0	21.2	21.0	124
26.	Etawah	"	39.8	21.8	21.0	161
27.	Faizabad	"	69.6	19.4	18.0	112
28.	Farrukhabad	"	45.4	21.4	21.0	163
29.	Fatehpur	"	47.2	21.4	21.0	178
30.	Firozabad	"	54.8	21.1	20.0	155
31.	Ghaziabad	"	31.7	22.2	22.0	142
32.	Ghazipur	"	57.7	20.7	20.0	130
33.	Gorakhpur	"	57.9	20.3	20.0	114
34.	Hamirpur(UP)	"	60.9	20.6	20.0	138
35.	Hardoi	"	52.4	21.0	20.0	105
36.	Hardwar	"	26.8	22.5	22.0	127
37.	Hathras	"	46.5	21.3	21.0	159
38.	Jalaun	"	54.2	21.0	20.0	118
39.	Jaunpur	"	63.0	19.8	19.0	200
40.	Jhansi	"	57.9	21.0	20.0	114
41.	Kanpur Dehat	"	39.8	21.8	21.0	113
42.	Kheri	"	64.8	20.5	20.0	142
43.	Lucknow	"	42.9	22.2	22.0	105
44.	Mahoba	"	61.0	20.2	20.0	146
45.	Mainpuri	"	59.8	21.0	20.0	169
46.	Mathura	"	46.9	21.5	21.0	194
47.	Mau	"	56.8	20.7	20.0	146
48.	Meerut	"	32.6	21.6	22.0	138
49.	Mirzapur	"	67.2	20.1	20.0	137
50.	Muzaffarnagar	"	31.2	22.0	21.0	154
51.	Pauri Garhwal	"	7.5	24.7	25.0	106
52.	Pilibhit	"	59.2	20.5	20.0	157
53.	Pithoragarh	"	20.2	23.1	22.0	99

Appendix - X (Continued)

Sr. No.	State/district	Level of FLR	Age at marriage < 21 years (%)	Mean	Median	Total Marriages (#)
54.	Pratapgarh	Medium	74.2	19.8	19.0	155
55.	Rae Bareli	"	61.4	20.4	20.0	127
56.	Saharanpur	"	30.3	22.1	21.0	132
57.	Shajahanabad	"	61.2	20.3	20.0	147
58.	Sitapur	"	59.7	20.6	20.0	134
59.	Sonbhadra	"	59.8	20.3	20.0	87
60.	Sultanpur	"	67.2	19.4	19.0	125
61.	Tehri Garhwal	"	16.7	23.3	22.0	102
62.	Udhamsingh Nagar	"	34.6	22.0	22.0	133
63.	Unnao	"	56.0	21.1	20.0	100
64.	Uttarkashi	"	25.8	22.8	22.0	89
65.	Varanasi	"	58.3	21.0	20.0	120
66.	Dehradun	High	8.4	24.9	25.0	119
67.	Kanpur Nagar	"	26.9	23.1	22.0	119
68.	Nainital	"	20.9	23.9	23.0	139
15	**West Bengal**					
1.	Bankura	Medium	18.9	24.2	24.0	159
2.	Barddhaman	"	27.4	24.5	24.0	190
3.	Birbhum	"	29.4	23.2	22.0	136
4.	Dakshin Dinajpur	"	25.7	24.3	24.0	144
5.	Darjiling	"	22.9	24.8	24.0	153
6.	Jalpaiguri	"	25.3	24.3	23.5	170
7.	Koch Bihar	"	24.6	23.8	24.0	134
8.	Maldah	"	22.8	23.8	24.0	149
9.	Medinipur	"	19.5	23.9	24.0	174
10.	Murshidabad	"	43.5	21.9	21.0	184
11.	Nadia	"	17.5	24.8	24.0	143
12.	Puruliya	"	30.8	23.4	22.0	159
13.	South 24 Parganas	"	23.6	24.0	23.0	157
14.	Uttar Dinajpur	"	24.5	24.1	24.0	155
15.	Haora	High	12.7	25.9	25.5	158
16.	Hugli	"	17.1	25.3	25.0	164
17.	Kolkata	"	11.7	27.0	27.0	120
18.	North 24 Parganas	"	14.1	26.3	26.0	135
16	**Andman & Nicobar**					
1.	Nicobar	Medium	0.0	27.4	26.0	75
2.	Andaman	High	4.3	25.3	25.0	69
17	**Arunachal Pradesh**					
1.	East Kameng	Low	51.1	22.0	20.0	47
2.	Tawang	"	7.7	25.1	24.0	26
3.	Tirap	Low	17.6	24.2	25.0	17
4.	Changlang	Medium	35.8	23.0	22.0	67
5.	Dibang Valley	"	31.6	23.5	22.0	38
6.	East Siang	"	56.5	21.5	20.0	46
7.	Lohit	"	28.9	23.4	23.0	38
8.	Lower Subansiri	"	38.2	23.0	21.5	34
9.	Papum Pare	"	40.0	23.2	22.0	25
10.	Upper Siang	"	21.7	22.9	23.0	23
11.	Upper Subansiri	"	24.6	23.6	23.0	69
12.	West Kameng	"	34.1	23.1	22.0	41
13.	West Siang	"	17.4	24.9	25.0	46

Appendix - X (Continued)

Sr. No.	*State/district*	*Level of FLR*	*Age at marriage < 21 years (%)*	*Mean*	*Median*	*Total Marriages (#)*
18	**Chandigarh**					
1.	Chandigarh	High	9.3	24.9	25.0	54
19	**Dadra & Nagar Haveli**					
1.	Dadra & Nagar Haveli	Medium	46.6	21.4	21.0	116
20	**Daman & Diu**					
1.	Daman	Medium	11.9	24.4	25.0	160
2.	Diu	High	17.0	24.3	24.0	147
21	**Delhi**					
1.	Delhi	High	12.7	24.4	24.5	102
22	**Goa**					
1.	North Goa	High	1.7	29.1	29.5	116
2.	South Goa	"	1.5	28.6	28.0	132
23	**Himachal Pradesh**					
1.	Chamba	Medium	6.3	24.8	24.0	175
2.	Kinnaur	"	13.7	24.4	24.0	102
3.	Kullu	"	13.0	24.4	24.0	108
4.	Lahul & Spiti	"	11.0	25.0	24.0	73
5.	Mandi	"	4.8	24.7	24.0	168
6.	Sirmaur	"	13.3	24.0	24.0	150
7.	Bilaspur	High	5.6	24.9	25.0	144
8.	Hamirpur	"	5.8	25.5	26.0	172
9.	Kangra	"	1.3	26.2	26.0	152
10.	Shimla	"	7.8	26.1	26.0	116
11.	Solan	"	8.4	24.3	24.0	178
12.	Una	"	1.8	25.9	26.0	165
24	**Jammu & Kashmir**					
1.	Anantanag	Low	7.7	25.1	25.0	26
2.	Badgam	"	34.1	22.3	22.0	44
3.	Baramula	"	15.2	25.9	25.0	66
4.	Doda	Low	1.5	26.5	26.0	67
5.	Kupwara	"	18.2	24.6	25.0	44
6.	Kargil	Medium	13.4	23.6	24.0	82
7.	Kathua	"	0.9	28.5	28.0	107
8.	Leh	"	16.4	24.1	24.0	55
9.	Pulwama	"	23.3	23.0	23.0	30
10.	Punch	"	3.1	24.5	24.0	65
11.	Rajauri	"	0.9	23.6	24.0	107
12.	Srinagar	"	30.8	21.3	22.0	26
13.	Udhampur	"	3.4	23.9	23.5	88
14.	Jammu	High	0.0	27.0	27.0	64
25	**Lakshadweep**					
1.	Lakshadweep	High	9.2	25.7	26.0	98
26	**Manipur**					
1.	Bishnupur	Medium	17.9	26.1	25.0	134
2.	Chandel	"	21.3	24.8	25.0	75
3.	Churachandpur	"	15.0	25.4	25.0	107
4.	Senapati	"	19.6	25.3	25.0	56
5.	Tamenglong	"	24.0	24.6	24.0	104
6.	Thoubal	"	16.4	25.5	25.0	146

Appendix - X (Continued)

Sr. No.	State/district	Level of FLR	Age at marriage < 21 years (%)	Mean	Median	Total Marriages (#)
7.	Ukhrul	"	18.5	26.7	27.0	54
8.	Imphal	High	10.9	28.0	27.0	92
27	**Meghalaya**					
1.	East Garo Hills	Medium	39.4	22.5	23.0	33
2.	Jaintia Hills	"	0.0	25.4	26.0	15
3.	Ri Bhoi	"	68.6	20.2	20.0	35
4.	West Garo Hills	"	33.3	24.3	24.0	6
5.	West Khasi Hills	"	51.3	21.3	20.0	39
6.	East Khasi Hills	High	52.6	21.3	20.0	19
28	**Mizoram**					
1.	Chhimtuipui	Medium	26.0	23.9	24.0	50
2.	Aizwal	High	23.9	24.5	24.0	134
3.	Lunglei	"	12.3	26.3	25.0	65
29	**Nagaland**					
1.	Kohima	Medium	69.4	20.0	20.0	49
2.	Mon	"	24.4	22.8	22.5	82
3.	Phek	"	31.6	22.1	22.0	19
4.	Tuensang	"	4.5	24.9	24.0	88
5.	Zunheboto	"	32.3	22.3	22.0	124
6.	Mokokchung	High	9.4	25.2	24.0	32
7.	Wokha	"	7.7	25.1	25.0	52
30	**Pondicherry**					
1.	Karaikal	High	4.2	26.4	26.0	96
2.	Mahe	"	1.1	29.7	29.0	186
3.	Pondicherry	"	0.8	27.5	27.0	130
4.	Yanam	"	13.4	24.7	24.0	67
31	**Sikkim**					
1.	North Sikkim	Medium	28.1	24.5	24.0	64
2.	South Sikkim	"	29.7	23.2	22.0	37
3.	West Sikkim	"	20.9	24.0	23.0	91
4.	East Sikkim	High	9.2	25.8	25.0	120
32	**Tripura**					
1.	North Tripura	Medium	8.4	27.5	27.0	131
2.	South Tripura	"	6.8	27.2	28.0	133
3.	West Tripura	High	6.2	28.6	28.0	146

FLR = Female literacy rate